PHILOSOPHY OF MIND IN THE LATE MIDDLE AGES AND RENAISSANCE

Characterized by many historically significant events, such as the invention of the printing press, the discovery of the New World, and the Protestant Reformation, the years between 1300 and 1600 are a remarkably rich source of ideas about the mind. They witnessed a resurgence of Aristotelianism and Platonism and the development of humanism. However, philosophical understanding of the complex arguments and debates during this period remain difficult to grasp.

Philosophy of Mind in the Late Middle Ages and Renaissance provides an outstanding survey of philosophy of mind in this fascinating and still controversial period and examines the thought of figures such as Aquinas, Suárez, and Ficino.

Following an introduction by Stephan Schmid, thirteen specially commissioned chapters by an international team of contributors discuss key topics, thinkers, and debates, including:

- mind and method,
- the mind and its illnesses,
- the powers of the soul,
- Averroism,
- intentionality and representationalism,
- theories of (self-)consciousness,
- will and its freedom,
- external and internal senses,
- Renaissance theories of the passions,
- the mind-body problem and the rise of dualism, and
- the 'cognitive turn' in logic.

Essential reading for students and researchers in philosophy of mind, medieval philosophy, and the history of philosophy, *Philosophy of Mind in the Late Middle Ages and Renaissance* is also a valuable resource for those in related disciplines such as religion, literature, and Renaissance studies.

Stephan Schmid is Professor for the History of Philosophy at the University of Hamburg, Germany. He mainly works on Late Medieval and Early Modern philosophy, focusing on debates in metaphysics, epistemology, and philosophy of mind, with a special interest in how these discussions are carried forward in present day analytic philosophy. He has published on Aquinas, Scotus, Ockham, Suárez, Descartes, Spinoza, Malebranche, and Hume and is the author of *Finalursachen in der frühen Neuzeit* (2011).

The History of the Philosophy of Mind
General Editors: Rebecca Copenhaver and Christopher Shields

The History of the Philosophy of Mind is a major six-volume reference collection, covering the key topics, thinkers and debates within philosophy of mind, from Antiquity to the present day. Each volume is edited by a leading scholar in the field and comprises chapters written by an international team of specially commissioned contributors.

Including a general introduction by Rebecca Copenhaver and Christopher Shields, and fully cross-referenced within and across the six volumes, *The History of the Philosophy of Mind* is an essential resource for students and researchers in philosophy of mind, and will also be of interest to those in many related disciplines, including Classics, Religion, Literature, History of Psychology, and Cognitive Science.

VOL.1 PHILOSOPHY OF MIND IN ANTIQUITY
edited by John E. Sisko

VOL.2 PHILOSOPHY OF MIND IN THE EARLY AND HIGH MIDDLE AGES
edited by Margaret Cameron

VOL.3 PHILOSOPHY OF MIND IN THE LATE MIDDLE AGES AND RENAISSANCE
edited by Stephan Schmid

VOL.4 PHILOSOPHY OF MIND IN THE EARLY MODERN AND MODERN AGES
edited by Rebecca Copenhaver

VOL.5 PHILOSOPHY OF MIND IN THE NINETEENTH CENTURY
edited by Sandra Lapointe

VOL.6 PHILOSOPHY OF MIND IN THE TWENTIETH AND TWENTY-FIRST CENTURIES
edited by Amy Kind

PHILOSOPHY OF MIND IN THE LATE MIDDLE AGES AND RENAISSANCE

The History of the Philosophy of Mind, Volume 3

Edited by Stephan Schmid

LONDON AND NEW YORK

First published 2019
by Routledge
2 Park Square, Milton Park, Abingdon, Oxon OX14 4RN

and by Routledge
605 Third Avenue, New York, NY 10017

First issued in paperback 2020

Routledge is an imprint of the Taylor & Francis Group, an informa business

© 2019 selection and editorial matter, Stephan Schmid; individual chapters, the contributors

The right of Stephan Schmid to be identified as the author of the editorial material, and of the authors for their individual chapters, has been asserted in accordance with sections 77 and 78 of the Copyright, Designs and Patents Act 1988.

All rights reserved. No part of this book may be reprinted or reproduced or utilised in any form or by any electronic, mechanical, or other means, now known or hereafter invented, including photocopying and recording, or in any information storage or retrieval system, without permission in writing from the publishers.

Trademark notice: Product or corporate names may be trademarks or registered trademarks, and are used only for identification and explanation without intent to infringe.

British Library Cataloguing-in-Publication Data
A catalogue record for this book is available from the British Library

Library of Congress Cataloging-in-Publication Data
Names: Schmid, Stephan, editor.
Title: Philosophy of mind in the late middle ages and renaissance / edited by Stephan Schmid.
Description: New York : Routledge, 2018. | Series: The history of the philosophy of mind ; Volume 3 | Includes bibliographical references and index.
Identifiers: LCCN 2017060252 | ISBN 9781138243941 (hardback : alk. paper) | ISBN 9780429508172 (e-book)
Subjects: LCSH: Philosophy of mind—History. | Philosophy of mind—History—16th century.
Classification: LCC BD418.3 .P4843 2018 | DDC 128/.209023—dc23
LC record available at https://lccn.loc.gov/2017060252

ISBN 13: 978-0-367-73414-5 (Vol III, pbk)
ISBN 13: 978-1-138-24394-1 (Vol III, hbk)

ISBN: 978-1-138-24392-7 (Vol I, hbk)
ISBN: 978-1-138-24393-4 (Vol II, hbk)
ISBN: 978-1-138-24395-8 (Vol IV, hbk)
ISBN: 978-1-138-24396-5 (Vol V, hbk)
ISBN: 978-1-138-24397-2 (Vol VI, hbk)
ISBN: 978-1-138-92535-9 (6-volume set, hbk)

Typeset in Times New Roman
by Apex CoVantage, LLC

CONTENTS

List of contributors — vii
General introduction — xi
REBECCA COPENHAVER AND CHRISTOPHER SHIELDS

Introduction to volume 3: Aristotelianism, Humanism, and Platonism – three pillars for thinking about the mind — 1
STEPHAN SCHMID

1 **Mind and method** — 22
DOMINIK PERLER

2 **Medical approaches to the mind in the late Middle Ages and the Renaissance** — 41
GUIDO GIGLIONI

3 **The soul and its parts: debates about the powers of the soul** — 63
PAUL J.J.M. BAKKER

4 **Averroism and the metaphysics of intellect** — 83
JEAN-BAPTISTE BRENET

5 **The function of the intellect: intentionality and representationalism** — 101
PAOLO RUBINI

6 **Late medieval theories of (self-)consciousness** — 125
SONJA SCHIERBAUM

CONTENTS

7 **Debates about the will and its freedom**   144
SYDNEY PENNER

8 **Late scholastic debates about external and internal senses: in the direction of Francisco Suárez (1548–1617)**   165
DANIEL HEIDER

9 **Renaissance theories of the passions: embodied minds**   185
SABRINA EBBERSMEYER

10 **Dualism and the mind-body problem**   207
SANDER W. DE BOER

11 **The immortality of the soul**   229
LORENZO CASINI

12 **Late scholastics and Renaissance humanists on the passions in moral action**   250
EILEEN C. SWEENEY

13 **Renaissance facultative logic and the workings of the mind: the "cognitive turn"**   270
MARCO SGARBI

Index   291

CONTRIBUTORS

Paul J.J.M. Bakker is Professor of Medieval and Renaissance Philosophy at Radboud University (Nijmegen, The Netherlands). His research focuses on themes related to the philosophy of mind such as the relations among soul, mind, and body; the soul's powers or 'faculties'; knowledge and perception; the rise of psychology as an independent scientific discipline. He mainly works on published and unpublished commentaries on Aristotle's book *On the Soul* (*De anima*) from the late 13th to the late 16th century. He is also involved in a series of editorial projects. Most recently, he has published (with Michiel Streijger) the first two volumes of the critical edition of John Buridan's questions commentary on Aristotle's *Physics*: John Buridan, *Quaestiones super octo libros Physicorum Aristotelis* (*secundum ultimam lecturam*). *Libri I-II* (Leiden: 2015) and *Libri III-IV* (Leiden: 2016). He is currently preparing the third and final volume of this edition. He co-edits the book series *Medieval and Early Modern Philosophy and Science* (Leiden: Brill) and is a member of the editorial board of *Vivarium* (Leiden: Brill).

Jean-Baptiste Brenet is Full Professor of Philosophy at the University of Paris 1 Panthéon-Sorbonne. His research and teaching focuses on the history of medieval Arabic and Latin Philosophy, Psychology, Philosophy of Mind, Metaphysics and Cosmology. Among many others, he is the author of *Je fantasme. Averroès et l'espace potentiel* (Lagrasse, Verdier, 2017); *Averroès l'inquiétant* (Paris, Belles Lettres, 2015); *Les possibilités de jonction. Averroès-Thomas Wylton* (Berlin, de Gruyter, 2013); *Transferts du sujet. La noétique d'Averroès selon Jean de Jandun* (Paris: Vrin 2003); and Thomas d'Aquin, *Les créatures spirituelles*, introduction, traduction et notes (Paris: Vrin 2010). In addition, he has published various articles in *Arabic Sciences and Philosophy*, *Archives d'Histoire Doctrinale et Littéraire du Moyen Âge* and *Revue des Sciences Philosophiques et Théologiques*, amongst others.

Lorenzo Casini has received his PhD in Philosophy (2006) at the University of Uppsala, where he continues to conduct his research, dealing mainly with philosophical psychology in Renaissance philosophy. He is the author of several papers, published in anthologies or peer-reviewed journals, which discuss topics related to natural philosophy and moral psychology in authors such as Ficino, Pomponazzi, Porzio, Valla, and Vives.

Sander W. de Boer works as a policy adviser at the University of Groningen and is a former member of the Philosophy department there. He is interested in the history of philosophical psychology, especially in the intersections of natural philosophy and metaphysics. He is the author of *The Science of the Soul. The Commentary Tradition on Aristotle's De anima, c. 1260–c. 1360* (Leuven University Press 2013). His most recent paper, co-authored with Han Thomas Adriaenssen, is 'Between Atoms and Forms: Natural Philosophy and Metaphysics in Kenelm Digby', *Journal of the History of Philosophy* (forthcoming).

Sabrina Ebbersmeyer is Associate Professor for the history of philosophy at the University of Copenhagen, Denmark. Working primarily on Renaissance and Early Modern philosophy, her research focuses on debates in moral psychology, philosophy of mind, and historical epistemology, with a special interest in the concept of humanism, the relation between emotion and cognition, and the role of gender in the history of philosophy. She has published on numerous Renaissance philosophers, including Petrarch, Ficino, and Telesio, as well as on Descartes, Elisabeth of Bohemia, and Leibniz. She is the author of *Sinnlichkeit und Vernunft* (München: Fink 2002) and *Homo agens* (Berlin, New York: de Gruyter 2010). Her recent publications include "Humanism", in *The Cambridge History of Moral Philosophy*, ed. by Sacha Gelob and Jens Timmermann (Cambridge: Cambridge University Press, 2017), pp. 192–207.

Guido Giglioni is Associate Professor of History of Philosophy at the University of Macerata, Italy. He is the author of *Francesco Bacone* (Rome: Carocci 2011) and *Immaginazione e malattia: Saggio su Jan Baptiste van Helmont* (Milan: Angeli 2000). His recent articles and chapters include "Medicine of the Mind in Early Modern Philosophy", in *The Routledge Handbook of the Stoic Tradition*, ed. by John Sellars (London: Routledge, 2016), pp. 189–203; "*Cupido, sive Atomus; Dionysus, sive Cupiditas*: Francis Bacon on Desire", in *Francis Bacon on Motion and Power*, ed. by G. Giglioni, James Lancaster, Sorana Corneanu and Dana Jalobeanu (Dordrecht: Springer, 2016), pp. 153–173; and "Delusion, Drowsiness and Discernment: Degrees of Awareness in Renaissance Dream Activity", in *Cognitive Confusions: Dreams, Delusions and Illusions in Early Modern Culture*, ed. by Ita Mac Carthy, Kirsti Sellevold and Olivia Smith (London: Legenda, 2016), pp. 89–109.

Daniel Heider is an Associate Professor at the Faculty of Theology, University of South Bohemia (České Budějovice). He is also employed as a researcher at the Institute of Philosophy of the Czech Academy of Sciences (Prague). In his research he focuses on early modern scholastic philosophy, especially on the philosophy of Jesuits headed by Francisco Suárez. His monographs include *Suárez and his Metaphysics. From the Concept of Being via Transcendental Unity to the Kinds of Transcendental Unity*, Prague: Filosofia, 2011 (in Czech) and *Universals in Second Scholasticism. A Comparative Study with Focus on the Theories of Francisco Suárez S.J. (1548–1617), João Poinsot O. P. (1589–1644) and Bartolomeo Mastri da Meldola O.F.M. Conv. (1602–1673)/Bonaventura Belluto O.F.M. Conv. (1600–1676)* (Amsterdam/Philadelphia: John Benjamin Publisher, 2014), among others.

Sydney Penner teaches philosophy at Asbury University. His research focuses on late medieval and early modern scholasticism, with particular attention to Francisco Suárez. He has published articles on early modern scholastic discussions of free will, final causation, and the metaphysics of relations.

Dominik Perler is Professor of Philosophy at Humboldt-Universität zu Berlin and Member of the Berlin-Brandenburg Academy of Arts and Science. His research focuses on medieval and early modern philosophy, mostly in the areas of philosophy of mind, epistemology, and ontology. His books include *Ancient and Medieval Theories of Intentionality* (ed., 2001); *Theorien der Intentionalität im Mittelalter* (2002); *Zweifel und Gewissheit. Skeptische Debatten im Mittelalter* (2006); *Transformationen der Gefühle. Philosophische Emotionstheorien 1270–1670* (2011, English translation in preparation); *Partitioning the Soul: Debates from Plato to Leibniz* (ed., 2014); and *The Faculties: A History* (ed., 2015).

Paolo Rubini is a staff member of the Leibniz Edition at the Berlin-Brandenburg Academy of Sciences and Humanities (BBAW). He is interested in the philosophy of nature and theories of cognition from the late Middle Ages to Early Modern period with particular focus on the Aristotelian "tradition" and Leibniz. He has published on Malebranche and is author of *Pietro Pomponazzis Erkenntnistheorie. Naturalisierung des menschlichen Geistes im Spätaristotelismus* (Leiden: Brill, 2015).

Sonja Schierbaum is currently working as a Post-Doc at the University of Hamburg, Germany on her project on the compatibility of freedom and rationality regarding actions. The project focuses on early modern positions (Leibniz, Crusius). It is funded by the German Research Foundation. She is the author of *Ockham's Assumption of Mental Speech – Thinking in a World of Particulars* (Leiden: Brill, 2014). She co-edited a volume on medieval theories of self-knowledge with Dominik Perler: *Selbstbezug und Selbstwissen. Texte zu einer mittelalterlichen Debatte* (Klostermann: Frankfurt/M., 2014).

Stephan Schmid is Professor for the History of Philosophy at the University of Hamburg, Germany. He mainly works on Late Medieval and Early Modern philosophy, focusing on debates in metaphysics, epistemology and philosophy of mind, with a special interest in how these discussions are carried forward in present day analytic philosophy. He has published on Aquinas, Scotus, Ockham, Suárez, Descartes, Spinoza, Malebranche, and Hume and is the author of *Finalursachen in der frühen Neuzeit* (Berlin, New York: de Gruyter 2011).

CONTRIBUTORS

Marco Sgarbi is Associate Professor of History of Philosophy and Vice-provost for Communication and Development at the Università Ca' Foscari, Venice. He is the PI of the ERC Starting Grant 2013 on "Aristotle in the Italian Vernacular: Rethinking Renaissance and Early-Modern Intellectual History (c. 1400–c. 1650)". He has been a Jean-François Malle-Harvard I Tatti Fellow at Villa I Tatti, The Harvard University Center for Italian Renaissance Studies and the Frances A. Yates Short-Term fellow at the Warburg Institute. He is the editor of *Philosophical Readings*, a quarterly online journal, and of the *Bloomsbury Studies in the Aristotelian Tradition*.

Eileen C. Sweeney is Professor of Philosophy at Boston College. She is the author of *Logic, Theology, and Poetry in Boethius, Abelard and Alan of Lille: Words in the Absence of Things* (Palgrave/MacMillan, 2006) and *Anselm of Canterbury and the Desire for the Word* (Catholic Univ. Press, 2011) and the author of many articles on Medieval Philosophy in the 12th and 13th centuries. Her present research is on the history of theories of the passions from the Middle Ages into the Modern period and on the development of the notion of science from the 12th to 13th centuries.

GENERAL INTRODUCTION

Rebecca Copenhaver and Christopher Shields

How far back does the history of philosophy of mind extend? In one sense, the entire history of the discipline extends no further than living memory. Construed as a recognized sub-discipline of philosophy, philosophy of mind seems to have entered the academy in a regular way only in the latter half of the twentieth century. At any rate, as an institutional matter, courses listed under the name 'Philosophy of Mind' or 'The Mind-Body Problem' were rare before then and seem not to have become fixtures of the curriculum in Anglo-American universities until the 1960s.[1] More broadly, construed as the systematic self-conscious reflection on the question of how mental states and processes should be conceived in relation to physical states and processes, one might put the date to the late nineteenth or early twentieth century.

One might infer on this basis that a six-volume work on *The History of Philosophy of Mind* extending back to antiquity is bound to be anachronistic: we cannot, after all, assume that our questions were the questions of, say, Democritus, working in Thrace in the fifth century BC, or of Avicenna (Ibn-Sînâ), active in Persia in the twelfth century, or of John Blund, the Oxford- and Paris-trained Chancellor of the see of York from 1234–1248, or, for that matter, of the great German philosopher and mathematician Leibniz (1646–1716). One might on the contrary think it *prima facie* unlikely that thinkers as diverse as these in their disparate times and places would share very many preoccupations either with each other or with us.

Any such immediate inference would be unduly hasty and also potentially misleading. It would be misleading not least because it relies on an unrealistically unified conception of what *we* find engaging in this area: philosophy of mind comprises today a wide range of interests, orientations, and methodologies, some almost purely *a priori* and others almost exclusively empirical. It is potentially misleading in another way as well, heading in the opposite direction. If we presume that the only thinkers who have something useful to say to us are those engaging the questions of mind we find salient, using idioms we find congenial, then we will likely overlook some surprising continuities as well as instructive discontinuities across these figures and periods.

Some issues pertinent to mental activity may prove perennial. Of equal importance, however, are the differences and discontinuities we find when we investigate questions of mind assayed in earlier periods of thought. In some cases, it is true, we find it difficult to determine without careful investigation whether difference in idiom suffices for difference in interest or orientation. For instance, it was once commonplace to frame questions about mental activity as questions about the soul, where today questions posed about the nature of the soul and its relation to the body are apt to sound to many to be outmoded or at best quaintly archaic. Yet when we read what, for instance, medieval philosophers investigated under that rubric, we are as likely as not to find them reflecting on such core contemporary concerns as the nature of perception, the character of consciousness, the relation of mental faculties to the body, and the problem of intentionality – and to be doing so in a manner immediately continuous with some of our own preoccupations.

That said, even where upon examination we find little or no continuity between present-day and earlier concerns, this very difference can be illuminating. Why, for instance, is the will discussed so little in antiquity? Hannah Arendt suggests an answer: the will was not discussed in antiquity because it was not discovered before St. Augustine managed to do so in the third century.[2] Is she right? Or is the will in fact discussed obliquely in antiquity, enmeshed in a vocabulary at least initially alien to our own? On the supposition that Arendt is right, and the will is not even a topic of inquiry before Augustine, why should this be so? Should this make us less confident that we have a faculty rightly called 'the will'? Perhaps Augustine not so much discovered the will as *invented* it, to give it pride of place in his conception of human nature. A millennium later Thomas Aquinas contended that the will is but one power or faculty of the soul, as an intellectual appetite for the good (*ST* I 82, resp.). Is he right? Is the will as examined by Augustine and Aquinas the same will of which we ask, when we do, whether our will is free or determined?

A study of the history of philosophy of mind turns up, in sum, some surprising continuities, some instructive partial overlaps, and some illuminating discontinuities across the ages. When we reflect on the history of the discipline, we bring into sharper relief some of the questions we find most pressing, and we inevitably come to ask new and different questions, even as we retire questions which we earlier took to be of moment. Let us reflect first then on some surprising continuities. Three illustrations will suffice, but they could easily be multiplied.

First, consider some questions about minds and machines: whether machines can be conscious or otherwise minded, whether human intelligence is felicitously explicated in terms of computer software, hardware, or functional processes more generally. Surely such questions belong to our era uniquely? Yet we find upon reading some early modern philosophy that this is not so. In Leibniz, for instance, we find this striking passage, known as 'Leibniz's mill':

> Imagine there were a machine whose structure produced thought, feeling, and perception; we can conceive of its being enlarged while maintaining the same relative proportions, so that we could walk into it as we can walk into a mill. Suppose we do walk into it; all we would find there

are cogs and levers and so on pushing one another, and never anything to account for a perception. So perception must be sought in simple substances, not in composite things like machines. And that is all that can be found in a simple substance – perceptions and changes in perceptions; and those changes are all that the internal actions of simple substances can consist in.

(*Monadology* §17)

Leibniz offers an argument against mechanistic conceptions of mental activity in this passage, one with a recognizably contemporary counterpart. His view may be defensible or it may be indefensible; but it is certainly relevant to questions currently being debated.

Similarly, nearly every course in philosophy of mind these days begins with some formulation of the 'mind-body problem', usually presented as a descendant of the sort of argument Descartes advanced most famously in his *Meditations*, and defended most famously in his correspondence with Elisabeth of Bohemia. Centuries before Descartes, however, we encounter the Islamic polymath Avicenna (Ibn-Sînâ) wondering in detail about the question of whether the soul has or lacks quantitative extension, deploying a striking thought experiment in three separate passages, one of which runs:

One of us must suppose that he was just created at a stroke, fully developed and perfectly formed but with his vision shrouded from perceiving all external objects – created floating in the air or in space, not buffeted by any perceptible current of the air that supports him, his limbs separated and kept out of contact with one another, so that they do not feel each other. Then let the subject consider whether he would affirm the existence of his self. There is no doubt that he would affirm his own existence, although not affirming the reality of any of his limbs or inner organs, his bowels, or heart or brain or any external thing. Indeed he would affirm the existence of this self of his while not affirming that it had any length, breadth or depth. And if it were possible for him in such a state to imagine a hand or any other organ, he would not imagine it to be a part of himself or a condition of his existence.

(Avicenna, *'The Book of Healing'*)

Avicenna's 'Floating Man' or 'Flying Man', reflects his Neoplatonist orientation and prefigures in obvious ways Descartes' more celebrated arguments of *Meditations* II. Scholars dispute just how close this parallel is,[3] but it seems plain that these arguments and parables bear a strong family resemblance to one another, and then each in turn to a yet earlier argument by Augustine,[4] more prosaically put, but engaging many of the same themes.

The point is not to determine who won the race to this particular argument, nor to insist that these authors arrive at precisely the same finish line. Rather, when we study each expression in its own context, we find illuminating samenesses and differences, which in turn assist us in framing our own questions about the character of the quantitative and qualitative features of mind, about the tenability of solipsism, and about the nature of the human self. One would like to know, for instance, whether such a narrow focus on the internal states of human consciousness provides a productive method for the science of mind. Or have our philosophical forebears, as some today think, created impediments by conceiving of the very project in a way that neglects the embodied characteristics of cognition? From another angle, one may wonder whether these approaches, seen throughout the history of the discipline, lead inexorably to Sartre's conclusion that 'consciousness is a wind blowing from nowhere towards objects'?[5] One way to find out is to study each of these approaches in the context of its own deployment.

For a final example, we return to the birthplace of Western philosophy to reflect upon a striking argument of Democritus in the philosophy of perception. After joining Leucippus in arguing that the physical world comprises countless small atoms swirling in the void, Democritus observes that *only* atoms and the void are, so to speak, really real. All else exists by convention: 'by convention sweet and by convention bitter, by convention hot, by convention cold, by convention colour; but in reality atoms and void' (DK 68B9). This remark evidently denies the reality of sensible qualities, such as sweetness and bitterness, and even colour. What might Democritus be thinking? By judging this remark alongside his remaining fragments, we see that he is appealing to the variability of perception to argue that if one perceiver tastes a glass of wine and finds it sweet, while another perceiver tastes the same glass and finds it bitter, then we must conclude – on the assumption that perceptual qualities are real – that either one or the other perceiver is wrong. After all, they cannot both be right, and there seems little point in treating them as both wrong. The correct conclusion, Democritus urges, is that sensible qualities, in contrast to atoms and the void, are not real. The wine is neither sweet nor bitter; sweetness and bitterness are wholly subjective states of perceivers.

Readers of seventeenth- and eighteenth-century British philosophy will recognize this argument in Locke and Berkeley. Locke presents the argument to support his distinction between primary and secondary qualities: primary qualities being those features of objects that are (putatively) *in* objects, independently of perception, such as number, shape, size, and motion; secondary qualities being those features of objects subject to the variability of perception recognized by Democritus. Locke struggles with the reality of secondary qualities, sometimes treating them as ideas in our minds and other times as dispositions of the primary qualities of objects that exist independently of us. Democritus, by contrast, aligning the real with the objective, simply banishes them to the realm of convention. And Berkeley appeals to the same phenomenon on which Locke founds his famous distinction – the variability of perception – to argue that the distinction is unsustainable and thus embraces the anti-Democritean option: the real is the ideal.

We may ask which if any of these philosophers deserves to be followed. As an anecdotal matter, when beginning philosophy students grasp the point of arguments from the variability of perception, they become flummoxed, because before having their attention focussed on the phenomenon of variability, most tend to think of sensible qualities as intrinsic monadic properties of the external objects of perception. This issue in the philosophy of perception, straddling as it does different periods and idioms, remains a live one, proving as vivid for us as it was for Democritus and Locke.

When we find similar philosophical arguments and tropes recurring in radically different periods and contexts throughout the history of philosophy, that is usually at least a strong *prima facie* indication that we are in an area demanding careful scrutiny. Unsurprisingly, arguments concerning the nature of perception and perceptible qualities offer one telling illustration. Still, we should resist the temptation to find continuities where none exist, especially where none exist beyond the verbal or superficial. We should moreover resist, perhaps more strongly still, the tendency to minimize or overlook differences where they appear. One of the intellectual joys of studying the history of philosophy resides precisely in uncovering and appreciating the deep discontinuities between disparate times and contexts.

On this score, examples abound, but one suffices to illustrate our point. The title of a widely read article written in the 1960s posed a provocative question: 'Why Isn't the Mind-Body Problem Ancient?'.[6] This question, of course, has a presupposition, namely that the mind-body problem is in fact *not* ancient. It also seems to betray a second presupposition, namely that there is *a* mind-body problem: a single problem that that engages philosophers of the modern era but that escaped the ancients. This presupposition raises the question: what *is* the single, unified, mind-body problem that the ancients failed to recognize? In fact, when we turn to the range of questions posed in this domain, we find a family of recognizably distinct concerns: the hard problem, the explanatory gap, mental causation, and so on. Not all these questions have a common orientation, even if they arise from a common anxiety that the mind and the body are at once so dissimilar that inquiring into their relationship may already be an error, and yet so similar in their occupation and operation as to obliterate any meaningful difference.

We might call this anxiety *categorial*. That is, it has seemed to various philosophers in various eras that there is some basic categorial distinction to be observed in the domain of the mental, to the effect that mental states belong to one category and physical states to another. That by itself might be true without, however, there being any attendant problem. After all, we might agree that there is a categorial distinction between, say, biological properties and mathematical properties, and even that these families of properties are never co-instantiable. After all, no number can undergo descent with modification, and no animal can be a cosine. That is hardly a problem: no one expects numbers to be biological subjects, and no one would ever mistake an organism for a mathematical function. The problem in the domain of the mental and physical seems to arise only when we assume that some objects – namely ourselves – exhibit both mentality and physicality, and do so in a way that is systematic and unified. Bringing these thoughts together we arrive at a mind-body problem: if mental and physical properties are categorially exclusive while we ourselves are mental and physical at once, we must be what we cannot be, namely subjects of properties that cannot coincide.

In this sense, Cartesian dualism might be regarded as a solution to the mind-body problem, at least *this* mind-body problem, one which simply concedes its conclusion by affirming that minds and bodies are irredeemably different sorts of substances displaying different sorts of properties. Needless to say, this 'solution' invites a series of still more intractable problems concerning the interaction of these postulated disparate substances, about the location of the mental, and so forth. Even so, when the Cartesian expedient is rejected on these or other grounds, the old problem re-emerges, in one guise yielding an equally desperate seeming sort of solution, namely the total elimination of the mental as ultimately not amenable to a purely physicalistic characterization.[7] Eliminativism, no less than Cartesianism, solves the mind-body problem by effectively by concession.

One should accordingly look afresh at the problem as formulated. In fact, when one asks *what* these purportedly mutually excluding properties may be, several candidates come to the fore. Some think properties such as *being conscious* are mental and cannot possibly be physical, perhaps because conscious states are ineliminably subjective, whereas all physical properties are objective, or because mental properties are essentially qualitative, whereas physical properties are only quantitative. Descartes' own reasons, though disputed, seem to have been largely epistemic: possibly one can doubt the existence of one's body, whereas it is impossible, because self-defeating, to doubt the existence of one's own mind or mental states (*Meditation* II). If these property-differences obtain in these domains and are in fact such as to be mutually exclusive, then we do now have the makings of a mind-body problem.

Returning, then, to the question pertinent to our study of the ancient period, we may ask: do the ancients draw these sorts of categorial distinctions? If so, why do they fail to appreciate the problems we find so familiar and obvious? Or do they in fact fail to draw these categorial distinctions in the first place? If they do not, then one would like to know why not. One can imagine a number of different options here: one could fault the ancients for failing to pick up on such starkly categorial differences; one could credit them for astutely avoiding the conceptual muddles of Cartesianism. Some argue, for instance, that Aristotelian hylomorphism embraces a framework of explanation within which Cartesian questions simply cannot arise, thereby obviating an array of otherwise intractable problems.[8] Although we do not attempt to litigate these issues here, one can appreciate how an investigation into ancient approaches to philosophy of mind yields palpable benefits for some modern questions, even if and perhaps precisely because such questions were not ancient.

Needless to say, we never know in advance of our investigations whether the benefits of such study are forthcoming. To make such discoveries as can be made in this area, then, we need ask a set of questions similar to those we asked regarding the mind-body problem, *mutatis mutandis*, for other philosophical problems in the mental domain, broadly construed, as they arise in other periods of philosophy beyond ancient philosophy as well.

If we proceed in this way, we find that the study of the history of philosophy of mind offers the contemporary philosopher perspectives on the discipline which, however far below the surface, may yet guide our own inquiries into the mental and physical, and into the character of mental and physical states and processes. This is, of course, but one reason to engage the studies these six volumes contain. Other researchers with a more purely historical orientation will find a wealth of material in these pages as well, ranging across all periods of western philosophy, from antiquity to that part of the discipline that resides in living memory. Our historical and philosophical interests here may, of course, be fully complementary: the history of philosophy of mind takes one down some odd by-ways off some familiar boulevards, into some dead-ends and cul-de-sacs, but also along some well-travelled highways that are well worth traversing over and again.

Notes

1 A perusal of the course offerings of leading universities in the US tends to confirm this. To take but one example, which may be multiplied, a search of the archives of the University of Notre Dame lists one course in 'Philosophy of Mind' offered as an advanced elective in 1918 and 1928, 1929, but then no further course until 1967, when 'The Mind-Body Problem,' began to be offered yearly off and on for two decades. In the 1970s, various electives such as 'Mind and Machines' were offered intermittently, and a regular offering in 'Philosophy of Mind' began only in 1982. This offering continues down to the present. While we have not done a comprehensive study, these results cohere with archive searches of several other North American universities.
2 Arendt sees prefigurations in St. Paul and others, but regards Augustine as 'the first philosopher of the will and the only philosopher the Romans ever had' (1978, vol. ii, 84).
3 For an overview of these issues, see Marmura (1986).
4 On the relation between Descartes and Augustine, see the instructive treatment in Matthews (1992).
5 Sartre (1943: 32–33).
6 Matson (1966). Citing Matson's question, King (2007) went on to pose a continuing question of his own: 'Why Isn't the Mind-Body Problem Medieval?'. In so doing, King meant to oppose Matson, who had claimed that the one should not assume that medieval philosophers, although writing in a recognizably Aristotelian idiom, similarly failed to engage any mind-body problem. After all, he noted, in addition to their Aristotelianism, they accepted a full range of theistic commitments alien to Aristotle.
7 Eliminativism about the mental has a long a chequered history, extending at least as far back as Broad (1925) (who rejects it), but has its most forceful and accessible formulation in Churchland (1988)
8 Charles (2008) has advanced this sort of argument on behalf of hylomorphism.

Bibliography

Arendt, Hannah. 1978. *The Life of the Mind*, vols. i and ii. New York: Harcourt Brace Jovanovich.
Broad, C. D. 1925. *The Mind and Its Place in Nature*. London: Routledge & Kegan.
Charles, David. 2008. "Aristotle's Psychological Theory". *Proceedings of the Boston Area Colloquium in Ancient Philosophy* 24: 1–29.

Churchland, P. M. 1988. *Matter and Consciousness*. Cambridge, MA: MIT Press.
King, Peter. 2007. "Why Isn't the Mind-Body Problem Medieval?" In *Forming the Mind: Essays on the Internal Senses and the Mind/Body Problem From Avicenna to the Medical Enlightenment*, 187–205. Berlin: Springer.
Marmura, Michael. 1986. "Avicenna's Flying Man in Context". *The Monist* **69**(3): 383–395.
Matson, Wallace. 1966. "Why Isn't the Mind-Body Problem Ancient?" In *Mind, Matter, and Method: Essays in Philosophy and Science in Honor of Herbert Feigl*, 92–102. St. Paul: University of Minnesota Press.
Matthews, Gareth. 1992. *Thought's Ego in Augustine and Descartes*. Ithaca: Cornell University Press.
Sartre, Jean-Paul. 1943. "Une Idée fondamentale de la phénomenologie de Husserl: L'intentionalité". In *Situations I*. Paris: Gallimard.

INTRODUCTION TO VOLUME 3

Aristotelianism, Humanism, and
Platonism – three pillars for thinking about
the mind

Stephan Schmid

The years between 1300 and 1600 constitute a rich and complex period in the history of philosophy. Nonetheless – or rather because of this – its philosophy is still quite poorly understood, and systematic reconstructions of its theories are still largely lacking. Admittedly, we have an increasingly broad overview of the rich variety of philosophical works written, translated and read in these times. On top of that, a growing number of critical editions and translations of pivotal thinkers of this period have made their ideas accessible. Last but not least, outstanding research has been conducted into selected authors and debates in this period, and there have even been attempts to formulate a detailed narrative of the philosophical developments of the period.[1]

Nevertheless, our philosophical understanding of the arguments and debates promoted by the thinkers of these times is still dim. Especially in comparison to our philosophical understanding of their medieval predecessors or, to an even greater extent, their early modern successors. Unlike these periods, the intellectually complex centuries between 1300 and 1600 do not even have a clear historiographical label. There are in fact two labels circulating – "Late Middle Ages" and "Renaissance" – and their use tends to depend on the intellectual tradition one has in mind. The first label is mainly applied to authors working within the scholastic-Aristotelian tradition, whereas the term "Renaissance" is often reserved for non-Aristotelian, predominantly humanist, authors of our period who decidedly distanced themselves from scholasticism.[2] What is more, these terms are often employed in a normatively "thick" sense in that they not only descriptively single out a certain period or tradition but, at the same time, present it in an evaluative light. The "late medieval" label often exhibits pejorative overtones, presenting late medieval philosophers as adherents of a decaying school of quibblers who not only failed to develop any original philosophical ideas, but even distorted the philosophical insights of their high scholastic predecessors.[3] The "thick" aspects of the "Renaissance" label are even more pronounced. Exponents of the Renaissance are typically imagined as thinkers who turned away from the fruitless brawling of Aristotelians and instead collected and studied ancient texts and shook off the paralyzing dogmas of medieval Aristotelianism.[4] The evaluative connotation of these labels is a holdover from their influential interpretation by Jacob Burckhardt (1860). Ever since Burckhardt's vivid account of this period, many have been tempted to share his view of the Renaissance as the cradle of modernity, where sophisticated humanists liberated the intellectual culture from sterile and retrograde Aristotelian dogmatism – a view that, as we will see, the humanists themselves were all too happy to promote by means of scornful polemics against scholasticism. And even though scholars have become aware of the problematic aspects of these labels and have tried to purge them of their evaluative character,[5] these evaluative overtones are still widespread in popular science, where the prevailing view is that Renaissance humanists were progressive and scholastics conservative.[6]

What, then, makes the intellectual landscape between 1300 and 1600 so hard to grasp? First of all, this period is characterized by many historically significant events. These include the rediscovery of ancient literature, its rapid dissemination due to the invention of the printing press (around 1450), the fall of Constantinople (1453), the discovery of the New World (1492) and the Protestant Reformation (1517), along with many others. These events did not leave the intellectual life unaffected; newly discovered ancient texts often coming from Constantinople (which was increasingly threatened and ultimately conquered by the Ottomans) questioned deeply entrenched orthodoxies; the ability to print led to a proliferation of books and thereby of views and opinions, while the discovery of America and the Reformation gave rise to fundamental questions about the relation between religion, church and state and the moral and political rights of native Americans.[7]

Moreover, a growing number of educated people – diplomats, lawyers, physicians and merchants – became interested in the newly discovered texts and theories and discussed them outside of the universities, which were dominated by Aristotelianism until late into the 17th century. In these new intellectual circles, the rediscovered ancient sources led to a revival of many ideas of Stoic, Pythagorean, Epicurean, Platonist and Sceptical origin. Often these ideas were combined to form inclusive and explanatorily powerful worldviews that sometimes drew on Galenism (a medical tradition going back to the Greek physician Claudius Galen) or included even strands of occult-magical theories. And although these discussions were initiated by non-academic circles, they rarely left the teachings in the universities unaffected, as will become clear with regard to many of the problems of the philosophy of mind that are addressed in this volume. In this way, the period between 1300 and 1600 became a unique biotope of intellectual creativity and experimentation in which many views were devised and explored and were often sought to be reconciled, inspired by a belief in a *philosophia perennis* – an all-encompassing, true philosophy of which all previously established philosophical theories reveal but individual aspects.

The philosophical landscape between 1300 and 1600 is thus complex and hard to chart. Yet, this is precisely what the following chapters attempt to do, at least with respect to selected strands of discussions about problems of the philosophy of mind. Some of these problems are familiar to us, for example, the problems of (self-)consciousness, freedom or immortality. Others might strike contemporary readers as alien, for instance, the problem of the unity of the intellect, debates about the powers of the soul or the interplay of external and internal senses. At any rate, it will be helpful to have a rough idea about the historical, systematic context of these debates. This context was very different from ours, not only giving rise to questions that might appear strange to us, but also leading philosophers to think about more familiar problems in a way that many will find no less alien. In order to provide some of this context, the remainder of this introduction will present three debates drawing upon three influential intellectual traditions that decisively shaped thinking about the mind in this period. The traditions are (i) scholastic Aristotelianism and its debates about the mind and soul, (ii) humanism and its critique of scholasticism and (iii) Platonism.

Before we start exploring these three traditions and their debates, a few clarifying remarks are in order: The first thing to note is that the three portraits cannot provide more than a rough overview of the debates involving the three selected intellectual currents, which figure prominently in the debates addressed in subsequent chapters. My discussion is thus oversimplifying and far from complete and exhaustive.[8]

The second important point to note is that the three movements do not represent mutually exclusive intellectual traditions. This is because these movements are defined by criteria that are partly doctrinal and partly methodological; while Aristotelianism and Platonism are characterized by their distinctive philosophical views, the humanist tradition is marked by its shared interest in the philological, scholarly and rhetorical questions raised by the newly available ancient texts. Consequently, being a humanist does not preclude one from endorsing Aristotelian or Platonist views. To the contrary, the main exponent of Renaissance Platonism, Marsilio Ficino, was a great humanist. And not every Platonist in this period simply rejected Aristotle's views wholesale. As I have already mentioned and as we will see with regard to Ficino, many of them exhibited a conciliatory attitude and sought to reconcile many different philosophical views by integrating them into one comprehensive philosophical system. Moreover, even the scholastic tradition, which was naturally committed to Aristotle, did not shy away from incorporating Platonist strands in its reasoning, most of which were taken from Augustine. With regard to our topic, the most salient Platonist element adopted by many scholastic authors may be the view that the mind is a distinctively active entity that requires radically different explanations than natural phenomena.

The third point to stress is that the three debates outlined below are not exclusively concerned with questions of the philosophy of mind. These questions will be explored in later chapters. The goal of the following sections is rather to sketch out the general framework within which debates about the nature of the mind and its states took place and to explain how those debates gave rise to questions about the mind that today might strike us as foreign. In order to demonstrate how the topics discussed in the remainder of this volume relate to the framework constituted by the three traditions, the introduction will end by briefly connecting the particular problems taken up by the subsequent thirteen chapters to the intellectual developments outlined in the next three sections.

1 Aristotelian hylomorphism, the soul and the mind

When philosophers ask about the mind and its nature, they are looking for an explanation of our capacities for perceiving, feeling, thinking and willing. How is it possible that we can know various things, make decisions and control and direct our actions? Aristotle famously answered these questions by appealing to capacities, which he sought to elucidate by integrating them into a more comprehensive account of vital capacities in general. For Aristotle mental capacities are merely a particularly elaborate type of vital capacity, such as digestion, growth and procreation, but unlike the latter, mental capacities are not shared by all living beings. The principle or ground of all these vital capacities is referred to by Aristotle as *the soul*. But of course a name in itself does not yet provide a substantial answer; one needs to know precisely what this soul is and how it gives rise to the capacities of a living being.

Aristotle answered these questions by appealing to his hylomorphist framework, according to which all material substances are composed of matter and form, which account for different aspects of a given substance. While a substance's form (Greek: *eîdos, morphé*) accounts for its specific capacities and hence for its belonging to a certain species, its matter (Greek: *hýle*) accounts for its concrete existence and the distinctive exercise of its natural capacities. In keeping with this general metaphysical framework, Aristotle famously explained that "the soul is . . . the form of a natural body having the capacity of life" (*DA* II.1, 412a19–21). The soul is thus the form or principle through which a "natural organized body" (*DA* II.1, 412b5) performs its various vital functions.

A major advantage of Aristotle's hylomorphist theory of the soul is that it offers the prospect of a neat and elegant solution to the famous mind-body problem, a problem that preoccupies so many philosophers today. On Aristotle's account, this problem immediately dissolves as an ill-formed question. As he himself noted, once we conceive of the soul as the form of a natural organized body, "there is no need to enquire whether soul and body are one, any more than whether the wax and its shape are one, or generally whether the matter of a thing is the same with that of which it is the matter" (*DA* II.1, 412b6–8).

But Aristotle's theory of the soul as the form of a living body is not free of problems either. A particularly persistent difficulty, which stimulated many discussions among scholastic authors between 1300 and 1600, arises from the fact that the Aristotelian soul is supposed to serve as a principle for *all* living beings and their activities, which of course differ widely. Apart from displaying certain biological functions, violets, dogs and humans have little in common. In order to account for the differences among living beings, Aristotle distinguished different parts of the soul, which he characterized as distinct kinds of the soul. While all living beings share a nutritive soul, which is responsible for basic vital functions, animals also have a sensitive soul, which accounts for their perception and their ability to move, while humans additionally possess a rational or intellective soul, which allows them to grasp universal essences.⁹ This suggestion accounts for the differences among living beings at the price of making the soul more complex. And this gives rise to further questions. In particular, one wonders what these parts of the soul actually are. Are they distinct from one another, and if so, how? Are they localized in different parts of the body? And how do they all come together to comprise a unified soul that can function as *the* form of the human body? These questions only become more urgent once we take into account another central claim of Aristotle's psychology: the immateriality of the intellect (or rational soul). As Aristotle argued in *De anima* III.4 (429a22–25), "the part of the soul which we call intellect (*noûs*) . . . cannot reasonably be conceived to be mixed with the body", for otherwise one could not account for the intellect's ability to grasp all essences. The precise form of this argument need not concern us here (it is a matter of contentious debate).[10] It is, however, a remarkable historical fact that virtually all scholastic authors accepted Aristotle's line of reasoning – not least because the claim of the immateriality of the intellect or mind allowed them to reconcile Aristotelianism with their Christian belief in an immortal soul. And this lent even greater urgency to the problem of how the immaterial mind or intellect can be part of a soul, which is characterized as the form of the living body. This problem, which provoked a lot of discussion in the Late Middle Ages and the Renaissance, has been aptly called the "mind-soul problem".[11]

Medieval authors mainly suggested three answers to this problem. Many scholastic authors between 1300 and 1600 took up these suggestions and often refined and developed them.

The most radical solution to this problem was to deny it. The mind-soul problem is only a problem if we assume that the intellect or mind is in fact a part of the soul. Exactly this assumption was rejected by the Arabic commentator Averroes, who argued that the intellect is a supra-individual entity, which human beings can indeed cognitively access, but which is no part or constituent of their individual souls.[12] In the 13th century this view was defended by Siger of Brabant and subject to an equally prominent and decisive attack by Thomas Aquinas.[13] The rejection of the supra-individuality of the intellect even gained institutional support from the Parisian Bishop Stephen Tempier, who included the Averroist claim that there is no individual intellect in his famous list of condemned theses (*articuli*) in 1277.[14] Despite these powerful headwinds, however, Averroism was no sinking ship. It soon found new adherents in the 14th century, above all in John of Jandun (c. 1285–1328), whose Averroist teachings remained influential up until the 16th century.[15]

Thomas Aquinas, by contrast, defended the individuality of our intellect by arguing for the unitarian view that each human has a single, undivided soul by which s/he can engage in various activities (such as digestion, perception and thought) provided s/he is equipped with the right bodily organs. This suggestion, however, faces an obvious difficulty: How can the intellect be a part of the soul conceived as the form of the human body, given that it is immaterial and thus separable from the body? Aquinas solves this difficulty by arguing that the soul, as a particularly noble form, has an operation and a power that is independent of corporeal matter.[16] However, this solution seems to presuppose that the soul's immaterial intellectual power is distinct from the soul as the form of the human body. Yet Aquinas was happy to accept this presupposition anyway, arguing that the soul must be distinct from its powers. In his view, the soul must be distinct from its powers since otherwise we would have to say that soul makes us constantly perceiving or thinking as it makes us constantly living, which is absurd.[17] Instead of being integral constituents of the soul, Aquinas explained that "all the powers of the soul . . . flow from the essence of the soul, as from their principle".[18] Accordingly, we do not call the soul rational, sensitive or nutritive because it is constituted by really distinct parts, but because it can give rise to the corresponding rational, sensitive or nutritive powers.[19]

This distinction between the soul and its powers was fiercely attacked by many scholastic authors after Aquinas, perhaps most rigorously by William of Ockham. As he pointed out, Aquinas's argument for the soul's essence being distinct from its powers turns on an equivocation of the Latin term "*potentia*", which can be translated as both "possibility" and "power". Recall that Aquinas argued that the powers of the soul must be distinct from the soul since, unlike the living being's state of being alive, these powers need not be constantly actualized. But why should we assume that the powers of the soul have to be constantly actualized if they are involved in, and thus are as actual as, the soul's essence? This only makes sense if one conceives of powers as possible states that have to be actualized if they are part of the actual essence of the soul. However, the powers of the soul are not potential states; they are actual features of the soul by means of which it can engage in various operations, and so nothing speaks against these powers being included in the soul's actual essence.[20] For Ockham, then, there is no need to postulate faculties or powers in addition to the soul. The will and intellect, he explains, are not two distinct faculties. Instead,

> there is one single substance of the soul that is able to have distinct acts for which there can be different denominations. Insofar as it produces (or is able to produce) an act of thinking it is called 'intellect', and with respect to an act of wanting is called 'will'.[21]

It is thus unnecessary to conceive of the soul's powers as additional entities that are somehow distinct from it. Powers, on Ockham's account, are but essential capacities of the soul.

This is surely an ontologically attractive view of cognitive faculties. But Ockham's parsimony with regard to powers entails ontological costs elsewhere. For given that the immaterial power of the intellect is identical with the soul, this soul cannot be identical with the sensitive soul, which is equipped with the material capacities of perception.[22] Indeed, Ockham himself adduced this argument in support of pluralism, that is, the view that the human being is composed of several distinct forms:[23]

> It is not the case that what is numerically the same form is both extended and non-extended, both material and immaterial. But in a human being the sensitive soul is extended and material, whereas the intellective soul is not. . . . Therefore ‹the sensitive soul is really distinct from the intellective soul›.[24]

For Ockham, then, the sensitive soul as a material power must be really distinct from the intellective or rational soul as an immaterial power such that there is no solution to the mind-soul problem. But neither is this a real problem. We simply have to acknowledge that "a human being has just one total existence, but several partial existences".[25]

As this brief survey makes plain, Aristotle's basic suggestion to conceive of the soul as the form of the human body leaves many questions unresolved. Aristotelian philosophers throughout Late Antiquity and the Middle Ages were happy to develop Aristotle's basic idea in various directions, all of which led to unique problems and gave rise to new questions. The same applies to Aristotelian authors from Ockham to Suárez.[26] In one way or another all of them had to take a stance on the question about the status of the soul, the parts and faculties of the soul and their interrelations as they struggled to provide a coherent account of the soul, one that not only accommodates their general hylomorphist assumptions and central Christian beliefs such as their belief in the immortality of the soul, but also proves phenomenologically adequate in explaining our experience as cognitive agents. The following chapters will trace at least some of their attempts to do so.

2 Humanist culture, its rediscovery of texts and critique of scholasticism

The period between 1300 and 1600 is perhaps most famous for the rise of humanism, an intellectual culture based on studying and imitating classical literature. The movement had its roots in the northern Italy of the 14th century, but soon spread to other European countries. Nowadays, a humanist is typically conceived as someone who has a special appreciation for humanity and is concerned about human needs, interests and welfare and values the realization of our capacities quite independently of any theist or other supernatural foundation.[27] Renaissance humanists, by contrast, are not characterized by a strictly codified ethical attitude or a distinct philosophical viewpoint, nor did they pursue a particularly secular agenda. And even though many of them were sympathetic to the importance of human values, it was not their primary concern to argumentatively defend those values. Their common goal was rather the study and imitation of ancient Latin and Greek literature.[28] Far from being professional philosophers, typical Renaissance humanists were experts in "the humanities". They were scholars devoted to the *studia humanitatis*, which consisted of subjects like grammar, rhetoric, poetry, history and moral philosophy and formed a body of discrete academic disciplines distinct from the philosophical and theological studies now known as scholasticism.[29]

One should thus resist the still popular view that Renaissance humanists formed a unified school with a distinct *Menschenbild* that eventually defeated scholastic Aristotelianism and prepared the way for Descartes' alleged discovery of the subject.[30] And even though many humanists became famous for their relentless critique of the philosophy of the schools, more recent scholarship has shown that scholasticism and humanism co-existed until the end of the 16th century in a more or less complementary fashion; while late medieval scholastics were primarily concerned with philosophical questions of logic, metaphysics and natural philosophy, Renaissance humanists focused on grammar, rhetoric, poetry and, to some extent, ethics.[31]

However, it would be equally wrong to claim that Renaissance humanists were philosophically irrelevant. On the one hand, humanism established a new intellectual culture outside of institutional boundaries. This made it possible not only to question fundamental assumptions and objectives of scholastic philosophy, but also to explore new ways of approaching philosophical questions. And these developments were pivotal for the rise of the anti-Aristotelian philosophy of the 17th century, which flourished almost exclusively outside of academia – at least in the beginning. On the other hand, humanists rediscovered many ancient ideas and philosophical views and provided philosophers of the period between 1300 and 1600 with new texts and better translations and taught them to read Greek. All this had a decisive impact on scholastic philosophy, too. The newly available material held out the prospect of worldviews that were as comprehensive and coherent as the one envisaged by Aristotle. And in light of the late-ancient commentaries on Aristotle and the growing ability to approach his work in the original Greek, even Aristotle's own views appeared to be much harder to pin down than was usually assumed. Let me briefly elaborate these points.

Scholastic philosophy was a highly professional enterprise, whose discussions were conducted and regimented by a shared set of authorities (such as Aristotle and Augustine) and a shared tradition of commenting on the same texts (such as Peter Lombard's *Four Books of Sentences* and many of Aristotle's works). While this allowed scholastic philosophers to tackle philosophical questions at an unprecedented (and for a long time nonpareil) level of precision and sophistication, it also made the discussions so specialized that their significance became hard for outsiders to appreciate. Indeed, for a long time there hardly were any outsiders capable of criticizing scholastic debates. For typically those who had access to higher education and thus were able to weigh in on intellectual controversies had already been raised within the scholastic tradition. This changed when humanists established an intellectual culture parallel to scholastic philosophy that enabled them to take a critical look at the latter. And indeed many humanist thinkers made use of this possibility. In fact, the sheer volume of humanist polemics against scholasticism is surely one of the reasons why 19th-century historians of ideas tended to portray Renaissance humanism as a genuine philosophical school with a distinct anti-scholastic agenda.

Anti-scholastic polemics of this kind are already to be found in Francesco Petrarch (1304–1374), the father of humanism. Apart from a general lament over the bad style of the scholastics' technical Latin and the fruitlessness of their considerations, scholastic treatment of Aristotelian ethics and syllogistic were particularly popular targets of his scorn. For example, Petrarch complained that studying Aristotle's *Nicomachean Ethics* made him more learned at best, but not a better person, such that Aristotle failed to attain his self-proclaimed goal of making us good in practice, rather than teaching us what the good is in theory (see *NE* II.2, 1103b27–28). On Petrarch's view, this goal is much more easily achieved by studying edifying literature of classical Latin, such as the exhortations of Cicero and Seneca.[32] Petrarch's attack against Aristotelian syllogistic was no less severe. For example, he warned his friends not to get involved with Aristotelian dialecticians, "who take their highest pleasure in the debate and whose goal is not finding the truth, but to quarrel".[33] Other humanists, by contrast, were not as dismissive of logic and tried to reform it rather than reject it altogether. A telling example on this score is Lorenzo Valla (c. 1406–1457), who tried to reform classic Aristotelian dialectics by integrating it into the framework of rhetoric. Valla suggested that dialectics or logic should be considered as a part of invention, which, alongside arrangement, style, memory and delivery, is one of the five canons of classical rhetoric.[34] Only on this conception can dialectics be turned into a truly fruitful enterprise, one that enables the orator to successfully defend his arguments. For this purpose, however, logic should widen its repertoire and explore other kinds of argumentation that are capable of convincing without being formally valid. Moreover, as a branch of rhetoric, logic or dialectics should be concerned not only with the truth-values of sentences, but also with their epistemic status (their credibility), which in turn depends on many contextual factors that determine the effectiveness of arguments (how difficult is the proposed chain of reasoning, how common are its examples, how agreeable is its style?).

In light of these deep reservations towards scholasticism, many humanists sought to explore non-Aristotelian approaches to philosophy as presented in the newly available texts of the Epicurean, Sceptical or Platonist tradition. In the next section, we will see how the rediscovery and translation of Platonic dialogues and other Platonist writings led to a revival of Platonism. These new approaches were often discussed in newly founded intellectual circles, which functioned as semi-institutionalized forums for non-academic philosophy. Famous examples include the Platonic Academy in Florence, which was sponsored by the Medici family and frequented by Marsilio Ficino, and the Accademia Cosentina in Consenza in Southern Italy, which was led by Bernardino Telesio, among others.

The formation of humanist circles under the patronage of wealthy citizens is indicative of another characteristic of humanist culture: humanist rhetorical skills and erudition were highly valued among lawyers, physicians, diplomats and politicians. By the beginning of the 16th century, humanist education had become so fashionable that wealthy families all over Europe wanted their children to benefit from a humanist education in Latin and Greek. The pedagogical success of the humanists also had an impact on the higher education provided by universities. For example, the Lutheran curriculum established by Philip Melanchthon and Johann Sturm required students to read Aristotle's *Nicomachean Ethics* and the New Testament in the original Greek. And in a similar vein, the Jesuits required their students to study the works of Cicero, Virgil and other classical texts before being introduced to scholastic philosophy. As a result, by the middle of the 16th century most professors and students at European universities were able to read Greek.[35]

By ensuring that philosophers had access to increasingly accurate texts and could even read some of them in the original Greek, the humanist tradition had probably the most decisive impact on scholastic philosophy between 1300 and 1600. Humanists exposed a wide range of inauthentic texts that were attributed to Dionysius the Aeropagite or even Aristotle, who was credited with more than a hundred works that are now considered spurious.[36] Moreover, they made various late-ancient commentaries on Aristotle available, which shed new light on Aristotle's doctrine. One example that is particularly important for the debates treated in this volume is Alexander of Aphrodisias's treatise on *De Anima*, which was translated into Latin by Girolamo Donato in 1495.[37] Drawing on Aristotle's definition of the soul as the form or "first actuality" of the organic body, Alexander insisted that the human soul is essentially bound to the human body.[38] Even though the Latin West knew Alexander's radical position from his critical discussion of Averroes in his *Long commentary on De anima*,[39] Donato's full translation of Alexander's treatise made it possible to appreciate the latter's arguments in their entirety. Alexander's materialist view of the soul was especially intriguing for philosophers at the northern Italian universities of Padua and Bologna, where Aristotle's *De anima* was customarily taught as a basis for the study of medicine.[40] At the same time, however, these philosophers were well aware of the epistemological, metaphysical and theological difficulties inherent in this view. As far as epistemology is concerned, Alexander's denial of the rational soul's separability seemed to rule out that humans can grasp the essences of all things, since Aristotle famously argued that the intellect must be separable from the human body in order to be capable of understanding all things. As regards metaphysics, Alexander's radically hylomorphist conception of the soul entailed that the soul cannot survive the death of the body and hence cannot be immortal, and it goes without saying that such a view was contrary to received theological opinion. Nonetheless, not all philosophers were willing to reject Alexander's radically hylomorphist conception of the human soul. A particularly famous example of a thinker who sought to cope with these difficulties is Pietro Pomponazzi (1462–1525), who for this reason will figure prominently in the subsequent chapters.[41]

Now, even though many humanists had strong reservations towards scholastic philosophy, which they often portrayed as useless quibbling, their philological skills and achievements still provided scholastic discussions with new material and even contributed to the development of these debates until they were ultimately dismissed by the proponents of the *science nouvelle* of the 17th century.

3 Platonist cosmology: Marsilio Ficino's conception of the immortal soul

Another fruit of Renaissance humanism was the rise of Platonism in the 15th century. A common objection frequently raised against Aristotelian authors, namely that they employed a cumbersome language and engaged in useless technical discussions, could hardly be directed against the carefully composed and rhetorically brilliant dialogues of Plato. To the contrary, many humanists admired Plato's dialogues for their stylistic elegance and literary qualities. What is more, Platonist metaphysics provided a framework that could neatly be combined with a Christian worldview, as Augustine (354–430) demonstrated and as the humanist Petrarch pointed out, writing as a pagan, "Plato could not fully grasp the truth, but he saw it and came closer to it than the rest".[42]

A pivotal representative of the Platonist tradition in the Renaissance was Marsilio Ficino (1433–1499). While very few texts of Plato's corpus were available in Latin until the 15th century (such as, the *Meno*, *Phaedo* and bits of the *Timaeus* and *Parmenides*), Ficino translated all the Platonic dialogues into Latin and wrote detailed commentaries on Plato's *Parmenides*, *Sophist*, *Philebos*, *Timaios*, *Phaidros* and, most famously, the *Symposium*. Apart from this, Ficino translated Plotinus's *Enneads* and many other works of the Platonic and Pythagorean tradition into Latin and thus made many of them accessible to the Western world. But Ficino also had a systematic interest in developing Plato's worldview, which he tried to substantiate and expand by including ideas from Neoplatonist authors such as Plotinus, Iamblichus and Proclus, as well as Augustine. With regard to the philosophy of mind, his monumental *Platonic Theology on the Immortality of the Soul* is especially pertinent. In this work, which consists of no less than eighteen books, Ficino explores the theological advantages of adopting a Platonist worldview when attempting to account for the immortality of the soul and its absolute dependency on God.

In line with his Platonist predecessors, Ficino conceived of the soul as an immortal and individual entity that naturally strives to be reunited with God by contemplating his eternal essence. This conception of the soul stands in stark contrast to certain variants of Aristotelianism that we have already encountered, namely Alexander of Aphrodisias's position that the soul is inseparable from the body and hence as mortal as the body and Averroes's view that humans share one supra-individual intellect.

What is crucial about Ficino's philosophy of mind is that both his positive theory of the soul as an immortal and individual entity and his rejection of rival views are based on very general cosmological considerations about the order of the universe. According to Ficino's Platonist worldview, reality is characterized by several layers of being that are hierarchically organized around God, who figures as the ultimate cause and end of the universe: He is its ultimate cause by virtue of being its creator and he is its end or goal insofar as all creatures, to the degree they are active, imitate God. Now, this multifarious dependence of creatures on God pertains not only to their existence, but also to their intelligibility. As products of God, they share, by their very nature, a certain likeness to God and thus qualify as imperfect images or copies of their creator. As a result, they can only be understood through their precise relation to God, whom they imitate and mirror to varying degrees of perfection.[43]

Ficino's conception of reality as a hierarchically organized whole with different layers that are intelligible through one another and ultimately by reference to God has crucial epistemological, methodological and ethical implications.

Epistemologically, Ficino's Platonist view of reality requires us to understand everything in reference to and ultimately through God, who has created everything according to his ideas. Now since our minds are themselves but products and images of God, these divine ideas are imprinted in them as certain "formulae", by which "God gives the mind enduring power to attain ideas in understanding". It is by activating those imprinted or innate formulae that we are able to grasp God's ideas and thus acquire an insight in the nature of things.[44]

Methodologically, Ficino's Platonist worldview yields a clear principle for how the universe and its structure ought to be studied. This principle is "that in the divinity of the created mind, as in a mirror at the centre of all things, we should first observe the works of the Creator, and then contemplate and worship the mind of the Creator".[45] In other words, we should try to activate our innate formulae in order to grasp God's ideas, which in turn enable us to understand God's works. Since these works bear a certain likeness to their creator, contemplating his works allows us to finally recognize God. Ficino himself strictly follows this methodological principle in writing his *Platonic Theology* by ascending to God via an examination of the nature of bodies, qualities, the soul and angels (book I) and then returning from an examination of God (book II) to a deeper analysis of the subordinate levels of being by reference to their divine origin (book III). In particular, he studies the nature of the soul by alternating between an analysis of its distinctive position in the order of reality and a comparison of its features to those found among the four other kinds of beings (i.e., bodies, qualities, angels and God), which takes up the remaining eighteen books of the *Platonic Theology*.

Last but not least, Ficino's Platonist view of reality has an important ethical implication. Given that God is the goal and end of everything in general, he is also the goal of our lives in particular, so that our happiness can only consist in the contemplation of his essence. On account of this, Ficino attributes a decisive ethical and religious purpose to his Platonist musings: They should free us from our wretched preoccupation with sensory thoughts and bodily goods by leading us to the immaterial principles of things, which are ultimately founded in God.[46]

This is undoubtedly an impressive worldview. The crucial question we are facing now is why Ficino thought himself able to draw any substantial views about the soul and the mind from this general cosmological picture. The main goal of his *Platonic Theology* is to prove the immortality of the soul and thereby to refute the radicalized Aristotelian positions of Averroism and Alexandrism. Ficino devoted no less than ten books of his *Platonic Theology* to this goal (books V–XIV, with the remaining four books, XV–XVIII, dedicated to further questions about the soul). Even a rough summary of his reasoning is outside the scope of this introduction. Let me therefore present just a few arguments that give an impression of Ficino's general strategy for defending the immortality of the individual soul.[47]

The most crucial element of Ficino's cosmological picture with regard to his defence of the immortality of the individual soul is the view that among the five levels of being, namely God, angels, soul, quality and body, the (human) soul occupies a central position. This makes the soul a mediator between the material and immaterial realm of the universe, which, according to Ficino, furnishes it with two additional, crucial features. As a mediating entity, the human soul must first belong to the immaterial part of reality and thus be itself an immaterial entity, and second it must somehow cling to material reality, which it does by being attached to the body it animates and from which it receives sensations.[48]

This is enough to establish the soul's immortality, as Ficino argues in a range of proofs in book V of his *Platonic Theology*. Ficino's first argument, for instance, seeks to demonstrate the soul's immortality based on the consideration that, as a linking entity between the immaterial and material, the soul must be the first principle of motion of material bodies. As first movers, Ficino submits, souls have to move forever since they must bear the source of movement in themselves. Accordingly, the soul must "supply life to itself"[49] and can thus never die.

Other arguments draw on the consideration that as an active power that is superior to qualities in the order of being, the soul must be independent of matter and thus immaterial so that it is indivisible and immune to all forms of corruption (*PTh*. V.5 and V.6).

Doubtlessly, Ficino's derivations of the soul's immortality from its central position in the cosmos are sketchy and often rely on inferences that are not fully self-evident. However, to criticize his arguments on these grounds would be to misunderstand Ficino's overall argumentative strategy. It is not his aim to derive truths about the nature of things from undeniable first principles that can be understood regardless of what they entail. If this were Ficino's aim, he would have been better off just presenting a single, conclusive argument and carefully justifying its individual steps. But this is not how Ficino proceeds. Rather, he provides a whole battery of considerations that collectively establish the immortality of the soul in that they converge on a comprehensive picture that makes a compelling case for conceiving of the soul as an immortal and immaterial entity.

Similarly, Ficino appeals to the central cosmological position of rational souls when defending the individuality of the intellect against Averroism. Ficino begins his refutation of Averroes[50] by arguing that he is committed to the view that the supra-individual "intellect is not a form such that it can perfect, give life to, and govern body, and adhere to body such that a single composite results from matter and from the intellect's substance, a composite whose being is one".[51] He then goes on to reject this view – and hence the Averroist position of the unicity of the intellect – by arguing that a mind incapable of giving life to its body cannot figure as a mediator between the material and the immaterial.[52]

Contrary to Alexander, Ficino argues that it is the human soul's central cosmological position and its corresponding function as a link between the material and immaterial realms of reality that explains why humans must have their own intellects. And similar to his refutation of the soul's mortality, Ficino's strategy to defend the soul's individuality consists in submitting that individual rational souls are necessary for a fully intelligible cosmos that mirrors the self-sufficient intelligibility of its creator. Averroes is wrong, according to Ficino, because the human soul can only figure as a mediator between two divine and two material levels of reality (God and angels on the one hand, qualities and bodies on the other) if it has its own individual intellect by which it can animate and govern its body.

Unlike the humanist criticism levelled against Aristotelian ethics and syllogistic mentioned in the previous section, Ficino addressed the views of his Aristotelian opponents directly. He did not doubt the legitimacy of their philosophical enterprise in general, but he did question the validity of some of their particular claims. By devising a comprehensive Platonist worldview, Ficino articulated a serious philosophical alternative to the Aristotelianism of his day, an alternative that found adherents not only due to its comprehensiveness and coherence, but also due to its degree of explanatory and conciliatory power to integrate almost every philosophical view that had ever been defended in the history of philosophy as a legitimate, yet incomplete, and sometimes even distorted, description of a limited aspect of the complex but integrated, intelligible structure of the universe. This enabled Ficino to present his Platonist worldview as the most accurate restoration of what he called the *prisca theologia*, the original, divinely revealed truth, which philosophers had increasingly distorted.

4 Conclusion

Because they played a major role in shaping the overall intellectual landscape between 1300 and 1600, Aristotelian hylomorphism, Renaissance humanism and Platonism are three important pillars for thinking about the mind in this period. However, as already mentioned, these three traditions are far from being the only elements of the philosophy of mind in this period. In this respect, it is particularly worth noting that there was a longstanding medical tradition that built on Galen's work by approaching the mind and its functions from a medical-empirical point of view.[53] Nonetheless, all the debates about the philosophy of mind between 1300 and 1600 that will be taken up in this volume build on at least one of these three pillars. Let me conclude by explaining how they do so and how the various problems treated in the subsequent chapters are connected with one another.

The first two chapters are concerned with different ways of approaching the philosophy of mind between 1300 and 1600. While Dominik Perler (Chapter 1) presents three different philosophical schools of the Later Middle Ages (Aristotelianism represented by Buridan, Platonism represented by Ficino and Pyrrhonian Scepticism represented by Montaigne) which all deploy distinctive methods in addressing questions about the mind, Guido Giglioni (Chapter 2) focuses on the tradition of Galenism, which drew on the medical study of human anatomy in attempting to explain the functioning of the mind and its illnesses.

The remaining chapters are devoted to various topics concerning the different operations of the mind and its nature (Chapters 3–11) and the psychological foundations of other disciplines. As seen in the first section, Aristotelians agreed that the soul is a principle of life and has various parts or faculties. But they widely disagreed on how these faculties relate to one another and how the existence of such a plurality of faculties is compatible with the soul's unity. In Chapter 3 Paul J.J.M. Bakker traces some Late Medieval voices on this debate.

Among the three parts of the human soul distinguished by Aristotle, the highest part, the rational soul, consists of will and intellect and is characteristic of human beings. It is this rational soul that turned out to be particularly problematic. How, for instance, does it manage to grasp universals? As seen above, Averroes famously thought that this question can only be answered on the assumption of a single supra-individual intellect shared by all humans. This conclusion found influential spokesmen in the 13th and 14th century, whose defence allowed Averroism to flourish as a serious philosophical position until the 17th century. In Chapter 4 Jean-Baptiste Brenet reconstructs the beginning of this Late Medieval debate about the unity of the intellect.

Apart from the metaphysical status of the different mental faculties, the precise account of their operations was no less controversial. A startling feature of our mind is that it endows us with intentionality, that is, with the capacity to think *about* various things. In Chapter 5, Paolo Rubini explores how philosophers from Ockham to Suárez tried to explain the intentionality of intellectual thoughts by refining or even opposing the famous model suggested by Thomas Aquinas. Another startling feature of our mind is that it renders us conscious. But how does it do that? In Chapter 6 Sonja Schierbaum presents three sophisticated Late Medieval attempts to crack this perennial problem.

Besides the intellect, the other component of our rational soul, the will, proved to be equally problematic. Then, as today, philosophers wondered how we should conceive of its freedom. In Chapter 7, Sydney Penner discusses a range of different Late Medieval views on this matter.

In addition to the operations of the rational soul – the soul's highest part – the functioning of its lower, perceptual faculties was also disputed. These disputes are traced in the following two chapters, which are concerned with Late Medieval debates about the activation of internal and external senses (treated by Daniel Heider in Chapter 8) and Renaissance theories of emotions, which take these psycho-physical phenomena as occasion to return to a Platonist-Stoic concept of spirit by means of which our minds can be seen as embodied beings in a panpsychist universe (as Sabrina Ebbersmeyer argues in Chapter 9).

The two chapters that follow are devoted to broader considerations about the metaphysical status of the mind. In Chapter 10, Sander W. de Boer explores Late Medieval and Renaissance debates about mind-body dualism, a view that, as he shows, was never embraced by the authors of the period, even though a few of them came very close to accepting it. In Chapter 11, Lorenzo Casini provides a survey of Renaissance debates about the immortality of the soul.

Finally, the last two chapters are concerned with the psychological foundations of morality and logic. As Eileen C. Sweeney argues in Chapter 12, Late Medieval and Renaissance authors of the scholastic and humanist tradition increasingly disputed the intrinsic connection between passions and morality, a link that was widely accepted by ancient and Medieval authors. And in Chapter 13, Marco Sgarbi shows how the Aristotelian doctrine of our capacity to grasp the first principles of scientific demonstrations led German philosophers to examine the scope of our epistemic faculties in anticipation of Kant's critical philosophy, while British philosophers transformed this doctrine into an empiricist framework.[54]

5 Acknowledgements

This volume owes its existence to a range of people and institutions. I would like to thank them here. First and foremost, I am grateful to the authors of the chapters of this volume. They presented and commented the first drafts of their chapters at a conference entitled "Late Medieval and Renaissance Accounts of the Mind" that took place at the Humboldt-Universität zu Berlin on October 23–25, 2014, and turned these drafts into the substantial chapters collected in this volume. Moreover, I am grateful to Joshua Crone for his work as a style editor, who helped integrate and unify the following chapters also on a linguistic level. Both, our conference and Josh's work, was generously funded by the Fritz Thyssen Foundation. For convincing the Fritz Thyssen Foundation that our project is indeed worth being funded I am deeply indebted to Dominik Perler. Last but not least, I would like to thank the main editors of the series of this volume, Rebecca Copenhaver and Christopher Shields, who not only initiated, but also supervised and accompanied the emergence of this volume in the best possible way. In planning the present volume I have particularly profited from my discussions with Dominik Perler and Christopher Shields, whose perceptive and knowledgeable comments at our conference, I am sure, have not only helped me, but all authors of this volume.

Notes

1 An outstanding attempt on this score is Pasnau 2011. A systematic overview of the philosophy of these times is to be found in Schmitt 1988, Hankins 2007a and in parts in Pasnau 2009.

2 This tendency is evident in Ueberweg (1924: 1–2) as well as in Kenny, Kretzmann & Pinborg 1982, which focuses almost exclusively on Aristotelian authors from the 13th to the 16th century.
3 This dismissive view of Aristotelianism after Aquinas is prominently found in Gilson 1949.
4 Doubtlessly pointed, these views are only slightly exaggerated versions of what one actually finds in enthusiastic portrayals of the time between 1300 and 1600 – perhaps most famously in Burckhardt 1860 – and in philosophical historical overviews such as Ueberweg (1924: 6–7).
5 See for instance Copenhaver & Schmitt (1992: 21), who emphasize use of "the term 'Renaissance' . . . [to] apply . . . to European history from early fourteenth to early seventeenth century, avoiding any prior commitment to a stronger sense of the term than this chronological use". Here Schmitt 1983 is a particularly notable work, which tracks the rich humanist engagement with Aristotelian texts, a tradition Schmitt calls 'Renaissance Aristotelianism'.
6 A telling example is Greenblatt 2012.
7 For a discussion of some of the debates incited by the latter question see Doyle 2007.
8 For more background see Schmitt 1988, Copenhaver & Schmitt 1992 and Hankins 2007a.
9 See *DA* II.2 413a21–b24, and for a discussion of Aristotle's conception of the parts of the soul see Johansen (2012: 47–71).
10 For a discussion see Sisko 1999 and Caston 2000.
11 By Pasnau 2007.
12 Averroes changed his view on this matter several times and treated the subject of the human intellect in no less than seven works; see Davidson (1992: 261–265). The only work on this subject known to the medieval Latin world was his *Long commentary* [*Commentarium magnum in Aristotelis De anima libros*], in which he defended the view of there being only one eternal supra-individual intellect shared by all humans. This view was subsequently discussed under the label Averroism. For more on this, see Chapter 4 in this volume.
13 Siger defends his Averroist position of the unity of the intellect in his *Quaestiones in tertium de anima*. Aquinas's most extensive refutation of this view is to be found in his treatise *De unitate intellectus contra Averroistas*.
14 For more on the condemnation of 1277 see Chapter 7 in this volume and Wippel 2002.
15 Apart from Chapter 4 in this volume, see also Brenet 2003 on Jandun's Averroism and Akasoy & Giglioni 2013 on Averroism in the Renaissance.
16 See his *STh*. I, q. 76, art. 1 corp. and Bazán 1997 for a discussion.
17 See his *STh*. I, q. 77, art. 1, corp.
18 *STh*. I, q. 77, art. 1, corp.
19 *STh*. I, q. 77, art. 1, ad 7.
20 See *Reportatio* II, q. 20 (*OTh* V: 428), and for further exploration of Ockham's criticism on Aquinas on this score, Perler 2015, 114–123.
21 *Reportatio* II, q. 20 (*OTh* V: 436), the translation is from Perler 2013: 28, who provides a wonderfully clear account of Ockham's 'procedural account' of faculties. See also Chapter 3 in this volume.
22 Some authors of the 14th century, such as Gregor of Rimini and John Buridan, tried to avoid this conclusion by distinguishing between the soul's power and the necessary conditions of its exercise. By appealing to this distinction they could argue that humans have only one immaterial soul, which is not distinct from its powers, while nonetheless conceding that the soul can exercise some of these powers only if the soul is conjoined to the body. For more on this strategy see Chapter 3 in this volume.

23 Note that Ockham offered several arguments in defence of pluralism. For a systematic discussion of all of them, see Perler 2010.
24 *QQ* II.10 (*OTh* IX: 159); transl. Kelly & Freddoso (1991: 134), slightly modified.
25 *QQ*. II.10 (*OTh* IX: 161); transl. Kelly & Freddoso (1991: 136), slightly modified.
26 For an overview of how the debate between Averroists, Thomist unitarians and Franciscan pluralists developed throughout the Renaissance see Michael 2000.
27 This conception of humanism is particularly evident in Sartre 1948.
28 This characterization of humanism is particularly emphasized by Witt (2000: 22), who holds that "a litmus for identifying a humanist was his intention to imitate ancient Latin style".
29 See Kristeller (1961: 110).
30 This narrative is given by Burckhardt 1860, but can also be found in Cassirer (1927: 130 & 201), who maintained that the Renaissance gave rise to new questions about the nature and importance of self-awareness, which were then clearly articulated by Descartes and Leibniz.
31 For more on the relation between humanism and scholasticism, see Hankins 2007b, Kristeller (1961: 92–119) and Schmitt 1983.
32 See Petrarch, *Own Ignorance*, 315.
33 Petrarch, *Familiaria* I.7 (3), 79.
34 See his *DD* II proem. 3 (vol. 2: 3). For a detailed discussion, see Nauta 2009 and Copenhaver & Nauta 2012.
35 For more on the educational influence of humanism and further references see Copenhaver & Schmitt (1992: 31).
36 Schmitt & Copenhaver (1992: 33–34).
37 For a detailed history of Alexander's doctrine of the soul see Keßler 2011.
38 Alexander of Aphrodisias, *Enarratio De anima* IV: 34–35.
39 More precisely in his *Commentarium magnum*, III.5, 395–398.
40 See Park & Keßler (1988: 457).
41 See Chapters 5 and 11. For more on Pomponazzi's philosophy of mind in general see Rubini 2015.
42 Petrarch, *Own Ignorance*, 321–322.
43 See *PTh*. V.10.2 (vol. 2: 59).
44 See *PTh*. XII.4.3 (vol. 4: 45–46). Ficino describes the process of activating these innate formulae by comparing it to the production of images by our sensation and phantasy; cf. *PTh*. VIII.1.2–5, XII.2.2 and XII.3.4.
45 *PTh*. Proem (vol. 1: 11).
46 See ibid.
47 For further discussion of Ficino's arguments, see Chapters 1 and 11.
48 Ficino argues for the intermediary position of the soul in his *PTh*. III.2.
49 *PTh*. V.1.2 (vol. 2: 13).
50 Note that as in many Renaissance debates about Averroism, Ficino's "Averroes" might not be identical with the historical Andalusian philosopher Ibn Rushd, but rather "a construct that he assembled from his study of Thomas Aquinas", as Copenhaver (2009: 444) argued.
51 *PTh*. XV.1.3 (vol. 5: 13).
52 Cf. his *PTh*. XV.2.2 (vol. 5: 29–30).
53 For more on such approaches see Chapter 2 of this volume.
54 This chapter has profited from helpful comments and suggestions by Therese Scarpelli Cory, Sander de Boer, Rebekka Hufendiek, Katja Krause, Sydney Penner, Dominik Perler, Paolo Rubini, Magali Roques, Christopher Shields and Marco Sgarbi. I am grateful to all of them.

Bibliography

Primary sources

Alexander of Aphrodisias. *Enarratio De anima ex Aristotelis institutione* (= *Enarratio De anima*). E. Keßler & Ch. H. Lohr (eds) & G. Donatus (trans.). Reprint of the first edition Brescia, 1495. Stuttgart-Bad Cannstatt: Frommann-Holzboog, 2008.
Aristotle. *De anima* (= *DA*). R. D. Hicks (trans.). Cambridge, UK: Cambridge University Press, 1907.
———. *Nikomachean Ethics* (=*NE*). In *The Complete Works of Aristotle*, vol. 2, J. Barnes (ed.). Princeton: Princeton University Press, 1984.
Averroes. *Commentarium magnum in Aristotelis De anima libros*. F. S. Crawford (ed.). Cambridge, MA: Mediaeval Academy of America, 1953.
Ficino, Marisilio. *Platonic Theology* (= *PTh*), 6 vols. M. J. B. Allen & J. Hankins (trans. & eds). Cambridge, MA: Harvard University Press, 2001–2006.
Petrarch, Francesco. *On His Own Ignorance* (=*Own Ignorance*). In *Invectives*, D. Marsh (ed.). Cambridge, MA: Harvard University Press, 2003.
———. *Familiaria: Bücher der Vertraulichkeiten*, vol. 1, books 1–12. B. Widmer (ed.). Berlin, New York: de Gruyter, 2005.
Siger of Brabant. *Summa Theologiae* (= *STh*). P. Carmello (ed.). Torino: Marietti, 1961.
———. *Quastiones in tertium de anima*. B. Bazán (ed.), 1–69. Louvain: Publications Universitaires, 1972.
———. *On the Unity of the Intellect Against the Averroists* (=*De unitate intellectus contra Averroistas*). B. H. Zedler (trans.). Milwaukee: Marquette University Press, 2004 (Latin text in *Opera Omnia*, Editio Leonina, vol. 43, 291–314. Rome, 1976).
Valla, Lorenzo (Laurentius). *Dialectical Disputations (Repastinatio dialectice et philosophie)* (= *DD*), 2 vols. B. P. Copenhaver & L. Nauta (eds. & trans.). Cambridge, MA: Harvard University Press, 2012.
William of Ockham. *Opera philosophica et theologica* (= *OPh* and *OTh*), 17 vols. G. Gál, J. Wey, S. Brown, et al. (eds). St. Bonaventure: The Franciscan Institute, 1967–1988.
———. *Quodlibetal Questions*, vol. I & II, Quodlibets 1–7 (= *QQ*). A. J. Freddoso & F. E. Kelley (trans.). New Haven, London: Yale University Press, 1991.

Secondary sources

Akasoy, A. & Guido, G. (eds). 2013. *Renaissance Averroism and Its Aftermath: Arabic Philosophy in Early Modern Europe*. Dordrecht, The Netherlands: Springer.
Bazán, B. C. 1997. "The Human Soul: Form *and* Substance? Thomas Aquinas' Critique of Eclectic Aristotelianism". *Archives d'histoire doctrinale et littéraire du Moyen Âge* **64**: 95–126.
Brenet, J.-B. 2003. *Transferts du sujet: la noétique d'Averroès selon Jean de Jandun*. Paris: Vrin.
Burckhardt, J. 1860. *Die Cultur der Renaissance in Italien: ein Versuch*. Basel: Schweighauser.
Cassirer, E. 1927. *Individuum und Kosmos in der Philosophie der Renaissance*. Berlin: Teubner.

Caston, V. 2000. "Aristotle's Argument for Why the Understanding Is Not Compounded With the Body". *Proceedings of the Boston Area Colloquium in Ancient Philosophy* **16**: 135–174.

Copenhaver, B. 2009. "Ten Arguments in Search of a Philosopher: Averroes and Aquinas in Ficino's Platonic Theology". *Vivarium* **47**(4): 444–479.

Copenhaver, B. & Nauta, L. 2012. "Introduction". See Valla, *DD* (2012).

Copenhaver, B. & Schmitt, Ch. 1992. *Renaissance Philosophy*. Oxford, New York: Oxford University Press.

Davidson, H. A. 1992. *Alfarabi, Avicenna, and Averroes on Intellect: Their Cosmologies, Theories of Active Intellect and Theories of the Human Intellect*. Oxford, New York: Oxford University Press.

Doyle, J. 2007. "Hispanic Scholastic Philosophy". See Hankins (2007a), 250–269.

Gilson, E. 1949. *Being and Some Philosophers*. Toronto: Pontifical Institute of Mediaeval Studies.

Greenblatt, S. 2012. *The Swerve: How the Renaissance Began*. London: Vintage.

Hankins, J. (ed.). 2007a. *The Cambridge Companion to Renaissance Philosophy*. Cambridge, New York: Cambridge University Press.

———. 2007b. "Humanism, Scholasticism, and Renaissance Philosophy". See Hankins (2007a), 30–48.

Johansen, T. 2012. *The Powers of Aristotle's Soul*. Oxford, New York: Oxford University Press.

Kenny, A., Kretzmann, N. & Pinborg, J. (eds). 1982. *Cambridge History of Later Medieval Philosophy*. Cambridge, New York: Cambridge University Press.

Keßler, E. 2011. *Alexander of Aphrodisias and His Doctrine of the Soul: 1400 Years of Lasting Significance*. Dordrecht, The Netherlands, Leiden: Brill.

Kristeller, P. O. 1961. *Renaissance Thought*. New York: Harper.

Michael, E. 2000. "Renaissance Theories of Body, Soul, and Mind". In *Psyche and Soma: Physicians and Metaphysicians on the Mind-Body Problem From Antiquity to Enlightenment*, J. N. Wright & P. Potter (eds), 147–172. Oxford, New York: Oxford University Press.

Nauta, L. 2009. *In Defense of Common Sense: Lorenzo Valla's Humanist Critique of Scholastic Philosophy*. Cambridge, MA: Harvard University Press.

Park, K. & Keßler, E. 1988. "The Concept of Psychology". See Schmitt (1988), 455–463. Cambridge, New York: Cambridge University Press.

Pasnau, R. 2002. *Thomas Aquinas on Human Nature*. Cambridge, New York: Cambridge University Press.

———. 2007. "The Mind-Soul Problem". In *Mind, Cognition and Representation*, J. M. M. H. Thijssen & P. J. J. M. Bakker (eds), 3–19. Aldershot: Ashgate.

——— (ed.). 2009. *The Cambridge History of Medieval Philosophy*, 2 vols. Cambridge, MA: Cambridge University Press.

———. 2011. *Metaphysical Themes: 1274–1671*. Oxford: Clarendon Press.

Perler, D. 2010. "Ockham über die Seele und ihre Teile". *Recherches de théologie et philosophie médiévales* **77**: 313–350.

———. 2013. "What Are Faculties of the Soul? Descartes and His Scholastic Background". *Proceedings of the British Academy* **189**: 9–38.

———. 2015. "Medieval Debates on Faculties". In *Faculties: A History*, D. Perler (ed.). Oxford, New York: Oxford University Press.

Rubini, P. 2015. *Pietro Pomponazzis Erkenntnistheorie: Naturalisierung des menschlichen Geistes im Spätaristotelismus*. Leiden: Brill.
Sartre, J.-P. 1948. *Existentialism and Humanism*. Ph. Mairet (trans.). London: Methuen.
Schmitt, Ch. 1983. *Aristotle and the Renaissance*. Cambridge, MA: Harvard University Press.
———. (ed.). 1988. *Cambridge History of Renaissance Philosophy*. Cambridge, New York: Cambridge University Press.
Schmitt, Ch. & Copenhaver, B. 1992. *Renaissance philosophy*. Oxford, New York: Oxford University Press.
Shields, Ch. 2007. *Aristotle*. London: Routledge.
Sisko, J. 1999. "On Separating the Intellect From the Body: Aristotle's *De Anima* III.4, 429a10-b5". *Archiv für Geschichte der Philosophie* **81**: 249–267.
Ueberweg, F. 1924. *Grundriß der Geschichte der Philosophie*, vol. 3: *Die Philosophie der Neuzeit bis zum Ende des XVIII. Jahrhunderts*. Berlin: Mittler.
Wippel, J. F. 2002. "The Parisian Condemnations of 1270 and 1277". In *A Companion to Philosophy in the Middle Ages*, J. J. E. Gracia & T. B. Noone (eds), 65–73. Malden, MA: Blackwell.
Witt, R. 2000. *"In the Footsteps of the Ancients": The Origins of Humanism From Lovato to Bruni*. Leiden: Brill.

1

MIND AND METHOD

Dominik Perler

1 Introduction

Any substantial theory of the mind has to deal with a number of intriguing questions. What kind of entity is the mind? How is it related to the body? Why and how can it produce activities such as thinking, willing and remembering? There is no doubt that late medieval and Renaissance philosophers offered elaborate answers to these questions, thus presenting detailed theories of the mind. But how did they proceed when building up their theories? To what kind of explanatory principles did they appeal? What kind of conceptual tools did they use? And how did they apply these tools?

These questions concerning their method are as important as those dealing with their account of specific problems. In fact, it is often impossible to understand their solution to a given problem without paying attention to the method they used for solving it. A closer look at the method is, of course, required for an understanding of every theory of the past, for every theory is shaped by explicit or implicit assumptions about how one should proceed in the analysis of a phenomenon. But it is of particular importance for an adequate understanding of theories of the mind developed in the period between 1300 and 1600 since there was no commonly accepted method in that period. Instead, we see a pluralism of methods inspired by Aristotelian, Platonist and Hellenistic traditions. These traditions did not simply succeed each other in a linear order. That is to say there was not simply an Aristotelian tradition that dominated up to the late fourteenth century, followed by a Platonist tradition in the fifteenth century and a Hellenistic tradition in the sixteenth, as a traditional historiographical scheme might suggest. Rather, Aristotelianism was present throughout the three centuries and coexisted with an increasing number of Platonist and Hellenistic strands.[1] The question to be asked is therefore not how an Aristotelian method was replaced by a Platonic or a Hellenistic one. The crucial questions rather are: What use did individual authors make of the various methods that were available? How did they reinterpret and eventually transform them? And how did they apply them in order to solve specific problems concerning the mind?

In the following I want to address these questions by focusing on three authors: John Buridan, who worked in the Aristotelian tradition; Marsilio Ficino, who was inspired by Platonism; and Michel de Montaigne, who was strongly influenced by Pyrrhonian scepticism. Before starting with an analysis of these authors, we should take into account three basic facts that are significant for all late medieval and Renaissance thinkers. First of all, they mostly spoke about the soul (*anima*), not about the mind (*mens*). This is much more than a terminological issue since most philosophers, especially those working in the Aristotelian tradition, considered the soul to be an all-embracing principle of life, responsible not just for higher cognitive functions, but also for lower vegetative and sensory ones. Consequently, they did not simply ask how and why thinking is possible; they were equally interested in processes like digestion and sensation. In fact, they often compared higher processes to lower ones, analyzing their similarities as well as dissimilarities. Hence, it is important not to contrast the mind as a well-defined entity with the body and to ask how late medieval and Renaissance authors conceived of the former. The relevant questions are rather how they explained higher processes in relation to lower ones and how they accounted for their unity. Or, in short, one should look at the way they dealt with the mind-soul problem, not just with the mind-body problem.[2]

The second general point to bear in mind is that there was no sharply defined discipline called 'psychology' in the period between 1300 and 1600. Psychology as a special field of investigation was developed in the modern period; not until the late nineteenth century did it emerge as an independent discipline that was institutionally recognized as a branch of science.[3] Of course, pre-modern authors widely discussed psychological phenomena, and some even talked about a 'science of the soul' (*scientia de anima*).[4] But this science was not considered an autonomous discipline. Instead, it was seen as a discipline that partly dealt with metaphysical issues (e.g., the status of the soul and its faculties) and partly with physical ones (e.g., the functioning of sensory organs). That is why the science of the soul was not classified on the same level as other sciences; it was treated as a branch of metaphysics, of physics or of both. This had an immediate consequence for methodological debates. The vexing problem for many authors was how and to what extent the science of the soul could borrow methods from metaphysics and physics. Moreover, authors influenced by scepticism asked if it was possible to speak about a science at all. Can we really spell out a set of general principles that apply to our own soul as well as to every other human soul? Or should we limit ourselves to describing particular phenomena we experience in our soul? These questions show that it was not simply the status of a science of the soul that was at stake, but the very possibility of a science dealing with subjectively experienced phenomena.[5]

Finally, it is important to note that debates about the appropriate method were closely linked to metaphysical discussions. This is hardly surprising, given the non-autonomous status of psychology. If psychology is partly a sub-discipline of metaphysics, basic problems in psychology turn out to be metaphysical problems. In particular, problems concerning the intellect, the immaterial part of the soul, are metaphysical problems because metaphysics taken in the strict sense is precisely about immaterial, imperishable entities.[6] But other parts of the soul, too, require metaphysical analysis when metaphysics is taken in a larger sense, namely as the discipline that investigates basic principles and categories of being. Metaphysical issues are at stake as soon as one asks what kind of entity the soul and its parts are, what kind of essential features they have and what kind of principles are required for explaining them. It would therefore be inadequate to look for a 'pure method' that is free from all metaphysical assumptions. On the contrary, it is precisely the commitment to fundamental metaphysical claims (or, in the case of the sceptics, the suspension of metaphysical claims) that distinguishes various ways of examining the mind in the period between 1300 and 1600.

2 John Buridan: an Aristotelian approach

In 1255 Aristotle's writings in natural philosophy officially became part of the curriculum at the University of Paris. This meant, of course, that from then on *De anima* was regularly taught and commented on in the Arts Faculty – not just in Paris, but in all the newly established universities.[7] When lecturing on this text, many masters were interested not only in details concerning the functioning of the soul, but in the entire program Aristotle had set up for the study of the soul. How should the soul be analyzed? What kind of concepts should be used to classify and describe it? And how should these concepts be related to those used in other fields? The increasing interest in these questions is manifest in the very structure of the commentaries on *De anima*. Fourteenth-century authors included more and more sections that did not deal with specific parts of Aristotle's text, but with its overall aim and the method it proposed. John Buridan, a master who spent his entire academic career at the Arts Faculty in Paris, is a telling example. In his commentary written between 1347 and 1357/58, he addressed a number of general problems concerning the appropriate way of studying the soul, thus engaging in a methodological debate.[8]

Buridan opens the debate with a very general question: What is the specific object of the science of the soul?[9] At first sight, this question looks quite naïve. Is it not evident that this science is about the soul, thus differing from other sciences that have their own object (metaphysics deals with being *qua* being, physics with being in motion, etc.)? A closer look at the context reveals, however, that Buridan is far from being naïve. In the fourteenth century, at least two objections had been raised against the seemingly natural answer. First, Ockham had insisted on the fact that no science deals directly with things in the world. Its first object is always a sentence or a plurality of sentences about things in the world, for these are the only items that are immediately grasped and understood by the intellect.[10] Therefore, we cannot say that the science of the soul has the soul as its proper object. Its object is rather a number of sentences about the soul – sentences that exist as long as there are speakers forming them. The second objection goes even deeper and has its root in Aristotle's own text. Let us grant for a moment that the science of the soul deals with something in the world. Why should that thing be just the soul and not the soul-body composite, given that Aristotle had emphasized that the soul is not a distinct thing added to the body but the principle of life present in the body? The soul does not seem to be an entity that could be studied apart from the body.

Buridan is fully aware of these problems. In response to Ockham he grants that in some sense only linguistic items are the immediate object of the science of the soul.[11] But the important point is that this science deals with terms of first imposition, i.e., with terms that directly signify things in the world, and consequently with sentences that are about these things. Our sentences are nothing but linguistic means that enable us to speak about things. This reply shows that Buridan applies his general theory of direct signification, which he develops in his philosophy of language, to the special case of our talk about the soul.[12] The simple fact that we need to make use of linguistic signs in order to acquire and exchange knowledge of the soul does not prove that our direct objects are just signs; objects should not be conflated with necessary means.

The second objection is more difficult. Like Aristotle, Buridan does not conceive of the soul as a thing added to the body. It is rather the principle of actuality, unity and life for the body.[13] How then can there be a science that deals just with the soul? Buridan stresses that "although the soul is inseparable from the body and could not function without the body, it is still possible to study the soul in itself by studying attributes and predicates that are suited to the soul in itself, not to the entire body".[14] He explains this point by contrasting the study of the soul with the study of the ensouled body. The first examines just the functions of the soul, whereas the second analyzes them insofar as they are present in a living animal. What does that mean? Let me illustrate the contrast by adducing an example.

Suppose that you want to examine the visual faculty in human beings. There are two ways of doing that. You can ask what a visual faculty is, what its distinctive features are, how it is related to other faculties and to the human being as a whole. When choosing this line you will not look at the visual apparatus in a given human being. You will wonder, quite generally, what it means for a human being to have a visual faculty, and you will describe the relationship between this faculty and other faculties by assigning a certain function to each of them. In the end you will ideally draw some kind of functional map that indicates the place of the visual faculty in the network of all the faculties. But you can also proceed in a different way, namely by looking at a specific human being, by examining her eyes, i.e., the lens, nerves, muscles, etc. they consist of, and the way they produce visual representations. You can then compare the eyes of this human being to that of another one, perhaps even to the eyes of non-human animals, and you will detect striking similarities. In the end you will attain detailed physiological and optical knowledge of various eyes.

This example shows that there are two ways of studying the soul. We can either draw a general map of the soul and its functions without looking at the way the functions are realized in this or that particular body, or we can give a detailed account of various functions insofar as they are materially present in a body. The way we choose has, of course, an immediate consequence for the appropriate method. If we decide to draw a general map, we do not need to enter into physiological or anatomical details. We simply start with the standard picture we have of human beings or other animals and then try to schematize the functions we ascribe to them.

But what can we learn when we proceed in this way? Buridan answers this question by focusing on the faculties that are ascribed to the soul as its 'attributes'. An everyday observation of human beings shows that they have a vast number of faculties designed to produce various activities, among them digesting, seeing and thinking. Does that mean that faculties are distinct causes, each with its own range of activities, and that all the faculties together form some kind of causal net? Several late thirteenth- and fourteenth-century authors drew exactly this conclusion, speaking about faculties as entities that are formally (or even really) distinct from each other.[15] Buridan vigorously rejects this position, defending instead the thesis that the soul is a single, undivided entity. Faculties are nothing but powers of this entity, and powers are not distinct things but ways of acting. So, when we speak about the visual and the rational faculty we simply say that there is a single soul that is able to act in at least two ways; it can produce both acts of seeing and acts of thinking. The crucial point is that it is one and the same thing that can act in both ways. Buridan mockingly remarks: "For if someone is a father of several children, he does not have to be several fathers; and if something is diverse from several things, it does not, on that account, have to be several diversities".[16] As it is one father that can beget many children, so it is one soul that can bring about many activities; distinct effects do not require distinct causes.

But are there not different *types* of effects? Acts of seeing clearly differ from acts of thinking; therefore, not all acts can be compared to children, who all belong to the same type of effect. So, should we not concede that there are at least different causes for different types of effects? Not according to Buridan. In his view, the soul as a single cause produces different types of acts only because it is active in different parts of the body, which have their own structure. Thus, eyes are built in such a way that the soul produces acts of seeing when it becomes active in them. But in principle it could produce the same type of acts if it were present in another part that displays the same structure. Buridan illustrates this point with a thought experiment.[17] Imagine that God were intervening in nature and forming an eye in a foot. Could the foot then see? Yes, Buridan responds, because the soul would then be active in a bodily part that has the appropriate structure for acts of seeing.[18] This fanciful case shows that it is in fact a single, undivided soul that can, at least in principle, produce every type of act. There is no plurality of sub-souls, i.e., of faculties acting as distinct causes, distributed all over the body and responsible for different types of acts.

From a methodological point of view, it is remarkable that Buridan pursues a *reductionist strategy*, arguing that it is superfluous to posit many agents in order to explain many types of acts. We simply need to refer to (i) a cause that is present in the entire body and (ii) different bodily parts that diversify the activity of that cause according to their structure. Equally remarkable is the way we can arrive at this insight. We do not need to engage in an elaborate empirical investigation that reveals the structure of each and every bodily part. We need only reflect upon the functioning of a faculty in order to realize that a faculty is simply a way in which the soul, the only causal principle, acts.

This way of examining the soul is also of crucial importance when we talk about the mind, which is nothing but the rational faculty. As soon as we adopt the reductionist strategy we will realize that there is no such thing as the mind added to other entities and producing a special type of acts. The mind is simply the soul insofar as it brings about acts of thinking and willing. Therefore, we should always appeal to the soul as the only cause if we want to explain what is responsible for particular rational acts. The only thing that is special about these acts is that they do not depend on a specific bodily part. Following Aristotle, Buridan claims that they are fully immaterial.[19] That is why the soul produces them without being bound to the heart, the brain or some other material organ.

This last point gives rise to the suspicion that the reductionist strategy has, after all, its limits. Is Buridan not compelled to distinguish between a soul that depends on the body and produces many acts that range from digesting to seeing, and another soul that is independent from the body and brings about immaterial acts of thinking and willing? This would be exactly Ockham's position. He had affirmed that it is inevitable to posit an immaterial, non-extended soul in addition to a material, extended one.[20] This claim had paved the way for a form of dualism in the fourteenth century – not soul-body dualism, of course, but soul-mind dualism.[21] The cause responsible for mental acts was set apart from the cause producing vegetative and sensory acts.

Buridan is familiar with this position but clearly rejects it, objecting that it threatens the unity of human beings (since if they had two souls and hence two substantial forms they could not be real unities) and, even worse, that it mixes up the functioning of the soul with its existence.[22] The fact that the soul can produce acts of thinking and willing without using a specific organ only shows that one of its functions does not depend on the body. But this does not prove that it must be a special entity existing in addition to another soul that acts in the body. Once we understand this crucial point, we can assign all the acts to the same soul. We simply need to specify under what circumstances (in other words, with or without a bodily organ) the soul performs a certain activity.

No doubt, the claim that the soul can act independently of any bodily organ is hardly self-evident and needs justification.[23] What matters here, however, is not Buridan's detailed argumentation for this claim but the method he chooses. He incorporates a study of the mind into a study of the soul and argues that we first need to be clear about the status and functioning of the mind. This is only possible if we realize that the soul can act in a specific (namely rational) way without requiring a special cause that is distinct from all other causes. We arrive at this conclusion not through empirical investigation, but by reflecting upon the relationship between causes and acts, i.e., upon the fact that one and the same cause can act in different ways, with or without a material basis. It is therefore a *metaphysical* reflection that enables us to work out an explanation of mental activities and to present a general map of the soul.

3 Marsilio Ficino: a Platonic approach

The Aristotelian program of a science of the soul was continued and further elaborated by many philosophers throughout the late medieval period.[24] Yet, in the fifteenth century, it was complemented and to some extent also opposed by a Platonic program. One of its most prominent defenders was Marsilio Ficino. His principal work, written between 1469 and 1474 and published in 1482, shows from its very title that he was indebted to the Platonic tradition. *Platonic Theology*, its main title, is a direct reference to Proclus's work of the same title; *On the Immortality of the Soul*, its subtitle, is an allusion to a part of Plotinus's *Enneads* (IV.7) and one of Augustine's earlier writings. In the very first sentence of this comprehensive work, Ficino invokes "Plato, the father of philosophers" as his authority.[25] However, the Plato he has in mind is not simply the Athenian philosopher, but a thinker interpreted and transformed by a series of later thinkers, both pagan and Christian.

What Ficino sees at the core of the Platonic program is an all-embracing theory of the structure of the world. This theory explains not only what kind of things there are, but also how they are related to each other, how they act and are acted upon, and how they form a fully coherent universe together. Only when we understand the place human souls occupy in this universe can we fully grasp what kind of entities they are and what kind of activities they can perform. That is why Ficino takes it to be of crucial importance not to focus on individual souls and their cognitive achievements, but on souls in general, that is, on their status and function in a well-ordered universe. Moreover, he takes it to be a basic fact that the human soul is "like a mirror in which the image of the divine countenance is readily reflected".[26] By analyzing the structure of the human soul we can therefore gain an insight into the divine intellect.

These programmatic statements show that Ficino has at least two goals in mind. First, he wants to assign a special place to the human soul, and second, he intends to emphasize its godlike and hence privileged status. To do so, he sketches a cosmological model that presents the entire universe as consisting of five hierarchically ordered levels of beings: bodies, qualities, souls, angels and God.[27] This model is directly inspired by Proclus and shows that Ficino intends to renew a Neoplatonic vision of the world.[28] It is characteristic of this vision that we can look at things in the world in both an ascending and a descending way. That is, we can start with the lowest level and ask why things on that level, namely bodies, are possible and why they exhibit a certain structure. To answer these questions we ascend to a higher level of things and from there to a still higher one, etc., until we finally arrive at the fifth and highest level where we find God, the most perfect and self-sufficient being, one that needs no other thing for its existence. But we can also start with God as the highest cause from which everything else flows. We can then ask what flows from God and descend to a lower level of things, and from there to a still lower one, etc., until we finally arrive at the lowest level, namely that of bodies which fully depend on higher things. It is significant for this procedure that in ascending we indicate *explanatory relations* since we give an account of lower things by appealing to higher ones. We say, for instance, that the movement of bodies cannot be explained unless we refer to higher things that set them in motion, and we add that there need to be still higher things so that the moving things can have some power. By contrast, in descending we indicate *causal relations* since we make clear what stems or flows from higher things. Thus, we say that God causes angels as fully immaterial but dependent beings, and we then add that angels act upon lower things and cause them to exhibit certain features. The important point is that the two types of relations match each other; what explains a certain thing is the cause of that thing. That is why we can always go upwards and downwards in the scale of beings and try to find the causal relations that match the explanatory relations.

In pursuing this strategy Ficino implicitly subscribes to two basic methodological principles. The first is the Principle of Sufficient Reason (PSR). To be sure, unlike Leibniz and other later rationalists, Ficino does not explicitly mention it, but it dominates his entire philosophical program, for in his view nothing can be accepted as a brute fact.[29] For everything that exists we need to give a reason, i.e., we need to explain why it exists and why it displays certain features. This is the driving force behind Ficino's thesis that we should always go upwards in the scale of beings and look for higher things that enable us to understand why lower things exist the way they do. And we need to proceed in this search for an explanation until we arrive at something self-explanatory. Like earlier Christian Neoplatonists and later rationalists Ficino takes this self-explanatory entity to be God, an entity that is always fully actual and therefore not in need of being actualized by something else. The second implicit methodological principle is the Principle of Perfection (PP), according to which whatever accounts for something else has to be more perfect than what it accounts for. Should it lack a higher degree of perfection, it would not have the power to bring about specific features or even the sheer existence of another thing. In light of this principle, it is hardly surprising that Ficino assigns a hierarchical structure to things in the world. There cannot be just a vast number of natural substances that all exist on the same level and act on each other. Admittedly, there are many things on a given level, say many bodies, but the crucial point is that they could not exist and eventually act on each other if there were no higher, more perfect things to make them act.

This appeal to two methodological principles has an immediate consequence for an explanation of the human soul. Since it is part of the hierarchically ordered universe, it needs to be explained like everything else (according to the PSR), and what accounts for its existence needs to be a higher, more perfect being (according to the PP). What is special about the human soul is, of course, that it occupies the third of a total of five levels, thus inhabiting the middle of the universe.[30] Hence, it is not merely something that can be explained (namely in relation to angels and God as higher things), but equally something that can be invoked in explaining other entities (namely bodies and qualities as lower things). Or in short, the soul is an explainable explainer. It is therefore quite understandable that Ficino focuses on the soul in its relation to higher as well as lower things. But what can we explain when we look at this double relation?

To answer this question we need to examine the way the soul is related to bodies on the first level and to God on the fifth. Bodies, the lowest of all things, are purely passive and inactive things that have no power in themselves. They cannot move or bring about a change. Qualities, things on the second level, cannot be responsible for a change either, because they are simply added to or taken away from bodies and do not cause any organic process. It is therefore indispensable to have an active entity that brings about such a process. This is precisely the soul, as Ficino points out: "When it fills bodies, moving them from within, it gives them life".[31] The decisive point is that the soul is not simply present in a part of a given body, leaving the other parts untouched. It is rather present in the entire body, thus making it a living thing that is able to move, grow, initiate a change and act upon other bodies. As soon as the soul is removed, the body returns to the status of an inert, completely passive thing.

In defending this view Ficino accepts some form of dualism, conceding that the soul is a special entity added to and detachable from the body. To be sure, this is a rather broad form of dualism, for not just rational human souls, but all things that give life to inert bodies are taken to be souls. Like traditional Aristotelians, Ficino ascribes a soul to every living creature. Moreover, he ascribes a soul to every celestial sphere, as indeed he must; for how would they rotate if they were not united with an active entity that makes them move?[32] This shows that the third level of beings comprises all sorts of principles of activity. What, then, makes the human soul so special on that level? It is the fact that it is related not just to bodies, but also – and even immediately – to God. Of course, all souls are related to God insofar as he is the creator of everything. But human souls are related to him in a special way because they mirror him. Consequently, they have a rational faculty just like God, a faculty that enables them to produce thoughts and chains of reasoning. This leads Ficino to the following definition of the human soul: "It is life which understands discursively, and gives life to the body in time".[33] This might appear like a fairly traditional definition. But a closer look reveals that it nicely captures the middle position of the human soul. This soul is related to bodies on the first level, to which it gives life and therefore activity, and at the same time to God on the fifth level, from whom it receives rationality and therefore the ability to understand. The definition also shows that the human soul is indeed some kind of explainable explainer; it explains life and motion in bodies, and its ability to understand can be explained as a godlike feature.

From a methodological point of view, two points are noteworthy in this attempt to define the human soul as standing in a double relation. The first point concerns its causal dimension. If the soul is not only an entity that acts upon bodies, but also one that is acted upon by higher things, it is important to know what all these relations are. How can the soul occupy a middle place in a causal chain? This question is particularly pressing because Ficino does not simply refer to external efficient causes when spelling out this chain. That is, he does not say that a cause is an agent that acts from the outside upon another thing. When describing the soul's activity he stresses that the soul acts *in* the body, and when talking about divine omnipotence he similarly emphasizes that God acts *in* all lower things, including human souls.[34] He obviously has a form of internal causation in mind. This has an important consequence for the explanatory scheme that is to be applied to the soul. When we speak about its operations, we should make clear how internal causation works. How can God act in the soul, and how can the soul in turn act in a body? Or to put it generally, how can there be a series of nested causal relations? It is precisely this problem of causation that was now open to debate. The interesting point, methodologically speaking, is that this problem did not emerge from an empirical observation of various activities of the soul. It was the Neoplatonic conception of a universal flow of causes according to which every cause is present in the effect that gave rise to it.

A second point to be noted is that Ficino's relational account of the human soul inevitably poses the immortality problem. If the soul mirrors God and if God is even present in the soul, it cannot be as perishable as a body. It must be an immaterial and hence immortal entity. Ficino adduces numerous arguments for this thesis, ranging from the soul's impassivity and indivisibility to its independent existence.[35] What matters here is less the detailed structure of the arguments than the procedure Ficino follows when introducing them. He starts with cosmological reflections upon the status of the human soul in a well-ordered universe. These reflections lead him to the conclusion that an entity mirroring the immortal God and constantly participating in his causal power must itself be immortal. A specific thesis about the status of the human soul is therefore the immediate – or even inevitable – consequence of a certain way of thinking about the soul. And the method of relational analysis, i.e., of looking at the soul as standing in explanatory and causal relations to higher as well as lower beings, has an immediate impact on the characterization of the soul.

4 Montaigne: a sceptical approach

Both Aristotelian and Platonic conceptions of the soul were widely discussed throughout the fifteenth and sixteenth centuries. Yet, the rediscovery of Pyrrhonian scepticism (Sextus Empiricus's *Outlines of Scepticism* were translated into Latin in 1562) gave rise to a different approach to the soul, one that did not simply add another theory to the stock of existing ones but radically questioned the possibility of constructing a theory. It might be an exaggeration to speak of a 'Pyrrhonian crisis' since the philosophers participating in sceptical discussions do not seem to have experienced a personal or intellectual crisis.[36] But the Pyrrhonian influence undoubtedly sparked a lively debate about the appropriate way of talking about the soul. This is most evident in the *Essais*, which Montaigne wrote and constantly revised in the period between the 1570s and his death in 1592. In the preface to the reader he famously remarks that his only ambition is to speak about himself: "Thus, reader, I am myself the matter of my book".[37] And in the very last chapter he states: "I study myself more than any other subject. That is my metaphysics, that is my physics".[38] Quite obviously, Montaigne does not mean to continue an Aristotelian or Platonic tradition that aims at presenting a general theory of the human soul or mind. He refrains from making general statements that would define or classify soul and mind, providing instead a detailed description of the phenomena he experiences in himself.

One might wonder if this permanent self-examination and self-presentation really involves the use of a philosophical method. Does Montaigne not simply refuse to engage in a theoretical discussion about the soul, thus adopting an anti-philosophical attitude? Tempting as this interpretation might be,[39] it is inadequate because it is precisely the application of a philosophical method that leads him to the avowal that he can describe nothing but himself. This is the Pyrrhonian method which, characterized in broad terms, consists in a four-step procedure.[40] First, the sceptic collects all kinds of phenomena and realizes that he can set out oppositions among them; for every phenomenon he can find an opposing one. Second, he notices that the opposed phenomena are equipollent, i.e., none of them is more evident or more convincing than the opposed one. Third, this leads him to the conclusion that there is no reason to approve of one and to reject its opposite; he completely suspends his judgement. Fourth, he no longer feels under constraint to come up with a judgement and reaches a state of mental tranquillity.

Montaigne is clearly aware of this method and makes extensive use of it. This is most evident in the 'Apology for Raymond Sebond', the long chapter dealing with animals.[41] Instead of simply arguing for the traditional thesis that only human beings can think, he adduces many phenomena against this thesis. In fact, he cites plenty of historical reports and stories about the cleverness of animals, thereby referring to phenomena that present animals as intelligent agents. These phenomena turn out to be as impressive and compelling as the counter-phenomena. According to Montaigne, we should therefore suspend the traditional judgement that animals are incapable of reasoning. Once we have done that we reach a relaxed attitude or even a state of tranquillity; we can play and communicate with animals without being under pressure to constantly evaluate them as non-rational beings.

To be sure, Montaigne does not slavishly follow the Pyrrhonian method. He modifies it by making it more dynamic. For instance, he permanently gathers new phenomena and counter-phenomena without ever resting. Consequently, he never arrives at the point where he could finally suspend every judgement and become fully relaxed. There is no final tranquillity. Moreover, he does not suspend every judgement. Following Christian doctrine, he holds that there is an omnipotent, benevolent God without ever neutralizing this claim.[42] This shows that he has, after all, some convictions that are not open for debate.[43] But it is clear that he applies the Pyrrhonian method to every area besides that of basic theistic convictions. And in all these areas he is even more radical than a traditional sceptic because he is never satisfied with a given set of phenomena. He incessantly augments their number and is constantly involved in a process of comparing and evaluating them.

This radical use of the Pyrrhonian method has an immediate consequence for the study of the soul: It is impossible to make general statements about it. All one can do is to collect phenomena and counter-phenomena. And phenomena are not objective facts, but subjective appearances. That is why Montaigne can only speak about himself, i.e., about his own appearances. Thus, he cannot endorse the general thesis that the human soul is rational. He must confine himself to noticing that his own soul *appears* to be rational because it seems to come up with chains of reasoning. More radically, he must limit himself to the observation that there is something that *appears* to be his soul, whatever it might be doing. But he cannot present a conclusive argument that would prove the existence of the soul, much less its rationality or immateriality. It is therefore quite understandable that he warns the reader to be aware that he only talks about himself; a mere report of appearances should not be conflated with the assertion of a solid theory.

From a methodological point of view, it is remarkable that Montaigne does not refrain from presenting a theory about the soul simply because he has given up every philosophical ambition and now confines himself to telling anecdotes and talking about personal experiences. It is rather a philosophical insight that makes him so cautious. This insight is based on the reasoning that if we do not want to uncritically accept a number of general theses as self-evident, we need to start with things that are evident to us. These are the phenomena that immediately present themselves. If we then compare them to counter-phenomena, as the sceptical method suggests, we will realize that we are not entitled to prefer one set of phenomena to another and to construct a theory that is based on them. Only a scrupulous examination of a wide range of phenomena will protect us from making unwarranted dogmatic claims; and this examination will never come to an end. We will always be confronted with new phenomena that will challenge seemingly uncontroversial ones.

It is clear that this way of proceeding does not lead to an alternative to an established theory, be it Platonic, Aristotelian or Stoic. It rather undermines every attempt to construct a theory of the soul. But does it lead to anything more than the negative conclusion that a general theory is impossible? There is indeed a positive conclusion since in the process of constantly examining phenomena some general patterns become recognizable – patterns that may not be sufficient ground for an all-embracing theory, but that nevertheless enable Montaigne to say something about his own soul as it appears to him.

The first and most important thing he recognizes is that he cannot find anything like reason or mind as a stable and reliable faculty of the soul that would produce enduring thoughts. Reason is "an instrument of lead and of wax, stretchable, pliable, and adaptable to all biases and all measures".[44] Whenever he is confronted with a new phenomenon he tends to come up with a new judgement that replaces an older one and that will in turn be replaced in the future. Reason runs, as it were, from one judgement to the next and eventually gives up each of them in the light of new phenomena. It therefore amounts to self-delusion to think that we have a faculty of reason that produces stable thoughts. It is even more self-delusory to assume that this faculty is superior to all other faculties, in particular to perception and imagination, which are often said to produce nothing but unstable and unreliable states. Thoughts are as unstable and unreliable as tokens of perceptions and imaginations. Hence, there is no reason to assume that we should always trust reason as the highest and most reliable faculty.

In drawing this conclusion Montaigne radically revises the traditional picture of the human soul. Unlike traditional Aristotelians he no longer subscribes to the thesis that there is a hierarchy of faculties culminating in reason, and unlike Neoplatonic authors he no longer holds that human reason is a godlike faculty that somehow mirrors divine perfection. In his view, we should give up the idea of a hierarchical order and treat reason as one faculty among many, one that is neither inferior nor superior to the others.[45] Doing so not only enables us to overcome the tendency to set reason apart from all other faculties, but also leads us to re-evaluate the so-called lower faculties. We can pay more attention to perception and imagination and realize that they are as important as reason, for they enable us to detect new phenomena. Moreover, they make us sensitive to the singularity of each phenomenon and thereby prevent us from making general claims. It is therefore hardly surprising that Montaigne devotes entire chapters to the cognitive function of these faculties, showing that it would be inadequate to conceive of them as untrustworthy. In particular, it would be inappropriate to think of imagination as a faculty that constantly leads us astray. It can be inventive and productive when it presents us possible scenarios we tend to dismiss in our rational thoughts.[46] To be sure, Montaigne does not make a final statement about the status and interrelation of our faculties. This would amount to a dogmatic claim and therefore to a violation of the sceptical method. But his detailed examination of the productive function of imagination shows that he revises the traditional view of the faculties, a devaluation of reason going hand in hand with a revaluation of the so-called lower faculties.

The application of the sceptical method leads to still another important result. Defenders of traditional theories often assume that the soul is a stable entity that somehow grounds all activities. Thus, Aristotelians call the soul a substantial form that makes all activities possible, and Platonists even think of it as an entity that can be separated from the body and exist on its own. No matter how they describe this entity in detail, they are in agreement in assuming that it must be an enduring thing. It is precisely this agreement that is challenged by Montaigne's sceptical method. In limiting himself to the description of phenomena he realizes that there is no distinct thing he could grasp, much less an enduring thing. He confesses: "I do not portray being: I portray passing. Not the passing from one age to another, or, as the people say, from seven years to seven years, but from day to day, from minute to minute".[47] This is first and foremost true of the way he paints himself. There is no stable, enduring thing to describe. All he can capture is a number of phenomena that change from minute to minute. It is an open question whether or not there is something underlying all of them and holding them together. The mere experience of permanently changing phenomena does not allow Montaigne to claim that there is such a thing, much less that it is a substantial form or an immaterial substance. That is why he makes no positive statement about the soul as a special entity.

Why then does Montaigne constantly use the pronoun 'I'? Does this not presuppose an enduring soul or even a self to which this pronoun refers? Indeed, something is referred to, and Montaigne often seems to be talking about a soul or a self. But in doing so he does not commit himself to positing a special entity. If there is a self, it is the conglomerate of all phenomena described as a unified thing. That is why Montaigne emphasizes the importance of writing. In writing about himself he collects all kinds of phenomena and establishes a more or less unified thing, thus constructing a self that persists through time. So, in the end there is a soul or a self, but it is nothing more than a construction. Montaigne does not shy away from drawing this conclusion: "I have no more made my book than my book has made me – a book consubstantial with its author".[48] The book made him because it was in the process of collecting phenomena and putting them together that a self emerged. But it would be inappropriate to assume that there was a well-defined self right from the beginning; the self was made, not simply discovered.

It is at this point that the radicalism of Montaigne's sceptical method becomes visible. It does more than simply undermine traditional theories by questioning the validity of general statements about the soul. It even questions the assumption that there is a given thing – a soul or a self – that can be discovered and metaphysically explained in a theory.

5 Conclusion

I hope the three examples given above make clear that there was no unified account of the soul in the period between 1300 and 1600. There was not even a unified method. In fact, it is precisely the controversy over an adequate method that characterizes philosophical debates during the three centuries in question. These debates were inspired not only by the rediscovery of ancient texts, but also by the awareness of a systematic problem, namely the tension we face when we deal with the soul. On the one hand, we are all familiar with it because we are all ensouled bodies. It should therefore be quite easy to describe it; we simply need to study what we find in ourselves. Unlike physics or astronomy, the science of the soul can focus on an object that is immediately present to each of us. On the other hand, it seems impossible to study this object since it is not a material thing that can be inspected and compared with other material things. It is not even a thing that is readily grasped since we only have access to acts or states in us, not to the naked soul. Buridan nicely captures this tension by making the seemingly paradoxical statement that the science of the soul is both the easiest and the most difficult science. In his view, it is "the most certain and easiest as regards the thing to be thought" since we all have immediate access to acts of the soul, but it is also "the most difficult for us, and consequently the most uncertain, as regards what does the thinking" since we never grasp the thing responsible for all the acts.[49] How then should we approach the soul? And what kind of knowledge can we gain of it? It is this fundamental question that motivated the authors discussed in this chapter to adopt radically different methods.

As we have seen, Buridan starts with a description of the acts that are immediately given, yet without confining himself to presenting a simple list of acts. He rather focuses on the faculties that make acts possible and then analyzes their relation to the soul. Moreover, he does not just examine the faculties that make his own acts possible; he pays attention to all the faculties that are responsible for human as well as non-human acts. This leads him to a general metaphysical picture of the soul and its faculties. The interesting point is that he starts with what is 'most certain and easiest', namely with the presence of individual acts, and then goes beyond that by looking for their metaphysical foundation. In doing so, he follows the famous Aristotelian maxim that in examining what is most certain for us (namely the acts) we can eventually arrive at what is most certain in nature (namely the soul).[50] This is possible because we can indicate the cause that is responsible for all acts. Buridan even thinks that we can specify the cause, namely a single soul that acts in various ways, and thereby rule out false causal explanations. This might be called an *empiricist method* that starts with the observation and classification of particular acts and then builds up a general theory.

Marsilio Ficino proceeds in a different way, namely by adopting a *rationalist method*. His starting point is a general metaphysical picture, which we can draw simply by reflecting upon different types of beings and their relations. When we proceed in this way, we learn that the human soul occupies a middle place in the universe and that it is therefore related both to higher and lower things. Moreover, we learn that it has specific features, for instance intrinsic activity and immortality. It is quite significant that Ficino starts with what is most difficult, namely with an explanation of the metaphysical status of the soul, and then moves on to what seems the 'most certain and easiest', namely the presence of acts we all experience. The crucial point is that, on this account, we cannot give an adequate explanation of what seems most evident and certain unless we locate the soul within a broad metaphysical picture. This is why Ficino rejects the empiricist idea of accepting empirically observed facts as self-evident. Instead, he pursues the rationalist strategy of refusing to accept brute facts and looks for an all-embracing picture that explains all facts, including those concerning the soul.

Montaigne pursues still another strategy. As a sceptic, he cannot build up a general theory on the basis of empirically observed facts. Nor can he start with an all-embracing theory and then apply it to given facts. He cannot even accept objectively given facts. All he can rely on are subjective phenomena that are to be set in contrast with counter-phenomena. That is why he cannot make a final judgement about the soul and its acts. He rather adopts a *method of abstention*, in which both empiricist and rationalist strategies that would justify final judgements are to be avoided. Of course, Montaigne insists on the importance of experience, but it is not the kind of experience an empiricist would appeal to. He does not refer to cases of objectively observable experience in order to use them as the basis for inductive reasoning that would lead to general judgements. He rather reports cases of subjective experience in order to show that they constantly change, that they are always dissimilar and that they do not warrant any general judgement.[51] It is therefore not surprising that he categorically denies that we could ever go beyond what is 'most certain and easiest' and reach a general theory of the soul. More radically, he denies that there is a realm of things that are the most certain and the easiest, for even the phenomena that are immediately present to us are far from easy to understand. Therefore, we must confine ourselves to reporting how we construct a coherent and constant soul out of a large number of phenomena.

It is this diversity of methods that is characteristic of the period between 1300 and 1600 – a period that, far from being a time of transition or decline as presented in traditional textbooks, was rather a time of tension and productive conflict between radically different approaches to the mind.

Notes

1 In fact, more commentaries on Aristotle were written in the fifteenth and sixteenth centuries than in the thousand years before. It is therefore legitimate to speak about a 'Renaissance of Aristotle' in that period, as Bianchi 2007 argues.
2 For a concise description of the first problem, see the Introduction to this volume and Pasnau 2007.
3 On the origins of psychology as a discipline, see Hatfield 1995 and Vidal 2006.
4 On the definition and demarcation of this science, see Zupko 1997, Bakker 2007 and de Boer 2013.
5 Sceptics thought that we can never go beyond a description of phenomena, whatever their content may be, thus questioning the possibility of every science and not just of a science of the soul. On this strategy, which became prominent in the late sixteenth century, see Larmore 1998.
6 This view can be traced back to Simplicius and was prominent in the sixteenth century; see Bakker (2007: 153).
7 On the reception of *De anima*, see Perler 2008 and Friedman & Counet 2013.
8 On the dating, see de Boer (2013: 13). On the place this text occupies in Buridan's project of developing a comprehensive theory of science, including a science of the soul, see Zupko (2003: 164–182) and Biard 2012.
9 *QDA* I, q. 1. To be precise, Buridan speaks about the *subiectum scientiae*, meaning thereby not the investigating subject, but the domain that is investigated.
10 See *Expositio*, prol. (OPh IV: 8–10).
11 *QDA* I, q. 1, n. 20.
12 On this background, see Biard (2012: 93–142).
13 See *QDA* II, qq. 1–3.

14 *QDA* I, q. 1, n. 12.
15 Duns Scotus and his followers spoke about a formal distinction, Thomists about a real distinction. For an analysis of various positions, see Pasnau (2011: 574–605), Perler 2015, and Chapter 3 of this volume.
16 *QDA* II, q. 5, n. 18.
17 For a detailed analysis of this thought experiment, which was also discussed by other fourteenth-century authors, see de Boer (2013: 211–16, 276–279).
18 *QDA* II, q. 5, n. 21.
19 *QDA* III, q. 17, ad 1.
20 See *Quodlibeta* II, q. 10 (OTh IX: 156–161) and an analysis in Perler 2010.
21 See Lagerlund 2004 and Chapter 10 of this volume.
22 See *QDA* II, q. 4, nn. 15–20, and *QDA* III, q. 17.
23 Buridan himself concedes that it is "miraculous" how the immaterial soul can be present in the material body and act without using a bodily organ; see *QDA* II, q. 9, n. 25. This is the position to be defended according to faith, not according to reason and natural evidence. If we were strictly following reason, Buridan holds, we would have to defend the thesis that the soul is "educed from matter" and therefore always bound to the material body. On this distinction between two positions, see Zupko (2003: 179–182) and Biard (2012: 361–362).
24 See Salatowsky 2006 and Bakker 2007.
25 *PTh*, proem., vol. 1: 9.
26 *PTh*, proem., vol. 1: 9.
27 *PTh* I.1, vol. 1: 17.
28 On his sources, see Allen 1982.
29 On the general structure of the PSR, see Della Rocca 2010.
30 For an analysis of these levels, see Kristeller (1972: 55–72).
31 *PTh* III.2, vol. 1: 237.
32 *PTh* IV.1, vol. 1: 249.
33 *PTh* III.2, vol. 1: 243.
34 *PTh* II.4 and III.1, vol. 1: 141–143 and 237–239.
35 Books V–XIV are entirely devoted to a discussion of these arguments. For an analysis, see Kristeller (1972: 307–334) and Chapter 11 of this volume.
36 Popkin 2003 coined the term 'Pyrrhonian crisis'. For a critical assessment, see Perler 2004.
37 *E*, 3/2. (The first reference applies to the French edition, the second to the English translation.)
38 *E* III.13: 1072/821.
39 His first readers, among them Malebranche, reacted in that way, characterizing him as a literary figure who did not contribute anything substantial to philosophical debates. On the controversial status of Montaigne as a philosopher, see Conche 1987 and Hartle 2003.
40 See Sextus Empiricus, *OS*, I.8–10, and a concise analysis in Annas & Barnes (1985: 19–30).
41 He explicitly refers to Pyrrhonism in this chapter (*E* II.12: 502–6/371–5). For a detailed analysis, see Wild (2006: 43–134).
42 *E* II.12: 440–1/321–2.
43 This leads some interpreters (e.g., Brahami 1997) to the conclusion that he is a fideist who overcomes scepticism. However, this interpretation overlooks Montaigne's remark that even his faith is not a set of convictions based on rational arguments, but only a view he has become accustomed to in his social context: "We are Christians by the same title that we are Perigordians or Germans." (E II.12: 445/325). Even theistic

claims can therefore be rephrased as claims about something that *appears* to be the case in the Christian context.
44 *E* II.12: 565/425; also ibid. 559/419.
45 In *E* II.12: 537/401 he rejects the idea of a hierarchically ordered soul that looks like an 'imaginary republic'.
46 This is most evident in *E* I.21, where he explains the force of imagination. For an analysis, see Westerwelle 2002.
47 *E* III.2: 805/611.
48 *E* II.18: 665/504.
49 *QDA* I.4, nn. 9–10.
50 *Phys.* I.1, 184a21–23.
51 In the very last chapter, which bears the programmatic title 'On Experience', he speaks about an "ingenious mixture on the part of nature" that does not allow for any systematic inference; see *E* III.13: 1070/819.

Bibliography

Primary sources

Aristotle. *The Complete Works*, 2 vols. J. Barnes (ed.). Princeton: Princeton University Press, 1984.
Ficino, Marsilio. *Platonic Theology* (= *PTh*), 6 vols. M. J. B. Allen & J. Hankins (trans. & eds.). Cambridge, MA: Harvard University Press, 2001–2006.
John Buridan. *Quaestiones de anima* (= *QDA*). P. King, P. Sobol & J. Zupko (trans. & eds.). Dordrecht, The Netherlands: Springer, forthcoming.
Montaigne, Michel de. *The Complete Essays*. D. M. Frame (trans.). Stanford: Stanford University Press, 1979.
———. *Les Essais* (= *E*). P. Villey (ed.). Paris: Presses Universitaires de France, 1999.
Sextus Empiricus. *Outlines of Scepticism* (= *OS*). J. Annas & J. Barnes (trans.). Cambridge: Cambridge University Press, 1997.
William of Ockham. *Quodlibeta septem*. In *Opera Theologica* IX, J. C. Wey (ed.). St. Bonaventure: The Franciscan Institute, 1980.
———. *Expositio in libros Physicorum Aristotelis* (= *Expositio*). In *Opera Philosophica* IV, V. Richter & G. Leibold (eds). St. Bonaventure: The Franciscan Institute, 1985.

Secondary literature

Allen, M. 1982. "Ficino's Theory of the Five Substances and the Neoplatonists' *Parmenides*". *Journal of Medieval and Renaissance Studies* **12**: 19–44.
Annas, J. & Barnes, J. 1985. *The Modes of Scepticism: Ancient Texts and Modern Interpretations*. Cambridge: Cambridge University Press.
Bakker, P. J. J. M. 2007. "Natural Philosophy, Metaphysics, or Something in Between? Agostino Nifo, Pietro Pomponazzi, and Marcantonio Genua on the Nature and Place of the Science of the Soul". In *Mind, Cognition and Representation*, P. J. J. M. Bakker & J. M. M. H. Thijssen (eds), 151–177. Aldershot: Ashgate.
Bianchi, L. 2007. "Continuity and Change in the Aristotelian Tradition". In *The Cambridge Companion to Renaissance Philosophy*, J. Hankins (ed.), 49–71. Cambridge: Cambridge University Press.

Biard, J. 2012. *Science et nature. La théorie buridanienne du savoir*. Paris: Vrin.
Brahami, F. 1997. *Le scepticisme de Montaigne*. Paris: Presses Universitaires de France.
Conche, M. 1987. *Montaigne et la philosophie*. Paris: Editions de Mégare.
De Boer, S. 2013. *The Science of the Soul: The Commentary Tradition on Aristotle's De anima, c. 1260–c. 1360*. Leuven: University Press.
Della Rocca, M. 2010. "PSR". *Philosophers' Imprint* **10**(7): 1–13.
Friedman, R. L. & Counet, J.-M. (eds). 2013. *Medieval Perspectives on Aristotle's De anima*. Louvain: Éditions de l'institut supérieur de philosophie & Peeters.
Hartle, A. 2003. *Michel de Montaigne: Accidental Philosopher*. Cambridge: Cambridge University Press.
Hatfield, G. 1995. "Remaking the Science of Mind: Psychology as a Natural Science". In *Inventing Human Science*, C. Fox, R. Porter & R. Wokler (eds), 184–231. Berkeley: University of California Press.
Kristeller, P. O. 1972. *Die Philosophie des Marsilio Ficino*. Frankfurt a.M.: Klostermann.
Lagerlund, H. 2004. "John Buridan and the Problem of Dualism in the Early Fourteenth Century". *Journal of the History of Philosophy* **42**: 369–387.
Larmore, Ch. 1998. "Scepticism". In *The Cambridge History of Seventeenth-Century Philosophy*, D. Garber & M. Ayers (eds), 1145–1192. Cambridge: Cambridge University Press.
Pasnau, R. 2007. "The Mind-Soul Problem". In *Mind, Cognition and Representation*, J. M. M. H. Thijssen & P. J. J. M. Bakker (eds), 3–19. Aldershot: Ashgate.
———. 2011. *Metaphysical Themes 1274–1671*. Oxford: Clarendon Press.
Perler, D. 2004. "Was There a 'Pyrrhonian Crisis' in Early Modern Philosophy?". *Archiv für Geschichte der Philosophie* **86**: 209–220.
———. (ed.). 2008. *Transformations of the Soul: Aristotelian Psychology 1250–1650*. Leiden: Brill (= *Vivarium* **46**(3)).
———. 2010. "Ockham über die Seele und ihre Teile". *Recherches de théologie et philosophie médiévales* **77**: 313–350.
———. 2015. "Faculties in Medieval Philosophy". In *The Faculties: A History*, D. Perler (ed.), 97–139. Oxford: Oxford University Press.
Popkin, R. 2003. *The History of Scepticism: From Savonarola to Bayle*. Oxford: Oxford University Press.
Salatowsky, S. 2006. *De anima: Die Rezeption der aristotelischen Psychologie im 16. und 17. Jahrhundert*. Amsterdam: Benjamins.
Vidal, F. 2006. *Les sciences de l'âme: XVIe–XVIIIe siècle*. Paris: Champion.
Westerwelle, K. 2002. *Montaigne: Die Imagination und die Kunst des Essays*. München: Fink.
Wild, M. 2006. *Die anthropologische Differenz: Der Geist der Tiere in der frühen Neuzeit bei Malebranche, Descartes und Hume*. Berlin: de Gruyter.
Zupko, J. 1997. "What Is the Science of the Soul? A Case Study in the Evolution of Late Medieval Natural Philosophy". *Synthese* **110**: 297–334.
———. 2003. *John Buridan: Portrait of a Fourteenth-Century Arts Master*. Notre Dame: Notre Dame University Press.

2

MEDICAL APPROACHES TO THE MIND IN THE LATE MIDDLE AGES AND THE RENAISSANCE

Guido Giglioni

1 Introduction: the mind, the body and the unconscious

From antiquity up to the early modern period, there has always been an intellectual figure who sits rather uncomfortably between the boundaries of established disciplinary divisions. We might call him the "physician philosopher" or the "philosopher physician." Hippocrates (c. 460–c. 375 BC) was saluted, initially by Plato (427–347 BC) and then by Galen (129–216?), as the first to have embodied this role, that is, the natural philosopher concerned with human health in holistic terms, or the therapist with an eye to the health of the cosmos, which he treats as one all-encompassing living being (ζῷον; *animal* in Latin). In both cases, philosophy was perceived as being closely connected to medicine. In *De naturalibus facultatibus* (*On the Natural Faculties*), Galen described Hippocrates as the author of a distinctive medical philosophy which he had proudly inherited and fully articulated. He systematized the Hippocratic view of nature and presented it as a force capable of preserving itself by enacting interconnected sequences of inborn propensities, in other words, by assimilating external materials, giving them anatomical shape and physiological function and finally eliminating all that resisted assimilation. Tendencies of attraction and repulsion were the primal drives of nature: "All natural beings (τὰ ὄντα) have a faculty through which they attract their specific quality" (*De naturalibus facultatibus* I, XIV, 55).[1] This principle of "specific attraction" (ἡ ὁλχή τοῦ συμμέτρου) and the fact that it took place without apparent conscious perception (τὸ χωρὶς λογισμοῦ) were for Galen the defining traits of nature (II, III, 85).

Until the eighteenth century, the medical view of the mind remained inextricably intertwined with a genuinely Hippocratic notion of nature. Within this framework, "nature" was supposed to have faculties of its own (οἰκεῖαι δυνάμεις), which allowed every living being to grow in all directions and to be fashioned in every single part while processing flows of external and internal matter through elaborate sequences of assimilation and evacuation (I, XV, 60). In this sense, the basic stages of life were nutrition, growth and formation. Unsurprisingly, in *De naturalibus facultatibus* Galen had characterized nature as being "creative" (τεχνική) in every single particle of the body. Indeed, nature was the original artist, in that the way it built natural bodies was a paragon of efficiency and ingenuity, clumsily imitated by human beings every time they fashioned their artefacts working from the outside in. In a manner that could not be replicated by technology, nature shaped every single part of matter by following the opposite route, from the inside out (II, III, 82).

At the risk of oversimplifying, we might sum up this point by saying that, while philosophers (especially Aristotle) concentrated their attention on the very notion of spontaneous *activity* and its conditions – conditions that in the end transcended nature and resided in the action of "external" forms (θύραθεν; *ab extrinseco* in Latin) – physicians since Hippocratic times were more interested in phenomena of *reactivity* and in the many ways in which nature responded to events, both external and internal. Another closely related *longue-durée* development in the field of medical philosophy is (certainly not by accident) the evolution of the notion of irritability, which can be traced from Galen to Jean-Baptiste Lamarck in the nineteenth century.[2] The kind of nature that had been championed by physicians since antiquity was not simply a source of motion, but a principle of responsiveness, seen as capable of adjusting itself to a whole universe of ever changing circumstances. Reactivity from within and from below (plants and viscera), rather than activity from without and from above (planetary intellects and astral influences), implied that the organization of the body was pluralistic and collective, based on flexible conglomerates of individual vital principles and a diversity of specific faculties. What is more, nature seemed to display original forms of pre-mental intentionality in the way in which the natural faculties responded to reality by attracting and rejecting, absorbing and transmitting, selecting and shaping. From its very beginnings, the medical philosophy of nature elaborated a sophisticated notion of reactive, plural and unconscious perception, with specific links to the faculties of imagination and desire. It was a consistent tradition that connected the legendary Hippocrates of pre-Socratic Cos to the eighteenth-century image of Hippocratic wisdom espoused by the Montpellier physicians in France by way of the extraordinarily influential interpretation of Hippocratic vitalism provided by Paracelsus (1493–1541) and his followers, through whom the renown vital principles of the Hippocratics (τά ἐνορμῶντα; *impetum facientia* in Latin) became the *archeus* of the chemical philosophers.[3]

Because of the way in which the philosophical and medical legacies of antiquity had been received and systematized during the Middle Ages, philosophy and medicine emerged out of the thirteenth and fourteenth centuries as two distinct traditions corresponding to two different ways of looking at nature and its possible transformations: the "path" of the philosophers (*via philosophorum*), which tended to focus on the soul (*anima*) and the "animal" faculties, and the "path" of the physicians (*via medicorum*), with its emphasis on nature and the "natural" faculties.[4] It was certainly no accident that the tradition of confronting philosophers with physicians became a successful genre of medical writing, from Pietro d'Abano's *Conciliator differentiarum quae inter philosophos et medicos versantur* (*The Reconciler of the Differences between Philosophers and Physicians*, composed around the beginning of fourteenth century) to Girolamo Cardano's *Contradicentia medica* (*Medical Contradictions*, written at different times throughout his life starting in the 1520s). More specifically, with respect to the mind, the Galenic approach to the study of the cognitive faculties was so deeply ingrained in the educational system of the late Middle Ages and the Renaissance that it managed to rival the most advanced results of philosophical investigations.

From late antiquity until at least the end of the seventeenth century, the most significant differences between physicians and philosophers in their attitudes towards the mind concerned, firstly, how to interpret the role of "temperaments" (that is, the specific combinations of material qualities in specific parts of the body at the level of fibres, tissues and microstructures, known in Greek medicine as κράσις and variously translated into Latin as *temperamentum*, *temperatura*, *temperies* and *complexio*), secondly, how to assess the contribution of natural and vital faculties to the emergence of perceptual abilities in the general economy of bodily life (that is, the role of unsentient powers in fostering and preserving life), and, finally, how to explain the functions and dysfunctions of the mind in all those situations in which a disassociation emerged between the faculties of the soul, the states of the body and the surrounding reality. It is these three questions that I am going to address in the following three sections.

2 The mind and its bodily temperament

Although identified since the Middle Ages as the prominent representative of the medical tradition of antiquity, Galen had from the very beginning insisted that his main aim was to build a medical philosophy. It was certainly no accident that he wrote several works dealing with the mind and the treatment of its disorders: *De cuiuslibet animi peccatorum dignotione et medela* (*The Diagnosis and Treatment of the Errors of the Mind*); *Quod animi mores corporis temperamenta sequantur* (*The Habits of the Mind Follow the Temperaments of the Body*); *De placitis Hippocratis et Platonis* (*The Opinions of Hippocrates and Plato*); *De moribus* (*On Habits'*). To this list we should now add *De indolentia* (*On Avoiding Grief*), a treatise discovered by Véronique Boudon-Millot in 2005 in the Vlatadon monastery in Thessaloniki.[5] In all these works, Galen demonstrated a loosely agnostic position regarding the nature of the mind and its possible immortality.[6] This does not mean that he completely ruled out the existence of incorporeal souls. On the contrary, plenty of evidence attesting to intelligent design in nature and the reality of premonitory signs had convinced him that there could be immaterial substances of a higher order acting in nature.[7] Regarding the human soul, however, Galen was more inclined to embrace an agnostic position. At the end of his life, he tentatively hypothesized that the soul emerged out of the shaping of the bodily temperaments, as a "form" resulting from a specific combination of material qualities and powers.[8]

During the Renaissance, at a time when Galen's medicine was undergoing an extraordinary revival, the "temperamental" account of the soul (that is, the view according to which the cognitive and ethical faculties of the soul depended on the individual constitution of the body) became the standard Galenic position among physicians and several philosophers, such as Marsilio Ficino (1433–1499), Symphorien Champier (1471–1538) and Jean Fernel (1497–1558). One of the authors to draw the most radical consequences from Galen's theory of the mind was the Spanish physician Huarte de San Juan (c.1530–1592). In the *Examen de ingenios para la ciencias* (*An Appraisal of the Natural Aptitudes for the Different Disciplines*), originally published in 1575 and republished posthumously in revised form in 1594, Huarte applied Galen's views on the mind to his study of human ingenuity in all its possible professional embodiments. In the "Letter to the Reader," he defended the Galenic principle that the soul depends on the anatomical parts of the body (*el ánima está sujeta al temperamento y compostura del cuerpo*).[9] Concerned with the possibility of theological misunderstandings, he reinforced his thesis by adding religious and biblical arguments: "When God created Adam and Eve, before He filled them with wisdom, He arranged their brain in such a way that they could receive knowledge with ease and the brain could be a convenient tool for them to speak and argue."[10] The fact remained, however, that in Huarte's *Examen*, the human mind was characterized in terms of natural and bodily constraints: "The intellect (*el entendimiento*) has its beginning, growth, balance and decline, like human beings, the rest of the animals and plants."[11]

In the middle of the sixteenth century, another physician with high philosophical ambitions produced an original synthesis of Platonic, Aristotelian and Galenic motifs: Jean Fernel.[12] Like Huarte, he too adhered to Galen's view that the different faculties of the soul were correlated to different bodily organs, instruments and seats (*substantia, instrumentis et sede*).[13] From an anatomical point of view, the substance of the brain (*cerebri substantia*), distributed to the whole body through the spinal cord and the nerves, was both the seat and the organ of the cognitive functions and voluntary motions. Although Fernel regarded the brain as the dwelling place of the mind (*humanae mentis arx et domicilium*) and the source (*fons et origo*) of all motions, sensations and thoughts, he did not go so far as to identify the activity of thinking with either a specific bodily process determined by the complexion of the brain or with the working of spirits and innate heat.[14] In Fernel's *Physiologia* (originally published in 1542), the human being resulted from a harmonious blend (*concentus*) of natural, vital and sentient faculties unified by the mind, which added the higher functions of reason and intelligence to the rest of the animal operations based on the senses.[15] The intelligent faculty of the mind (*intelligentia*) was then divided into different powers (*patibilis, agens, componens, iudicans, ratiocinatrix, contemplans, deliberans, artifex* and *effectrix*). They all dealt with abstract representations of things (*species*) and culminated in the faculty of rational will (*voluntas*), which brought the deliberations of the intelligence (*consilii conatus*) to completion and was identified as the last of the mental faculties (*omnium facultatum intelligentiae postrema*).[16]

Fernel is an interesting case of a physician who, besides having a competent grasp of the most recent trends in contemporary anatomy, was steeped in Platonic philosophy and underwent all the characteristic stages of humanist training. A few decades earlier, in 1538, a professional humanist had published an original account of the mind and its faculties that stood out for its attention to the concrete details of bodily life and the latest findings of medical science. The humanist was Juan Luis Vives (1493–1540), who was fascinated by the ways in which the mind unfolded its powers in the manifold circumstances of human life. The work, entitled *De anima et vita* (*On Soul and Life*, 1538), represents a unique combination of moral philosophy, rhetorical expertise and medical knowledge.[17] From the very beginning of the treatise, the study of the vital functions and the emotions is presented as the foundation of ethics, both private and public, with major applications in the domain of politics.[18] Vives highlighted how the higher faculties of the mind depended on the balanced exercise of the non-mental functions of life (*altrix, attrahens, retentrix, purgatrix, expultrix, distributiva, incorporatrix*), on their permeating every single part of the body and operating without the mind being aware of their work.[19] For Vives, the functions of the soul required a body that could serve as a suitable subject of life and whose parts and instruments (*calor, humor* and *spiritus*) offered a proper dwelling place for reason, since the soul, Vives continued, "is said to inhabit the body." The way in which he acknowledged the "temperamental" conditions of mental powers proves that Vives had fully assimilated the legacy of Galenic psychosomatics.[20]

3 Conscious and unconscious

The "temperamental" view of the mind examined above stressed the link between mental operations and bodily actions. However, the relationship between the mind and the body was not the only critical element in the various attempts to explain how the mind oriented itself in the world it inhabited. Between the most abstract cognitive performances of the intellect and the merely mechanical reactions of the body there lay a vast, largely unknown and unknowing area of corporeal life. From Aristotle and Galen on, this area had been assigned to the so-called "natural" (vegetative) and "vital" faculties, while the conscious and voluntary operations of the soul had been confined to the domain of "animal" functions. Since ancient times, philosophers and physicians agreed that souls were entities characterized by the exercise of intentional movement and sentient perception. And yet countless vital phenomena demonstrated at each moment that many operations were involuntary and unconscious. In order to justify this apparent gap between life and soul, authors had variously resorted to a number of disparate solutions such as natural instinct, habit, unsentient perception, plastic activity and vegetative adroitness. The seminal incipit of Galen's *De naturalibus facultatibus* is worth recalling here because of its clarity and concision:

> Since perception and voluntary motion are specific properties of animals, while growth and nutrition are also common to plants, one should look at the former as effects of the soul (ψυχή), at the latter as effects of nature (φύσις).
>
> (*De nat. fac.*, I, I, 1)

Galen distinguished between three main natural faculties – generation (γένεσις), growth (αὔξησις) and nutrition (θρέψις) – and other faculties considered as their subservient "handmaids." For instance, he regarded generation as compounded of alteration (ἀλλοίωσις) and formation (διάπλασις) (I, v, 11). He then added the faculties of attraction (ὁλκή), assimilation (ἐξομοίωσις), expulsion (ἀπόκρισις), addition (πρόσθεσις), adhesion (πρόσφυσις) and absorption (ἀνάδοσις) (I, II, 7; VIII, 19; XI, 25). In Galen's account of the natural faculties, the ability to anticipate future developments in the transformations of life (πρόνοια) and the capacity to perform purposeful actions (τέχνη) were embedded in the very core of nature's activity, and there was no need to invoke mental and conscious operations (II, III, 80). In the most general terms, he defined nutrition as assimilation of food by the feeding principles, a process based on acts of recognition and transformation (I, II, 7; II, IV, 89). Galen described the formative or shaping faculty as endowed with exquisitely "artistic" skills (I, VI, 15). Moreover, specific parts of the body manifested specific abilities: a blood-making faculty in the veins and the liver, a digestive faculty in the stomach and a pulsific faculty in the heart (I, IV, 9–10).

As already mentioned in the previous section, Galen never expressed a definitive opinion about the essence and role of the rational soul. To the contrary, he concentrated all his efforts on understanding nature and its activity in the animal body. He clearly ruled out the hypothesis that nature had a soul (as had always been intimated by the Platonists); and yet, in line with the principles of Hippocratic naturalism, he characterized nature as a fully autonomous power that is capable of performing a number of extremely complex operations in the bodies of natural beings. In defending his view of nature, Galen rejected in the clearest terms any explanation of natural functions that relied on mechanical principles (for instance, the theories formulated by Erasistratus and Asclepiades of Bithynia in the third and second centuries BC, respectively). Galen's nature operated through specific powers capable of attracting and selecting the proper nutrients, constantly transforming the metabolized food into bodily constituents and finally regulating all the variables necessary for preserving life. In criticizing those physicians and philosophers who had deprived nature of its "artistic" (τεχνική) character, its provident attitude (προνοητική) and its range of specific faculties (οἰκείαι δυνάμεις), Galen pitted his opponents against Hippocrates, who right from the beginning had posited one vital substance subject to countless forms of alteration and ruled by nature "according to art and justice" (I, XII, 29).

In the Galenic framework of unsentient faculties, nature manifested its "art" and "justice" by assimilating the suitable and rejecting the unsuitable. And yet the ontological chasm between "natural" (non-sentient) activity and "animal" (sentient) perception remained the great problem in Galen's metaphysics of life. When the myriad parts of a living body were all busy attracting, selecting, transforming and expelling matter, did they have any knowledge of their incessant activity? Combining Hippocratic and Platonic motifs, and relying on the latest anatomical findings by the Alexandrine anatomists Erophilus (335–228 BC) and Erasistratus (c. 304–250 BC), Galen assigned the sensory-motor functions of the body to the brain and the nervous system. He located the sentient part of the soul (τὸ αἰσθητικὸν μόριον) in the ruling power of the mind (τὸ ἡγεμονικόν) located in the brain; from there the ἡγεμονικόν branched off via the nerves to all the parts of the body and controlled both the vital and the cognitive faculties. All innervated parts were therefore considered to be endowed with sensibility and intentional motion.[21] A question, nevertheless, remained open: how could one account for the large number of unconscious operations in the body without assuming the participation of the brain and the nerves?

How to understand the elusive relationship between unconscious nature and conscious sentience remained one of the most controversial points in the medical philosophy inspired by Galen from the Middle Ages to the early modern period. While Aristotelian philosophy was the main counterpart in this centuries-old debate, currents of Platonism and Stoicism had added nuance and complexity to the discussion by the early days of the Renaissance. This is already evident in Pietro d'Abano's *Conciliator differentiarum*, which, as mentioned in the previous section, represents one of the most systematic and comprehensive attempts to provide a synthesis of medical and philosophical knowledge between the Middle Ages and the Renaissance. More specifically, Pietro devoted Difference 57, entitled "Whether the vital power is yet another faculty or not," to analyzing the vital operations of the body, which physicians traditionally viewed as intermediary faculties between the physical operations of nutrition and the mental acts underlying the various activities of knowledge.

It is a particularly important *Differentia* due to both the scope and the detail of Pietro's analysis of questions surrounding of the faculties of the soul. Pietro sets up the discussion by differentiating between the philosophical and the medical approach. He begins by expounding the philosophical position, dissecting the whole process of bodily life into thirty-four or thirty-five acts involving motion, appetite and knowledge. The account is a tour de force of analytical precision and is worth summing up here. In two in-folio pages of densely written prose, Pietro outlines a detailed atlas of the principal faculties of the soul involved in such disparate activities as digestion, breathing and thinking. Aristotle's division of the principal powers of the soul into vegetative, sensitive and rational operations represents the starting point. The first sequence of faculties refers to the characteristic acts of unsentient life. These powers are then distinguished into the vegetative faculties of growth and reproduction (*nutritiva, augmentativa* and *generativa*).

One type of reproductive function is universal and corresponds to the generation of biological species; the other has a narrower scope and involves the generation of individual organisms. The former is located in the organs of generation, the latter in the liver, where the nutritive and augmentative faculties are further subdivided into attractive, digestive, retentive and expulsive powers.[22]

The shift from the self-preserving and instinctive functions of life to the operations of voluntary motility and conscious sentience occurs with the power controlled by sensation and appetite. "The sensitive faculty or soul" is defined in traditional Aristotelian terms as "perfection of an organic body insofar as it apprehends and is moved by the appetite." Pietro then divides this faculty into two powers, one capable of perceiving (*comprehensiva*), the other of controlling all kinds of motion (*motiva*). The motive power is differentiated into the faculty that instigates motion and the one that accomplishes it. The power that initiates motion by giving orders is located in the heart and is further distinguished into a "concupiscible" tendency (capable of seizing suitable substances, i.e., the *congrua*) and an "irascible" tendency (capable of rejecting harmful substances, i.e., the *nociva*). In the domain of knowledge, the faculty of perceiving (*comprehensiva*) is also divided into two principal functions: one is subject to the grasp of the external five senses (*manifesta*), while the other is hidden (*occulta*) and refers to the internal senses. The faculty of the internal senses is further differentiated into two, depending on whether the faculty deals with the "forms" (that is, less abstract representations) or the "intentions" (that is, more abstract representations). Regarding the former, if the forms are simple, the possibilities are three: common sense (*sensus communis*), corresponding to the function of general perception (*comprehensio*); simple imagination (*imaginatio vel phantasia*), corresponding to the functions of retention and preservation of knowledge; and complex imagination (*imaginativa*), which is further subdivided into animal (*brutalis*) and rational (*cogitativa*) powers and corresponds to the ability to combine the representations of the senses in innumerable ways. The faculty of perception that deals with intentions is divided in two depending on the level of abstraction, that is, on whether the material conditions of knowledge are included or not. When the intention is abstracted and the material circumstances of its abstraction (*appenditia*) are retained, the results are the estimative faculty (*aestimativa*, i.e., when the soul discards the form) and the allied faculties of memory (*conservativa, reminiscitiva* and *memoria*, i.e., when the soul retains the form). In this case, the faculty of perception (*comprehensiva*) culminates in a form of syllogistic ability that can only be performed by a human mind. When the intention is abstracted without its accompanying material and empirical conditions, then we have the rational faculty (*virtus rationalis vel humana*), which Pietro defines as "the perfection of the organic body taken as a whole, which processes the universals by going through processes of inner deliberation or meditation."[23]

Pietro's anatomy of the cognitive faculties does not end here, though. Following the Aristotelian model, he distinguishes the rational power into a theoretical (*speculativa*) and a practical faculty (*activa*). The practical power of reason is in turn twofold:

> [E]ither its action produces an immediate beginning in external matter, as in the case of art (*ars*), which represents the right way of making things (*recta ratio factibilium*), or it acts within itself, as if it were dealing with the actions of human beings, and this is practical wisdom (*prudentia*), which is the right way of doing things (*recta ratio agibilium*).[24]

The theoretical faculty, by contrast, is "the power which is informed by the universal form devoid of matter." This, too, takes on two modalities, depending on whether the function occurs in potentiality or in actuality. Potentiality has three levels, paired with three kinds of intellects: "material" intellect, which is a pure substratum devoid of form; "potential" intellect, containing the first principles of the mind (*intelligibilia per se nota*); and intellect "of perfection," which "can understand in actuality what it wants." This threefold intellect, says Pietro, is called potential intellect by Aristotle. When the intellect understands that it is understanding itself, then it is called intellect in actuality (*in effectu*), which is when "the intellect that is said to be adapted from the outside (*accommodatus ab extrinseco*)" is joined and united with the human intellect.[25] Pietro explains that by active intellect Aristotle meant that part of the human soul which, in relation to the potential intellect, acted as the light with respect to colours. When united with the active intellect, the material intellect "will understand everything," and the human being will finally be able to be "assimilated to God." At the end of this complex but carefully thought-out analysis, Pietro even provides a numerical summary made up of thirty-four/thirty-five principal elements:

> If we carefully calculate all these steps, it is apparent that the chain of the powers of the soul (*catena virium animae*) consists of thirty-four or thirty-five rings, including the subservient faculties. They are: four qualities [heat, cold, moisture and dryness]; four natural powers acting as subservient operations [attractive, excretive, alterative and retentive]; six powers acting as ruling operations [nutritive, augmentative, generative (with respect to both individuals and species) and formative (with respect to both each single part of the body and the body as a whole)]; two vital powers [appetitive and irascible]; a motive one in the heart, which following the contraction of the muscular fibres is differentiated into 529 [motions] according to their number; five apprehensive powers that are externally visible [sight, hearing, smell, taste and touch]; seven that perceive in a hidden way [common sense, simple imagination, complex imagination, animal imagination, cogitative and estimative faculties, and reason]; five or six that act in a universal way [practical reason, i.e., art and prudence; theoretical reason, i.e., material intellect, potential

intellect and complete intellect; copulation with active intellect]. And of these rings, the intellect in actuality, adapted or acquired, is the only one that rules over all other powers and is served by them.[26]

Pietro's discussion confirms that, when it came to the faculties of the soul, the main difference between philosophers and physicians lay in the former's reluctance to add a special vital power to the list of natural and animal faculties. The reason was that for the philosophers the functions of life (such as the heartbeat, the pulsating motion of the arteries, the production of vital spirits and the preservation of innate heat) were evenly distributed between the unsentient operations of digestion and growth, on the one hand, and the voluntary motions of the soul and the senses, on the other. The vital functions that physicians thought were performed by the heart could simply be assigned to the natural power of the soul (which Pietro also called *cibativa*, i.e., "nourishing," or *plantativa*, i.e., "plant-like").

It is interesting to note how Pietro d'Abano's account criticizes Averroes (1126–1198), the renowned Aristotelian interpreter and physician, for adding a further faculty – the "discerning" power (*discretiva*) – to the list of natural faculties. For Pietro, to assume the existence of a discerning ability was pointless, for the power to distinguish and recognize was implied in both the attractive and expulsive faculties.[27] Pietro's discussion of Averroes's *discretiva* was no minor point. In choosing whether or not to include a "discerning" ability among the natural faculties of the body, one gave a specific answer to the question of whether the vegetative activity of the body implied a form of tacit knowledge and, if so, whether this knowledge was directly supervised by the mind or was rather a distinctively biological function. This is when the observation of plant life becomes crucial, as it had been for Plato and Aristotle.[28] In Galen's opinion, plants had the ability to move. This motion was in fact a complex sequence of insensible operations through which they regulated their life; plants were able to attract specific nutrients, expel foreign matter, transform and assimilate food and finally retain all that was useful for the general economy of their vital functions. As we have already seen, in *De naturalibus facultatibus* Galen had distinguished four principal natural faculties: attractive, excretive, alterative and retentive. He had left unsolved the question of whether the formative power was implied in these four faculties or whether it was a different function altogether; indeed, he postulated a higher level of creative "wisdom." In the secret motions of plants, in the growth of animal organisms, in the way in which the most primordial operations of life were unceasingly performed in a living body, knowledge seemed to surpass all examples of human ingenuity.[29]

It is therefore safe to say that the way in which successive generations of physicians and anatomists systematized their knowledge of the vital processes had momentous consequences for a long-term history of the mind. The medical view of the unconscious, as elaborated by Galen and later reinterpreted by Arabic, Hebrew and Latin physicians, led to an understanding of life and its natural and vital functions (including the cognitive ones) that was fundamentally pluralistic and decentralized. At the end of his life, Galen delved for one last time into the question of where to look for the ultimate sources of life production within animal organisms. In *De propriis placitis*, he suggested that one had to focus on the anatomical parts themselves, concentrating one's attention on the most elementary combinations of material particles and qualities. It was once again a way of reminding both physicians and philosophers that bodily temperaments played a decisive role in the functions of life. And precisely there, in the original laboratories of the natural faculties, each part of matter could be seen as an autonomous living being, a true ζῷον. This amounted to saying that every individual animal consists in fact of many, indeed innumerable, animated organisms:

> Among the remedies that are beneficial to us, some act according to one or two qualities, others through the specific property of the substance as a whole. The same is certainly true of the operations of nature, for some occur through one or two qualities, others through the substance as a whole, such as the digestions in the stomach, blood production in the liver and the processes of growth and nutrition in each single part of the body. These activities take place in every part of the living being (ζῷον), for every part regulates itself following the faculties called "natural," which the living being has in common with plants, as if each part were a living being capable of preserving itself, (καθάπερ τι ζῷον ἑαυτὸ διασῷζον), for it attracts what is suitable for itself, expels what is foreign, and transforms, alters and assimilates to its own nature every element that has been attracted.[30]

Galen was here outlining the principles of what we might call "digestive pluralism," the view that at any moment, each part of the body was performing transformative operations based on the four principal natural faculties: attraction, excretion, alteration and retention. In this sense, each part behaved as if it were a ζῷον, an autonomous living being. Inevitably, given the complexity and diversity of the system, issues of conflict and consent were more pronounced in the medical than in the philosophical tradition. The reason was that, from an anatomical point of view, the mind was constantly exposed to the task of reconciling the parallel lives of countless vital principles with the many constraints imposed by the preservation of the living being as a whole, and this happened every time a metabolic change was performed. From the philosophers' perspective, by contrast, the mind was viewed from the very beginning as more confidently in control of the bodily situation. In some cases, it didn't even have to meddle with the body at all, for it was supposed to be a completely immaterial principle.

A Renaissance author who made full use of the Galenic notion of unsentient knowledge in attempting to mediate the doctrine of natural faculties with a newfound appeal to the Platonic notion of the mind was the aforementioned Cardano (1501–1576). In his book devoted to the interpretation of dreams, Cardano argued that, strictly speaking, God alone had the ability to be fully aware of himself (*seipsum cognoscere*). The rest of nature could only rely on varying degrees of self-consciousness:

> [W]ith the exception of God, all things that act act in a natural way [that is, unconsciously], and not as a creative mind. I mean, the elements [earth, water and air] move and know the end of their own motions, but they do not know how they move. The plants nourish themselves, grow and produce flowers and fruit; they do not know, however, how they do it. The animals move their muscles without thinking about it (*imprudenter*); and yet they do it in the right way, which is something that we also experience within ourselves.[31]

A "mind," Cardano continued, was certainly operating in each of the heavenly intelligences, in demons and human beings, but it was an incorporeal power that did not govern bodies in an unmediated way. While nature ruled the bodies, it was the intellect that understood through the mind.[32]

Before concluding this section on the conscious and unconscious faculties of the soul, I would like to hint briefly at another case of Renaissance hybridization of philosophy and medicine in which the Hippocratic notion of unknowing nature was mediated with a series of innovative opinions concerning the mind. I am referring to Paracelsus and his many followers throughout Europe. Reinterpreting Hippocratic motifs in a highly original way, Paracelsus argued that knowledge was already embedded in nature and unremittingly being objectified in infinite productions of exquisite formative skill. More radical than any other contemporary appropriation of the medical doctrine of natural faculties, Paracelsus's theory explained the functions of the mind as resulting from the actions of a myriad of vital principles, which he called *archei*. In this respect, the Paracelsian mind was inherently plural and centripetal. Life, even in its most complex manifestations, emerged out of an entangled mass of teeming individuals, all alive and perceiving. However unified into particular centres of action and knowledge, natural beings in Paracelsus's cosmos resulted from infinite agglomerations of desiring and knowing *archei*.[33] In his *Idea medicinae philosophicae* (*A Model of Philosophical Medicine*, 1571), Petrus Severinus (1542–1602), who successfully translated Paracelsus's obscure ideas (phrased in the opaque idiom of a local German dialect) into a systematic account written in the more familiar jargon of international Latin, explained that seeds contained elements of knowledge (*scientiae*), technical skills (*artes*) and propensities to make things (*dispositiones mechanicae; mechanici rerum processus*).[34] Above all, seeds and *archei* were made up of images and streams of imaginative energy that were always in the process of reacting to material stimuli and being transformed into increasingly abstract trends of representative activity. It is true that Severinus characterized Paracelsus's *archei* as "mechanical" agents (*spiritus mechanicus*). By *machina*, however, Severinus meant first and foremost a "tool" that could be used by a vital principle. There could therefore be a "machine" only when there was a natural agent endowed with a basic level of "selfhood" capable of using and controlling instruments and organs. By opening up the possibility of countless chemical applications, the way in which Paracelsus and the Paracelsians had transformed the originally Hippocratic view of a "digestive" selfhood had a deep impact on how processes of thought and imagination were envisaged. Cognitive and mental operations were presented as collective organizations of multiple forces, with natural tendencies to be displaced from central and permanent sources of knowledge and life. The balance between centre and periphery, internal and external, parts and the whole was therefore constitutively precarious. As we will see in the next section, the anatomical mind was constantly faced with the possibility of disorder and had a tendency to lose its equilibrium to an extent that had no parallel in the philosophical mind.

4 Delusions

Since the time the short treatise on *Sacred Disease* was composed by a Hippocratic author sometime during the fifth century BC, physicians had always stressed the delicate nature of the relationship linking the mind to its body and the external world. Delusions loomed large in the world of doctors, who often had to deal with illnesses in which the osmosis between the mental and non-mental aspects of a patient's life was part of a broader overlapping between representation and reality. Antonio Guaineri (d. around 1455), who studied and taught medicine at the University of Pavia, described melancholy and madness (*mania*) as "specific unnatural states of the brain" that were caused by "a disorder of the imaginative or the estimative faculty, or of both faculties at the same time." In recalling the various divisions of the internal senses in his influential treatise on mental illnesses, *De aegritudinibus capitis* (*On the Diseases of the Head*, originally published in 1473), he referred, as was often the case with physicians, to Avicenna. For Guaineri, the critical element in determining the specific nature of mental illness was the degree of self-awareness involved in assessing the boundaries separating the mind from reality:

> [W]e experience within ourselves that there is one power that perceives all the acts of the external senses; none of these is capable of self-perception (*sui actus perceptivus*), but perceives its own object. For instance, sight perceives colour, hearing sound, and so on with all the other senses. None of these objects is vision or hearing itself. Therefore, as we perceive ourselves seeing, hearing, tasting and the like, this activity cannot be reduced to any of the external senses. It is for this reason necessary to assign the task of performing this function to a specific power of the brain; this is what philosophers call "common sense," the seat of which is in the anterior area of the first ventricle of the brain.[35]

As a physician, Guaineri largely followed the Galenic tradition in locating the Aristotelian function of unifying the information conveyed by the senses (a function that was crucially accompanied by awareness) in the first ventricle of the brain. In Guaineri's scheme, Aristotle's common sense was also the starting point for the visualizing powers of the mind. Through Avicenna, Guaineri articulated the different levels of the imagination by meticulously mapping their location in the cavities of the brain:

> The rear area [in the first ventricle of the brain] is where the imagination (*fantasia*) is located; its function is to retain the representations of the sensible objects when they fade away. After the acts and operations of the common sense, we then include another power of the brain, which forms complex aggregates of representations, compounds and divides them, draws inferences from one element to another, and so constructs syllogisms. This virtue, insofar as it assists the intellect, is called cogitative faculty (*cogitativa*), insofar as it assists the estimative faculty (*extimativa*), it is called imaginative faculty (*imaginativa*). Its location is in the anterior area of the second ventricle.[36]

As we have seen in the first section of this chapter, the "temperamental" nature of all cognitive operations (*animi mores*) was one of the most enduring and influential legacies of the Galenic tradition. Along these lines, Guaineri argued that the disorders of the imagination and, more specifically, of the cogitative faculty might result from the malfunctioning constitution of the temperament in the corresponding part of the ventricle, or in the faulty quality of the humours and spirits circulating in it. More complex disorders of the internal senses (*ratio* or *extimatio*), however, derived from an impairment affecting the way in which the higher intellective functions processed mental notions from sensible representations:

> [T]hrough this power not only do we abstract intelligible representations from sensible images, such as representations of friendship and enmity and the like, but through it we also judge what is suitable and unsuitable for us, and what we should avoid or pursue. This faculty is located in the rear area of the second ventricle. And when that part of this ventricle or the spirit contained in it behave in an unnatural way, reason or the estimative function in man are perturbed.[37]

It is interesting to note that in Guaineri's account common sense and memory did not play a particularly significant role in triggering the specific diseases of the imagination and reason (*melancholia* and *mania*). Situated in the rear ventricle of the brain, the faculty of storing and preserving the representations of things was said to preserve these representations exactly as they had originally been received (*tales quales*):

> I saw some people suffering from melancholy who, once they recovered their health, remembered the things they had seen and done in their

bouts; and memory represents now the species in the same way as it received them at the time. In the common sense, too, in my opinion, no impairment (*laesio*) takes place, for it judges the matter as faithfully as reported by the external senses.[38]

This means that problems of recognition and self-identity, as already mentioned, started only at the level of the imagination and its various shades of replicating activity. The imaginative faculty, Guaineri argued, erred in assuming that "that which does not exist is real." The faculty that made a mistake here was one of the many functions within the power of the imagination, not the senses, the common sense or memory. This was what happened to people affected by delirium (*frenetici*),

> who, as a result of vapours rising to the visual faculty, think that they are seeing dead people or other things, depending on the various nature of those vapours or the strength (*fortificatio*) of some of the species stored in the upper echelons of the imagination (*fantasia*).

Sometimes, Guaineri continued, these vapours could reach the hearing faculty, and then patients thought that they were hearing flutes and other musical instruments. In all these cases, it was the malfunctioning of the imagination that destabilized the economy of cognitive faculties and their relations with the surrounding reality:

> [T]his happens in the imaginative faculty (*imaginativa*) and not in the common sense; therefore, by falsely imagining, the estimative faculty (*extimativa*) often thinks that what should be pursued should be avoided. Judging from all these cases, these two powers alone are injured in episodes of madness and melancholy: the imaginative and the estimative faculties.[39]

From Constantine the African, who in the eleventh century translated an influential treatise on melancholy by Ishaq ibn 'Imran (d. 908), to Robert Burton (1577–1640), who wrote a celebrated, seventeenth-century survey of melancholic affections, the dominant model of the faculties of the mind that physicians and natural philosophers had used to account for a whole host of mental illnesses had largely been based on the way the imagination responded to internal and external stimuli.[40] Thomas Fienus (1567–1631), a physician and a professor of medicine at Louvain, explained delusions as originating from a surplus of empathetic responsiveness in the faculty of the imagination and from a disruption of the natural bond connecting the powers of knowledge, desire and motion in the body. The author of a popular book on the powers of the imagination (*De viribus imaginationis*, published in Louvain in 1608), Fienus blamed the faculty of producing representations of things for distorting the natural link between the senses and reality:

> The reason that those who see other people eating sour things perceive the same sour taste in their mouth and those who imagine pain sometimes may feel pain is not because those representations (*species*) of taste and pain cause real taste or pain, but depends on the deception of the sensitive faculties caused by the imagination. It is through the imagination that we think we see what we do not see, hear what we do not hear and touch what we do not touch, as very often happens with people affected by melancholy.[41]

Rather than confining its role to facilitating the shift from sense perceptions to memory and the intellect, the imagination might sometimes interfere during certain critical phases of the mind's construction of its representational world. In keeping with centuries of medical investigations, Fienus was once again attributing melancholic delusions to both corporeal distempers (mainly excesses of black bile) and bouts of mental concentration:

> Melancholy often occurs because of a defect of the body, often merely as a result of a mental fault deriving from representations (*species*) that are impressed too deeply in the imagination, as happens to those who become melancholic due to excesses in religious zeal, study or love.[42]

Fienus did not rule out the possibility that, when delusions are directly caused by a disorder of the imagination, they might be treatable by inducing imaginary impressions opposite to the pathological ones.[43] This point was later brought to its natural conclusion by a former student of Fienus at Louvain, Jan Baptiste van Helmont (1580–1644), who in his posthumous medical epitome, *Ortus medicinae* (*The Dawn of Medicine*, 1648), argued that all illnesses, not just mental ones, were caused by a breakdown of the imagination. Indeed, as a follower of the chemical revolution initiated by Paracelsus, Helmont viewed the vital and sentient organization of the body in terms of multiple, intertwined, "archeal" associations. All physiological and pathological processes were ruled by combinations of local and peripheral imaginings unremittingly streaming from countless *archei*. Most of the time, these currents of representative processes were in agreement with each other, and this helped maintain the healthy balance of the organism. Often, though, the harmony of the imagination was disrupted by conflicting representations. These clashes among imagining *archei* coincided with the beginning of a disease, which for this reason was indistinguishably physical and mental. In Helmont's medical philosophy, the mind was immaterial and separated from the body, therefore immune to passions and illnesses. It was the body, as a vital substratum susceptible to the effects of the imagination, that was entirely at the mercy of bodily drives and corporeal desires.[44]

The view of mental sanity as precariously poised between the life of the body and the various faculties of knowledge can be seen as the most significant legacy resulting from the medical understanding of the mind and its powers. With his emphasis on the imagination, Helmont was not the only one in the first half of the seventeenth century to contend that threats of delusion were looming large in the life of human beings. Tommaso Campanella (1568–1639), an Italian philosopher who also produced a comprehensive and systematic account of medicine, the *Medicinalium iuxta propria principia libri septem* (*Seven Books of Medicine According to His Own Principles*, 1635), traced the origin of mental illness back to the very beginnings of sentient life in every single part of nature.[45] In his *Universalis philosophia* (*Universal Philosophy*, 1638), his imposing metaphysical summa, Campanella advanced the original theory that every perception (in both animate and inanimate beings) was a momentary lapse into insanity. Since the first stage in knowing something was to take on some of the characteristics of the object of knowledge and to become somehow "like" it, true and "healthy" knowledge meant to recognize oneself in the known object and thus strengthen one's identity as a perceiving subject. The problem was that for Campanella the possibility of becoming alienated was always lurking in every act of knowledge. "To know (*scire*) is to become another thing (*alienari*); to become another thing is to become mad (*insanire*), that is, to lose one's own being (*perdere proprium esse*) and to acquire someone else's being (*acquirere alienum*)."[46]

By pointing out that a propensity for delusion was built into the very mechanisms of perception, Campanella put the finishing touches, as it were, on the explanatory framework that considered the dividing lines between knowledge (mind), the body (temperament) and life (natural and vital faculties) to be inherently fleeting and osmotic. Possibilities for misrecognition and mistakes already loomed large at the level of nutrition and metabolism, where all the parts of the body were involved in discerning suitable substances from unsuitable ones. They all revealed that a form of elementary selfhood was in effect in the primal operations of life. We may call this kind of agency the "digestive self."

5 Conclusion: medical philosophy and the digestive self

A few words are in order to clarify the notion of a "digestive" self and its relationship with the mind. Between the fourteenth and seventeenth centuries, philosophers and physicians argued whether the mind, as a faculty involved in cognitive operations of a high level of abstraction and awareness, could be seen as the sum of increasingly complex bodily functions (from the natural powers acting in the homogeneous parts of the body to the nervous system centred around the brain), or whether the mind should be regarded as a special cognitive power irreducible to any form of bodily organization, no matter how composite and elaborate. In this chapter, we have surveyed the most salient features of a tradition that, from antiquity to the early modern period, conveyed a distinctively medical consideration of the mental functions. According to this characteristic point of view, individual living beings, such as plants and lower animals, not to mention entire anatomical regions within sentient animals of a higher degree of complexity (for example, the heart, the liver, the stomach and the intestines), were able to perform the most delicate biological operations without requiring the activity of conscious perception. These sophisticated instantiations of natural life could therefore be regarded as autonomous manifestations of vital energy, foreshadowing forms of life-sustaining selfhood; without being actual souls or substances endowed with cognitive faculties, living structures such as plants, internal organs and vital tissues were nevertheless capable of enacting patterns of intentional and purposeful action. Centuries of observation and speculation in the domains of anatomy and therapy had thus led several physicians, natural philosophers and masters of arts in universities to associate even the most abstract functions of the mind with the vital and material conditions of the body. This also meant that, far from being the expression of logical and linguistic competencies existing only in thought, the operations of the mind could be described as sophisticated forms of vital discernment whose roots were to be found in nature at large. In other words, sentient animals could feel and intelligent humans understand because the ability to distinguish and select was already at work in the most elementary functions of digestion and reproduction.

Among the various contributions to the philosophy of the mind made by the medical disciplines (including anatomy, practical medicine, materia medica and prophylaxis), this chapter has concentrated on three particularly influential themes: the extent to which the activity of thinking was deemed to depend on bodily structures and vital processes (regardless of whether those structures and processes involved the brain, the blood and the spirits); the interplay of conscious and unconscious operations in governing the life-preserving functions of the body; and, finally, the possibility that the mind could be subject to states of delusion, false belief and fixed opinion. The question of the "temperamental" nature of thinking had been associated from the outset with a number of specific relationships linking the faculties of the soul to the parts of the body. At the beginning of the fourteenth century, Pietro d'Abano had summed up the established view among physicians in very clear terms: "three are the principal organs, namely, the heart, the brain and the liver; the powers, therefore, are related to them as if they were their bases or roots."[47] In discussing the question of how the natural, vital and animal powers were all connected to each other in performing their functions, Pietro reminded his readers that on this matter physicians held a view that was different from the model espoused by scholastic philosophers, who located the soul in the heart.

The temperamental underpinnings of mental operations presupposed the existence of different levels of anatomical complexity. Physicians had long connected the emergence of awareness in human and non-human animals to the specific composition of bodily organs (formless and shaped structures, tangible and pneumatic parts). For this reason, it was quite common for philosophers and physicians to study the interplay of conscious and unconscious operations in parallel with the difference between plants (unsentient) and animals (sentient). Plants were able to move and to choose between substances that could be assimilated (food) and substances that could harm the organism (poison). They were also able to separate nourishing from superfluous substances, which then needed to be expelled from the organism. And yet animals too, even those endowed with a mind, contained within themselves a "plant-like" dimension (*plantativa*, to revisit Pietro d'Abano's expression). That the vital operations of assimilation, expulsion and shaping entailed an ability to discern and recognize could not be ruled out, and this involved two crucial consequences concerning the status of the mind. Firstly, it proved that cognitive propensities were already at work in the most elementary operations of nature. Secondly, it demonstrated that to distinguish between internal knowledge and external reality was a much more difficult task than philosophers had anticipated. Just as the digestive and plant-like characteristics of vegetative life blurred the boundaries between the mind and the specific bodily complexion it inhabited, so the representations of the senses, the imagination and the intellect obfuscated the contours separating the subject from the object of knowledge. In this light, it is certainly no accident that the study of delusion in its various forms had always been a large part of the theoretical and practical commitments involved in the medical approach to the mind.

Notes

1. See also *De naturalibus facultatibus*, I, II, 5; II, IV, 88–89.
2. See Temkin 1964; Giglioni 2008, 2013.
3. On the evolution of Hippocratism during the early modern period, see Smith 1979; Lonie 1981; French 1990.
4. See Schmitt 1985.
5. See Rothschild & Thompson 2014.
6. On Galenism and its influences on the philosophy of the mind see Temkin 1973; García Ballester 1988; Donini 2008; Jouanna 2009; Gill 2010.
7. Galen, *De propriis placitis*, 94. All translations from languages other than English are mine.
8. *De propriis placitis*, 64, 86.
9. Huarte de San Juan, *Examen de ingenios para la ciencias*, 50. See also ibid, pp. 113–115,
10. *Examen*, 50.
11. *Examen*, 103. On Huarte see Serés 1990.
12. Fernel, *Universa medicina*, 212.
13. *Universa medicina*, 219.
14. *Universa medicina*, 50.
15. *Universa medicina*, 221.
16. *Universa medicina*, 202–203. For further discussion of Fernel's theory of faculties, see Chapter 3 of this volume.
17. For more on the moral aspects of Vives's work, see Chapter 12 of this volume.
18. Vives, *De anima et vita*, sig. 3ᵛ.
19. *De anima et vita*, 5–7.
20. 42–43. On *De anima et vita*, see Del Nero 2008.
21. Galen, *De propriis placitis*, 80–82.

22 Pietro d'Abano, *Conciliator controversiarum*, 83ᵛab.
23 *Conciliator controversiarum*, 83ᵛb.
24 The *ratio agibilium* is further distinguished into *monastica*, *oeconomica* and *politica*, depending on whether the emphasis is on the individual mind, the family or the community (*Conciliator controversiarum*, 83ᵛbG).
25 *Conciliator controversiarum*, 83ᵛbGH.
26 *Conciliator controversiarum*, 84ʳaB.
27 *Conciliator controversiarum*, 83ᵛaH.
28 See Giglioni 1999.
29 This point was also stressed by Vives in his *De anima et vita*, 14 ("quum tota plantae vita introrsum spectet, exterorum orba et ignara").
30 Galen, *De propriis placitis*, 98.
31 Cardano, *Somniorum Synesiorum libri quatuor*, II, 390–392.
32 *Somniorum Synesiorum libri*, 392. On Cardano's view on the mind, see Giglioni 2014, 2005–2007.
33 See for instance Paracelsus, 58.
34 Severinus, *Idea medicinae philosophicae*, 42.
35 Guaineri, *De aegritudinibus capitis*, 37ʳa. On Guaineri, see Mugnai Carrara 2003.
36 *De aegritudinibus capitis*, 37ʳa.
37 *De aegritudinibus capitis*, 37ʳb.
38 *De aegritudinibus capitis*, 37ʳb.
39 *De aegritudinibus capitis*, 37ʳb – 37ᵛa.
40 See Strohmaier (1998: 161–162).
41 Fienus, *De viribus imaginationis*, 154.
42 *De viribus imaginationis*, 200.
43 *De viribus imaginationis*, 200.
44 On Van Helmont and imagination, see Giglioni 2000.
45 Campanella, *Medicinalium libri*, 308–309.
46 Campanella, *Universalis philosophia*, I, 20a.
47 Pietro d'Abano, *Conciliator controversiarum*, 83ᵛaE.

Bibliography

Primary sources

Campanella, Tommaso. *Medicinalium iuxta propria principia libri septem*. Lyon: Jean Pillehotte, 1635.

———. *Universalis philosophiae, seu metaphysicarum rerum, iuxta propria dogmata, partes tres, libri 18*, 3 vols. Paris: Denis Langlois, 1638.

Cardano, Girolamo. *Somniorum Synesiorum libri quatuor*, 2 vols. J.-Y. Boriaud (ed.). Florence: Olschki, 2008.

Fernel, Jean. *Universa medicina*. G. Plancy (ed.). Frankfurt: Claude de Marne and the Heirs of Johann Aubry, 1607.

Fienus, Thomas. *De viribus imaginationis tractatus*. Leiden: Officina Elzeviriana, 1635.

Galen. *De propriis placitis*. In Galen, *L'anima e il dolore*, I. Garofalo & A. Lami (eds). Milan: Rizzoli, 2012.

Guaineri, Antonio. *De aegritudinibus capitis*. In Guaineri, *Practica*. Lyon: Constantin Fradin, 1517.

Huarte de San Juan, Juan. *Examen de ingenios para las ciencias*. G. Serés (ed.). Barcelona: Círculo de Lectores, 1996.

Paracelsus, Theophrastus. *Liber de lunaticis*. In *Sämtliche Werke*, vol. I, 14, K. Sudhoff & W. Matthiessen (eds). Munich and Berlin: Oldenbourg and Barth, 1922–1933.

Pietro d'Abano. *Conciliator controversiarum quae inter philosophos et medicos versantur*. Venice: Heirs of Lucantonio Giunti, 1565 (repr. Padua: Antenore, 1985).

Severinus, Petrus. *Idea medicinae philosophicae, fundamenta continens totius doctrinae Paracelsicae, Hippocraticae, et Galenicae*. Basel: Sebastian Henric-Petri, 1571.

Vives, Juan Luis. *De anima et vita libri tres*. Basel: Robert Winter, 1538.

Secondary literature

Del Nero, V. 2008. "A Philosophical Treatise on the Soul: *De Anima et Vita* in the Context of Vives' Opus". In *A Companion to Juan Luis Vives*, C. Fantazzi (ed.), 277–314. Leiden: Brill.

Donini, P. 2008. "Psychology". In *The Cambridge Companion to Galen*, R. J. Hankinson (ed.), 184–209. Cambridge: Cambridge University Press.

French, R. 1990. "Sickness and the Soul: Stahl, Hoffman and Sauvages on Pathology". In *The Medical Enlightenment of the Eighteenth Century*, A. Cunningham & R. French (eds), 88–110. Cambridge: Cambridge University Press.

García Ballester, L. 1988. "Soul and Body: Disease of the Soul and Disease of the Body in Galen's Medical Thought". In *Le opere psicologiche di Galeno*, P. Manuli & M. Vegetti (eds), 117–152. Naples: Bibliopolis.

Giglioni, G. 1999. "Girolamo Cardano e Giulio Cesare Scaligero: Il dibattito sul ruolo dell'anima vegetativa". In *Girolamo Cardano: Le opere, le fonti, la vita*, M. Baldi & G. Canziani (eds), 313–339. Milan: Angeli.

———. 2000. *Immaginazione e malattia: Saggio su Jan Baptiste van Helmont*. Milan: Angeli.

——— 2005–2007. "*Mens* in Girolamo Cardano". In *Per una storia del concetto di mente*, E. Canone (ed.), 2 vols, II, 83–123. Florence: Olschki.

———. 2008. "What Ever Happened to Francis Glisson? Albrecht Haller and the Fate of Eighteenth-Century Irritability". *Science in Context* **21**(4): 465–493.

———. 2013. "Jean-Baptiste Lamarck and the Place of Irritability in the History of Life and Death". In *Vitalism and the Scientific Image in Post-Enlightenment Life Science, 1800–2010*, S. Normandin & C. T. Wolfe (eds), 19–49. Dordrecht, The Netherlands: Springer.

———. 2014. "Humans, Elephants, Diamonds and Gold: Patterns of Intentional Design in Girolamo Cardano's Natural Philosophy". *Gesnerus* **71**(2): 237–257.

Gill, Ch. 2010. *Naturalistic Psychology in Galen and Stoicism*. Oxford: Oxford University Press.

Jouanna, J. 2009. "Does Galen Have a Medical Programme for Intellectuals and the Faculties of the Intellect?". In *Galen and the World of Knowledge*, C. Gill, T. Whitmarsh & J. Wilkins (eds), 190–205. Cambridge: Cambridge University Press.

Lonie, I. M. 1981. "Hippocrates the Iatromechanist". *Medical History* **25**(2): 113–150.

Mugnai Carrara, D. 2003. "Guaineri, Antonio". In *Dizionario Biografico degli Italiani*, vol. 60, 111–115. Rome: Istituto della Enciclopedia Italiana.

Rothschild, C. K. & Thompson, T. W. (eds). 2014. *Galen's De Indolentia: Essays on a Newly Discovered Letter*. Tübingen: Mohr Siebeck.

Schmitt, Ch. B. 1985. "Aristotle Among the Physicians". In *The Medical Renaissance of the Sixteenth Century*, A. Wear, R. K. French & I. M. Lonie (eds), 1–15. Cambridge: Cambridge University Press.

Serés, G. 1990. "Huarte de San Juan: De la 'naturaleza' a la 'politica'". *Criticón* **49**(1): 77–90.

Smith, W. D. 1979. *The Hippocratic Tradition*. Ithaca: Cornell University Press.

Strohmaier, G. 1998. "Reception and Tradition: Medicine in the Byzantine and Arab World". In *Western Medical Thought From Antiquity to the Middle Ages*, M. D. Grmek & B. Fantini (eds) & A. Shugaar (trans.), 139–169. Cambridge, MA: Harvard University Press.

Temkin, O. 1964. "The Classical Roots of Glisson's Doctrine of Irritation". *Bulletin of the History of Medicine* **38**(4): 297–328.

———. 1973. *Galenism: Rise and Decline of a Medical Philosophy*. Ithaca: Cornell University Press.

3

THE SOUL AND ITS PARTS

Debates about the powers of the soul

Paul J.J.M. Bakker

1 Introduction

Medieval and Renaissance debates about the soul and its parts, or powers, arose from a set of brief remarks in Aristotle's book *On the Soul* (*De anima*). According to Aristotle, all vital operations of a living organism are ultimately caused by one single principle: the soul (*psychē, anima*). In addition to his notorious definition of the soul as "the first actuality of a natural, organic body having life potentially" (*De anima* II.1, 412a27–28), he proposed a second, more straightforward description of the soul as the principle "by which primarily we live, perceive and think" (*De anima* II.2, 414a12–13).[1] The diversity of the operations mentioned in this second definition (live, perceive and think) prompted the question of how a *single* principle can actually produce such *diverse* effects. Is it possible for one single soul to bring about such different processes as digestion, growth, procreation, movement, sense perception, imagination, higher order cognition and volition? Or does the very diversity of operations make it necessary to assume a multitude of souls coexisting in a human being instead of one single soul?

At the same time, since Aristotle speaks about the soul as a "principle (*archē*) characterised by the powers of self-nutrition, sensation, thinking, and movement" (*De anima* II.1, 413b11–12), the question arose how exactly these 'powers' are related to their basic principle, the soul. Are they somehow distinct from the soul itself? Or are they ontologically identical with it? And vice versa, is the soul itself anything else than a set of powers or capacities? How many different powers do we need to assume to account for the various operations? On what grounds do we accept certain distinctions (e.g., between a power of vision and a power of nutrition) and reject others (e.g., between a power of seeing white and a power of seeing yellow)? How are these powers related to one another and to the different parts of the body?[2]

In the Middle Ages and the Renaissance, Aristotle's brief and sketchy remarks about the soul's powers were further elaborated and synthesised into a full-scale 'faculty psychology,' a theory according to which the soul is 'composed' of a set of powers (*potentiae*), forces (*virtutes*) or faculties (*facultates*), each directed to a specific category of objects and responsible for certain kinds of operations.[3]

If such powers are seen as entities distinct from the soul itself, they are usually characterised as the 'immediate' principles of the vital operations, the soul itself being the 'remote' or 'ultimate' cause. In other words, the powers of the soul are described as intermediary (causal) entities between the soul itself and its operations. Medieval and Renaissance Aristotelians typically described the relation between the soul and its powers as a process of emanation (*fluxus*), in which the powers 'flow forth' from the soul's essence. As a rule, they distinguished between three basic types of powers: vegetative, sensitive and intellective (or rational). But beyond these three basic types, individual authors proposed various, often highly sophisticated systems of psychic faculties and sub-faculties.[4]

Besides Aristotle's remarks, two Christian theological sources influenced medieval and Renaissance debates about the soul's powers. The first is Augustine's book *On the Trinity* (*De Trinitate*). Contrary to Aristotle (who speaks about *all* powers of the soul, the vegetative, sensitive and intellective), Augustine focuses specifically on the powers of the *rational* soul: memory, understanding and will. In the Middle Ages and the Renaissance, Augustine was often quoted as saying that the three rational powers constitute "one life, one mind, and one substance" and hence are identical with one another. But in other passages he seems to say precisely the opposite, namely that memory, understanding and will are three distinct powers.[5] The second influential source, the short, anonymous twelfth-century treatise known as the *Liber de spiritu et anima*, exhibits the same 'vertical' approach as Aristotle (focusing on all the powers of the soul), as opposed to the 'horizontal' approach we find in Augustine, who only speaks about the powers of the rational soul. This anonymous treatise was often quoted to support the claim that the soul and its powers are identical, the powers of the soul differing from the soul itself "only in name."[6]

A convenient starting point for studying late medieval and Renaissance discussions of the powers of the soul is Thomas Aquinas (d. 1274).[7] Aquinas argued that every hylomorphic substance contains *one* single substantial form, which accounts not only for its essential unity and identity over time but also for *all* its operations. In the case of a human being, this unique substantial form is the intellective soul.[8] But to explain the variety of operations carried out by a human being, Aquinas argued that the intellective soul possesses different powers. As the immediate principles of the soul's operations, the powers are distinct from one another and from the soul's essence. Aquinas's principal (theological) argument in favour of this view is based on the distinction between God and creatures. God, in virtue of His simplicity, operates immediately through his essence, not through distinct intermediary powers. Hence in God, and *only* in God, there is a full identity of operations, powers and essence. In created substances, powers and essence are distinct from one another.[9] Another (psychological) argument is based on the assumption that the soul, according to its essence, is what accounts for the fact that a human being (or any other living organism) "is always actually alive," from birth to death. The soul's powers, however, are not always actualised, at least not all of them. For example, human beings are not continuously engaged in acts of seeing or thinking. According to Aquinas, this implies that the powers of the soul are not fully identical with the soul's essence.[10]

If this is indeed the case, the question arises what kind of entities such powers are. Aquinas suggests two possible ways of answering this question. In one sense, arguing along the lines of Aristotle's *Categories*, he claims that the powers are 'accidents' of the soul and belong to the ontological category of quality. But following Aristotle's discussion of the five predicables in the *Topics*, Aquinas argues that the powers are not accidents, but 'proper attributes' (*propria*) of the soul. Aristotle's example of a proper attribute is a human being's ability to learn grammar. This ability is not part of the essence of being human, but it is necessarily consequent upon it. Hence, saying that the powers are the soul's proper attributes implies that they are not included in the soul's essence, yet are inseparable from it.[11] This intimate relation between the soul and its powers is implied by the traditional emanation metaphor, namely that all psychic powers naturally 'flow forth' from the soul's essence. According to Aquinas, this emanation is not a kind of change (*transmutatio*) but a process by which "one thing naturally results from another, for example colour from light."[12]

But even though all psychic powers emanate from the soul's essence, they do not all have the same subject (*subiectum*) or bearer. According to Aquinas, the *intellective* powers, intellect and will, have the soul's essence as their subject, because they do not require bodily organs to carry out their operations; it is the soul itself that performs acts of understanding and willing. The *vegetative* and *sensitive* powers, on the other hand, require bodily organs to perform their operations. Hence, these powers have the whole human composite as their subject, both soul and body.[13] This difference in subject between the intellective powers, on the one hand, and the vegetative and sensitive powers, on the other, entails that the former remain fully functional after death, when the soul subsists without the body, whereas the latter remain intact only potentially or, as Aquinas says, "virtually."[14]

Finally, to answer the question on what grounds the existence of specific psychic powers can be established, Aquinas takes his cue from Aristotle's statement according to which *powers* are distinguished in virtue of their *acts* and their *objects* (*De anima* II.4, 415a14–22). But a distinction between psychic powers cannot be based upon random, accidental differences between objects. For example, the difference between a white swan and a black swan does not justify postulating two distinct powers of seeing white and seeing black. To avoid a meaningless proliferation of powers, Aquinas argues that only a difference in something that the power is "concerned with *per se*" justifies postulating a distinct power. In other words, powers are distinguished in virtue of their proper objects. This admittedly vague (and possibly circular) claim allows him to accept a distinction between, e.g., the power of vision (being *per se* concerned with colour) and the power of hearing (having sound as its proper object), but to reject a distinction between a power of seeing white and a power of seeing black.[15]

In the period between 1300 and 1600, Aquinas's account often served as a starting point for discussing the powers of the soul. In this chapter I shall examine two radically opposed views. First, I shall examine a group of fourteenth-century writers whose goal is to identify the powers of the soul with the soul itself to the furthest possible extent. Second, I shall discuss two sixteenth-century authors who describe the powers of the soul as more or less independent causal agents really distinct from the soul itself. In the final section I shall briefly examine some critics of the notion of psychic faculties. Throughout this chapter I shall focus on questions concerning the relation between the *soul and its powers*, on the one hand, and on questions concerning *the powers of the soul and the organs of the body*, on the other.

2 The real identity of the soul and its powers

Aquinas's view of the powers of the soul as the immediate principles of the soul's operations fell out of favour in the fourteenth century. Around 1300, John Duns Scotus (d. 1308) was already arguing that there is no compelling reason to assume that a single, undivided principle such as the soul cannot produce a multitude of operations by itself without distinct, intermediary powers. Nevertheless, in order to satisfy philosophical and theological 'authorities' on this issue, Scotus felt the need to admit the existence of psychic powers that are 'formally distinct' from the soul itself.[16] One decade later, William of Ockham (d. 1347) went one step further, arguing that the powers of the soul are *really identical* with the soul itself and that the variety of vital operations can be explained (at least partly) in terms of the soul's relation to the body.

2.1 William of Ockham

Ockham's discussion of the powers of the soul is based upon his view of the metaphysical constitution of human beings. According to Ockham, human beings (unlike plants and animals) possess *two* really distinct souls, a sensitive soul and an intellective soul, both of which have the metaphysical status of a substantial form.[17] His principal argument in favour of this view draws on the empirical observation that we sometimes experience mutually exclusive desires simultaneously, one by sensitive appetite, the other by intellective appetite. In Ockham's view, such conflicting experiences can only be explained by assuming distinct sensitive and intellective souls. Ontologically speaking, the difference between these two souls is that the former is material and extended according to the extension of the body, whereas the latter is immaterial and indivisible (in Ockham's terms: "present as a whole in the whole body and in every part of it").[18] In accordance with this ontological difference, Ockham offers separate accounts of the powers of the *intellective* soul and those of the *sensitive* soul.

Concerning the former, Ockham argues that there is no real distinction between these powers and the soul itself; intellect and will are really identical with one another and with the essence of the intellective soul. According to Ockham, 'intellect' can be defined as "the essence of a soul capable of understanding," whereas 'will' can be defined as "the essence of a soul capable of willing." The only difference between these two definitions resides in the fact that to understand and to will are two really distinct *acts*. But the principle that causes these acts is really one and the same thing, namely the intellective soul.[19] Consequently, Ockham describes 'intellect' and 'will' as 'connotative terms' primarily signifying the intellective soul itself, but also connoting its distinct acts of understanding and willing. Apart from this distinction at the level of *acts*, there is no distinction between intellect and will. Ockham's principal argument in favour of the 'indistinction' (or real identity) of intellect and will is his famous principle of parsimony, according to which it is simply unnecessary to posit distinct psychic powers to explain how the soul performs acts of understanding and willing.[20]

Ockham also applies the principle of parsimony in his account of the powers of the *sensitive* soul. In his view, there is no real distinction between, e.g., the powers of vision and hearing as such, leaving aside the 'accidental dispositions' of the body needed for acts of seeing and hearing. Nor is there a real distinction between these powers and the sensitive soul. According to Ockham, the sensitive soul is itself the immediate cause of all its operations. There is no need to assume distinct intermediate psychic entities such as the power of vision or the power of hearing. However, on a broader understanding of the notion of 'power of the (sensitive) soul,' Ockham has no trouble accepting the apparently opposite claim that there *is* a real distinction between the various powers, and between those powers and the soul. On this broader understanding, the notion of 'power of the (sensitive) soul' *includes* those of the body's dispositions that the soul requires to perform its operations. For example, the notion of the 'power of vision' taken in this broader sense includes, besides the sensitive soul, the bodily organ needed for the act of seeing, in other words, the eye. It is obvious that the bodily dispositions involved in operations of the sensitive soul are really distinct from one another and from the sensitive soul, because these dispositions are qualities of the *body*, not of the *soul*. Therefore Ockham concludes that the powers of the sensitive soul, taken broadly as including the bodily dispositions necessary for the powers to act, are really distinct both from one another and from the sensitive soul.[21]

To clarify his point, Ockham further elaborates on the relation between the sensitive soul and the body. In his view, the sensitive soul (which includes all vegetative and sensitive powers) is divisible into parts that command different parts of the body. For example, the part of the sensitive soul that commands the eye is called the 'power of vision.' Another part of the sensitive soul that commands the ear is called the 'power of hearing.' According to Ockham, these parts of the soul are *homogenous*. In other words, the distinction between the power of vision and the power of hearing does not originate within the sensitive soul itself, but precisely in its relation to the various parts of the body.[22] Nevertheless, according to Ockham, the distinction between the powers is *real*, for the simple reason that one power can cease to function while others remain undamaged. Applying this principle, Ockham even goes so far as to admit that human beings possess *two* really distinct powers of vision (one for each eye). But this real distinction between powers is entirely dependent on the structure of the body, not on the sensitive soul as such.[23]

The fact that the parts of the soul are homogeneous implies that one part is not exclusively suited to cause one specific activity rather than another. Every homogeneous part is, in and of itself, capable of causing the full range of operations produced by the sensitive soul. This makes it possible for parts of the soul to 'change organs' in a certain way. For example, it is conceivable that the part of the soul that normally commands the eye might subsequently command the ear. The dispositions of the body determine which act is caused by a specific part of the sensitive soul. Hence, if the dispositions required for vision that are normally present in an eye miraculously occur elsewhere in the body, for example in a foot, the part of the soul present in the foot will produce acts of seeing in the foot just as the part present in the eye causes acts of seeing. In this hypothetical situation, the dispositions required for vision will be precisely the same in the eye and in the foot. Hence, the homogeneous parts of the soul present in both parts of the body will produce precisely the same acts.[24]

To conclude, Ockham argues that sensitive powers are homogeneous parts of the sensitive soul that command specific parts of the body, where certain dispositions are found. Thus, for example, the power of vision is that homogeneous part of the sensitive soul that commands the eye (or another part of the body where similar dispositions are available). The power of hearing is another homogenous part of the same sensitive soul that commands the ear. Only regarding the power of touch does Ockham offer a somewhat different account, because it is unclear what exactly the organ of touch is (as Aristotle had already pointed out). According to Ockham, the power of touch is in fact identical with the sensitive soul as a whole because human beings are able to have tactile sensations by means of any part of their bodies where the dispositions necessary for touch are found.[25]

Many fourteenth-century writers further elaborated on Ockham's view.[26] To illustrate Ockham's influence, I shall briefly examine the accounts given by a physician (Thomas Del Garbo), a theologian (Gregory of Rimini) and a philosopher (John Buridan). These authors strengthen the double tendency present in Ockham's account. On the one hand, they identify the powers of the soul with the soul itself to the furthest possible extent. On the other hand, they explain the variety of (sensitive) operations performed by the soul in terms of its relation to different parts of the body.

2.2 Thomas Del Garbo

Thomas Del Garbo (d. 1370) offers a general account of the soul that closely resembles that of Ockham. He considers it 'likely' (although not demonstrable) that the intellective soul and the sensitive soul are two distinct substantial forms. His argument is the same as the one given by Ockham, namely that we sometimes experience contrary sensitive and intellectual desires at the same time. Such experiences suggest that the sensitive and the intellective souls are two distinct substantial forms.[27] Thomas also states, like Ockham, that the intellective soul is present "as a whole in the whole body and in every part of it." This has to be accepted on the authority of faith, because it cannot be demonstrated by reason nor derived from experience. Probably for this reason, Thomas has little more to say about the intellective soul and its operations. Instead, he focuses on the sensitive soul. Assuming that the latter is indeed a distinct substantial form, it must therefore be of the same nature as the soul of non-human animals. Now we know from experience that when certain parts of the body of, say, a worm are cut off, they continue to react to sensitive stimuli. In Thomas's view, this counts as empirical evidence that the sensitive soul is divisible and extended according to the extension of the body.[28]

To elaborate on this point, he raises the question of how the sensitive soul informs the various parts of the body. One possible (Aristotelian) answer to this question is that the heart constitutes the soul's principal subject, whereas other parts of the body are informed only indirectly, because the working of the soul is transmitted from the heart to other parts of the body by means of 'animal spirits.' On this cardiocentrist account, the soul is present in the heart 'essentially' but in other parts of the body only "through the soul's powers." Support for this view can be found in Aristotle's comparison of the relation between the soul and the parts of the body with a well-ordered city, in which "there is no more need of a separate monarch to preside over each several task," because "the individuals each play their assigned part as it is ordered" (*De motu animalium* 10, 703a28–b2).[29] Thomas rejects this view, because *all* parts of the body perform the soul's operations equally. In his view, there is no reason to think that the operation of the heart is more directly caused by the soul than the operations of other parts of the body. This can only be explained if the soul itself informs *all* parts of the body in the same 'essential' manner.

Thomas applies Ockham's principle of parsimony in arguing that the powers of the soul are not 'things' (*res*) distinct from the soul itself.[30] He understands 'power of the soul' to be a connotative term that primarily signifies the soul, but also refers secondarily to its acts. For example, when we speak of the 'power of vision' we primarily signify the soul itself and secondarily its act of seeing. Given that acts of the sensitive soul always involve specific parts of the body, Thomas concludes that the term 'power of vision' primarily signifies the soul and secondarily the eye, the organ needed to perform acts of seeing.[31] He also shares Ockham's view that the distinction between the various powers of the soul does not originate within the sensitive soul itself, but precisely in its relation to the various organs of the body. Hence, he argues that, from the point of view of the sensitive soul itself, all powers are present in each and every part of the body. From this perspective, one can say that vision is equally present in the eye as in a foot. But insofar as acts of seeing require colour perception, which can only take place through a specific bodily organ, the soul can be said to exercise its power of vision in the eye and in no other part of the body.[32]

Thomas thus offers a 'medicalised' version of Ockham's view. Since, as a physician, he has little to say about intellect and will, his theory is limited to the powers of the sensitive soul. He applies Ockham's analysis of the powers as connotative terms to the powers of the sensitive soul. Moreover, he tries to confirm Ockham's view of the sensitive soul as divisible and extended by giving empirical evidence (the dissection of worms). Finally, he rejects cardiocentrism, claiming that the sensitive soul informs all parts of the body in the same 'essential' way.

2.3 Gregory of Rimini

Gregory of Rimini (d. 1358) also elaborates on Ockham's view, although his point of departure is different. Whereas Ockham argues that human beings possess two really distinct souls, Gregory rejects the idea of a distinct sensitive soul. In his view, *all* operations performed by a human being are caused by one unique substantial form: the intellective soul.[33] Yet in spite of their disagreement concerning the number of souls, Gregory and Ockham offer largely similar accounts of the soul's powers. While Ockham differentiates between the powers of the sensitive soul and the powers of the intellective soul, Gregory distinguishes between the sensitive and the intellective powers of the unique (intellective) soul.[34]

With respect to the soul's *intellective* powers, he argues along the same lines as Ockham that there is no real distinction between intellect and will and that both are really identical with the intellective soul itself. Gregory's main argument in favour of this identity thesis is again the principle of parsimony.[35] Gregory also follows Ockham in treating 'intellect' and 'will' as connotative terms that primarily signify the soul's essence while also connoting acts of understanding and willing. Both terms designate the soul as an undivided and indivisible whole, but they also indicate the various kinds of acts the human (intellective) soul is capable of performing. Only in this sense is Gregory willing to accept the common labelling of intellect and will as 'parts' or 'powers' (in the plural) of the soul. This common way of speaking does not imply that intellect and will are really parts of the soul, let alone distinct things, but only that the soul has different 'functions' (*officia*) that can be designated separately.[36]

Gregory also uses Ockham's principle of parsimony to argue that there is no real distinction between the soul and its *sensitive* powers.[37] But given that the soul's sensitive operations always involve the body, the question arises what role the body and its organs play in performing such operations. To answer this question, Gregory argues that acts of the sensitive soul are, strictly speaking, acts of the soul alone. In his view, the soul is the only subject or 'bearer' of sensory acts. The body and its organs merely play the role of a 'medium' or a 'messenger' (*nuntius*) between the sensible object and the soul, where sensation takes place. Gregory's most important argument in favour of this view is a theological '*post mortem*' argument, according to which sense images, acquired through sense perception, have to remain preserved in the soul after death. Otherwise, the disembodied soul would lack a distinct memory of specific sensible objects (and hence would remain ignorant of the reasons for its reward or punishment). According to Gregory, the only way to guarantee that sense images are remembered after death is to assume that the (unique, immortal) soul alone is the 'bearer' of acts of sensation.[38]

2.3 John Buridan

Another influential follower of Ockham is John Buridan (d. ca. 1361). Yet, just like Gregory of Rimini, Buridan disagrees with Ockham on the question of the number of souls and substantial forms in a human being. According to Buridan, human beings have only *one* substantial form, the intellective soul, which accounts for *all* operations.[39] With respect to the powers of the soul, there is one important respect in which Buridan's approach differs from that of both Ockham and Gregory. Instead of offering separate accounts of the sensitive and intellective powers, Buridan proposes *one* single theory for *all* powers of the soul. His account is based upon a distinction between a narrow and a broad understanding of the notion 'power of the soul' (precisely the same distinction Ockham made with respect to the powers of the sensitive soul). Taken in a narrow sense, the notion 'power of the soul' refers to what Buridan calls the soul's 'principal' powers. In this sense, the notion refers precisely to the powers of the soul leaving aside the bodily dispositions necessary for these powers to act. According to Buridan, this narrow sense constitutes the proper meaning of the notion 'power of the soul.' In a broader sense, the notion of 'power of the soul' stands for what Buridan labels the soul's 'instrumental' powers. In this second sense, the notion 'power of the soul' denotes *either* the powers of the soul together with anything the powers need to exercise their operations, in particular the dispositions of the body, *or* these bodily dispositions themselves.[40]

Appealing to this distinction, Buridan claims that the principal powers of the soul are *really identical* with the soul itself. In speaking of the 'principal' powers, we can only say that a human soul has multiple powers in the sense that it is able to perform a variety of *acts*. According to this variety of acts, we can use different words to describe the soul as vegetative, sensitive or intellective. But these different words do not imply the real existence of vegetative, sensitive or intellective psychic powers distinct from one another and/or from the soul itself. On the contrary, it is the soul itself that 'principally' performs all its acts, no matter how different they are.[41] However, with respect to the soul's 'instrumental' powers, Buridan (just like Ockham) makes what appears to be the opposite claim, namely that the powers are *really distinct* both from one another and from the soul itself. But the contradiction between the two claims is only apparent, because the principal powers are powers of the *soul*, whereas the instrumental powers are powers of *soul and body* together (or, in other words, powers of the animated *body*). The latter are called 'powers of the *soul*' only because the soul uses them as instruments. Insofar as these instrumental powers are *bodily* powers, they are really distinct both from one another and from the soul itself. For example, the instrumental power of nutrition is distinct from the instrumental power of vision because the respective bodily dispositions required for nutrition and vision are really distinct.

And precisely the same goes for the intellective (instrumental) power, which differs from the power of vision in that the latter needs sense images and a specific bodily organ to act (the eye), whereas the former needs mental representations and performs its operations without any bodily organ at all.[42]

Moving from Ockham and Thomas Del Garbo to John Buridan via Gregory of Rimini, we witness an increasing simplification concerning the relation between the soul and its powers together with an increasingly strong emphasis on the relation between soul and body. Ockham distinguishes between two really distinct souls in a human being and offers two distinct accounts of the powers of the intellective soul and those of the sensitive soul. Thomas Del Garbo 'medicalises' Ockham's view, focusing on the powers of the sensitive soul and their bodily counterparts. Gregory of Rimini simplifies Ockham's view by recognizing not two souls but one, the intellective soul, while nonetheless proposing separate accounts of the soul's intellective and sensitive powers. John Buridan further simplifies the theory. Like Gregory, he recognises only one soul in a human composite, the intellective soul. But unlike Gregory, he offers one single account of *all* powers of the soul. In Buridan's view, all that is needed to explain how the soul can produce such a wide variety of operations is a distinction between principal and instrumental powers. The former are fully identical with the soul itself. Hence, in the case of a human being, *all* principle powers of the soul are immaterial, indivisible and immortal, precisely because they are really identical with the intellective soul. Only at the level of instrumental powers does it make sense to differentiate between vegetative and sensitive powers, on the one hand, and intellective powers, on the other. However, instrumental powers are not just powers of the soul, but powers of *soul and body* together.[43]

3 The real distinction of the soul and its powers

In sharp contrast with Ockham and his fourteenth-century followers, many fifteenth- and sixteenth-century writers described the powers of the soul as distinct intermediary entities between the soul and its operations. Here I shall focus on two particularly outspoken advocates of this view: the Spanish Jesuit philosopher and theologian Francisco Suárez (d. 1617) and the French physician Jean Fernel (d. 1558).[44]

3.1 Francisco Suárez

At first glance, Suárez's discussion of the powers of the soul seems to be a straightforward defence of Aquinas's view.[45] Like Aquinas, Suárez argues that the intellective soul is the only substantial form of a human being. It accounts for *all* operations (including the sensitive and the vegetative ones). The 'pluralists,' arguing that the intellective, sensitive and vegetative 'parts' of the soul are in fact distinct substantial forms (and not merely different aspects of one unique human soul), not only jeopardise the unity of a human being but also leave unanswered the question of how these three completely different forms relate to and interact with one another.[46] Suárez also seems to adopt Aquinas's view concerning the soul and its powers. His main thesis, that the "powers of the soul are really (*realiter*) distinct from the soul itself" is, in his own words, the view of Aquinas and "all his followers."[47]

Against the Ockhamist view that the powers of the soul are "in no way" distinct from the soul's essence Suárez uses Aquinas's (theological) argument concerning the difference between God and creatures. Only in God is there absolutely no distinction between essence and operative powers. In created substances, these items are distinct entities.[48] Suárez also argues that the soul's powers are distinct from one another because of their respective acts; intellect differs from will because acts of understanding differ from acts of willing. If the soul's powers are really identical with the soul itself, there seems to be no way to distinguish between one power and another, because "two items that are really identical with a third must be really identical with one another." Hence, we would be entitled to attribute the operation of one power to another (saying, e.g., that the intellect wills or that the will understands), rendering the very notion of 'powers of the soul' meaningless.[49] Taking his criticism of the Ockhamist view as his starting point, Suárez makes two claims, with different degrees of certitude. His first claim, presented as 'certain' (*certa*), is that the powers of the soul must be distinct from the soul itself '*ex natura rei.*' In other words, the distinction between the soul and its powers is not merely conceptual, but has at least some kind of real 'underpinning.'[50]

According to Suárez's second claim, which concerns the precise nature of this underpinning, it is 'most plausible' that the powers of the soul are 'really' (*realiter*) distinct from the soul itself. Although Suárez claims that he agrees with Aquinas on this point, there is in fact an important difference between Suárez's defence of a real distinction between the soul and its powers, on the one hand, and Aquinas's view, on the other. According to Aquinas, psychic powers are the soul's 'proper attributes.' As such, they do not belong to the soul's essence, but are naturally consequent upon it. For Aquinas, the powers of the soul are indeed something real, because they are the immediate principles of the soul's operations, and hence the distinction between the soul itself and its powers is not merely conceptual. But Aquinas does not claim that the powers of the soul are 'really' distinct from the soul itself. By defending the latter thesis, Suárez goes beyond Aquinas's view. Although he considers most of Aquinas's arguments less than convincing, there is one argument he finds compelling enough to accept that a real distinction between the soul and its powers might at least be 'plausible.' This is again the (theological) argument concerning the difference between God and creatures, according to which God's essence, power and operation are fully identical, whereas in created substances, essence and operative powers are really distinct entities.[51]

The fact that Suárez describes the powers of the soul as really distinct entities makes the question of their causation particularly important for him. The most delicate issue in this respect concerns *efficient* causality. Is the soul the efficient cause of its own powers? Suárez realises that there are good reasons to deny this.

If the soul were indeed the efficient cause of its powers, it should be able to restore powers that have been damaged. Hence, the soul of a blinded person should be able to bring back the power of vision.[52] Despite such arguments, Suárez endorses what he calls the 'common opinion,' according to which the soul efficiently causes its own powers. The main question for him is precisely *how* the efficient causality of the soul functions vis-à-vis its powers. In his view, a two-tier process of causation is at work here. On the one hand, it is God who, by an act of 'creation,' causes the soul itself or the 'substance' of the soul. On the other hand, it is the soul that produces its own powers by a distinct causal act of 'emanation.'[53]

To justify his view that the 'creation' of the soul's substance and the 'emanation' of the soul's powers are two distinct causal acts produced by two different agents, Suárez describes the following imaginary scenario:

> Imagine that God creates the substance of the soul but impedes any power from emanating from it. . . . In that case the substance of the soul would remain without intellect and will. But if God then removed the impediment and left the soul to its own nature, intellect and will would certainly emanate from it, just as in the first instant of its [i.e., the soul's] . . . creation.[54]

Under normal circumstances, the 'creation' (by God) of the soul's substance and the 'emanation' of its powers (from the soul's essence) occur simultaneously. For this reason, Suárez follows Aquinas in arguing that the act by which God creates the substance of the soul also implies the 'co-creation' of the soul's powers, because the latter are naturally consequent upon the soul's substance. But Suárez's imaginary scenario demonstrates that logically speaking these two acts are really distinct. Hence, the one can occur without the other, since it is at least logically possible for the 'substance of the soul' to exist without its powers emanating from it.[55] This view of the relation between the substance of the soul and its powers seems to imply that, for Suárez, the soul is not a real unity. Although human beings possess only one substantial form, the intellective soul, the soul itself can only be called a 'unity by aggregation' (*unum per aggregationem*), in that it is composed of a 'substance' (produced by creation) and a bundle of really distinct powers (produced by emanation).[56] Suárez thus radicalises the distinction between the soul and its powers, describing the former as a bare essence without powers and the latter as separately produced, causal agents.

3.2 Jean Fernel

A similar tendency is visible in the works of Jean Fernel. Although Fernel's account of the soul's powers is cast in a vocabulary that differs from the uniform technical language of Suárez and his scholastic predecessors, their views can be easily compared. According to Fernel, a living being possesses only one single soul, which is present as a whole in the whole body.[57] The most fundamental function of the soul is to give life. Since life comes in three different manifestations or 'degrees' – that of plants, animals and human beings – there must be different kinds of soul as well, namely 'natural,' 'sentient' and 'intelligent.' Here Fernel introduces his notion of 'parts' of the soul. Plants possess only one single natural soul. Human beings also possess one single soul, an intelligent soul. But the human soul includes a natural 'part' as well as a sentient 'part.' In nonhuman animals, the latter is not a 'part' of the soul, but a sentient soul in its own right, which includes a natural 'part.' Hence, in human beings, the intelligent, the sentient and the natural are contained as parts of the soul, which, taken as a whole, is an intelligent soul.[58] The different parts of the soul include a variety of 'faculties' (*facultates*). Fernel defines a 'faculty' of the soul as "the power and potentiality that the soul brings out from ... its bosom, and presents for the performance of functions."[59] More specifically, speaking of a 'faculty of the soul' is like referring to

> an indwelling and homegrown property of the soul, which is itself an accident, but so deeply within the soul that most people would take it for the soul's essence.[60]

Yet, according to Fernel, faculties of the soul are *not* the same thing as the soul's essence. They are "powers that percolate from it." The soul's essence brings several activities into being 'of itself,' but in so doing it uses its faculties as instruments. That the faculties of the soul are not identical with the soul may be deduced from the fact that they sometimes perish while the soul's essence remains intact. For example, I may lose my faculty of vision without therefore dying. This is precisely what constitutes the difference between psychic parts and faculties:

> A faculty differs from a part of the soul particularly in its ability to be parted from the substance of the soul; no part could be separated without the total breakdown and destruction of the soul at the time. Though a faculty is implanted in the soul, it is as an inherent accident.[61]

Fernel suggests two possible ways to understand the idea that faculties are 'accidents' of the soul. On the one hand, he describes faculties in terms of *relations*, pointing out that we ascribe different faculties to the soul, because the soul "behaves differently towards the things it does." According to this description, the faculties of the soul can be compared with the different relations one person may have vis-à-vis other persons (e.g., the relation of being a father, an uncle, a child, etc.).[62] On the other hand, he treats the faculties as *qualities* of the soul by comparing them with the healing properties of a drug. The relevant point of comparison here is that both the healing properties of a drug and the powers of the soul can be characterised in terms of 'more and less,' since a drug can have more or less effective healing properties while its essence remains the same. Likewise, the soul's faculties admit of more and less while the soul itself remains the same.[63]

Fernel agrees with Aristotle that the intelligent part of the human soul occupies a special position, because it does not need "the agency of any bodily instrument."[64] The other two parts of the human soul use bodily instruments.[65] He offers detailed analyses of the interaction between the natural and sentient parts of the soul (and their respective faculties) and the body. With respect to the natural part, he agrees with Aristotle that its seat is the heart, "the citadel of life."[66] From there, its faculties (generative, nutritive and augmentative) are distributed evenly over the whole body by means of 'vital heat.' Vital heat is described as the "carrier and instrument of the soul and its faculties." From the heart, "it streams out into all of the body."[67] Concerning the sentient (or 'animal') part of the soul, Fernel rejects Aristotle's view according to which this part is also located in the heart.[68] He argues that the sentient part "dwells deep in the body of the brain as though in its own stronghold."[69] The most important faculties of this part of the soul are (1) the faculties of *external* sensation (i.e., vision, hearing, smell, taste and touch), (2) the faculties of *internal* sensation (imagination, common sense and memory) and (3) the *appetitive* faculty (including the faculty of movement). Concerning external sensation, Fernel draws a vivid picture of how the sentient soul uses intermediary agents to perform its functions in various parts of the body:

> It was unsafe for this essence of the soul, located in the brain as if in a citadel, to perform functions in remote extremities of the body, unless it used henchmen and (so to speak) intermediaries of its powers. Accordingly, the soul sends out spirits like servants and porters carrying the powers it distributes from itself, each power to discharge its own function, and sends them . . . into all the bodily parts that lie outside that citadel.[70]

Just as vital heat is described as the instrument of the natural part of the soul, so the animal spirits are called the "first instruments" of the sentient part of the soul.[71]

In Fernel's physiological account, the theory of the powers of the soul reaches an even higher degree of elaboration and sophistication than in Suárez's writings. According to Fernel, the human soul is composed of three 'parts,' each of which comprises a set of 'faculties' (and 'sub-faculties'), which do not directly interact with the various parts and organs of the body, but make use of intermediate carriers such as vital heat and animal spirits to perform their functions.

4 Conclusion: criticism of faculty psychology

The elaborate and sophisticated accounts given by Suárez, Fernel and others became the target of severe criticism and ridicule. Among the most famous are Molière's mockeries of the scholastic doctors hiding their ignorance behind imaginary and mysterious entities such as the 'dormitive power' of opium and the 'purgative power' of rhubarb. Equally celebrated is Montaigne's criticism of his 'learned' contemporaries for the endless fragmentation of the human soul into parts and powers other than those that he considers 'natural' (discoursing, reasoning and remembering).

But similar critiques of the notion of 'powers of the soul' had been formulated much earlier by writers belonging to different intellectual traditions. For example, Galen suggested that speaking of 'faculties' of the soul is basically a way of manifesting our ignorance, not a way of providing a substantial explanation: "so long as we are ignorant of the true essence of the cause which is operating, we call it a *faculty*."[72] Within the scholastic tradition as well, the powers of the soul came to be seen as problematic entities. Sixteenth-century Aristotelians such as Pietro Pomponazzi (d. 1525) and Francesco Piccolomini (d. 1607) tried to sidestep the debate about the distinction between the soul and its powers by declaring the issue unsolvable or irrelevant. Pomponazzi claimed that the problem of the relation between the soul and its powers belongs to the same category as the unanswerable question of whether the number of stars is even or odd.[73] Piccolomini simply declared the problem to be a non-issue, arguing that Aristotle himself never spoke of any *distinction* between the soul and its powers in the first place.[74] While Pomponazzi and Piccolomini criticised the discussion about the distinction between the soul's powers, Fernel, the humanist champion of faculty psychology, went one step further, raising the following question concerning the explanatory value of the four sub-faculties of the soul's nutritive power (attractive, expulsive, concoctive and retentive):

> Will you say that everyone who discusses medicine or debates it daily is wrong to talk ... of a faculty drawing in whatever in the food is best attracted, an expelling faculty ejecting what is foreign, a concocting faculty digesting food, also a fourth one enclosing it?[75]

Unlike Fernel, the 'new' philosophers of the seventeenth century would almost certainly answer this question in the affirmative. They rejected the Aristotelian metaphysical framework of hylomorphism and replaced it by theories that were compatible with the mechanistic principles of the new physics. Even though the mechanist philosophers often accepted the basic taxonomy of faculties established by their predecessors to describe the vegetative functions of organisms, the explanatory account of these functions in terms of psychic powers became obsolete. To explain and understand phenomena such as digestion, growth and movement one simply needed to understand the internal structure of the body and the mechanical laws of nature. On the other hand, the cognitive powers of human beings (including sense perception and imagination, which the Aristotelians attributed to the sensitive soul) at least partly survived early modern criticism and, embedded in new metaphysical frameworks, became the focus of intense discussions in seventeenth-century philosophy. They occupied a central place in rationalist metaphysics, in corpuscularian theories of sense perception and in the development of new methods for guiding the understanding and for acquiring certain knowledge.[76]

Notes

1 On Aristotle's two definitions of soul, see Ackrill 1979 and Frede 1995.
2 On Aristotle's view of the powers of the soul, see Johansen 2012.
3 For an overview of Medieval and Renaissance faculty psychology, see Künzle 1956 and Perler 2015.
4 The basic, threefold distinction of powers is mentioned, for example, by Avicenna, *Liber de anima seu sextus de naturalibus* I.5 (ed. Van Riet: 79–80). John of La Rochelle, *Tractatus de divisione multiplici potentiarum animae* (ed. Michaud-Quantin) offers a detailed overview of various systems of powers of the soul. For a later example (taken from Gregor Reisch's *Margarita philosophica*), see Park (1988: 466).
5 On Augustine's ambiguous role in the debate on the powers of the soul, see Künzle (1956: 7–38).
6 One of the most often quoted passages from this treatise is the following: "It (the human soul) is called soul when it nourishes, spirit when it contemplates, sense when it senses, intellect when it is wise, mind when it understands, reason when it discerns, memory when it remembers, will when it consents. But these do not differ in *substance*, as they do in *name*, because all these are one soul" (*Liber de spiritu et anima* [ed. Migne: 788–789]).
7 For a discussion of Aquinas's view, see Künzle (1956: 171–218); Wippel (2000: 275–294); Pasnau (2002: 143–170); and King (2008: 258–266).
8 Thomas Aquinas, *Summa theologiae* I, q. 76, aa. 3–7.
9 *Summa theologiae* I, q. 77, a. 1, 236.
10 *Summa theologiae* I, q. 77, a. 1, 236–237.
11 *Summa theologiae*, I, q. 77, a. 1 ad 5, 237. Following the *Categories*, everything that exists must be *either* substance *or* accident. Given that the soul itself, as a substantial form, belongs to the category of substance, the soul's powers can only be accidents. Aquinas argues more specifically that the powers belong to the "second species of the category of quality," i.e., they are 'natural capacities' for doing or undergoing something easily (cf. Aristotle, *Categories* 9a14–19). The idea that the powers of the soul belong to the second species of the category of quality seems to have its roots in Simplicius's commentary on Aristotle's *Categories* (ed. Pattin: 332, 334, 340–341).
12 *Summa theologiae*, I, q. 77, a. 6, ad 3, 246.
13 *Summa theologiae*, I, q. 77, a. 5, 244–245.
14 *Summa theologiae*, I, q. 77, a. 8, 248–289. That the vegetative and sensitive powers remain intact 'virtually' implies that they will become functional again once body and soul are reunited after the resurrection of the body. See Pasnau (2002: 380).
15 *Summa theologiae*, I, q. 77, a. 3, 241. For a discussion of this claim, see Pasnau (2002: 172–189).
16 On Scotus's view, see King (2008: 266–268); Cross (2014: 145–149); Van den Bercken 2015.
17 William of Ockham, *Quodlibet* II, qq. 10 and 11 (ed. Wey: 156–164). On Ockham's view of the human soul and its powers, see King (2008: 269–271); Perler 2010; Perler (2013: 25–31); De Boer (2013: 219–221, 248–250).
18 *Quodlibet* II, q. 10, 156–158.
19 *Sent.* II, q. 20 (ed. Gál and Wood: 435).
20 *Sent.* II, q. 20, 436. Ockham nevertheless admits that "will is nobler than intellect" because acts of loving (*actus diligendi*) are nobler than acts of knowing (*actus intelligendi*). Likewise he admits that "intellect is prior to will" because acts of knowing precede acts of willing in the order of efficient causality. See *Sent.* II, q. 20, 441–442.
21 *Sent.* III, q. 4 (ed. Kelley and Etzkorn: 135–136).
22 *Sent.* III, q. 4, 136–137.

23 *Sent.* III, q. 4, 137–138.
24 *Sent.* III, q. 4, 138–139. The accidental dispositions of the body play an important role in Ockham's account of perceptual disorders such as blindness. When a person goes blind, neither her power of vision as such nor any other power of the sensitive soul ceases to exist. What ceases to exist is the accidental disposition of the body required for seeing.
25 *Sent.* III, q. 4, 139.
26 Ockham's view became the 'communis opinio' at Oxford. See Schepers (1972: 108). The late fourteenth-century theologian Marsilius of Inghen claims Ockham's view was generally accepted among the Masters of Arts of his day. Cf. *Sent.* I, q. 6 (ed. Santos-Noya: 268–271).
27 Thomas del Garbo, *Summa medicinalis*, I, tr. 5, q. 1 (1506), 53[rb]. The view that the distinction between the intellective and sensitive souls is likely, but not demonstrable, goes back to Ockham, *Quodlibet* I, q. 10, 63–64.
28 *Summa medicinalis*, I, tr. 5, q. 1, 53[rb].
29 *Summa medicinalis*, I, tr. 4, q. 1, 28[vb] – 29[ra].
30 *Summa medicinalis*, I, tr. 4, q. 1, 29[ra].
31 *Summa medicinalis*, I, tr. 5, q. 2, 53[va]; see also tr. 5, q. 18, 66[rb].
32 *Summa medicinalis*, I, tr. 5, q. 18, 66[ra–rb].
33 Gregory of Rimini, *Sent.* II, d. 16–17, q. 2 (ed. Trapp et al.: 333–353).
34 *Sent.* II, d. 16–17, q. 3, 354–355.
35 *Sent.* II, d. 16–17, q. 3, 368.
36 *Sent.* II, d. 16–17, q. 3, 370–371.
37 *Sent.* II, d. 16–17, q. 3, 355–356.
38 *Sent.* II, d. 16–17, q. 3, 362–363.
39 On Buridan's views of the soul and its powers, see Zupko (2003: 164–182); Biard 2008; De Boer (2013: 221–224, 241–248).
40 John Buridan, *De anima*, II, q. 5 (ed. Sobol: 66–67).
41 *De anima*, II, q. 5, 63–64.
42 *De anima*, II, q. 5, 64–65.
43 *De anima*, II, q. 5, 68–69.
44 In the fifteenth century, most Dominican authors defended Aquinas's view. Scotus's view, according to which the powers of the soul are 'formally' distinct from the soul's essence, strongly influenced Parisian handbook writers.
45 On Suárez's views on the soul and its powers, see Perler (2013: 13–25) and Shields 2013.
46 Francisco Suárez, *De anima*, disp. 2, q. 5 (ed. Castellote: 322–330).
47 *De anima*, disp. 3, q. 1, 58–60, 62.
48 *De anima*, disp. 3, q. 1, 60–62.
49 *De anima*, disp. 3, q. 1, 62.
50 *Ibid.*
51 *De anima*, disp. 3, q. 1, 70–72.
52 *De anima*, disp. 3, q. 3, 120–122.
53 *De anima*, disp. 3, q. 3, 130–132. Cf. *De anima* II, cap. 3, 582.
54 *De anima* II, cap. 3, 582.
55 *De anima*, disp. 3, q. 3, 132–134. Cf. *De anima* II, cap. 3, 583. Suárez does not simply speak about the *real* possibility of certain powers not functioning (properly), but about the *logical* possibility of certain powers being prevented from coming to be altogether. Concerning the real possibility of a loss of functions, Suárez argues that, in such cases, the bodily organs in which the powers reside are damaged, not the powers themselves. The soul is not able to repair a damaged organ, just as it cannot restore a severed hand.
56 *De anima* II, cap. 3, 583.

57 Jean Fernel, *Physiologia* V.12 (ed. Forrester: 367).
58 *Physiologia* V.2, 305–311.
59 Fernel, *Physiologia* V.2, 309. Cf. Jean Fernel, *De abditis rerum causis* II.5 (ed. Forrester: 459–461).
60 Fernel, *Physiologia* V.2, 309.
61 Fernel, *Physiologia* V.2, 311. By characterizing the faculties as 'accidents' of the soul, Fernel obviously means that the soul can remain intact when it loses certain faculties. This does not imply that the faculties can be separated from the soul and remain in (independent) existence, as is clear from the continuation of the citation: "A part of the soul is a substance, and as it were a share of it; it exists separately established in plants or beasts. But a faculty never exists in isolation and apart from the attachment to the soul it depends on."
62 Fernel, *De abditis rerum causis* II.5, 461. The description of the faculties of the soul in terms of relations goes back to Galen, *On the Natural Faculties* I.4 (ed. Brock: 17).
63 Fernel, *De abditis rerum causis* II.5, 463–465.
64 Fernel, *Physiologia* V.11, 357. Cf. also VII.5, 549.
65 Fernel, *Physiologia* V.14, 371.
66 Fernel, *Physiologia* V.13, 365.
67 Fernel, *Physiologia* V.12, 363–365. Concerning the natural part, Fernel defends the view that had been rejected by Thomas Del Garbo. See above, page 69 (and n. 29) of this chapter.
68 Fernel, *Physiologia* V.12, 365.
69 Fernel, *Physiologia* V.8, 337.
70 Fernel, *Physiologia* VI.13, 489.
71 *Ibid.*
72 Galen, *On the Natural Faculties* I.4, 17.
73 Pietro Pomponazzi, *Fragmenta super libros* De anima *Aristotelis*, II, *Utrum potentiae animae distinguantur realiter ab anima* (ed. Mojsisch).
74 Piccolomini, *De anima*, II, t.c. 33 (1602), 62^r.
75 Fernel, *De abditis rerum causis* II.5, 465.
76 On the importance of the cognitive faculties in seventeenth-century metaphysics and theories of cognition, see Hatfield 1998.

Bibliography

Primary sources

Avicenna. *Liber de anima seu sextus de naturalibus*. S. Van Riet (ed.). Leuven and Leiden: Peeters and Brill, 1972.

Fernel, Jean. *Physiologia*. See Forrester (2003).

———. *De abditis rerum causis*. See Forrester (2005).

Galen. *On the Natural Faculties*. A. J. Brock (ed.). Cambridge, MA: Harvard University Press, 1979.

Gregory of Rimini. *Lectura super secundum Sententiarum* (Dist. 6–18). A. D. Trapp, V. Marcolino & M. Santos-Noya (eds). Berlin: Walter de Gruyter, 1979.

John Buridan. *Quaestiones de anima (secundum ultimam lecturam)*. See Sobol (1984).

John of La Rochelle. *Tractatus de divisione multiplici potentiarum animae*. P. Michaud-Quantin (ed.). Paris: Vrin 1964.

Liber de spiritu et anima. J.-P. Migne (ed.). Paris, 1845 (*PL* vol. 40).

Marsilius of Inghen. *Quaestiones super quattuor libros Sententiarum. Vol. 1: Super primum quaestiones 1–7.* M. Santos-Noya (ed.). Leiden: Brill, 2000.
Piccolomoni, Francesco (Franciscus). *Expositio in tres libros De anima.* Venezia: Ioannes Antonius and Iacobus de Franciscis, 1602.
Pomponazzi, Pietro (Petrus). *Fragmenta super libros De anima Aristotelis.* B. Mojsisch (ed.). www.hs-augsburg.de/~harsch/Chronologia/Lspost15/Pomponatius/pom_fr0204.html.
Simplicius. *Commentaire sur les Catégories d'Aristote.* A. Pattin (ed.). Leiden: Brill, 1975.
Suárez, Francisco (Franciscus). *Commentaria una cum quaestionibus in libros Aristotelis De anima,* 3 vols. S. Castellote (ed.). Madrid: Editorial Labor, 1978–1991.
Suárez, Francisco (Franciscus). *De anima.* Paris: Ludovicus Vivès, 1856.
Thomas Del Garbo. *Summa medicinalis.* Venezia: Octavianus Scotus, 1506.
William of Ockham. *Quaestiones in librum secundum Sententiarum (Reportatio).* G. Gál & R. Wood (eds). St. Bonaventure: The Franciscan Institute 1981 (*OTh* vol. 5).
———. *Quaestiones in librum tertium Sententiarum (Reportatio).* F. E. Kelley & G. I. Etzkorn (eds). St. Bonaventure: The Franciscan Institute, 1982 (*OTh* vol. 6).
———. *Quodlibeta septem.* J. C. Wey (ed.). St. Bonaventure: The Franciscan Institute, 1980 (*OTh* vol. 9).

Secondary literature

Ackrill, John L. 1979. "Aristotle's Definitions of psuchè". In *Articles on Aristotle, 4: Psychology and Aesthetics*, J. Barnes, M. Schofield & R. Sorabji (eds), 65–75. London: Duckworth.
Bercken, John H. L. van den. 2015. "John Duns Scotus in Two Minds About the Powers of the Soul". *Recherches de Théologie et Philosophie médiévales* **82**(2): 199–240.
Biard, Joël. 2008. "Diversité des fonctions et unité de l'âme dans la psychologie péripatéticienne (XIVe–XVIe siècle)". *Vivarium* **46**(3): 342–367.
Boer, Sander W. de. 2013. *The Science of the Soul: The Commentary Tradition on Aristotle's De anima, c. 1260–c. 1360.* Leuven: Leuven University Press.
Cross, Richard. 2014. *Duns Scotus's Theory of Cognition.* Oxford: Oxford University Press.
Forrester, John M. 2003. *The Physiologia of Jean Fernel (1567).* Philadelphia: American Philosophical Society.
———. 2005. *Jean Fernel's On the Hidden Causes of Things: Forms, Souls, and Occult Diseases in Renaissance Medicine.* Leiden: Brill.
Frede, Michael. 1995. "On Aristotle's Conception of the Soul". In *Essays on Aristotle's De Anima*, M. C. Nussbaum & A. Oksenberg-Rorty (eds), 93–108. Oxford: Oxford University Press.
Hatfield, Gary. 1998. "The Cognitive Faculties". In *The Cambridge History of Seventeenth-Century Philosophy*, D. Garber & M. Ayers (eds), 953–1002. Cambridge: Cambridge University Press.
Johansen, Thomas Kjeller. 2012. *The Powers of Aristotle's Soul.* Oxford: Oxford University Press.
King, Peter. 2008. "The Inner Cathedral: Mental Architecture in High Scholasticism". *Vivarium* **46**(3): 253–274.

Künzle, Pius. 1956. *Das Verhältnis der Seele zu ihren Potenzen: Problemgeschichtliche Untersuchungen von Augustin bis und mit Thomas von Aquin*. Freiburg: Universitätsverlag.

Park, Katherine. 1988. "The Organic Soul". In *The Cambridge History of Renaissance Philosophy*, C.B. Schmitt, Q. Skinner, E. Kessler & J. Kraye (eds), 464–484. Cambridge: Cambridge University Press.

Pasnau, Robert. 2002. *Thomas Aquinas on Human Nature: A Philosophical Study of Summa theologiae 1a 75–89*. Cambridge: Cambridge University Press.

Perler, Dominik. 2010. "Ockham über die Seele und ihre Teile". *Recherches de Théologie et Philosophie médiévales* **77**(2): 313–350.

———. 2013. "What Are Faculties of the Soul? Descartes and His Scholastic Background". In *Continuity and Innovation in Medieval and Modern Philosophy: Knowledge, Mind, and Language*, John Marenbon (ed.), 9–38. Oxford: Oxford University Press.

———. 2015. "Faculties in Medieval Philosophy". In *The Faculties: A History*, Dominik Perler (ed.). Oxford: Oxford University Press.

Schepers, Heinrich. 1972. "Holkot contra dicta Crathorn. II. Das 'significatum per propositionem'. Aufbau und Kritik einer nominalistischen Theorie über den Gegenstand des Wissens". *Philosophisches Jahrbuch* **79**: 106–136.

Shields, Christopher. 2013. "The Unity of the Soul in Francisco Suárez". In *Medieval Perspectives on Aristotle's De anima*, R. L. Friedman & J.-M. Counet (eds), 359–382. Leuven: Peeters.

Sobol, Peter. 1984. *John Buridan on the Soul and Sensation: An Edition of Book II of His Commentary on Aristotle's Book on the Soul With an Introduction and a Translation of Question 18 on Sensible Species*. PhD Thesis, Indiana University.

Wippel, John. 2000. *The Metaphysical Thought of Thomas Aquinas: From Finite Being to Uncreated Being*. Washington, DC: The Catholic University of America Press.

Zupko, Jack A. 2003. *John Buridan: Portrait of a Fourteenth-Century Arts Master*. Notre Dame: Notre Dame University Press.

4

AVERROISM AND THE METAPHYSICS OF INTELLECT

Jean-Baptiste Brenet

1 Introduction, Averroes's "scandalous" noetics

In the narrow sense, "Averroism"[1] in the Latin world refers to all the readings that were favorable, from the rational point of view, to the doctrine of the intellect put forward by the Andalusian philosopher Averroes or Ibn Rushd (1126–1198) in his *Long Commentary on the* De Anima *of Aristotle*, which made its appearance in Paris the middle of the 1220s. Averroes's commentaries on Aristotle were so famous in the Late Middle Ages that he was commonly referred to as "the Commentator." Now, Averroes's theory of the intellect – or "noetics" for short – was forcefully rejected starting from the second half of the 13th century, both by the Catholic Church, which condemned it on two occasions in 1270 and 1277,[2] and by leading Christian theologians, such as Albertus Magnus (before 1200–1280), Bonaventure (1221–1274), and Thomas Aquinas (1225–1274), the latter of whom judged it to be not only blasphemous, but conceptually absurd.

In his 1270 pamphlet *De unitate intellectus contra Averroistas*, Thomas Aquinas delivered a masterful critique that would serve as a model and a reference for later challenges to the Averroists for generations to come.[3]

From a philosophical perspective, three specific arguments are rejected. They concern first and foremost[4] what the Scholastics call the "material" or "possible" intellect, namely the substratum of thought Aristotle talks about in *De anima* III, 4 (429a10–11) and III, 5 (430a14–15). The following positions are criticized:

(a) *The substantial separation of the material intellect*: The intellect is not, as Aristotle's hylomorphism dictates, a "soul," a form of the body (or at least, the highest power of a soul form of the body), but an autonomous substance, a reality by itself, ontologically independent from and superior to the body.
(b) *Its numerical unicity*: Apart from the agent intellect, there is only one single material intellect for all people, and not as many distinct intellectual powers as there are individuals.
(c) *Its* a parte ante *as well as* a parte post *eternity*: The one material intellect available to human beings is not only incorruptible; it is not generated or

created, but instead is eternal like the world itself, according to Aristotle's conception.

In Thomas Aquinas, the scandalous character of these three arguments can be summed up in a phrase: the impossibility of verifying the axiomatic proposition, "*hic homo intelligit*" ("this particular human being has intellectual understanding"). If the intellect is indeed separate in substance from the body, thought occurs outside of the individual, is extrinsic to him, and therefore it is not his. Neither does it, more generally, belong to human beings. If it is numerically one, there will only be one thinker and one thought for the entire species. This would mean the destruction of the very idea of individual intellectual personhood. Lastly, if the intellect is eternal, there cannot have been a first thinking person, and each person, heir to an already full eternal intellect, will never be able to learn or discover anything. Thought, always already completed in act, performed outside the person, no longer exists as a constituent *power* of the individual. The Commentator's noetics thus amounts to destroying singular rationality, the condition of all human life.[5]

Thomas Aquinas, of course, knew Averroes's solution, based on Aristotle's idea that "the soul never thinks without an image" (*De an.* III, 7, 431a16–17). Averroes, in fact, maintains that thought in act has "two subjects":[6] not only (a) the material intellect, a separate, unique, and eternal substratum of intelligible species, but also (b) individual images, from which these intelligible species are abstracted.[7] This would be the key that would make it possible to explain "the manner in which the action of this [separate and unique] principle that is the intellect may [also] be the action of this man here [or that man there]."[8] The individual manages to think via his images, which are required in the act of intellection, by "uniting" him individually to the separate intellect.

Thomas Aquinas, however, rejects this completely. First, if a human being is only united with the intellect via the image, a human being's humanity constituted by this intellect will not be primary (*secundum primam eius generationem*) and permanent, but secondary and fluctuating; it would depend on the appearance of the imagination as well as the back-and-forth nature of its activity. Second, the image cannot be a link between the intellect and the body. The intelligible, indeed, is only in the image *in potentiality*, and the intellect only receives it *in actuality* after its abstraction. The *separation* from the image is therefore the condition for the intellection of a species. In other words, a person who does not immediately accept the intellect as her form is incapable of thought. If the action of the intellect is not originally the individual's, as an action of *his* or *her* intellective power, we will not find a way to unite the individual and the intellect. And the problem is even more serious, since, third, the image is *only an object* for the intellect. It is to the intellect, in the act of thinking, what the color of a wall is to the eye that sees it. Now, says Thomas Aquinas, no one would argue that the color sees itself. The color does not see; it is seen. In Averroes, as a result, not only does a human being not think, but he or she is thought. Before Descartes, Averroism was rejected as an anti-*cogito* philosophy, where the human being is alienated and only an object of the intellect.

And Thomas Aquinas does not stop here. After presenting Averroes's position, he also explains the position of certain "Averroists," who were aware of the impasses Averroes's noetics lead to, and attempted to get around them by taking another path.[9] This position may be summed up as follows: (a) the intellect is united to the body as a mover; (b) the individual human is composed of this intellect and this body; (c) in this union by aggregation of a mover (the intellect) and the thing moved (the body), the action of a part is attributed to the whole; and (d) likewise, therefore, just as the action of the eye (a part of a human) is attributed to the human (the whole composed of the eye and the rest of the organs), the action of the intellect (the moving part of a human being) is attributed to the human being (the whole composed of the intellective moving part and its mobile, the body). The human being thinks, therefore, because (i) the intellect thinks, (ii) this intellect, *qua* mover, is a part of him, and (iii) the act of a part is an act of the whole. Lastly, (e) to support their argument, these "Averroists" put forward a cosmological paradigm. After positing that humans think with their intellects like they see with their eyes, we could thus say that a human thinks with his intellect as the heavens, composed of a separate intelligence and a sphere, thinks with its moving intelligence.

How does Thomas Aquinas respond to this? By arguing that none of it holds up. (a) This pseudo-unit by aggregation of a mover and a thing moved which we claim is valid for a human does not make him a genuine being;[10] (b) for this reason, a human, as a whole, does not act – since only a genuine being can act; (c) and the act of his supposed intellective part (the mover-intelligence) cannot be attributed to the whole (the person), since the act of the part is an act of the whole only in a genuine being (i.e., genuinely one, and not one that only has operational unity); (d) if, therefore, the intellect unites with the body as a mover (as these "Averroists" imagine it does), we cannot use the model of the eye (since the union of the eye with the rest of the body and the human being is not a moving force, but a unity comparable to that of a sailor and his boat; (e) yet nobody will say that the thought of the sailor, in his capacity as the moving part of the whole he forms with the boat, is the act of this whole. This thought (an immanent act, and not a transitive operation) remains his own, without transfer or extension; and (f) and using a cosmological paradigm, by claiming that a person (composed of a mover-intellect and a body) thinks like the heavens (composed of a mover-intelligence and a sphere) think, is an *assumptio difficilioris* where, in an absurd reversal of method, we would account for the obscure by the even more obscure.[11]

The goal of this chapter is to indicate briefly, on a number of points, how Averroism survived and responded to Thomas Aquinas's attacks. We have selected three major figures to serve as a framework for more detailed analyses:[12] first, Siger of Brabant, Aquinas's contemporary, then Thomas Wylton and John of Jandun, two thinkers active in Paris at the beginning of the 14th century.

2 Siger of Brabant's *Tractatus de anima intellectiva*

Let us begin with the *Tractatus de anima intellectiva* by Siger of Brabant (c. 1240–1277), which is generally recognized as a response to Thomas Aquinas's *De unitate intellectus* (1270).[13]

In Chapter III, Siger examines the relationship between the "intellective soul" and the body. We can, of course, accept that the intellective soul is the "act" of this body (*actus corporis*) – but in what way? Does it go as far as an ontological constitution? The intellective soul, in that case, would give being to the body and be united with it *in essendo*. Or is it only a union from the point of view of agency? The intellective soul would then be separated from the body *in esse*; it would not give the body its being, but would be linked to the body only *in operando*.

Siger's response is based on what the act of thinking (*intelligere*) involves. This act is two-sided.[14] On the one hand, it is in some way united to matter – since if this were not the case, it would not be true to say that it is *a human being* himself who thinks (*homo ipse intelligit*); rather, only the intellect would think. On the other hand, however, the act of thinking is separate from matter, since it does not occur in a bodily organ (like the act of seeing occurs in the eye). Thought, as such, does not take place in the body; it is immaterial. Consequently, it is clearly apparent from the nature of its act, that the intellective soul "is in one respect united to the body and in another respect separate therefrom."[15] It is a question of conceptualizing this very duality (which, on the one hand, protects *intellectuality*, and on the other, makes it the intellectuality *of a human being*, composed of a soul and a body).

As a first step,[16] Siger returns to his initial alternative and clearly posits, against what he considers to be Albert Magnus's and Thomas Aquinas's argument, that the intellective soul is separate from the body *in essendo* (it is not united to it as "the shape is united to the wax"; it does not give it its *esse*), but, in spite of everything, its separation is not complete, and the intellective soul is "united" to the body *in operando*.

But what does this *in operando* union of the intellect and the body, which are otherwise ontologically separate, mean? It means that the intellect, whose being does not depend on the body, needs the body in order to act, in other words, to perform intellection, inasmuch as, according to Aristotle, the intellective soul does not think anything without an image. Put another way, ontological autonomy is not functional independence. The intellect, as the power of thinking, is first empty and depends on what the imagination offers it in order to become active, since there is neither innate knowledge, nor self-actualization, nor divine illumination. This dependence goes far, because not only do we have to feel and imagine in order to think, but the soul does not even think except insofar as it imagines. The soul, in other words, always thinks *with* an image, and not only *from* it.[17] This, says Siger, does not make the body a "subject in which" (*subiectum in quo*) the activity of intellection takes place (which would degenerate into an absurd materialism that, in his view, Thomas Aquinas's argument leads back to), but an "object"[18] likely to give the activity of intellection content after abstraction.

However, Siger does not stop there. In response to Aquinas's critique regarding the too-weak nature of the union of the intellect and the body, Siger emphasizes the *naturalness* of this dependence on the image. The intellect does not accidentally require images of the body in order to think. It is in *its nature* to depend on them. From the point of view of its act, the intellect is made (*natus*) to be acted upon by the body like an object.

Siger clarifies his position by means of a subtle conceptual turn of phrase. The intellect in the act of thinking, he says, is by nature *operans intrinsecum ad corpus*.[19] The argument, whose complex origin undoubtedly has several sources,[20] is crucial to the history of Averroism. In fact, Siger does not mean that the intellect operates in the body, but, using a cosmological paradigm, *that it is intrinsic, as a part, to the whole it forms with the body*. This means that a human being is neither intellect nor body, but a whole, of which the intellect and body, although separate *in esse*, form two parts. A human is therefore well and truly human by virtue of the intellect,[21] but this does not mean, says Siger, that the intellect must unite with the body like the shape with the wax.

It is this, according to Siger, that makes it possible – even if he no longer explicitly cites Averroes – to respond to Thomas Aquinas. If the intellect is an "intrinsic agent" in its relationship with the body, we can say that, even though it is ontologically separate, it is the "form" and "perfection" of the body and that its act, thought, is attributed to the composite (a human being) it forms with this body. Put another way, the ontological separation of the intellect and the body does not do away with the individual's rationality if we understand that the intellect, though separate from the body *in esse*, is related to it by nature, in thought, and that it is an intrinsic agent in the human being.

Does a human being think? Siger's unhesitating answer is an affirmative "yes." Even though the activity of intellection only takes place in the intellect, and not the body, *the intellect is part of a human being, and its act can be attributed to the whole*. This means that, despite the ontological separation, there is a union between the intellect and the body that is strong enough for the intellect to appear as part of a human being, and its act is attributed to the whole.

Siger avoids, in his view, the two pitfalls of materialism and strict dualism. The intellect is not a material form, nor is it an ontologically separate substance that does not participate in any form of natural composition with the body. In its intellectual relationship with the body, it is an intrinsic agent that, despite the separation in being, brings about a *sui generis* unit, the human individual, to whom is attributed by metonymic transfer the operation of this internal actor, which he terms the *anima intellectiva*.

From this point of view, the *operans intrinsecum* appears to be a major concept of the third way, which is faithful to Aristotle and manages to link the necessary idea of the separation *in esse* with the idea of the intellect as "part" of the soul, as part of the human being. Furthermore, it even serves as a link, in line with the general definition of the soul given in *De anima* (even if in the broad sense and almost ambiguous), with the notion of the intellect as "form" and "perfection." Indeed, as

Siger notes at the end of his argument, "among philosophers" (*apud philosophos*), intrinsic movers, or intrinsic agents, are called the "forms" and "perfections" of the things they are related to.

All of Siger's efforts must thus be understood as an attempt, in keeping with Aristotle (and implicitly Averroes), to conceptualize a relationship between the intellect and the body that, despite their ontological separation, does not destroy the unity of the human being and undermine her rationality. How can we save Aristotelian hylomorphism when our starting point is the separation of the intellect (from the body)? How can we save the human being once we have saved thought? That is the question. Siger's answer is consistent, but, as he recognizes himself,[22] it leaves major difficulties concerning the individuality of thought unresolved.

In fact, Chapter VII on the unicity of the intellect (*utrum anima intellectiva mutiplicetur multiplicatione corporum humanorum*) appears to end with an admission of helplessness. Siger recognizes that he is unable to account for Aristotle's views on the individuation of thought, nor to do justice to what could be demonstrated by natural reason[23] Averroes himself had pointed out this difficulty: If there is only one intellect for all people, how do we distinguish the wise from the ignorant, the teacher from the student? Curiously, Siger does not manage to use – as John of Jandun, for example, does at a later date – his notion of *operans intrinsecum* here. As he suggests, however, we have to say that the intellect is unique, of course, but that it is composed of different wholes with different bodies, and that the operation resulting from its union with such and such a body having such and such phantasms is only specific to that body. The activity of intellection, in other words, is always an act of the intellect singularized by its union *in operando* with an imagining body that is itself singular.

But Siger, surprisingly, does not defend this argument to the end. What distinguishes an operation, he says, may either be the agent, the object, or the time at which the action is situated. Now, if the intellect is unique, nothing stops us from positing that two people can think of the same object at the same time and, therefore, that their act of thinking will be the same, which would be absurd.

Siger should have noted that the agent, even in this case, is not unique since two people always have two different imagining bodies, and their bodies enter into the particular whole they form with the intellect as a part. But he was unable to formulate this argument clearly; in his conclusion he admits to having long been in doubt about this question,[24] and he asserts that the next generation will be better equipped to answer it.

3 Thomas Wylton's *Quaestio de anima intellectiva*

The position of theologian Thomas Wylton (d. ca. 1327), active in Paris at the beginning of the 14th century, is original and strong.[25] In it we see the influence of Scotism; the presence of debates with other masters of the era; the emergence of unprecedented solutions (on knowledge of the singular, abstraction, and the basis for noetic unicity, etc.); and a direct confrontation with certain "Catholic" positions.

Wylton's question is whether it can be proven that the intellective soul is the form of the human body (*an intellectivam esse formam corporis humani possit ratione necessaria probari et convinci evidenter*).

It all comes down to what is meant by "form," according to the theologian. In this case, by "form" Wylton means an "informing" form of the human body, but not an "inherent" one. The concept of "informing form" refers to

> a form having a natural inclination, an order, and a dependence towards something else, in such a way that from itself and something else one composite is apt by nature to come to be, which by virtue of such a form is specifically distinguished from every other thing.

Wylton's argument (a position he later reversed for religious reasons) is that we can establish with Averroes that the intellective soul, likened to the material intellect, is indeed an "informing" form of this type for the body.[26] First, the active intellect must not be considered as part of the soul; it is "*a substance subsisting by itself*" that is first only an "assisting" form[27] for the possible intellect. Second, this possible intellect is indeed, in Averroes, *as among the Catholics*, "the first formal perfection of the human being" that distinguishes humans *intrinsically* from other species.[28] This means that the intellect, though subsisting (*subsistens*), is never separated (*separatus*) from what Wylton calls its "first perfectible," namely the "human nature" present in all the numerically distinct "supposits" of the species.[29] Consequently, as an informing form of the body, the intellect could not exist if this human nature did not. Therefore, the intellect, which essentially needs images, is not only unable to *operate* without the body, without the bodies of the human species (which also means that the activity of intellection is in no way an act specific to the intellect, but an act *of the composite*), but it quite simply cannot *be* without it. Therefore, the intellect is not "this certain thing complete in a species, but the principle of a species" (*hoc aliquid perfectum in specie, sed principium speciei*),[30] incapable of existing without its other principle. If the intellect, thus, is said to be "*abstractus*," this does not mean that it is "a form separated from the body according to being,"[31] but "a form non-mixed with matter." That is the first major point: The intellect is not mixed with a body's matter, but only exists with it. This, in Wylton's view, makes Averroes's position more coherent and even "truer" than the Catholic doctrine, inasmuch as the latter must accept that the human soul survives the death of its own body, while awaiting its resurrection, even though the soul is supposed to be its form.[32]

Two arguments, on the other hand, place Averroes in direct opposition to the Catholic Church's position: the unicity of the intellect, which, according to the Commentator, is not multiplied by the number of human bodies, and its eternity in the future as well as in the past. As we have seen, the first justification Wylton gives for the argument of unicity is remarkable. It consists in saying that the intellect is one like its first correlate, namely the human species, or rather, as we have said, the human nature equally present in human supposits. In other words, a kind of realist ontology of the common nature forms the foundation of the noetic argument of unicity. Wylton makes two points on this basis. First, if we can distinguish in each person a common human nature and a *haecceitas*, then we can and must also distinguish the unique intellect, the perfection of human nature, on the one hand, and the individuated intellect as a form of a singular body, on the other. Second, phantasms are the cause of this individuation, inasmuch as they necessarily cooperate with the intellect in all acts of intellection. Put another way, the intellect is not the *causa totalis* of thought, but requires the intervention of agents that are both particular and adventitious, namely the images borne by individual bodies, so much so that neither the unicity nor the eternity of the intellect prevents us from conceiving the contingent and individual nature of all mental acts.[33]

4 John of Jandun's *Quaestiones super libros de anima*

John of Jandun (c. 1285–1328) has gone down in history as the "prince of the Averroists."[34] A contemporary of Wylton, whom he read and referenced, John of Jandun was involved in numerous debates with his colleagues and other leading lights of the era. In Paris he developed a doctrine of the intellect, in the name of Aristotle and Averroes, that would continue to influence later Averroism until the Renaissance.[35]

For him too, the noetic problem is above all whether the intellective soul is the substantial form of the human body. In his answer, Jandun is opposed to the two extreme, positive and negative views on this matter.

The first was that of Alexander of Aphrodisias, the great Greek commentator on Aristotle, who was very influential in the Arab world and whom the Latins read and knew mainly from what Averroes himself said about him.[36] Alexander of Aphrodisias's argument was that "the intellective soul is *the substantial form that formally gives being to the human body*, and is joined to the body in respect to being, like the shape in wax."[37] In Jandun's view, this is impossible. Such a position comes down to materializing the intellect, extending it, fitting it into dimensions, which does away with thought, whose existence depends on the immateriality – and therefore the *separation* – of its principle.

But the opposite argument, which consists in saying this time that the intellective soul, according to Aristotle and Averroes, *is not the form of the human body*, is no less false. In fact, as it is "unmixed" (*immixtus*); as "it has no other nature other than being called possible" (*non habere naturam nisi quod possibilis vocatus est*); as "it is not any being in actuality before intellection" (*nihil esse actu eorum quae sunt ante intelligere*); and as it is "separate" (*separate*), the intellect could not satisfy the common definition of the soul as the "first act of the body." Consequently, strictly speaking, the intellect cannot be a "soul."

But Jandun contests this, not only because, in his view, Aristotle's common definition of the soul covers the intellect, but also because, in Averroes, the intellect is clearly characterized as a form. If, therefore, it is false to say that the intellect is substantially united with the body, this does not mean that the intellect is not its form. The intellect, of course, is the form of the body, but the difficulty lies in determining in which sense this is the case.

For Jandun, in fact, two notions of "form" must be distinguished. In the first sense (1) the form of the body refers to "the perfection that gives being to the body and is joined to the body in respect to being;"[38] it is the principle giving it "its specific substantial being."[39] In the second sense (2) which echoes Siger of Brabant, the form of the body refers to "an intrinsic agent appropriate for the body,"[40] in other words, an agent

> (a) that is not distinct from the body by place or subject, (b) whose proper act depends properly and exclusively on this body, or on something existing in this body, such that this intrinsic agent and this body, even though they are not one thing from the point of view of being (the *esse* of one being the other's *esse*), they are nevertheless one thing in ‹the performance of› a proper work immediately dependent on one and the other.[41]

It is in this sense, according to John of Jandun, *that the intellect, in Aristotle and Averroes, is the form of the body*. The intellect is not substantially united with the human body. It does not give this body its being (which does not mean, however, that this body could *exist* without the intellect), but it is, in spite of everything, its form, in the way that the cosmic intelligence is the form of the heaven it moves, or in the sense that the sailor is the form of the boat he commands.

The intellect is therefore the form of the human body qua intrinsic agent, in other words, as the principle of operation that is internal *by nature* to the aggregate that is a human being, composed of the intellect and a body. Its proper act depends exclusively on the body (namely the images provided by the cogitative power specific to the human body), such that it is united with it, not ontologically, but by virtue of performing one and the same operation.

As Jandun notes, however, such a position immediately invites two objections: First (1), can we thus explain the self-evident fact that "man formally and properly understands"? Can we say that a human being thinks via this "form" that is ontologically extrinsic to his body, that is, the intellect? Put another way, can we respond to Thomas Aquinas? Second (2), does this noetic conception not lead to a dualism of forms within one and the same being? Apart from the intellect, which is a "form" as an intrinsic agent, should we not accept another form in the human being, tasked with giving the body its specific actual being? And does this not come down to destroying Aristotelian hylomorphism's principle of the unicity of the constitutive substantial form?

The first question (1), as we have seen, is the most famous of all. Jandun answers that his conception of the intellect as an "intrinsic agent" suffices. The intellect is not the form that gives being to the body, but it is joined to the body as an intrinsic operator and constitutes a unit that is sufficient for its act to be said of the whole it forms with this body, namely the human being.

There are several points that need to be explained here.

First, there is an error to be avoided, consisting in making the intellect a simple principle of operation related to a human being constituted independently from it. It is true, of course, that the intellect does not give being to the *body*, but we should not deduce from this that it is ontologically separate *from the human being*. Put another way, the intellect does not constitute the body's being, but inasmuch as it operates or may operate with the latter in the act of intellection, *it indeed gives the human his human beingness*.[42]

The argument is a crucial one. It means that the intellect not only gives the intellect/body composite *agency*, but that, *in this action, through it*, it gives this composite its *being. The intellect does not give being to the body, but it gives it to the human being, which it composes together with the body*.

To put it another way, the intellect is the mover of the body, but it is not a mover *for a human being*; as a mover of the body, indeed, it is a constituent of the *human beingness* of humans. In other words, the intellect, as an intrinsic agent, not only gives intellectual operation; by giving the activity of intellection to human beings, it also makes human beings be. This agency, or this power of acting, establishes human beingness.

Thus there are two mistakes, in fact, with respect to the intellect as an "intrinsic agent." The first consists in believing that it is intrinsic in that it operates within the body (whereas it is intrinsic *to the whole it forms with the body*). The second is that it only gives the operation, the agency, whereas it forms a being, via aggregation, to which it gives its own agency. We must therefore be careful with wording that presents the intellect as *forma dans operationem*. Indeed, the intellect does not give the operation (of thinking) to a (potentially thinking) being that is *otherwise already constituted*. The intellect, by singularly joining the body (constituted in itself, although ordered to the intellect), *constitutes* a potentially thinking being, the human, to whom it gives his agency.[43]

Consequently, as an intrinsic agent, the intellect makes *a human being* be, in that the latter emerges as an aggregate composed of two principal parts: the intellect and the body. And this is the key to the problem of thought. The idea in fact is that a human being, understood as an aggregate, thinks *ratione partis*,[44] even though this *pars* is not the substantial form of the other and is not, therefore, subjectively received in the other part. As Siger maintained and Jandun reiterates, the intellect composes a whole with the body that is sufficiently one so that we can see two genuine parts in it and posit that the act of the (intellective) part is predicated of the whole. And even if we are dealing with very different acts (one immanent, the other transitive), we can say that a human being thinks in the same way as the heaven moves itself. In other words, the human being, the composite, thinks even if the thought is the act of the intellect, which is not the substantial form of the body, and the heaven moves itself, even if motion, the act of moving, is the act of the intelligence, which is not the substantial form of the sphere.

But two objections are possible. Do we not say, indeed, that nothing acts except *insofar as it is in actuality*, and that only a being that is *truly one* can act? That is correct, says Jandun, and this is indeed the position he intends to defend with his argument. This is because there is more than one way of being in actuality for a composite. First, this can be done one way when the actual being of the form, of the formal part, is subjectively received in matter, which is the other part of this composite. Such a composite is one, then, because its form is "constituted in being by its subject." But this can be accomplished another way: A composite may be said (and be) in actuality when the actual being is *in only one of the two parts*, namely in the form, and this being is not received in the other part, matter. In this case, the composite is in actuality by virtue of the actuality of its formal part, in the same way we say of a blond-haired man that he is blond, the whole of him, even though only his hair is. Blondness, consequently, is absolutely applicable to the individual as a whole, whereas it is only in actuality on his head. The same applies here. A human, composed of the intellect and the body, is a being in actuality *ratione partis*, in other words, by the actuality of his intellective part.[45] And the same goes for unity: The intellect, of course, does not give being to the body; but, in spite of everything, there is unity between the intellect and the body *in respect to being*. For there is unity in respect to being, an ontological unity of the human composite, even if a) the intellect's being is not received in the body and, in addition, b) this body has its own *esse*. Indeed, the *esse*'s duality does not preclude the ontological unity of the composite inasmuch as the intellect's being is not distinct "by place and subject" from the body's being, and inasmuch as the act of the intellect depends properly and immediately on the act of the body.

What can we say at present about the objection concerning hylomorphism (2)? If the separate intellect is the form of the human being, are we not forced to accept two forms in the individual? Jandun accepts this without difficulty:

> When one says that another form must exist, I answer that this is true according to the opinion of Aristotle and the Commentator; it is indeed a question of the cogitative soul that is the noblest of material forms, and by it a human being is generable and corruptible, as the Commentator says in Commentary 33 of Book 3; and there is nothing bothersome in a human being having two proper forms, one giving his body substantial being, the other being the intrinsic agent thanks to which he is said to be thinking in the aforesaid manner; and this is above all because the human is the most perfect and noblest of beings on Earth.[46]

Put another way, it is obvious that, apart from the intellect, there needs to be another form that can give being to the body, an individual form inherent in matter by virtue of which the human being is generable and corruptible. For various reasons, which we can read in Aristotle's *De anima*, the intellect cannot take on this function (it cannot have an organ, be mixed, etc.); this is due to the sensitive soul, and more precisely the noblest of them all: the cogitative soul, which, for Jandun represents the last of the material forms and is employed by the intellect in its process of abstraction. Thus, there are two forms, or rather: *two proper forms of a human being*, in other words, two component and characteristic forms of his or her humanity.

This point is important. Jandun is in fact a proponent of what he himself, as part of a long history, calls the plurality and gradation of forms. He is convinced, for example, that the form by which Socrates is an animal (the form of genus), is really different than the form by which he is human (the form of species). His idea – inspired *inter alia* by Scotism – is that the form of the genus is potential and imperfect with respect to the form of the species, that it is anterior to it, and that it necessarily lays the groundwork for the information of prime matter by that specific form. The individual therefore includes several common forms, ordered to one another, and all subordinate to a single individual substantial form that is last in the order of generation and is only received in matter – its true subject – by the mediation of other forms. But we must distinguish this first level, where a real plurality of forms leading to a single substantial and proper form of matter meet, from a second level, this time ontologically separate from matter, where we find *a second proper form* to which all the others are also principally ordered. Thus humans differ from other species by reason of the intellect, *but also* by reason of the cogitative faculty. And it is crucial to distinguish these two respects, in which humans differ, in order to avoid inconsistency. This is what Jandun highlights:

> [T]he human is distinguished from other [species] by the intellect itself, as by an intrinsic agent that, by operating, relates to the body by nature in a way so as to only make one; and by the cogitative soul it is distinguished from other [species] as by a form that constitutes it in specific substantial being, and thus one and the other are, in different ways, its form.[47]

There is only one proper substantial form in a given mode (that of inherence, for example), but nothing prevents another proper form from existing in another mode. Jandun will repeat this later in the work, emphasizing the fact that the cogitative and intellective souls are indeed two souls (and not two powers of the same soul), or even that they are indeed two "substantial" forms (this latter term being ambiguous). Nonetheless a human being remains one because in a human these two forms are ordered in such a way that one form relates to the other "as its perfection." This is to say that the cogitative soul depends in its operation and existence on the intellective soul so that these two souls constitute a genuine unity.[48]

This conception of the human-aggregate also makes it possible for Jandun to respond to the problem of the individuality of thought. The intellect, of course, is unique and eternal, but it only operates by aggregating itself to the individual, adventitious phantasms of a particular body. It is not the intellect that thinks, but the individual, which refers not only to the cogitating body, but also to the composite of the cogitating body (the body where the cogitative faculty is inherent) and the intellect, which together with it forms *quid unum sufficienter*.

All thought occurs via and relative to certain phantasms. Consequently, for the same intelligible, there will always be different intellections, according to the different phantasms they conform to and depend on, both in order to be and to continue to exist. The intellections of the same intelligible are one relative to this intelligible (at least negatively, since, in this regard, there is nothing there to distinguish them), but they are numbered according to the phantasms they depend on.

5 Conclusion: the theoretical fruitfulness of Averroism

Several points emerge from the arguments we have briefly presented. Contrary to what E. Gilson said long ago, Averroism is not at all an "obstinate and stubborn Aristotelianism," satisfied with repeating Averroes and not offering anything conceptually fruitful. The Averroists, who should not be confused with one another, actively re-appropriated Aristotelianism's Greco-Arab heritage and worked meticulously on a certain number of problems that gave rise to modernity. With regard to the relationship between the separate intellect and the body, for example, Averroism does not content itself with taking a position, answering yes or no to the question of whether the intellect is the form of the body. What it does, in conformity with Averroes, and drawing upon a complex tradition, even goes so far as to question what a form is. What is a form? What are the conditions of information? Is there, for example, only information by inherence, or can we conceptualize something as a separate perfection, which requires rethinking the link between being, power, and agency? This is what Averroes, among others, attempts to conceptualize, and it is also what the Averroists worked on, and what earns their writings a place in the vivid history of rationality.

Thomas Aquinas reduced Averroism to a series of wrong answers, but the truth is rather that Averroism asks the right questions or raises good ones. Let us take the most obvious example. Averroism, as we have said, is for Aquinas a heterodox system, but first and foremost a senseless one; it undermines personal rationality in that it is not able to establish that humans think. And yet, the theoretical reality is different and more complex because the statement: "*hic homo intelligit*" ("this human thinks") or even *ego cogito*, which some merely wish to confirm or reject, is only apparently obvious. In fact, its defense requires a considerable number of non-trivial arguments.

And that is what Averroism does. Obviously, Averroism does not say: "a human being does not think." The Averroists ask: "What do we call thinking?" "What is a human being?" "What relationship is there, for example, between, thought and the *experience* of thought?" "What am I experiencing, when I say, that I experience myself thinking, if this is indeed the case?" And furthermore, in answer to their adversaries' claim that, in Averroism, a human being no longer acts, no longer acts his thought, and that the thought that occurs is not his own, Averroism asks: "What are the conditions for the effectuation and attribution, or the imputation, of agency?" "Does it go without saying that the notion of interiority, or of the subject, must intervene?" "Where do we place will in the framework of mental action, and to what effect?" "What do phantasms do, and what is their significance?"

Averroism raises all of these issues, and they effectively show the existence of problematic crossroads. The current in European thought that emerged with Thomas Aquinas and others, before disappearing as well, was always just one of its roads.

Notes

1. On this label, see Bianchi 2015; Brenet 2003, 2013a and 2013b; Calma 2011; and Hasse 2007a and 2007b. On Averroes's other commentaries on *De anima*, unknown to the Latin world, see Wirmer 2008; Ivry 1995, 1999.
2. On the condemnation of 1277, see in particular Piché 1999, Hissette 1977.
3. See A. de Libera 2004, 2007, 2008, 2014a.
4. The agent intellect is also involved, but the idea of a unique source of illumination – equivalent to god – was less problematic.
5. On Averroes's position and then Thomas Aquinas's critique, see the Black 1993, 1996, 1999, 2004, 2005 and Taylor 1999, 2004a, 2004b, 2009. See also Brenet 2009c; for an analysis of the "scandal" of Averroism in Europe, see Brenet 2015.
6. Cf. Averroes, *Long Commentary on the De anima*, III, c. 5, ed. Crawford: 400, l. 382.
7. On the theory of the two subjects, see Brenet 2005, 2003, 311f.
8. Thomas Aquinas, *De unitate intellectus*, ed. de Libera: §62, 137.
9. See Thomas Aquinas, *De unitate intellectus*; ed. de Libera: §66, 141.
10. Witness what Thomas Aquinas writes against Plato, for example in his *Quaestiones disputatae De Anima*, q. 11, ed. Bazán: 98–99, l. 160–179.
11. See Thomas Aquinas, *De unitate intellectus*, ed. de Libera: §68, 143; cf. Thomas Aquinas, *Summa Theologiae* I, q. 76, art. 1, sol., 209.
12. For a longer history of Averroism, *cf.* Kuksewicz 1968, 1978, Nardi 1958, Niewöhner-Sturlese 1994, Akasoy-Giglioni 2013.
13. On Siger, see, amongst others, Imbach-Putallaz 1997, Petagine 2004, Nardi 1945, Kuksewicz 1968, de Libera 2004, Calma 2011, Calma-Coccia 2006a, 2006b.
14. Siger de Brabant, *De anima intellectiva*, ed. Bazan: 80.
15. *Ibid.*, 80, l. 73–74.
16. *Ibid.*, 84, l. 67ff.
17. *Ibid.*, 84, l. 63ff.
18. On the body-subject, body-object distinction, and the anti-Averroist idea of the human being as a simple object of the intellect, see Brenet 2009a, 2012.
19. *Ibid.*, 85, l. 80.
20. On the notion of *operans intrinsecum*, see Brenet 2013a.
21. Siger de Brabant, *De anima intellectiva*, ed. Bazan, 87, l. 17ff.
22. *Ibid.*, chap. VII, 101ff.
23. *Ibid.*, 108, l. 83–87.
24. *Ibid.*
25. On this text and its author, see the Trifogli-Nielsen and Seńko editions; Brenet 2013b, 2009b, Kuksewicz 1968.
26. Thomas Wylton, *Quaestio de anima intellectiva*; ed. Trifogli-Nielsen: §84.
27. On this notion of assistance, see Brenet (2013b: 76ff.), de Libera 2014b.
28. Thomas Wylton, *Quaestio de anima intellectiva*, ed. Trifogli-Nielsen: §84.
29. *Ibid.*, §120, 124.
30. *Ibid.*, §124.
31. *Ibid.*, §141.
32. *Ibid.*, §124.

33 *Ibid.*, §113; 114.
34 For more on John of Jandun, see Brenet 2001, 2003, 2008, 2009b, Kuksewicz 1968.
35 Cf. Mahoney 2000, Hasse 2007a, 2007b.
36 In the Latin world, Alexander of Aphrodisias was considered to be a proponent of strict materialism who saw all souls – including the human soul – as the product of a physico-chemical blend of elements; on this misreading, cf. Brenet 2015.
37 John of Jandun, *Super libros Aristotelis de anima subtilissimae quaestiones*, col. 234b.
38 *Ibid.*, col. 239a.
39 *Ibid.*, col. 239b.
40 *Ibid.*, col. 239a.
41 *Ibid.*, col. 239a–b.
42 Cf. *ibid.*, col. 245: "per intellectum homo est homo. . ., sed illud esse hominem non est esse receptum in materia subiective."
43 If we think of the sailor, we must imagine, consequently, that the sailor is not the one who gives the boat, which otherwise exists, its act. The sailor, in a singular relationship with the ship (whose separate being is not, however, independent), makes a composite sailor-boat be (via his own being) to which he gives agency as such.
44 John of Jandun, *Super libros Aristotelis de anima subtilissimae quaestiones*, col. 245a.
45 *Ibid.*, col. 243.
46 *Ibid.*, col. 245.
47 *Ibid.*, col. 246.
48 *Ibid.*, col. 291.

Bibliography

Primary sources

Averroes. *Averrois Cordubensis commentarium magnum in Aristotelis de anima libros*. F. S. Crawford (ed.). Cambridge, MA, The Medieval Academy of America, 1953.

———. *Aristotelis opera cum Averrois commentariis*. Venice: Apud Junctas, 1562–1574; reprint Frankfurt am Main, Minerva, 1962.

John of Jandun. *Ioannis de Ianduno philosophi acutissimi super libros Aristotelis de anima subtilissimae quaestiones*. Venise, 1587; réimpr. Minerva, Frankfurt a. M., 1966.

Siger de Brabant. *Quaestiones in tertium De anima, De anima intellectiva, De aeternitate mundi*. B. C. Bazán (ed.), 1–69. Louvain: Publications universitaires, 1972.

Thomas Aquinas. *De unitate intellectus: Contra Averroistas, Opera Omnia*, Editio Leonina, vol. 43, 291–314. Rome: San Tommaso, 1976.

———. *Quaestiones disputatae De Anima*. B.-C. Bazán (ed.). Rome, Paris: Commissio Leonina, 1996.

———. *L'Unité de l'intellect contre les averroïstes, suivi des Textes contre Averroès antérieurs à 1270*. Texte latin, traduction, introduction, bibliographie, chronologie, notes et index par A. de Libera. In *Contre Averroès*. Paris: GF-Flammarion, 1994.

Thomas Wylton *Quaestio de anima intellectiva*. W. Seńko (ed.). In "Tomasza Wiltona *'Quaestio disputata de anima intellectiva'*". *Studia Mediewistyczne* **5**(1964): 75–116; the other questions follow on 117–190.

———. *On the Intellectual Soul*. L. O. Nielsen & C. Trifogli (eds). Oxford: Oxford University Press, 2010.

———. L'âme intellective. trans. J.-B. Brenet. In Id., *Les possibilités de jonction: Averroès-Thomas Wylton*. Berlin: de Gruyter, 2013.

Secondary sources

Akasoy, A. & Giglioni, G. (eds). 2013. *Renaissance Averroism and Its Aftermath: Arabic Philosophy in Early Modern Europe*. Dordrecht, The Netherlands: Springer.

Bianchi, L. 2015. "L'averroismo di Dante: qualche osservazione critica". *Le tre corone: Rivista internazionale di studi su Dante, Petrarca, Boccaccio* **2**: 71–109.

Black, D. L. 1993. "Consciousness and Self-Knowledge in Aquinas's Critique of Averroes's Psychology". *Journal of the History of Philosophy* **31**: 349–385.

———. 1996. "Memory, Individuals, and the Past in Averroes's Psychology". *Medieval Philosophy and Theology* **5**: 161–187.

———. 1999. "Conjunction and the Identity of Knower and Known in Averroes". *American Catholic Philosophical Quarterly* **73**: 161–184.

———. 2004. "Models of the Mind: Metaphysical Presuppositions of the Averroist and Thomistic Accounts of Intellection". *Documenti e Studi sulla tradizione filosofica medievale* **15**: 319–352.

———. 2005. "Psychology: Soul and Intellect". In *The Cambridge Companion to Arabic Philosophy*, P. Adamson & R. C. Taylor (eds), 308–326. Cambridge, New York: Cambridge University Press.

Brenet, J.-B. 2001. "Perfection de la philosophie ou philosophe parfait? Jean de Jandun, lecteur d'Averroès". *Recherches de théologie et philosophie médiévales* **38**(2): 310–348.

———. 2003. *Transferts du sujet: La noétique d'Averroès selon Jean de Jandun*. Paris: Vrin.

———. 2005. "Averroès a-t-il inventé une théorie des deux sujets de la pensée?". *Tópicos: Revista de filosofía* (Universidad Panamericana, México) **29**: 53–86.

———. 2006. "Vision béatifique et séparation de l'intellect au début du xive siècle: Pour Averroès ou contre Thomas d'Aquin?". *Freiburger Zeitschrift für Philosophie und Theologie* **53**: 310–342.

———. (ed.). 2007a. *Averroès et les averroïsmes juif et latin: Actes du colloque international, Paris 16–18 juin 2005*. Turnhout: Brepols.

———. 2007b. "Moi qui pense, moi qui souffre: la question de l'identité du composé humain dans la riposte anti-averroïste de Pierre d'Auriol et Grégoire de Rimini". In *Généalogies du sujet: De saint Anselme à Malebranche*, O. Boulnois (ed.), 151–169. Paris: Vrin.

———. 2008. "Âme cogitative, âme intellective: Jean de Jandun et la *duplex forma propria* de l'homme". *Vivarium* **46**: 318–341.

———. 2009a. "Corps-sujet, corps-objet: Notes sur Averroès et Thomas d'Aquin dans le *De immortalitate animae* de P. Pomponazzi". In *Pietro Pomponazzi entre traditions et innovations*, J. Biard & Th. Gontier (eds), 11–28. Amsterdam, Philadelphia: Grüner.

———. 2009b. "Jean de Jandun et la *Quaestio de anima intellectiva* de Thomas Wylton". *Freiburger Zeitschrift für Philosophie und Theologie* **56**: 309–340.

———. 2009c. "Thomas d'Aquin pense-t-il? Retours sur *hic homo intelligit*". *Revue des Sciences Philosophiques et Théologiques* **93**(2): 229–250.

———. 2012. "Sujet, objet, pensée personnelle: l'Anonyme de Giele contre Thomas d'Aquin". *Archives d'Histoire Doctrinale et Littéraire du Moyen-Age* **79**: 49–69.

———. 2013a. "Siger de Brabant et la notion d'*operans intrinsecum*: un coup de maître?". *Revue des Sciences Philosophiques et Théologiques* **97**: 3–36.

———. 2013b. *Les possibilités de jonction: Averroès-Thomas Wylton*. Berlin: de Gruyter.

———. 2015. *Averroès l'inquiétant*. Paris: Les Belles Lettres.

Calma, D. 2011. *Etudes sur le premier siècle de l'averroïsme latin: Approches et textes inédits*. Turnhout: Brepols.

Calma, D. & Coccia, E. 2006a. "Un commentaire inédit de Siger de Brabant sur la *Physique* d'Aristote (ms. Paris, BNF, lat. 16297)". *Archives d'Histoire Doctrinale et Littéraire du Moyen-Age* **73**: 283–349.

———. 2006b. *Les 'sectatores Averrois': Noétique et cosmologie aux xiiie-xive siècles. Freiburger Zeitschrift für Philosophie und Theologie* **53**: 133–344.

De Libera, A. 2004. *L'unité de l'intellect: Commentaire du De unitate intellectus contra averroistas de Thomas d'Aquin*. Paris: Vrin.

———. 2007. *Archéologie du sujet*, t. I. Paris: Vrin.

———. 2008. *Archéologie du sujet*, t. II. Paris: Vrin.

———. 2014a. *Archéologie du sujet*, t. III. Paris: Vrin.

———. 2014b. "Formes assistantes et formes inhérentes: Sur l'union de l'âme et du corps, du Moyen Âge à l'Âge classique". *Archives d'Histoire Littéraire et Doctrinale du Moyen-Âge* **81**: 197–248.

Hasse, D. N. 2007a. "*Averroica secta*: Notes on the Formation of Averroist Movements in Fourteenth-Century Bologna and Renaissance Italy". See Brenet (2007), 307–331.

———. 2007b. "Arabic Philosophy and Averroism". In *The Cambridge Companion to Renaissance Philosophy*, J. Hankins (ed.), 113–136. Cambridge: Cambridge University Press.

Hissette, R. 1977. *Enquête sur les 219 articles condamnés à Paris le 7 mars 1277*. Louvain-Paris: Publications universitaires-Vander-Oyez.

Imbach, R. & Putallaz, F.-X. 1997. *Profession: Philosophe. Siger de Brabant*. Paris: Cerf.

Ivry, A. L. 1966. "Averroes on Intellection and Conjunction". *Journal of the American Oriental Society* **86**(2): 76–85.

———. 1995. "Averroes's Middle and Long Commentaries on the *De anima*". *Arabic Sciences and Philosophy* **5**: 76–92.

———. 1999. "Averroes's Three Commentaries on De anima". In *Averroes and the Aristotelian Tradition: Sources, Constitution and Reception of the Philosophy of Ibn Rushd (1126–1198)*. Proceedings of the Fourth Symposium Averroicum (Cologne, 1996), G. Endress & J. A. Aertsen (eds), 199–216. Leiden, Boston, Köln: Brill.

Kuksewicz, Z. 1965. *Averroïsme bolonais au xive siècle*, édition de textes (Institut de philosophie et de sociologie de l'Académie polonaise des sciences). Wrocław-Varsovie-Cracovie: Ossolineum.

———. 1968. *De Siger de Brabant à Jacques de Plaisance: La théorie de l'intellect chez les averroïstes latins des xiiie et xive siècles*. Wrocław-Varsovie-Cracovie: Ossolineum.

———. 1978. "L'influence d'Averroès sur des universités en Europe centrale. L'expansion de l'averroïsme latin". In *Multiple Averroès*, J. Jolivet (ed.), 275–281. Paris: Les Belles Lettres.

Mahoney, E. P. 2000. *Two Aristotelians of the Italian Renaissance: Nicoletto Vernia and Agostino Nifo*. Aldershot: Ashgate.

Nardi, B. 1945. *Sigieri di Brabante nel pensiero del Rinascimento Italiano*. Roma: Edizioni Italiane.

———. 1958. *Saggi sull'Aristotelismo padovano del secolo XIV al XVI*. Firenze: Sansoni.

Niewöhner, F. & Sturlese, L. (eds). 1994. *Averroismus im Mittelalter und in der Renaissance*. Zürich: Spur Verlag.

Petagine, A. 2004. *Aristotelismo difficile: L'intelletto umano nella prospettiva di Alberto Magno, Tommaso d'Aquino e Sigieri di Brabante*. Milan: Vita e Pensiero.

Piché, D. 1999. *La condamnation parisienne de 1277*, texte latin, traduction, introduction et commentaire. Paris: Vrin.

Taylor, R. C. 1999. "Averroes's Epistemology and its Critique by Aquinas". In *Medieval Masters: Essays in Memory of Msgr. E. A. Synan*, R. E. Houser (ed.), 147–177. Houston: Center for Thomistic Studies: University of St. Thomas.

———. 2004a. "Separate Material Intellect in Averroes's Mature Philosophy". In *Words, Texts and Concepts Cruising the Mediterranean Sea: Studies on the Sources, Contents and Influences of Islamic Civilization and Arabic Philosophy and Science, Dedicated to Gerhard Endress on His Sixty-Fifth Birthday*, R. Arnzen & J. Thielmann (eds), 289–309. Leuven: Peeters.

———. 2004b. "Improving on Nature's Exemplar: Averroes's Completion of Aristotle's Psychology of Intellect". In *Philosophy, Science and Exegesis in Greek, Arabic and Latin Commentaries*, P. Adamson, H. Baltussen & M. W. F. Stone (eds), 107–130. London: Institute of Classical Studies.

———. 2009. "Intellect as Intrinsic Formal Cause in the Soul According to Aquinas and Averroes". In *The Afterlife of the Platonic Soul: Reflections on Platonic Psychology in the Monotheistic Religions*, M. Elkaisy-Friemuth & J. M. Dillon (eds), 187–220. Leiden: Brill.

Wirmer, D. 2008 (ed. & trans.). Averroes, *Über den Intellekt. Auszüge aus seinen drei Kommentaren zu Aristoteles' De anima, Arabisch-Lateinisch-Deutsch*. Freiburg im Breisgau: Herder.

5

THE FUNCTION OF THE INTELLECT

Intentionality and representationalism

Paolo Rubini

1 Introduction: intentionality of intellectual cognition in Aquinas

"Intentionality" is a modern concept introduced into philosophical terminology only around the end of the 19th century.[1] Nonetheless, philosophers had long been acquainted with the phenomenon addressed by this label, namely the fact that acts of cognition and other mental activities are about something, that they refer to something as their object or content. In this chapter I shall outline philosophical accounts of intentionality proposed between 1300 and 1600. Two major restrictions ought to be mentioned, however.

First, philosophers in this period tended to distinguish different kinds of cognitive acts in human beings. The main distinction, inherited from ancient psychology, was drawn between acts of sense perception (pertaining to the sensorial properties of things) and acts of intellection (concerning essences, the constitutive features of things). Sense perception was considered to be cognition of singulars, whereas intellectual knowledge was traditionally regarded as universal cognition. These two kinds of cognitive acts were conceived of as mutually interconnected; perceptual acts were supposed to lead (under ordinary conditions) to acts of intellection, which in turn were described as based (under ordinary conditions) on sense perception. In this chapter, however, I will only focus on intellectual cognition and set sense perception aside.[2] I will exclusively examine how philosophers accounted for the intentionality of acts of intellection that were usually taken to involve the cognition of universals. In particular, I will examine what function (if any) was assigned to *representations* in theories of intellectual cognition and how this assignment was linked to fundamental assumptions about the mind's ontology and causality.

The second restriction is even more severe. The centuries between 1300 and 1600 exhibit several different approaches to the nature and functioning of the mind.[3] The rediscovery of ancient sources restored access to epistemological theories that had been ignored or neglected for centuries. Besides traditional scholastic views we encounter an increasing number of independent accounts of cognition in this period, for example theories inspired by Neo-Platonic innatism (in Cusanus or Ficino) or Epicurean empiricism (in Fracastoro), whereas sceptical sources stimulated authors such as Gianfrancesco Pico, Sanchez or Montaigne to challenge established views.[4] In spite of these multifarious developments, I will restrict my attention to scholastic Aristotelianism, the philosophical tradition prevailing in the universities at that time. The reason for this choice is that discussions on intentionality within this tradition form a more homogeneous discourse. Accordingly, in the next three sections I will consider scholastic authors who epitomise emblematic views on intentionality, namely Ockham, several Renaissance Aristotelians and Suárez.

But first I will begin by outlining the account defended by Thomas Aquinas (1224/25–1274), a theory that formed the background of scholastic debates on intentionality between 1300 and 1600.[5] For, these debates can largely be understood as attempts to refute, rehabilitate or radicalise Aquinas's account or aspects of it.

In Aristotelianism, intentionality has from the beginning been conceived of in terms of *formal assimilation*. In a nutshell, a subject S bears a cognitive relation to an object O, if S shares the form of O. More specifically, if O is a sensible property of a thing, the cognitive relation occurs in an act of perception (or imagination); if O is the essence of a thing, the cognitive relation is embedded in an act of intellection. In both cases, the cognitive relation rests on the formal similarity between S and O, that is, on the fact that the form of O somehow also exists in S.[6] In the following I will refer to this conception as the formal assimilation account of intentionality (FAA).

Let me briefly flesh out this account. First, FAA evidently presupposes Aristotelian hylomorphism as its ontological framework.[7] Only on the assumption that things are compounded of matter and form(s) is it plausible to explain intentionality in terms of formal assimilation. Second, according to FAA the form of O shared by S does not exist in S in the same way as it exists in O. Aristotle points out that in acts of cognition forms are received by the subject "without matter" and thus deprived of their original status as properties or essences of things.[8] The form of O exists in S according to an "abstract" way of existing usually described by 13th-century scholastic Aristotelians as *intentional*.[9]

Moreover, FAA answers the basic question of intentionality – why cognitive acts refer to objects – in accordance with *direct realism*. By formally assimilating to objects, a subject gains direct access to them; no intermediary "internal" objects are required to explain intentionality. The task faced by scholastic Aristotelians was to spell out the psychological mechanism responsible for assimilation. How is it possible for S to share the form of O? In the following I will sketch out the influential answer articulated by Aquinas.[10]

First, Aquinas's account of intentionality draws on the *cognitive faculties* human beings are endowed with. These faculties – the external and internal senses and the intellect – are specific "powers" of receiving forms of objects in accordance with an "intentional" way of existing.[11] They originate from the human soul but reside in bodily organs – except for the intellect, which is regarded as an *immaterial* faculty of the soul. According to Aquinas, cognitive powers are essentially *passive*; their nature consists in their capability of being actualised by forms of objects and, consequently, of assimilating to them. These forms are in turn the efficient causes responsible for the cognitive faculties being actualised.[12] Thus, the intentionality of cognitive acts rests on a reception of forms that is but an affection of the subject's passive faculties. With regard to passivity, cognitive acts do not differ from other processes of (qualitative) change in nature, such as the burning of a straw. This is a naturalistic approach to intentionality insofar as the same principles that are supposed to explain natural changes in general are also adopted to explain why acts of cognition take place and refer to objects. Aquinas does not appeal primarily to a spontaneous mental capacity of grasping objects, but to cognitive faculties of the mind that work like ordinary dispositions of natural substances.[13]

The second basic element in Aquinas's account of intentionality – the assumption of representations – testifies to the same naturalistic attitude. Aquinas takes affections, and change in general, to require the *union* of a passive principle with an efficient one.[14] With regard to FAA this means that the subject's passive faculties need to be affected by the forms that are responsible for assimilation as efficient causes. Aquinas distinguishes two main cases.[15] (a) If a cognitive faculty comes into immediate contact with the actual form of an appropriate object, this very same form actualises the faculty's receptivity. This is how sight is affected by the actual form of light. (b) If the faculty cannot be immediately affected by the object's actual form, assimilation requires an intermediary actual form that (i) resembles the object's form as a "likeness" (*similitudo*) and (ii) actualises the faculty by direct union. Such intermediary forms are *representations* of the objects' forms, and Aquinas calls them *species*, or more precisely, *sensible* species if they represent sensory properties of things and affect the senses, and *intelligible* species if they represent non-sensory essences of things and affect the intellect. Both types play a dual role. As actual forms united with cognitive faculties, they trigger cognitive acts; as representations of the forms of objects, they provide these acts with content.

Aquinas's view on intelligible species can be outlined in four claims[16]:

(1) During earthly life, intelligible species are required for *all* acts of intellection. For, the objects of these acts are universal essences separated from individual matter, and as such they do not *actually* exist in nature, nor can they be grasped directly.[17]

(2) For this reason, intelligible species need to be *abstracted*
  (a) from sensory representations of individual things, called "phantasms",
  (b) by an active power of the soul, termed the "agent intellect".

(3) Being abstracted, intelligible species are immaterial. Consequently they can both
   (a) represent essences as universal objects of knowledge and
   (b) actualise the receptive intellect, a power of the soul that is passive but immaterial.

(4) Nonetheless, intelligible species are not objects of intellection, but *media* through which the receptive intellect grasps its objects by assimilating to them. Accordingly, Aquinas's assumption of species does *not* amount to a rejection of direct realism.[18]

To sum up, in order to explain the intentionality of intellectual cognition in accordance with FAA, Aquinas describes acts of intellection as actualisations of a receptive intellect and holds that their efficient causes are intermediary entities provided with representational content ("likenesses" of objects). In the second half of the 13th century, a similar account of intentionality was endorsed not only by theologians such as Albert the Great (ca 1200–1280) or Giles of Rome (ca 1243–1316), who strove to harmonise Aristotelianism with Christianity; even authors committed to a more "radical" Aristotelianism, such as the Averroist Siger of Brabant (ca 1240–before 1284), adopted the vocabulary of intelligible species (although in a different psychological framework).[19]

2 Against representations: direct realism according to Ockham

By the time of his death in 1274, Aquinas's account of intentionality was already being challenged by theologians more devoted to an Augustinian than an Aristotelian approach to psychology. Despite their hostility to his account, however, they did not completely reject its Aristotelian framework and vocabulary.[20] With regard to intentionality, they rarely questioned the core assumption of FAA, namely the idea that cognition involves assimilation of the knower to the known. Rather, they rejected the naturalistic orientation of Aristotelian psychology in general and of Aquinas's account of intentionality in particular. Their anti-naturalistic attitude is evident in two tendencies: (a) the proponents of a (more) Augustinian psychology were (more) inclined to appeal to supernatural factors (e.g., divine illumination) in their accounts of intentionality; (b) they tended to consider the soul's cognitive faculties as active powers that are efficient-causally responsible for the intentionality of acts of cognition. As a result, the assumption of intelligible species was sharply criticised. Authors such as Henry of Ghent (ca 1217–1293) and Peter John Olivi (1247/8–1296) epitomise the dissatisfaction with Aquinas's views on intentionality within the Augustinian camp.[21]

Around 1300, by contrast, an account of intentionality more akin to Aquinas's was defended by the Franciscan theologian John Duns Scotus (1265/66–1308). As has been noted, this was an attempt directed mainly against Henry of Ghent to restore the "possibility of natural intentional acts of cognition".[22] Scotus largely preserves the basic tenets of Aquinas's account; in particular, he maintains that a full-fledged explanation of intentionality requires the assumption of representations (intelligible species). But he introduces substantial refinements as well, for instance concerning knowledge of individuals. For the purpose of this chapter, two of his refinements are particularly noteworthy.

The first is his influential distinction between intuitive and abstractive cognition. According to Scotus, a cognition is *intuitive* if it is "of a present object as present and of an existing object as existing", *abstractive* if it "abstracts the object from existence and non-existence, presence and absence".[23] This distinction is cast in new terminology, but ultimately rests on a dichotomy already found in Aquinas, namely that intuitive cognition arises from the objects themselves, whereas abstractive cognition *merely* originates from representations (species, phantasms) of objects.[24] This distinction played a major role in discussions about intentionality in the 14th century, as we will see in Ockham.

Scotus's second refinement concerns the ontological status of objects of intellection, traditionally regarded as universal essences abstracted from matter. According to scholastic Aristotelians, universals are not actual entities separate from the individual material things they are abstracted from. But because they have an ontological foundation in these things, they are not fictional entities either. As Scotus points out, they do possess being, but "only a diminished being, as it is a known being".[25] Introducing the label *esse cognitum* (or *esse obiectivum*) enables Scotus to adequately distinguish universal objects of intellections not only from the individual things in which they are grounded, but also from the intelligible species by which they are represented and from the acts of intellection in which they are grasped; species and acts exist in the mind as qualities, whereas objects exist there with "known being".[26]

This distinction, too, played a pivotal role in later debates on intentionality. Scotists, as well as "independent" authors such as Peter Auriol (ca 1280–1322), generalised Scotus's view, arguing that due to its cognitive acts the mind is *always* immediately acquainted with entities that have objective being and can either resemble real things (in veridical acts) or be fictional (as in deceptive acts).[27] Such intermediary entities also figure as representations, although in an opposite way to species; they are not "causal pre-conditions", but "effects" of cognitive acts. In the following I will only touch upon this major development of late medieval representationalism while discussing Ockham.

Despite Scotus's refinements of the traditional account of intentionality, the strongest challenge came one generation later from his confrere, the controversial theologian William of Ockham (ca 1280–ca 1349). Ockham's criticism culminates in the rejection of any and all intermediary entities between object and subject, but it also affects the traditional conception of faculties. He deals with matters of intentionality in different theoretical contexts (logic, psychology, theology) and with different results at different stages of his philosophical development. Here, I will draw on topics from his commentary to the *Sentences*.

In the first place, Ockham's discontent with the traditional account pertains to the requirement of representations (species) as efficient causes of acts of intellection. His attitude towards this question is expressed in a passage where he discusses Aquinas's and Scotus's claim that intelligible species are necessary to explain how acts of intellection come to be:

> This view cannot be rejected with evidence *by means of natural reasons*. Nonetheless, it seems to me that the opposite part is more probable; for plurality must not be assumed without necessity. But whatever can be explained [*salvari*] with a species, can be explained without a species; hence it is not necessary to assume it.[28]

Ockham apparently considers the viewpoint of natural philosophy as non-committal for an account of intentionality. The assumption of representations might even be justified with regard to "natural reasons", but the only decisive criterion is the principle of ontological parsimony. Accordingly, intelligible species must be rejected as superfluous to an explanation of intentionality. But why?

In order to justify his view, Ockham appeals to Scotus's distinction between intuitive and abstractive cognition. He actually reshapes Scotus's schema, but the *ratio* of the distinction remains the same, in that intuitive cognition originates from its object, while abstractive cognition does not.[29] Ockham obviously takes for granted that "for an intuitive cognition to occur, it is only required to assume the intellect and the known thing, and no species at all".[30] But he considers intelligible species to be superfluous even to abstractive cognition, where objects cannot be the immediate cause of acts of intellection. To explain abstractive acts of intellection he assigns efficient causality not to intelligible species, but to "habits" (*habitus*) resulting in the intellect from previous intuitive acts of intellection. By grasping an object O a certain number of times, the intellect acquires the capacity for grasping O even if O is absent. Thus, no intelligible species is required for abstractive acts of intellection concerning O. All we need is an acquired disposition for grasping O in the intellect. For Ockham, abstractive acts of intellection rest in the end on intuitive acts of intellection. In other words, direct acquaintance with objects (as provided by intuitive acts) is the ultimate source of intentionality, whereas intelligible species are useless with regard to all questions they have traditionally been adduced for.[31]

However, two (joint) questions arise, both of which are pertinent to our topic. First, Ockham abides by the view that the intellect is an immaterial faculty.[32] But then how is it possible for material objects to immediately act upon the intellect, as intuitive cognition requires? The second question results from Ockham's nominalism, according to which intuitive acts of intellection only allow acquaintance with individuals.[33] Since Ockham takes abstractive cognition to rest on intuitive cognition, but rejects intelligible species abstracted from individuals, how is intellectual cognition of universals possible in his nominalistic framework? In his commentary to the *Sentences* he answers these questions in five steps:

(1) In acts of intuitive cognition, the intellect only grasps individual objects (individual essences of individual things). This direct access to individuals is the starting point of intellectual knowledge, or of concept formation.[34]
(2) Universals, which are the specific objects of acts of intellection, can exclusively be grasped in acts of abstractive cognition originating from acquired intellectual habits. In early passages of the *Sentences*, Ockham regards the object of these acts as a "fictional being", in other words, "a conceptual content in objective being, which determines the act".[35] Later on, when arguing against Auriol's doctrine of "apparent being", he conceives of universal knowledge rather as resulting from (abstractive) acts in which the intellect apprehends a plurality of similar individuals confusedly.[36]
(3) In both intuitive and abstractive acts the intellect behaves not merely as a passive faculty (acted upon by the object), but as an *active* one. For Ockham, receptive and "agent" intellect are not two different faculties of the soul (as they were for Aquinas), but two functional aspects of one and the same rational soul.[37]
(4) The intellect's active contribution is obviously required for intellection of universals; for in this case there is no actual object that can affect the intellect. Such a contribution is properly an act of *abstraction*; in early passages Ockham describes it as "production of the universal concept of a thing in objective being".[38]
(5) The intellect's activity is equally required for intellection of individuals in intuitive acts of cognition. In this case there is an object (normally a material object) that can affect the intellect, yet only as a "partial cause". If an (intuitive) act of intellection is to be accomplished, the "agent intellect" is required as an additional partial cause; the (immaterial) intellect causes an (immaterial) act, in which a (material) individual object is immediately grasped. This causal activity of the intellect, too, is abstraction, namely

> the one [that] consists in *partially causing* an intuitive or abstractive intellection together with an object or a habit. . . . This intellection is absolutely abstracted from matter, since it is in itself immaterial and possesses subjective being in something immaterial [i.e., in the intellect].[39]

In Ockham's view, it is this causal activity of the (immaterial) intellect that makes intuitive intellectual cognition of (material) individuals possible.

To sum up, Ockham's account of intentionality begins by tracing abstractive cognition (of universals and individuals) back to intuitive cognition (of individuals). It then explains the emergence of intuitive cognition by appealing to the efficient causality exerted by both the objects and the intellect. "With regard to this cognition, the agent intellect and the object are sufficient agents".[40] More precisely, the object's efficient-causal power is responsible for the *determinate* content of an intentional act; act *a* refers to object *A* and act *b* to object *B* because *A* is a (partial) cause of *a* and *B* of *b*. But the intellect's "causal power" (*virtus causativa*) is complementarily required to bring about *a* and *b* as acts referring to *A* and *B*, that is, as intentional acts provided with a determinate *content*.[41]

Such a view emphasises direct realism. After all, Ockham never appeals to representations such as intelligible species, not even in his account of abstractive cognition. Correspondingly, he also rejects Auriol's claim that the immediate objects of acts of intellection are not things in their real being, but things as they "appear" to the intellect, that is, with "objective being".[42] At least in Ockham's later writings this holds even for knowledge of universals; to grasp them, the intellect has no need of representations as causal preconditions, or as effects, of its acts. But to justify his radical version of direct realism, Ockham has to conceive of the intellect as equipped with a *primitively intentional* activity, that is, with a spontaneous capacity for interacting with things both causally and cognitively.

To be sure, Ockham endorses the view that the intentionality of intellectual cognition rests on causality. But he abandons Aquinas's naturalistic attitude, according to which efficient causality only pertains to the objects or to their "likenesses", namely the intelligible species as intermediary efficient causes of acts of intellection. Instead, Ockham reframes the intellect's causal role in line with Augustinian psychology; he assumes that the objects can only produce intentional acts thanks to the intellect's active capacity for interacting with them in both causal and cognitive terms. Leaving open the question how satisfactory this approach to intentionality is, I shall ask instead whether Ockham, with his uncompromising rejection of representations, also sacrifices FAA. Does he still conceive of intentionality in terms of sharing of form?

Some readers are disappointed to find that in several places Ockham describes the relation between intuitive acts of intellectual cognition and their objects (individual essences) in terms of similarity.[43] This suggests that, although he criticises the causal explanation of intentionality in Aquinas's account, he does not completely reject FAA; instead, he maintains that intentionality rests, at least partially, on a sharing of form. In other words, his radical commitment to direct realism does not prevent him from conceiving of the intentional relation between the intellect and its objects in terms of assimilation: "Previous to the act of intellection, no assimilation by means of a species is required. But sufficient is the assimilation that occurs through the act of intellection, which is a likeness of the known thing".[44]

Despite Ockham's conciliatory tone, it is not easy to understand how an individual essence of a material thing and an individual act of the immaterial intellect can share a form in any relevant sense.[45] But was this point really clearer in Aquinas's account? In any case, we should not forget that Ockham takes intuitive acts of intellectual cognition to be immediately (although only partially) caused by their objects, and in an Aristotelian framework it is a commonplace that a cause and its effect are similar to one another or share a form.[46] Accordingly, Ockham might have found it plausible that an act of intellection, being linked to its object as an effect to its (partial) cause, might necessarily be linked to it in terms of formal similarity, too (and thus have a determinate content). Apparently, Ockham's radical views on the intentionality of acts of intellection do not rely on abandoning FAA, but on rejecting representations as both epistemic and causal intermediaries of cognition.

3 The fortunes of representationalism between Ockham and Pomponazzi

Ockham's radical version of direct realism, which rules out any intermediaries between the intellect and its objects, found only a few emulators in the generations that followed.[47] In the 14th and early 15th century, even authors sharing similar views in matters of ontology (nominalism) and methodology (principle of parsimony), e.g., John Buridan (before 1300–after 1358), Gregory of Rimini (ca 1305–1358) or Pierre of Ailly (ca 1350–1420), did not entirely accept Ockham's views on intentionality. They retained intermediary entities such as species or phantasms in their accounts of abstractive cognition, where no object can be envisaged as the efficient cause of cognitive acts. Accordingly, they appealed to representations in order to explain the intellectual cognition of universals, a kind of cognition that is eminently abstractive. But even though they (partially) endorsed representationalism, they did not simply revert to Aquinas's account.[48]

This is evident in Gregory of Rimini, a theologian of the Augustinian order who was influenced by Ockham. In his commentary to the *Sentences* he applies the distinction between intuitive and abstractive cognition in order to account for intentionality; yet, he interprets this distinction differently than Ockham. For Gregory, abstractive cognition is indirect cognition not because it arises from habits in place of objects (as Ockham claimed), but because it rests on representations of objects (as was Scotus's view); in fact, the content of abstractive cognition is determined not by the object itself, but by the *medium* in which the object is to be grasped. However, Gregory (unlike Scotus) argues that such a medium (a phantasm, species or concept of the object) needs to be *known* in order to fulfil its function.[49] The medium determines the cognitive act not only as its efficient cause, but also as its *immediate* object. Acts of abstractive cognition are, in fact, intuitive acts in which objects of former acts of intuitive cognition are apprehended in place of external objects.[50] This requires that objects of former intuitive acts be stored in memory to serve as representations in acts of abstractive cognition.[51] In the end, cognition is always intuitive and rests on the intellect's capability to grasp objects affecting it; but these objects are sometimes internal and allow the intellect to cognise external objects indirectly, which is especially important when the things to be known are absent. As a result, Gregory endorses *indirect realism* in his account of abstractive cognition, advancing a position that postulates internal objects in order to explain intentionality.

This has consequences for a nominalist such as Gregory. On his view, only individuals can be directly cognised, whereas universals need to be cognised by means of representations made up by the mind – representations that resemble not only the individuals they originate from, but also all individuals similar to them. According to Gregory, the same holds for *concepts*. Concepts are representations that, due to their indeterminacy, apply to a plurality of similar individuals. With representations of this kind the intellect achieves "confused" knowledge of pluralities of individuals.[52]

Gregory's indirect realism was a remarkable departure not only from Ockham's account of intentionality, but also from the traditional one, according to which intellectual representations only figure as efficient causes of acts of intellection, and not as their objects. In the 14th and 15th century the traditional conception – the "orthodox" way of supporting direct realism – was usually shared by theologians devoted to Aquinas's and Scotus's views. In fact, Thomism and Scotism would play a major role in debates on intentionality up to the 17th century, particularly in the context of Iberian scholasticism. In the late Middle Ages, however, an account of intentionality committed to direct realism and relying on FAA was also defended by professors of philosophy who embraced Averroism, first in Paris, then in Italy. Inclined towards a naturalistic epistemology, these authors developed autonomous views that would strongly influence Renaissance-Aristotelian discussions about the intentionality of intellectual cognition. In the following I will summarise the position of John of Jandun (1280/85–1328), an influential representative of this strand of scholasticism.[53]

Averroists were Aristotelians convinced that neither the receptive nor the "agent" intellect are parts of the human soul, which they considered to be the form of the human body. Instead, they regarded both the receptive and the agent intellect as supra-individual, unique entities to which individual human beings are linked when acts of intellection occur. To account for intentionality, Averroists thus had to explain how human beings are connected with supra-individual acts of intellection and can plausibly be considered as (co-)subjects of these acts. Jandun's influential solution rests on the following assumptions:

(1) Intelligible species (as representations of universal essences) are necessary causal conditions for the receptive intellect to grasp its proper objects by formally assimilating to them. However, they are not efficient causes of these acts of assimilation, but specific *dispositions* (habits) for performing them.[54]
(2) The receptive intellect acquires such dispositions from *phantasms*, representations made up by the inner senses of humans and inhering in their bodily organs. Accordingly, phantasms figure as efficient causes of intelligible species.[55] After the receptive intellect (as subject of all acts of intellection) has acquired a species, this can be actualised by the agent intellect (as efficient cause of all acts of intellection).

To be sure, the active intellect must be involved in bringing about intelligible species, as otherwise phantasms (corporeal representations of individual objects) could not produce representations of universal objects in the immaterial receptive intellect.[56] Nonetheless, Jandun takes intelligible species to be efficient-causally dependent on phantasms rather than on the active intellect. This is a remarkable departure from the traditional account of intentionality; for Aquinas, phantasms were just the "material" from which intelligible species needed to be abstracted by the agent intellect.[57] By reshaping the causal role of phantasms, Jandun can ensure that acts of intellection, although occurring in the supra-individual intellect, are still dependent on individual human beings. Without the active support of human sensory representations, intellectual cognition would neither obtain nor have any content.

Jandun's views on intellectual cognition strongly influenced the debate on intentionality among professors of natural philosophy at Italian universities, especially Bologna and Padua, during the late 14th and the 15th century. In particular, the idea that phantasms exert efficient causality by "impressing" intelligible species into the receptive intellect was shared by authors such as Paul of Venice (1369/72–1429) and Gaetano of Thiene (1387–1465) and became commonplace in that philosophical biotope permeated by diffuse Averroism.[58]

In the late 15th century, however, Averroists grew suspicious of intellectual representations. Equipped with improved philological skills due to the spread of humanistic education,[59] they probably realised that the assumption of intelligible species was alien to Averroes's genuine account of intellectual cognition, in which representations play no role. As a result, after Ockham we find the utmost hostility against intelligible species among Italian professors of philosophy such as Nicoletto Vernia (1420–1499), Alessandro Achillini (1463–1512) or Agostino Nifo (1469/70–1538), who embraced Averroism at the turn of the 15th century for at least part of their career. Nifo was possibly the most radical; by appealing to the immateriality of the (supra-individual) receptive intellect, to the abstractive power of the (supra-individual) agent intellect and to the mere passivity of (individual) phantasms, he ruled out representations of intelligible objects as causal factors of acts of intellectual cognition.[60]

Nifo's understanding of intellectual intentionality emphasised elements of Neo-Platonic innatism in Averroistic psychology. For this reason it could not be accepted by philosophers oriented towards a naturalistic reading of Aristotle. The counterattack was started by Pietro Pomponazzi (1462–1525), a professor of natural philosophy in Padua and Bologna at the dawn of the 16th century. In a lecture delivered in 1503–1504 on Aristotle's *De anima* he reaffirmed intelligible species against criticism by contemporary Averroists, thereby initiating a long-term debate among Italian Aristotelians on the role of representations in intellectual cognition.[61] But Pomponazzi's defence of intelligible species was neither a revival of Aquinas's account of intentionality nor a restoration of Jandun's Averroism, as appears from his later *De immortalitate animae* (1516).

In psychology Pomponazzi follows the radical hylomorphism of the Greek commentator Alexander of Aphrodisias (fl. 200 CE), whose treatise *De anima* had been available in Latin since 1495.[62] According to radical hylomorphism, the human soul is but the form of the human body, a form as dependent on its bearer as any other material form; none of its "parts" or faculties is essentially "separable" from the body and its organs. As a result, Pomponazzi rejects the tenet that the human intellect is immaterial, a view shared by virtually all scholastic Aristotelians. His radical hylomorphism, which represents an attempt to construe Aristotelian psychology naturalistically, rules out both Averroism and Thomism as possible conceptions of the human intellect. The intellect can neither be a supra-individual entity, for it is the individual form of individual human beings, nor can it be immaterial; it can only be material and thus as perishable as the body itself.[63]

Like any other natural form, the body-dependent human intellect is the "causal principle" of its function (the cognition of universal essences) insofar as it is a passive disposition that needs to be actualised by an efficient-causal agent. As Pomponazzi points out:

> the intellect is moved by the body, since [Aristotle] says that knowing is just like sensing, and the receptive intellect is a passive power; and further on he says that its mover is a phantasm. But what needs a phantasm is inseparable from matter.[64]

In emphasising the intellect's sense-like passivity and its efficient-causal dependence on corporeal representations of the inner senses, Pomponazzi actually follows Jandun more than Alexander.[65] Indeed, Pomponazzi draws on the claim that phantasms, together with the agent intellect, are efficient causes of the intelligible species. However, he interprets the efficient-causal role of phantasms as proof of the corporeal nature of the receptive intellect – a conclusion Jandun would never have approved of. Moreover, from the idea of the intellect's efficient-causal dependence on phantasms he draws a striking consequence about the intentionality of intellectual cognition, as we will see in the following.

Pomponazzi agrees with the traditional account that genuine intellectual knowledge requires an immaterial intellect; for only in this case do acts of intellection rest on formal assimilation. In the separate "Intelligences" that move the heavens, for example, "who knows, what is known and the knowing are the same".[66] Being immaterial, they do not abstract their objects from corporeal representations, but apprehend them intuitively in themselves. The human intellect, by contrast, is always "moved" by phantasms; therefore:

> [it] cannot ... know a universal unqualifiedly but always sees the universal in the singular, as everyone can observe in himself. For in all cognition, however far abstracted, we form some bodily image. On this account the human intellect does not know itself first and directly; and it composes and thinks discursively, whence its knowing is in succession and time.[67]

The human intellect has no access to its objects directly, by means of assimilation, but can only grasp them indirectly, *in* bodily images of singular things, that is in phantasms; the intellect needs to use phantasms as sensory vehicles of universal contents, as *symbols* of essential forms. Accordingly, human intellectual cognition can only be a discursive process in which phantasms are transformed into symbols of intellectual objects by means of judgments and inferences. As a result, apprehension of universals is always "veiled", always mediated by sensory contents and hence "obscure" and "confused".[68] Pomponazzi's account of intellectual intentionality evidently abandons FAA in favour of indirect realism.

This entails two relevant consequences for our topic. First, phantasms become the real fulcrum in Pomponazzi's account of intentionality; for they are the unavoidable medium through which the human intellect discursively grasps its objects. Acts of intellection rest on representations of the inner senses not only in terms of efficient causality, but also with regard to their content, because intellectual cognition always requires phantasms suited to work as general symbols of intellectual objects. Accordingly, intentionality turns out to depend on the senses to a higher degree than usually assumed in scholastic Aristotelianism.

The second consequence concerns Pomponazzi's understanding of intelligible species. He still uses this notion, but evidently is no longer entitled to view intelligible species as intermediary entities enabling the intellect to assimilate to its objects. Rather, he describes them as representations with a double content.[69] Intelligible species originally are sensory representations of individual objects, but in virtue of the intellect's discursive activity they acquire a supplementary function as indirect vehicles of universal contents (essences) that they do not resemble in any way. Ultimately, Pomponazzi's radical hylomorphism in psychology promotes an innovative and no less radical account of intentionality.

4 Moderate views on representationalism in late Aristotelianism: Zabarella and Suárez

Pomponazzi's naturalistic approach to the human mind emphasises the intellect's efficient-causal dependence on representations of the inner senses. As a result, the mind's activity appears to be determined by bodily processes, just like the activity of any other material form. Later Renaissance Aristotelians equally inspired by Alexander, such as Simone Porzio (1496–1554) and Giulio Castellani (1528–1586), accepted this radical consequence.[70] With regard to intentionality, however, it appears questionable whether Pomponazzi can persuasively account for the discursive nature of intellectual representations (a central claim in his epistemology, as we have seen) by appealing to an essentially passive intellect. His picture of the mind seems to leave no room for active mental functions such as judging and reasoning.

Scholastic Aristotelians committed to the Christian doctrine obviously rejected Pomponazzi's naturalism.[71] Yet, his approach to the mind also found opponents among 16th-century professors of natural philosophy who still preferred Averroes's teaching over Alexander's. Authors such as Marcantonio Genua (1490/91–1563) and Francesco Piccolomini (1523–1607) even reshaped

Averroism in order to preserve the efficient-causal autonomy of the intellect. Following the newly available *De anima* commentary of the Neo-Platonist philosopher Simplicius (ca 490–ca 560), they assumed a universal *parallelism* between sensory and intellectual cognition. According to this view, whenever phantasms are supplied by the senses, the agent intellect autonomously makes the corresponding intellectual contents available to the receptive intellect; in turn, whenever the agent intellect spontaneously elicits acts of intellection in the receptive intellect, the inner senses themselves provide the corresponding images.[72] On this view, intentionality is not the result of a causal interaction between faculties, but rests on the basic fact that acts of intellection harmonise with acts of imagination.

Despite rejecting Averroism, Jacopo Zabarella (1533–1589), a professor of philosophy in Padua, was apparently reluctant to follow Pomponazzi's naturalism without restrictions. Influenced by Alexander, Zabarella embraced radical hylomorphism. According to him, the subject matter of psychology is the "ensouled body", and the soul is to be considered the "principle" of all vital (and cognitive) activities as it is the form and "nature" of the body.[73] The "rational soul" is no exception; the human intellect is the principle of universal cognition not as a separate entity, but as the form of the human body.[74] However, Zabarella did not conceive of the intellect as merely passive, and in this he showed a better understanding of Alexander's psychology than Pomponazzi.

His investigation of the human intellect in his treatises on natural philosophy (*De rebus naturalibus*) rests on the assumption that "[t]he soul is a principle in a double way: of the ensouled body as form, and of its functions as efficient cause".[75] Accordingly, cognitive acts cannot merely be considered as actualisations of passive bodily dispositions, but also as genuine activities arising from the soul as efficient cause. Zabarella takes the soul to play its efficient-causal role not directly, but through faculties. These are "aptitudes" for performing specific vital functions; they "emanate" from the soul, but reside in the body as "qualities" of its organs. As such, faculties are "conditions" under which the soul is able to unfold its efficient causality in union with the body.[76] With this conception Zabarella attempts to tie vital functions (in particular, cognitive acts) to a spontaneous activity of the soul, without trading hylomorphism for Neo-Platonic or Augustinian psychology; the subject of the vital functions is not the soul, but the living body in virtue of the soul's formal and efficient causality as specified through its faculties.[77]

To be sure, the intellect is a special faculty of the soul. Following tradition, Zabarella denies that the receptive intellect may reside in a bodily organ, since this would prevent it from grasping objects of any kind. Instead, the intellect must reside in the whole body (as its whole form) and be the immediate subject of the affections that trigger its acts of intellection.[78] What affects the receptive intellect, however, are not intelligible species (as in Aquinas's account of intentionality), but phantasms (as in Pomponazzi's or Jandun's), and the resulting affection are "impressed intelligible species".[79]

Yet, a decisive feature of Zabarella's account of intentionality is the claim that impressed intelligible species are not merely affections, but also acts of the receptive intellect:

> An intelligible species is called "intellection" as it is not only received, but simultaneously also judged, so that a received and judged species is the same as an intellection. The phantasm does not contribute to judging the species, but only to impressing it . . . with regard to the judgment the intellect's nature itself is the active principle of intellection.[80]

As a result, impressed species display a twofold structure as bearers of intentionality: on the one hand, they are likenesses of the objects to be grasped and thus representations of them; on the other hand, they are themselves cognitive acts (of judgments) about these objects. On account of this twofold structure, impressed species are responsible for the receptive intellect assimilating to its objects – a process Zabarella describes as "absorption" (*imbibitio*) of the objects into the intellect.[81]

What the intellect thereby assimilates to are not the phantasms that elicit its cognitive acts. For Zabarella, acts of intellection ultimately grasp the universal essences of the things represented by phantasms.[82] Accordingly, they are not simply acts of judgment, but also acts of abstraction. Following Alexander instead of Aquinas, Zabarella denies abstraction to be a function of the agent intellect; it is rather the receptive intellect that, once affected by phantasms, turns them into adequate representations, or likenesses, of universal essences.[83] Its autonomous capacity for performing acts of abstraction is thus a necessary condition of the intentionality of intellectual cognition.

Thanks to his conception of the soul's causality Zabarella can provide a more convincing account of the intentionality of intellectual cognition than Pomponazzi; in particular, he is in a better position for construing intellectual representations as acts of judgment in which universals are apprehended by means of phantasms. What is more, Zabarella avoids indirect realism. For although he agrees with Pomponazzi that the intentionality of acts of intellection depends on phantasms in both causality and content, he denies that phantasms are the immediate objects of intellectual cognition.

Note however that Zabarella's restoration of FAA and of direct realism is only to be had at the price of emphasising the role of the agent intellect, which he – again in line with Alexander – describes as a supra-individual, divine entity.[84] For only such an entity is supposed to make the intelligible content of phantasms accessible to the receptive intellect and thus immediately available for its acts of abstraction. In the end, the intentionality of intellectual cognition rests on this crucial contribution of the agent intellect.[85] Unfortunately, Zabarella's explanation of how this should work remains fairly obscure. In light of his naturalistic approach to psychology, the activity of the agent intellect must ultimately strike us as a kind of magic.

Late 16th-century Iberian Aristotelians, being mostly theologians (often Jesuits), could not approve of the naturalism of their Italian fellows; their aim was rather, as it had been for many Scholastics in the three centuries prior, to interpret Aristotelian psychology in accordance with Christian faith. But not everybody was willing to simply adopt Aquinas's (or Scotus's) position; some sought for autonomous answers to traditional debates and to new tendencies in Aristotelianism. One of them was Francisco Suárez (1548–1617), a Jesuit, theologian and influential figure in Iberian Scholasticism. His psychology bears some similarity to Zabarella's "moderate" naturalism. But the propensity to emphasise the soul's causal autonomy as a principle of cognition is even stronger in Suárez. With him, Augustinian and Neo-Platonic elements emerge once again in Aristotelian psychology.

In his commentary on *De anima*, Suárez accepts hylomorphism as the ontological framework of psychology. The soul figures as the principle of all vital (and cognitive) functions because it is the substantial form of the living body.[86] Like Zabarella, Suárez holds that the soul gives rise to its functions by means of faculties, or "powers", which inhere in bodily organs but originate from the soul in virtue of its efficient causality.[87] As to the cognitive powers themselves, Suárez assumes that they need to receive intermediary representational entities ("intentional species") in order to perform their acts. He justifies this claim with a typical argument from natural philosophy: unless we take into account "likenesses of the objects through which the objects can be unified with the powers", intentionality becomes inexplicable in all cases in which no immediate union between objects and cognitive powers occurs.[88] Thus, by maintaining that every cognition must be mediated by species, Suárez's account of intentionality remains fully in line with FAA.[89] Yet, because it emphasises the soul's activity and autonomy as a causal principle of acts of cognition, it weakens naturalism in comparison to Zabarella's account. Let me mention two major points on this score.

First, Suárez denies that mere reception of species in the soul's cognitive powers amounts to a proper act of apprehending objects. To be sure, species actualise the potentiality of powers, but a power that is actualised or "informed" by a species has not yet performed any cognitive act. The actualised power is rather an "integral instrument" that the soul, as the principal agent of cognition, uses to actually grasp an object.[90] To elucidate how the soul makes use of this "instrument", Suárez invokes a prominent tenet of Augustinian psychology, according to which it is due to the soul's *attention* that cognitive acts result from the reception of species. On this assumption, he explains why there is no automatism in cognition:

> That the power does not actually understand or cognise everything it has a species of, derives from another reason, namely that the power does not attend to the representation of all species, nor does it always use all of them in a vital way.[91]

By making the soul's attention a necessary condition for the formation of intentional acts, Suárez not only manages to accommodate a central theme of Neo-Platonic psychology within the Aristotelian framework; he also substantiates the idea that the soul is efficient-causally involved in cognition to a far greater extent than in Zabarella's account.

The second point manifests a complementary strategy. Suárez's conception of mental activity in his *De anima* commentary excludes any efficient-causal dependence of the intellect upon the inner senses. Instead, it emphasises the ontological dependence of the cognitive powers upon the soul. Being "rooted" in the same soul, intellect and imagination need not interact with each other to bring about acts of cognition; to the contrary, the soul as their common "root" ensures that they always cooperate in accordance with a certain "order" and "harmony" (*consonantia*).[92] This assumption of a basic parallelism between the operations of the sensory soul and those of the rational soul is directed against naturalistic accounts of intellectual intentionality typical of radical Aristotelianism. On Suárez's view, phantasms are far from being efficient causes of acts of intellection. Rather, the occurrence of a phantasm of O (an individual object) in the inner senses only indirectly prompts the agent intellect (as a power of the soul) to perform an act of abstraction from which an immaterial intelligible species representing the individual form of O originates.[93] As Suárez suggests, the phantasm of O is only an occasional cause of such an act or a prototype for its outcome, the intelligible species of O. Once the receptive intellect (a power that is passive and active at the same time) is informed by this species, the soul can perform an autonomous act of intellection by which it apprehends the individual form of O. Yet, the soul can also use the receptive intellect for a second act of abstraction by which it apprehends the form of O as a universal content. To accomplish this, the soul needs to compare similar intelligible species with one another.[94]

In assigning the abstraction of universals to the receptive intellect, Suárez echoes Alexander. Yet by maintaining that the intellect and the inner senses do not interact causally but rather act in a parallel fashion, he takes up a strand that can be traced back to the Italian Averroists influenced by Simplicius.[95] Once again, his conception of the intentionality of intellectual cognition adopts elements of Neo-Platonism within an Aristotelian framework of hylomorphism. This eclectic account enables Suárez to maintain central tenets of Aquinas's conception of intentionality, such as FAA and intelligible species, without jeopardising the mind's efficient-causal autonomy. Furthermore, it allows him to argue against indirect realism more persuasively than the radical Aristotelians, who stressed the intellect's efficient-causal dependence upon phantasms. Since according to Suárez intellectual representations are autonomously produced by the intellect in virtue of its "harmonious" coordination with the inner senses, phantasms do not even figure as efficient-causal, let alone epistemic, intermediaries of intellectual cognition.[96]

5 Conclusion

Between 1300 and 1600, the scholastic-Aristotelian debate on the intentionality of intellectual cognition reveals a range of constants. General ontological assumptions about the soul's nature determine to what extent representations (intelligible species or phantasms) are considered necessary for an account of the intentionality of intellectual cognition. Authors hostile to the idea of entities that mediate between cognitive acts and objects ascribe an irreducible intentional activity to the soul by reinterpreting Aristotelian vocabulary in line with Augustinian (or Neo-Platonic) psychology. Ockham is an eloquent example of this attitude. But his uncompromising rejection of species remains rather isolated, and other opponents of Aquinas's conception of intentionality (such as Gregory of Rimini) accept representations in their accounts of abstractive cognition. However, even within this Augustinian camp of scholastic Aristotelianism the vocabulary of FAA is usually preserved. In fact, the bone of contention turns out to be not FAA but the psychological mechanism employed in the traditional conception to explain assimilation. For this mechanism appears to clash with the picture of an active mind advocated by these authors, who are often theologians.

By contrast, scholastic Aristotelians who regard psychology as a part of natural philosophy usually insist on considering representations as necessary conditions for explaining the "union" between objects and intellect. This attitude, however, does not entail a mere restoration of Aquinas's account. The tendency emerging in this camp is rather to interpret sensory representations (phantasms) as the actual vehicles of intellectual cognition, whereas intelligible species are understood as mental acts in which phantasms are processed in order to represent intelligible objects. Pomponazzi draws radical consequences from this view; insisting on the intellect's efficient-causal dependence on phantasms, he rejects both the tenet of the intellect's immateriality and FAA, thus taking refuge in indirect realism to explain the intentionality of intellectual cognition. But Pomponazzi, too, remains an exception. Even a radical Aristotelian such as Zabarella conceives of intentionality in accordance with FAA and direct realism. To this end, he partially reframes hylomorphism in that he takes the soul to be the principle of cognitive acts as both a formal and efficient cause and emphasises the role of the agent intellect. This tendency is further strengthened by Suárez. In order to preserve the soul's efficient-causal autonomy and FAA, Suárez implements elements of Neo-Platonic psychology in his "species-friendly" account of intentionality.

Ultimately, the scholastic-Aristotelian debate on intentionality proves to be mainly a discussion about the psychological conditions of intellectual cognition. FAA is seldom challenged, whereas a different understanding of intentionality emerges only episodically, when the ontological presuppositions underlying Aristotelian psychology are questioned (for example, when Pomponazzi questions the intellect's immateriality). In fact, abandoning FAA would not become a generally acceptable philosophical option until the 17th century, once its hylomorphistic presuppositions had been rejected.

Notes

1 On the "history" of this concept see Crane 1998.
2 For accounts of sense perception see Chapter 8 of this volume.
3 See the Introduction and Chapter 1 of this volume.
4 On developments in epistemology in our period of interest see Popkin 1988.
5 Often referred to as the "standard" or "traditional" account of intentionality in the Middle Ages: see e.g. King (1994: 110); Spruit (1994: 24); Pasnau (1997: 11–12); Perler (2002: 31–32).
6 Main source is Aristotle, *DA* III.8 (431b21–432a5).
7 For an outline of Aristotelian hylomorphism see Introduction, section 1.
8 *DA* II.12, 424a17–24. Here Aristotle addresses sense perception.
9 With regard to Aquinas, see Pasnau (1997: 31–41); Perler (2002: 33–42).
10 For details see Pasnau (1997: 195–209); Perler (2002: 61–89). On Aquinas's psychology: Pasnau (2002: 143–170).
11 *STh* I.II, q. 22, art. 2, corp.
12 See e.g. *STh* I, q. 14, art. 2, corp.
13 Aquinas weakens his naturalism in psychology (a) by regarding the receptive intellect as an *immaterial* faculty and (b) by taking into account a spontaneously active "agent intellect" in addition. See below.
14 On Aquinas's account of change see Schmid (2011: 38–46).
15 *STh* I, q. 56, art. 3, corp. Aquinas's distinction is actually a tricotomy. I am simplifying.
16 See *STh* I, q. 84–85.
17 For Aquinas, universal forms only exist (individualised) in material things. See *STh* I, q. 86, art. 1, corp.
18 *STh* I, q. 85, art. 2. – By contrast, Aquinas takes intellectual cognition of individuals to be necessarily indirect, as based on reflections about phantasms. See *ibid.*, q. 84, art. 8, corp.
19 On Siger see Bazán (1981: 439–436). Averroistic psychology is addressed below, section 2.
20 About the "Augustinian-Aristotelian synthesis" in the late 13th century see Kuksewicz 1982.
21 On Henry see Pickavé 2015. On Olivi see Pasnau (1997: 67–69, 168–181); Perler (2002: 109–127).
22 Perler (2002: 186). On Scotus and Henry see Dumont 1998.
23 *Quodl.* VI (243b-244a). For orientation see Pasnau (2006: 296–300).
24 See Scotus, *Quodl.* XIII (521a–522b). On Aquinas's dichotomy see section 1 in this chapter.
25 *Ordin.* I, appendix A, n. 217.
26 For an overview and discussion see Perler (2002: 217–320). On Scotus's theory of cognition see Cross 2014.
27 On Auriol's representationalism see Tachau (1988: 85–112).
28 *Report.* II, q. 12–13 (256.5–9; my emphasis).
29 See *Report.* II, q. 12–13 (256–261). On Ockham's distinction between intuitive and abstractive cognition see Perler (2002: 342–360); Stump (1999: 181–188).
30 *Report.* II, q. 12–13 (268.2–4).
31 See *Report.* II, q. 12–13 (272–276) and as commentary Panaccio (2004: 27–31). On cognition by means of habits see Adams (1987: 515–525).
32 For textual evidence see below, footnote 39.
33 On Ockham's nominalism see Adams (1987: 13–69).
34 *Report.* II, q. 12–13 (284.1–5). This is an inversion of Aquinas's view; see above, footnote 18.
35 *Report.* II, q. 12–13 (304–24–305.1).
36 See *Ordin.* I, dist. 2, q. 8 (289–292). On concept formation and knowledge of universals in Ockham see Pasnau (1997: 76–85); Panaccio (2004: 23–27).

37 *Report.* II, q. 20 (442.23–443.3). On the ontological status of the rational soul in Ockham see above, Introduction, section 1.
38 *Report.* II, q. 12–13 (307.7–9). The intellect's active function in Ockham's later account of universal cognition is less clear.
39 *Report.* II, q. 12–13 (307.4–7; my emphasis).
40 *Report.* II, q. 12–13 (268.9–10).
41 *Report.* II, q. 12–13 (309.4–13).
42 Ockham discusses Auriol's position in *Ordin.* I, dist. 27, q. 3 (238–258).
43 See e.g. *Report.* II, q. 12–13 (276.13–19); a list of further occurrences in Perler (2002: 370). The question is extensively discussed in Panaccio (2004: 119–143); Adams (1987: 121–133). According to King (2005: 98), Ockham's claim that the act of intellection is a "likeness" of the object is an "empty formula".
44 *Report.* II, q. 12–13 (295.13–296.1).
45 For this reason Perler (2002: 371) prefers to speak of a vague "isomorphism" (instead of formal identity) in Ockham's account of intentionality. For a different approach see Panaccio (2004: 123–125). For a more optimistic interpretation of "similarity" in Ockham's theory of intuitive cognition see Brower-Toland 2007.
46 See e.g. Aquinas, *STh* I, q. 4, art. 3, corp.
47 On the reception of Ockham in England see Tachau (1988: 157–312).
48 On representations in Buridan, Gregory and Ailly see Spruit (1994: 301–305, 309–318, 354–357).
49 See *Lect.*, dist. 3, q. 3 (389.27–31).
50 See *Lect.*, dist. 3, q. 3 (391.11–17, 392.32–34).
51 See *Lect.*, dist. 3, q. 1 (358.28–30).
52 See *Lect.*, dist. 3, q. 1 (358.30–32, 362.20–35); q. 3 (396.20–23).
53 For details on Averroism see Chapter 4 of this volume.
54 See *SDA* III, q. 17 (308–311). On Jandun's epistemology see Brenet 2003.
55 Jandun explains how the inner senses cooperate to engender intelligible species in the receptive intellect in *SDA* III, q. 15–16 (304–307). On the agent intellect see *ibid.*, q. 23 (351).
56 Actually, Jandun does not exclude this possibility; see *SDA* III, q. 24 (359–361). See also below and Chapter 8 of this volume.
57 See *STh* I, q. 85, art. 1, ad 3.
58 On the development of Aristotelianism in Italy up to the 17th century see Poppi 1991 and Iorio 1991; with particular regard to theories of intellect, Kuksewicz (1968: 315–406); Kessler (1988: 488–500).
59 See Introduction, section 2.
60 On Nifo's position see Spruit (1995: 76–84).
61 For Pomponazzi's "rehabilitation" of intelligible species and the subsequent debate see Poppi (1970: 142–160).
62 On this translation see Introduction, section 2, and for Pomponazzi's reception of Alexander, see Kessler (2011: 57–66).
63 Pomponazzi's views on the intellect are expressed in *Immort.*, c. 9. For his refutation of Averroes's and Aquinas's accounts see *ibid.*, c. 4 and 8. Overview in Kessler (1988: 500–504).
64 *Immort.*, c. 9 (291; translation modified). References to Aristotle, *DA* III.4, 429a13–18; III.7, 431a14–15; 431b2–5.
65 Alexander rather emphasises the autonomy of the intellect as the cause of its acts. See *Anima* (85.23–86.3).
66 *Immort.*, c. 9 (327).
67 *Immort.*, c. 9 (319).
68 *Immort.*, c. 12 (340). On Pomponazzi's account of intentionality see Rubini (2015: 257–279).

69 *Immort.*, c. 10 (332–333); c. 12 (344).
70 See Kessler (1988: 519–523).
71 Their reaction led to the controversy on immortality in the 16th century. See Chapter 11 of this volume.
72 See Kessler (1988: 523–530); Spruit (1995: 164–173, 238–245).
73 *DNS*, c. 38 (119A-B).
74 See *DMH*, c. 7 (931–938). On Zabarella's theory of the intellect see Poppi (1972: 35–63); Kessler (1988: 530–534).
75 *DMH*, c. 1 (916A). On Alexander as a source for Zabarella's psychology see Kessler (2011: 50–56).
76 *DFA*, c. 4 (690E-F, 693B); c. 9 (706D-E). Zabarella's views on the soul's faculties are examined in Perler (2013: 290–293).
77 See e.g. *DSA*, c. 10 (854C-D).
78 See *DMH*, c. 13 (973B-974B).
79 See *DSI*, c. 5 (987B-988F). On Zabarella's account of intelligible species see Spruit (1995: 225–236).
80 *DSI*, c. 7 (999D-E). See *DSI*, 5 (989A-D).
81 See *DSI*, c. 5 (988B-C).
82 See *DSI*, c. 13 (972F-973).
83 See *DMA*, c. 6 (1016F-1017E). See also Alexander, *Anima* (83.2–84.14; 85.11–86.4; 87.11–18).
84 See *DMA*, c. 13 (1030F-1031E). For Alexander's view on the agent intellect see *Anima* (88.23–89.21).
85 See *DMA*, c. 6 (1017E-1018B).
86 See *IDA*, disp. 1, q. 1, n. 7–8.
87 See *IDA*, disp. 3, q. 3, n. 7. However, Suárez takes the intellect not to inhere in the body, but in the soul itself; see *ibid.*, n. 4.
88 *IDA*, disp. 5, q. 1, n. 3 (II: 286.52–53). On species as "instruments" that unify objects and powers see *ibid.*, q. 2, n. 1.
89 *IDA*, disp. 5, q. 2, n. 21 (II: 322.385–358). For Suárez views on intelligible species see Spruit (1995: 294–306).
90 *IDA*, disp. 5, q. 4, n. 16 (II: 366.252–256).
91 *IDA*, disp. 5, q. 2, n. 3 (II: 300.48–51).
92 *IDA*, disp. 9, q. 2, n. 12 (III: 96.528–537); q. 7, n. 6 (III: 202.1961–1966).
93 On the agent intellect see *IDA*, disp. 9, q. 2, n. 14–16. Its distinction from the receptive intellect is examined *ibid.*, q. 8.
94 See *IDA*, disp. 9, q. 3, n. 13 (III: 126–128). Ockham similarly distinguished two levels of abstraction. See above, section 2. On Suárez's account of knowledge of universals see Åkerlund (2009: 169–174); South (2002: 809–822).
95 Kessler (1988: 515–516) notes this similarity. A broader picture of Suárez's sources (with more emphasis on the Scotistic tradition) is to be found in Tropia 2014. For a causal analysis of the idea of parallelism ("sympathy") in Suárez's psychology see Knuuttila 2014.
96 See *IDA*, disp. 9, q. 7, n. 6.

Bibliography

Primary sources

Alexander of Aphrodisias. *De anima* (= *Anima*). In *Commentaria in Aristotelem Graeca. Supplementum Aristotelicum*, vol. II.1, I. Bruns (ed.), 1–100. Berlin: Reimer, 1887.

Aristotle. *De anima* (= *DA*). W. D. Ross (ed.). Oxford: Clarendon, 1961.
Gregory of Rimini. *Lectura super primum et secundum Sententiarum*, vol. I (= *Lect.* I). D. Trapp & V. Marcolino (eds). Berlin: De Gruyter, 1981.
John Duns Scotus. *Quaestiones quodlibetales* I–XIII (= *Quodl.*). In *Opera omnia: Editio nova iuxta editionem Waddingi*, vol. XXV. Paris: Vivès, 1895.
———. *Ordinatio. Liber primus. Distinctio tertia* (= *Ordin.* I, dist. 3). In *Opera omnia. Editio Vaticana*, vol. III, Vatican City, Typis Polyglottis Vaticanis, 1954.
John of Jandun. *Super libros Aristotelis De anima* (= *SDA*). Venice: Haeredes Hieronymi Scoti, 1587.
Pomponazzi, Pietro. *On the Immortality of the Soul* (= *Immort.*). W. H. Hay II & J. H. Randall Jr. (trans.). In *The Renaissance Philosophy of Man*, E. Cassirer, P. O. Kristeller, J. H. Randall Jr. (eds), 280–381. Chicago: CUP, 1948. Original edition: *De immortalitate animae*. Bologna, 1516.
Suárez, Francisco. *Commentaria una cum quaestionibus in libros Aristotelis De anima* (= *IDA*), 3 vols. S. Castellote (ed.). Madrid, Editorial Labor, 1978–1991.
Thomas Aquinas. *Summa theologiae* (= *STh*), 3 vols. P. Caramello (ed.). Turin-Rome: Marietti, 1952–1956.
William of Ockham. *Scriptum in librum primum Sententiarum. Ordinatio* (= *Ordin.* I). In *Opera theologica*, vol. II, S. Brown & G. Gál (eds). St Bonaventure: Franciscan Institute, 1970.
———. *Quaestiones in librum secundum Sententiarum. Reportatio* (= *Report.* II). In *Opera theologica*, vol. V, G. Gál & R. Wood (eds). St Bonaventure: Franciscan Institute, 1981.
Zabarella, Jacopo. *De facultatibus animae* (= *DFA*). In *De rebus naturalibus*, 683–728. Frankfurt: Zetzner, 1617.
———. *De mente agente* (= *DMA*). In *De rebus naturalibus*, 1007–1042.
———. *De mente humana* (= *DMH*). In *De rebus naturalibus*, 915–978.
———. *De naturalis scientiae consitutione* (= *DNS*). In *De rebus naturalibus*, 1–134.
———. *De sensu agente* (= *DSA*). In *De rebus naturalibus*, 831–856.
———. *De speciebus intelligibilibus* (= *DSI*). In *De rebus naturalibus*, 979–1006.

Secondary sources

Adams, M. McCord. 1987. *William Ockham*, 2 vols. Notre Dame: University of Notre Dame Press.
Åkerlund, E. 2009. "Suárez on Forms, Universals and Understanding". *Studia Neoaristotelica* **6**: 159–182.
Bazán, B. C. 1981. "*Intellectum Speculativum:* Averroes, Thomas Aquinas and Siger of Brabant on the Intelligible Object". *Journal of the History of Philosophy* **19**: 425–446.
Brower-Toland, S. 2007. "Intuition, Externalism, and Direct Reference in Ockham". *History of Philosophy Quarterly* **24**: 317–336.
Brenet, J.-B. 2003. *Transferts du sujet. La noétique d'Averroès selon Jean de Jandun*. Paris: Vrin.
Crane, T. 1998. "Intentionality". In *Routledge Encyclopaedia of Philosophy*, E. Craig (ed.), vol. IV, 816a–821b. London: Routledge.
Cross, R. 2014. *Duns Scotus's Theory of Cognition*. Oxford: OUP.
Dumont, S. 1998. "Henry of Ghent and Duns Scotus". In *Medieval Philosophy*, J. Marenbon (ed.), 291–328. London: Routledge.

Iorio, D. 1991. *The Aristotelians of Renaissance Italy: A Philosophical Exposition*. Lewiston: Edwin Mellen Press.

Kessler, E. 1988. "The Intellective Soul". In *The Cambridge History of Renaissance Philosophy*, Ch. Schmitt et al. (eds), 485–534. Cambridge: CUP.

———. 2011. *Alexander of Aphrodisias and His Doctrine of the Soul: 1400 Years of Lasting Significance*. Leiden: Brill.

King, P. 1994. "Scholasticism and the Philosophy of Mind: The Failure of Aristotelian Psychology". In *Scientific Failure*, T. Horowitz & A. I. Janis (eds), 109–138. Lanham: Rowman & Littlefield.

———. 2005. "Rethinking Representation in the Middle Ages: A Vade-Mecum to Medieval Theories of Mental Representation". In *Representation and Objects of Thought in Medieval Philosophy*, H. Lagerlund (ed.), 81–100. Aldershot: Ashgate.

Knuuttila, S. 2014. "The Connexions between Vital Acts in Suárez's Psychology". In *Suárez's Metaphysics in its Historical and Systematic Context*, L. Novák (ed.), 259–274. Berlin: De Gruyter.

Kuksewicz, Z. 1968. *De Siger de Brabant à Jaques de Plaisance. La théorie de l'intellect chez les averroïstes latins des XIIIe et XIVe siècles*. Wrocław: Ossolineum.

———. 1982. "Criticisms of Aristotelian Psychology and the Augustinian-Aristotelian Synthesis". In *The Cambridge History of Later Medieval Philosophy*, N. Kretzmann et al. (eds), 623–628. Cambridge: CUP.

Panaccio, C. 2004. *Ockham on Concepts*. Aldershot: Ashgate.

Pasnau, R. 1997. *Theories of Cognition in the Later Middle Ages*. Cambridge: CUP.

———. 2002. *Thomas Aquinas on Human Nature: A Philosophical Study of 'Summa theologiae' I^a 75–89*. Cambridge: CUP.

———. 2006. "Cognition". In *The Cambridge Companion to Duns Scotus*, T. Williams (ed.), 285–311. Cambridge: CUP.

Perler, D. 2002. *Theorien der Intentionalität im Mittelalter*. Frankfurt: Klostermann.

———. 2013. "How Many Souls Do I Have? Late Aristotelian Debates on the Plurality of Faculties". In *Medieval Perspectives on Aristotle's 'De anima'*, R. Friedman & J.-M. Counet (eds), 277–296. Leuven: Peeters.

Pickavé, M. 2015. "Causality and Cognition: Henry of Ghent's Quodlibet V, q. 14". In *Intentionality, Cognition, and Mental Representation in Medieval Philosophy*, G. Klima (ed.), 46–80. New York: Fordham UP.

Popkin, R. 1988. "Theories of Knowledge". In *The Cambridge History of Renaissance Philosophy*, Ch. Schmitt et al. (eds), 668–684. Cambridge: CUP.

Poppi, A. 1970. *Saggi sul pensiero inedito di Pietro Pomponazzi*. Padua: Antenore.

———. 1972. *La dottrina della scienza in Giacomo Zabarella*. Padua: Antenore.

———. 1991. *Introduzione all'aristotelismo padovano*. Padua: Antenore.

Rubini, P. 2015. *Pietro Pomponazzis Erkenntnistheorie: Naturalisierung des menschlichen Geistes im Spätaristotelismus*. Leiden: Brill.

Schmid, S. 2011. *Finalursachen in der frühen Neuzeit: Eine Untersuchung der Transformation teleologischer Erklärungen*. Berlin: De Gruyter.

South, J. 2002. "Singular and Universal in Suárez's Account of Cognition". *The Review of Metaphysics* 55: 785–823.

Spruit, L. 1994. *Species Intelligibilis: From Perception to Knowledge*, vol. I. Leiden: Brill.

———. 1995. *Species Intelligibilis: From Perception to Knowledge*, vol. II. Leiden: Brill.

Stump, E. 1999. "The Mechanism of Cognition: Ockham on Mediating Species". In *The Cambridge Companion to Ockham*, P. V. Spade (ed.), 168–203. Cambridge: CUP.
Tachau, K. 1988. *Vision and Certitude in the Age of Ockham: Optiks, Epistemology and the Foundation of Semantics*. Leiden: Brill.
Tropia, A. 2014. "Scotus and Suárez on Sympathy. The Necessity of the Connexio Potentiarum in the Present State". In *Suárez's Metaphysics in its Historical and Systematic Context*, L. Novák (ed.), 275–292. Berlin: De Gruyter.

6

LATE MEDIEVAL THEORIES OF (SELF-)CONSCIOUSNESS

Sonja Schierbaum

1 Introduction

The growing number of publications on medieval accounts of consciousness, including self-consciousness, indicates that more and more scholars do not question whether a substantial discussion of the problem of consciousness took place in the later middle ages, but rather assume that it did.[1] This assumption, of course, needs further qualification. As in contemporary debates, there is not just *the* problem of consciousness but, rather, a whole bundle of interrelated problems.[2]

If one accepts the widespread contemporary view that questions concerning the explanation of various cognitive functions, such as discriminatory abilities or the capacity for focusing attention, constitute at least part of the problem of consciousness, then this supports the view that at least in this sense there *is* a substantial medieval discussion of the problem of consciousness,[3] despite the fact that medieval authors do not use the term or any of its Latin correlates.[4] For instance, they attempt to account for the phenomenon of distracted attention by taking their cue from Augustine's famous remark in *De trinitate* about distinct but simultaneous mental acts or states (e.g., of seeing and hearing).[5] The authors thereby take as paradigmatic (if only implicitly) the case in which a cognitive state, e.g., of perceiving a thing, yields the subject's being (perceptually) aware or conscious *of* that thing.[6]

As regards *self*-consciousness, medieval authors clearly distinguish between being conscious of one's "self", that is, of one's soul in the Aristotelian sense, and being conscious of one's own mental acts.[7] Once again, they do not use the term "conscious" in this context but cast the discussion in terms of perceiving and cognizing. Roughly speaking, authors with a strong Aristotelian background tend to restrict cognitive access and hence the possibility of self-consciousness to one's acts, whereas authors with a strong Neo-Platonic or Augustinian background also tend to admit the possibility of cognitive access to one's own soul as an immaterial substance.[8]

In this chapter, I present three authors in the Aristotelian tradition. One reason for this choice is that, in contemporary debates, especially in analytically trained quarters, there is little or no interest in the problem of having cognitive access to and hence of being conscious of any "self" as an ontologically distinct thing.[9] The problem discussed by Ockham and Chatton in the fourteenth century and Suárez in the sixteenth will sound familiar to these readers, at least in the way I am going to present it.

In my presentation, I rely on Dretske's distinction between object-awareness and fact-awareness.[10] For instance, if Peter is aware of a cat because he sees it, then Peter has object-awareness of it. And if Peter is aware that there is a cat, then he has fact-awareness that there is a cat. Both object-awareness of external things and fact-awareness involving external things, but not mental acts, require only first-order states. I further distinguish objectual act-awareness as a higher-order object-awareness of an act. Accordingly, if Peter is aware of seeing a cat, then he has objectual act-awareness of seeing a cat. Lastly, if Peter is aware that he is seeing a cat, then I shall say that he has propositional self-awareness.[11] We can distinguish two non-propositional (i–ii) and two propositional (iii–iv) cases:

(i)   S is aware of an object o.
(ii) S is aware of being aware of o.
(iii) S is aware that o exists.
(iv) S is aware that she is aware of o.

Now the dispute between Ockham and Chatton in this matter turns on the following question: How does propositional self-awareness (iv) come about? Their approaches roughly correspond to those presented by same-order and higher-order theories. On the one hand, Ockham accounts for propositional self-awareness (iv) in terms of objectual act-awareness (ii), just as modern higher-order theorists account for a mental state's being conscious in terms of a higher-order act taking the state as its object; one becomes aware *that* one is seeing by being aware *of* the state of seeing (as an object).[12] On the other hand Chatton outright rejects Ockham's conception of an objectual act-awareness. He attempts to account for propositional self-awareness in terms of a same-order act-awareness related to one's first-order acts.[13] In short, Ockham thinks that (iv) requires both (i) and (ii), whereas Chatton denies the need for positing (ii).

In the discussion of these two approaches that I take to be representative of the late fourteenth century, I lay special emphasis on the central role assigned to *attention* in the respective accounts of self-consciousness. My assumption is that, according to the medieval authors, the scope of self-consciousness is limited by the scope of attention.[14]

Neither Ockham nor Chatton, however, made an attempt to locate and categorize attention itself within the overall cognitive system (the soul). For this reason, I finally turn to Suárez, who made a serious attempt to do so. I begin with Ockham's approach to self-consciousness.

2 (Self-)consciousness according to Ockham

What does it mean that Ockham (1287–1349) accounts for propositional self-awareness (iv) in terms of objectual act-awareness (ii)? In Ockham's terms, an intellectual higher-order act can provide objectual act-awareness of one's act as it occurs. Being a higher-order act, it is directed at a first-order act as its object, and it belongs to a class of cognitive acts that Ockham calls acts of "intuition". And if one has objectual act-awareness of one's act, one can become aware that one's act is occurring by judging that it is occurring. Ockham calls this act of judging "evident".

In his early *Ordinatio*, Ockham first presents intuition with respect to external particulars. In a corollary he also argues for the possibility of intuiting one's acts.[15] Ockham writes:

> [T]he intuitive cognition of a thing is the sort of a cognition by virtue of which it can be known whether a thing exists or not, such that if the thing exists, the intellect judges immediately that it exists and evidently recognizes that it exists.[16]

What does it mean that this intuition-based judgement is *evident*? By definition, if a judgement is *evident*, then what is judged is true. Also, Ockham states that "the intellect judges immediately (*statim*)". A subject cannot *merely* entertain the thought that a thing exists if he intuits the thing in question. Intuition-based thoughts leave no room for lack of truth commitment.[17] In Ockham's view, the subject cannot seriously doubt whether a thing *a* exists or not while intuiting it because the intuition of *a* includes a causal relation to *a* such that this relation would not obtain if *a* did not exist.[18] Acts of intuition are individuated by their (existing) object. As Ockham states in an often-quoted passage in the *Quodlibeta*:

> [intuitive cognition] is proper to particulars ... because it is immediately caused by a particular thing or is apt to be caused, and cannot be caused by another thing.[19]

This causal relation to its object provides intuitive cognition with the reliability needed to adequately fulfil its role of producing evident acts of judgement.[20] Ockham names contingent propositions of the form

(I) *a exists*

"first contingent propositions".[21] Now in his *Quodlibeta*, he also distinguishes a strictly analogous case of such a "first contingent proposition" concerning mental acts. He states:

> regarding the cognition of the intellect and volition a first contingent proposition can be formed which is evidently cognized by the intellect,

such as 'an act of the intellect exists' (*intellectio est*), 'an act of the will exists' *(volitio est)*.[22]

This kind of proposition about mental acts has the very same form as the kind of "first" proposition about external things, namely: *a exists*. Ockham argues that it is possible to know evidently that an act is occurring because it is possible to intuit the act. Existential present-tense thoughts about external things and thoughts about acts are structurally alike, except that in the case of the mental act it is the intuiting of the *act* in question that enables the subject to judge evidently about the act's existence. For instance, if Peter is seeing a dog, then his judgement about the existence of the act of seeing is correct due to the intuition of his seeing. Ockham calls intuitive acts of external things "direct" acts and intuitive acts of one's other mental acts "reflexive".[23] Direct acts are first-order acts, whereas reflexive acts are second-order acts. The latter are individuated causally by their objects, just as the former are individuated causally by their (external) objects. As Ockham states, this kind of assent to thoughts about one's act of seeing, for instance, is "caused by the intuition of that vision".[24] That is, the reflexive intuition of an act (partially) causes the act of assent, just as the intuition of an external thing does in the analogous case. I say "(partial) cause" here because a reflexive act of intuition is only necessary, but not sufficient for an ensuing act of evident judgement, just as the intuition of a particular thing *a* is only necessary for an act of judging evidently that *a* exists; what is further required is the forming of the thought in question.[25]

It seems odd that the subject should merely judge from a third-person perspective (e.g., "the act is occurring"), but not from a first-person perspective (e.g., "I am seeing" or "my act of seeing is occurring"). In the same *Quodlibet*, however, Ockham also speaks of first-person judgements.[26] But how can the intuition of an act give rise to judgements from the third-person as well as from the first-person perspective? Put differently, if objectual act-awareness (by means of reflexive intuition) can also cause awareness that *one* has that act *oneself*, is it not necessary to suppose that reflexive intuition makes one aware of one's act *as* one's own? The strict analogy between direct intuition of external things and reflexive intuition of one's act precludes this possibility, since, analogously, direct intuition does not make one aware of a thing *as* differing from oneself; one becomes aware of that *thing* and nothing else. It does not seem to be part of what one becomes aware *of* by means of an intuition whether the object one is aware of is distinct from oneself or whether it belongs to oneself; there is no mark of "mineness" that one would become aware *of* by means of a reflexive intuition, just as there is no mark of "otherness" that one would become aware *of* by means of a direct intuition.

Again, a direct act of intuition has an external object of which the subject becomes aware by means of the act; analogously, a reflexive act of intuition has a first-order act as an object of which the subject becomes aware by means of the reflexive act. What is further required to become aware that one has a certain cognitive act is the forming of a *first-person* thought. The question then is what enables a subject to correctly and non-arbitrarily ascribe the intuited acts to herself, in view of the fact that direct and reflexive acts are structurally alike.

How can one know then that the act one is aware of by reflexive intuition is in fact *one's own*? First, note that Ockham refers to an act of will to explain the fact that we do not reflect upon our acts *automatically*, but only by voluntarily drawing our attention to an act by means of another act.[27] Ockham writes:

> I say that the reflexive act is caused by the direct act as its object and by an act of will by means of which it *wants that act to be understood*. That, however, [the reflexive act] is caused by the direct act is obvious, because it necessarily depends on the direct act, since it can only be caused if the direct act exists. . . . It is obvious, however, that an act of will is required, because someone can understand something and nevertheless not perceive himself to understand, just as someone can see and nevertheless not perceive himself to see. If, however, the reflexive act were to be caused precisely by . . . the direct act, then immediately when it is posited and the direct act obtains, necessarily he would perceive himself to understand immediately, which is against experience.[28]

In his view, we are not automatically aware of our being aware whenever we are aware of something. As Ockham puts it, this is "against experience". By pointing to an act of will as a further necessary condition of reflexive intuition, Ockham also meets the objection of an infinite regress that Chatton takes to be implied by Ockham's conception of reflexive intuition.[29] Ockham clearly denies that we have objectual act-awareness (ii) whenever we have object-awareness (i). He concludes that, put crudely, we only become aware *of* our act if we are *willing* to become aware of it. The degree to which one is focussing on something is the result of one's willing.[30] Reflexive acts of intuition are conceived as acts by means of which one is *focussing* on one's act since reflexive acts are the result of a voluntary shift of one's attention. And this willing is also a rational act, since according to Ockham's Aristotelian psychology, intellect and will are the two powers of the rational soul.[31] But the question still remains how one can know that one is aware of one's *own* act, if it does not carry with it some mark of "mineness".

Suppose Peter is aware of the dog sitting in front of him because he sees it.[32] Peter can only become aware of his *seeing* the dog if he is aware of the *dog*, which implies that he is paying attention to the dog at least to some degree. This might sound trivial. Nevertheless, Ockham admits of cases of distracted attention where several acts of different powers, e.g., of seeing and hearing occur at the same time to the effect that the subject is paying attention *only* to the object of his act of seeing, and not to the object of his hearing, or vice versa.[33] As I take it, Ockham would agree with Dretske that what makes an act *conscious* is not that one is conscious *of* that act (by means of another act), but rather that one becomes conscious of *something* by means of it.[34] In Ockham's picture, one can only become aware of one's act if one is paying attention to the object of that act to a degree that exceeds the degree of not paying attention at all. Every such act is conscious in that it makes one aware *of* something. Therefore, those acts one can become aware *of* are *conscious* acts.[35]

Again, the problem seems to be that the fact that one is directed at one's own act is not part of what one becomes aware of by the reflexive act, since the latter has only a specific mental act as its object. It is, however, no arbitrary fact that one can shift one's attention from an external object *to* the act by means of which one is aware of the object if the act in question is *one's own*, that is, if it makes *oneself* aware of the thing. For example, if Peter is not aware of the dog because at least some of his attention is focused on seeing it, then he cannot draw his attention away from the dog to his act of seeing it. Only a conscious act of one's own can become the *object* of awareness in this reflexive way, since if one is not conscious of something by means of some act, one cannot voluntarily shift one's attention away from the thing to the very vehicle of that object-awareness.[36]

Even if one could be aware of the mental acts of *other* persons, there would be no danger of mistaking their acts for one's own.[37] According to Ockham, only one's own acts make one aware of s*omething* (different from the acts), without at the same time making one aware of the acts. In the case of mind-reading, however, the subject becomes aware of the act of another subject *only* in the manner of an object.[38] The act of another person never makes the mind-reading subject *merely* aware of an object without making her aware of the *act* (the vehicle of object-awareness).[39] Thus, if one *reflects* upon an act at all it *is* one's own. Hence, one can come to know in general which acts are one's own, namely those which one can reflect upon by a shift of attention.[40] This is what distinguishes first-person from third-person access: Only the former implies awareness of objects by means of acts which, at least initially, are not the *objects*, but only the *vehicles* of awareness, and which can *become* the objects of awareness by a voluntary shift of attention. Although Ockham's picture appears to leave no room for a sense of "mineness" *vis-à-vis* one's own acts, one can identify one's own acts non-arbitrarily as those acts which make one aware of their objects without making one aware of them without a shift of attention. It is possible to come to know that one can only reflexively grasp one's own acts, although this very fact is not part of what one becomes aware of by any reflexive act. For Ockham, it is not possible to entertain such thoughts without at the same time accepting them as true if one is reflexively intuiting the act in question. The ability to ascribe acts to oneself in this way is by no means without preconditions, since it presupposes some (linguistic) skills, such as the correct use of the first-person pronoun and the possession of concepts concerning, for instance, different kinds of mental acts.

Note that propositional self-awareness in Ockham's picture pertains to the intellectual level insofar as intellectual acts require both objectual act-awareness and the propositional awareness that one's act is occurring. In general, for Ockham awareness *that* one's act is occurring (iv) requires the objectual act-awareness *of* one's act (ii) insofar as the latter partially causes the former. This position is denied by Chatton, whose critique will be the subject of the next section.

3 (Self-)consciousness according to Chatton (including a critique of Ockham's account)

How does propositional self-awareness (iv) come about in Chatton's view? Chatton (c. 1285–1343) agrees with Ockham that one can become (propositionally) aware that one's act is occurring by judging that one's act is occurring. But he denies that this propositional self-awareness (iv) presupposes any objectual act-awareness of one's act as it occurs (ii) as a partial cause.[41] Chatton rejects Ockham's very conception of reflexive intuition, partly because he argues that an infinite regress would result if one assumes that every act is accompanied by a higher-order act in such a way that every act becomes the object of another act – an assumption he incorrectly ascribes to Ockham.[42]

Now Chatton somewhat boldly claims that *if* one happens to entertain a first-person thought about one's act as it occurs then this is sufficient to cause one to accept this thought as true. He writes:

> I say that the soul assents to what is signified by this [proposition] 'I am thinking about [a stone]' without any intuitive act. This is because apart from this proposition 'I am thinking about a stone' which is composed of abstractive cognitions . . . all that is required is that this [non-propositional intellectual act] be received in the mind.[43]

What does it mean that the thought, the "proposition" in Chatton's terms, has as its parts "abstractive" acts of cognition? Intuition is an intellectual cognition of things in their very presence, like perception, whereas abstractive cognition is of absent or even non-existing things, like imagination.[44] For Ockham, intuitive and abstractive cognition of particulars differ insofar as the former can cause evident judgements about a particular in its presence, whereas the latter cannot.[45] On the level of intellectual cognition, Chatton admits only of abstractive cognition. He agrees with Ockham that abstractive cognition is not sufficient to cause one to accept a first-person thought about one's act as true. That is, it is not sufficient to *have* such a first-person thought in order to accept it as true. Otherwise, merely imagining that one is doing something would cause one to accept as true *that* one is doing it.

But what does it mean that if the act about which one *is* entertaining a thought is "received in the mind" then the thought *is* (correctly) accepted as true? Let me stress that Chatton's point against Ockham is that if the "cognition of an act of the intellect" (that is, if the reflexive act directed at a direct act can cause one to accept the first-person thought *T* "I think of *a*" as true, then the direct act must be "all the more" capable of causing one's acceptance of *T*. Speaking in terms of awareness then, one does not become aware *that* one's act is occurring because one has objectual act-awareness *of* one's act, but because there is another kind of awareness related to one's act. At this point, Chatton refers to the "reception" of the act as a condition for a certain kind of awareness, which he introduces by distinguishing it from a first-order object-awareness. He writes:

> I confirm this, because the soul experiences something in a two-fold way: this is because it experiences something as an object, and [on the other hand] it experiences something in the way a living subject experiences its own act; since otherwise, it would go on to infinity, since if [the subject] would experience his act only as an object, there would therefore be another act whose object it is, and he would experience that act. Either, therefore, [he experiences the act] as an act and not as an object, and we have our case, or [he experiences the act] as an object by another act, and like that to infinity.[46]

In a first approximation, one can either (a) "experience" something as *an object* or (b) one can "experience" *one's own act* as a subject.[47] As regards (a), Chatton agrees with Ockham that *object*-awareness is had by means of cognitive acts; a cognitive act makes one aware of its (external) object. Chatton's point is that, if one could only become aware of one's act by means of another act having the former act as its object, then becoming aware of all of one's acts as they occur would imply an infinite series of simultaneously occurring acts. (He implicitly assumes that every act gives rise to another act whose object it is.) Therefore, he admits of the possibility of (b) "experiencing one's *act* as a subject" when it occurs. That is, a cognitive act makes the subject aware of its (external) object and, if such an act occurs, it gives the subject some awareness of itself. According to (b), however, the subject is not aware of this cognitive vehicle as yet another *object*, since this would require another act taking that act as an object. Rather, it seems that, by (b), the awareness of a thing is somehow marked as *one's own awareness*, simply because the act by means of which one becomes aware of the thing is "received" in oneself, and not in any other subject.[48] It is unclear, however, whether the "reception" of the act is supposed to include more than the mere occurrence of the act.[49]

Chatton's general idea seems to be this: If one *is* entertaining a first-person thought about one's act as it occurs, then one accepts this thought as true *because* the act is somehow marked as one's own act, due to its being "received" in oneself. Where Ockham makes it explicit that objectual act-awareness requires one's attention to be focused on one's act, Chatton leaves it open whether in general the mark of "mineness" implies any degree of attention at all.

However, is it not necessary to attend to some degree to one's act in order to readily accept one's thought about it as true? It seems phenomenologically inadequate that one could accept such a thought as true without paying any attention to the act one is judging. As regards the problems related to lack of attention,

Chatton discusses *only* the case where an act occurs without the subject becoming aware *that* it occurs. He writes:

> I confirm this, because someone can cognize a stone, but not form this complex 'I cognize a stone'. And if he does not form this complex ['I am cognizing stone'] (e.g. if he does not entertain this thought), no assent to the thing signified by the complex is caused; and as a consequence, he does not assent *that* he is cognizing [a stone]. And this is because perceiving that he cognizes or assenting that he cognizes [a stone] is an assent caused by the very act of cognizing a stone by means of the forming of the complex (e.g., by means of entertaining this thought).[50]

Chatton here applies his general idea to explain the lack of propositional self-awareness. If an act of, say, thinking about a stone occurs in a subject, but the subject does not form and thus entertain the thought *that* she is thinking about a stone, then she cannot become aware that she is thinking about a stone by accepting this thought as true. In the last two lines, Chatton reformulates again the two necessary conditions that are jointly sufficient for being or becoming aware *that* one's act is occurring, namely (a) the "reception" of an act within a subject together with (b) the subject's forming of a first-person thought about that act. If this account is to have any phenomenological plausibility, it should be able to answer the question how one comes to entertain such a first-person thought, assuming this does not happen at random. I am aiming again at the issue of attention. It is plausible that one would come to entertain thoughts about things one is paying attention to rather than about things one is not paying attention to. One difficulty in Chatton's account is that he remains silent as to *why* one suddenly comes to entertain a first-person thought in one case, but not in the other.

Consider the following example: Suppose that while reading a book Peter hears dogs barking. However, Peter does not pay any attention to the barking. Now, to provide Peter with a reason for entertaining a first-person thought, suppose that Anne asks Peter: "Do you hear those dogs barking?" Now what happens in Peter's cognitive apparatus? Although Chatton does not explicitly discuss such a case, it is plausible that Anne's question might lead Peter to turn his attention to *what* he is hearing. And since he is now focussing on the object of his hearing, it is plausible that the "mineness" of his *hearing* might thereby enter the scope of his attention as well. Chatton might say that the degree of attention one pays to one's *act* as the subject of that act depends on the degree of attention one pays to the *object* of one's act. If Peter now answers that he hears dogs barking, then he can accept the thought he thereby expresses as true because he is aware of his *hearing* the barking as the subject of that act, that is, he is objectually aware of the *barking* with the same degree of attention.

As for Ockham, propositional self-awareness for Chatton pertains to the intellectual level insofar as awareness that one's act is occurring implies the intellectual acts of forming a thought and of judging. For Chatton, it is the "mineness" of one's acts that causes one to accept that one's act is occurring if one entertains the thought that one's act is occurring. At some point, however, Chatton should consider the issue of attention, since it is unclear whether the "reception" of an act includes more than the mere occurrence of it. And its mere occurrence does not explain why one should come to have first-person thoughts about one's act. Chatton might add that one is brought to entertain such thoughts when one's attention is drawn – voluntarily or involuntarily – to an object one is aware of. Since every object-awareness carries the mark of "mineness", it is plausible that focussing on the object of an act might also bring its "mineness" into the scope of attention. For this reason I finally turn to the account of the sixteenth-century philosopher Francisco Suárez, who deals more explicitly with the issue of attention and its scope.

4 (Self-)consciousness according to Suárez: the role of attention

My aim in this section is not to present and discuss Suárez's account of (self-) awareness as a whole.[51] I only want to show that Suárez assigns an explicit role to attention, whereas Chatton, much more than Ockham, fails to realize the explanatory need to posit it within his account.

How does self-awareness come about according to Suárez? Like Ockham and Chatton before him, the Jesuit admits of the possibility of propositional self-awareness (iv): One can become aware that one's act is occurring. Suárez agrees with Ockham that it is by objectual act-awareness (ii) that one becomes aware that one's act is occurring. As Suárez states in his commentary on Aristotle's *De anima*,[52] "when I cognize that I cognize", then my act of cognizing that I am cognizing (say *a*) is a distinct act that is directed at my first-order act of cognizing *a*.[53] This is the "proper way" of cognizing one's own act. From this, Suárez distinguishes a further, "improper" way of cognizing one's act. The distinction divides sensory acts from intellectual ones; only the latter can be cognized in the proper sense. Suárez writes:

> The act of cognition can be cognized in two ways, namely properly in one way, as the object of another act, as when I cognize that I cognize; and then the act which [cognizes] is distinct from the one by means of which it is cognized. In the other way [the act itself] can be cognized in the act that is exercised, so to speak, not by another act, but by the same, as when I see a man. Since this vision is a vital cognitive action, therefore I see that I see in the act that is exercised, as it were, not because I am producing a reflexion, but solely because this change of *the object* happens vitally; and while I am actually seeing, I experience that I am seeing actually, as it were. And this second way is improper, but the first is [most proper].[54]

The problem as regards sensory acts is that it is not possible to account for propositional self-awareness (iv) – perceiving that one is perceiving – in terms of objectual act-awareness (ii) in the proper sense. The reason is that the intellect alone, and not the senses, can produce a reflexive act taking a first-order act of the same power as an object.[55] This is due to the fact that in Suárez's view the intellectual and the sensory soul are distinct entities.

Suárez's general idea is that the occurrence of any perceptual act – and more generally, of any cognitive act[56] – implies a certain degree of attention. Very roughly stated, there can only be cognition where there is attention. He is committed to the view that perception requires the reception of sensible species, just as intellectual cognition requires the reception of intelligible species.[57] The mere reception of such a vehicle of cognition, however, is merely necessary, but not sufficient for an act of cognition to obtain. What is further required is that the subject – "the soul" in Suárez's terms – be somehow attentive to the received species. If it is not, there is only a "dead" reception of the species, just as when "the species is received in the eye, but the man does not see, attending to other things".[58] But when the "soul attends", then "the species is received vitally in the power", and thus, an act of cognition obtains such that the subject cognizes something.

This attention is neither an additional power that is really distinct from the power of the senses or the intellect, nor is it an entity distinct from the soul itself; rather, it is a certain way (*modus*) in which the soul behaves as a whole.[59] It might be helpful to compare this to the ways a system such as a CD player can behave as a whole. Suppose there is a CD in the slot, but the machine is turned off. In this mode, the machine cannot play the music on the CD, even though the CD is in the machine. This mode of the machine bears some similarity to the "dead" reception of a species within a cognitive power. That the music on the CD can be played presupposes that the machine is turned on. The music can only be played in this mode, just as an act of cognition can only be produced if the soul is attentive to the species.[60]

Whereas Ockham remains silent as to *where* to locate attention within the cognitive system and how to classify it, Suárez takes attention to be a way or mode of the cognitive system as a whole and a *precondition* of cognition, and hence, of awareness in general.[61] Furthermore, Ockham views attention, like cognition, as basically intentional; one can draw one's attention to things as *objects* of cognition.[62] It is less clear whether for Suárez, the soul's attention is *only* intentional. In other passages Suárez also talks about the "change of the power", as when he says that "every cognition occurs by vital attention and change of the power".[63] Suárez claims that the attention involved in the production of the act also somehow extends to this very change of the cognitive power, where it seems clear that one does not attend to this change in the way of an object. Therefore, attention might also bear some non-intentional feature. According to Suárez, it is due to this latter aspect that one can be said (if only improperly) to become aware that one is seeing a man when one is seeing a man. As regards sensory (propositional) self-awareness, Suárez's argumentation runs roughly as follows.

(1) An act of perception can only be cognized while it is exercised, and not by a distinct perceptual act, but by itself, because[64] (2) an act of perception is a "vital cognitive action". (3) This means that there is attention involved to some degree which does not merely extend to the object of perception, but also, somehow, to the act of perception itself. For instance, if I am seeing a man, then I do not only attend to the man, but also (somehow) to my act of seeing. (4) Thus when I am seeing a man, I am not only aware of the man, but also, if only *improperly*, aware that I am seeing. What exactly is the aim of the distinction Suárez makes here? Like Ockham before him, Suárez agrees that as regards intellectual acts one can only become aware that one's act is occurring if one has objectual act-awareness. That is, propositional self-awareness (iv) implies objectual act-awareness (ii). The aim of the distinction is to explain the sense in which one can be said to have a kind of propositional self-awareness as regards one's perceptual act. As I see it, Suárez explains that one can be (perceptually) aware that one is perceiving when one is perceiving because one is *somehow* aware of one's perceptual act even though strictly speaking this awareness is not propositional awareness, which, as we have seen above, Suárez rules out for perceptual acts. Unlike Chatton, Suárez does not distinguish explicitly between (a) object-awareness and (b) the "experience" of "mineness" of such an awareness. The awareness pertaining to one's perceptual act, however, is not intentional insofar as the perceptual act is not directed at itself in the manner of an *object*.[65] Note that in the passage cited Suárez literally states that "I see that I see in the act that is exercised, as it were, . . . because this change of *the object* happens vitally". Why does he speak of the change of *the object* if, as he states in related passages, it is the change of the cognitive *power* that is somehow attended to?

I think it is because Suárez here refers to the perceptual act as the improper object of cognition that he speaks of the change of the *object*, and not of the *power*. Although it seems clear that it is by being somehow aware *of* one's perceiving that one becomes aware *that* one is perceiving, it is less clear how exactly this awareness *of* one's perceiving is to be characterized, that is, whether it is simply non-intentional or whether it is intentional in an improper sense.[66] However, it bears *some* likeness to Chatton's account in that it is by the mere actualization of the power that there is also some awareness related to one's *act*. Perhaps this awareness is also best described as some mark of "mineness" as in Chatton's case.

This awareness appears to be a by-product of the soul's attending to the species and hence to the production of an ensuing act that Suárez describes as a "change" in the power. Suárez thus admits of propositional self-awareness (iv) on the intellectual as well as the sensory level. The difference is that the former involves objectual act-awareness (ii) by means of a reflexive act, whereas the latter involves another kind of objectual act-awareness (ii) which is had by means of the perceptual act itself. Attention is most crucial in accounting for this act-awareness. Recall that Ockham can be taken to hold that an act is *conscious* if it makes the subject that has it conscious *of* something. Due to the constitutive role of attention in the occurrence of any act of cognition, it seems that for Suárez, an act is conscious not only if it makes the subject conscious *of* something (i), but also if it somehow makes the subject aware of the *act* itself (ii). Unlike Chatton, Suárez explains this two-fold awareness explicitly in terms of attention.

5 Conclusion

All three authors discussed here agree that we can have propositional self-awareness (iv), namely awareness *that* one's act is occurring. They disagree, however, on how this propositional self-awareness comes about. For Ockham, propositional self-awareness presupposes objectual act-awareness (ii) by means of a reflexive higher-order act, whereas for Chatton, propositional self-awareness presupposes the mark of "mineness" of one's awareness; in other words, this mark comes along with first-order object-awareness. Now Suárez agrees with Ockham that propositional self-awareness on the intellectual level presupposes objectual act-awareness by means of a reflexive higher-order act. However, he also seems to admit of propositional self-awareness on the sensory level. He explicitly accounts for the propositional perceptual self-awareness in terms of some kind of act-awareness. This, in turn, is accounted for in terms of the basic role of attention for cognition in general. To wit, Suárez makes attention a certain mode of the cognitive system (the soul) as a whole; as such, it is the precondition for any kind of cognition. For all three authors, the scope of self-awareness is limited by the scope of attention. They more or less explicitly acknowledged the central role of attention for the issue of (self-)awareness. But only Suárez made an attempt to locate and categorize attention itself within the overall cognitive system (the soul). Perhaps more could be learned about medieval conceptions of consciousness in general and self-consciousness in particular if the role, scope and location of attention came to be better understood.

Notes

1 For this tendency see Brower-Toland 2012; Perler 2014; Perler & Schierbaum (2014: 46–48); Rode (2014: 19–34), Yrjönsuuri 2006, 2007a.
2 For the contemporary debate, see Güzeldere (1997: 30–31) who structures these problems by distinguishing five different types of questions.
3 The kind of problem I am alluding to here is the so-called "easy" problem of consciousness as opposed to the "hard" problem of consciousness which pertains to the "what-it-is-like-to-have-it" question of undergoing mental states. From a contemporary perspective, the problem is that there is an explanatory gap between the scientifically explainable cognitive functions of mental states and their subjective feel. Cf. Chalmers (1995: 203).
4 On this terminological point see Perler (2014: 261–263).
5 Augustine, *De trin*. XI, c. 8, n. 15 (PL 42, 996). I use "(mental) act" and "(mental) state" interchangeably to designate an actual mental episode. Thereby, I try to account for the fact that the Latin expression "*actus*", in an Aristotelian sense, indicates the actualization of cognitive powers, as opposed to their mere potentiality. For the medieval usage of "actus" see also Panaccio (2004: 21).

6 In this chapter, I use the terms "conscious" and "aware" interchangeably. Dretske (1997: 773) puts it in the following way: "Being conscious of a thing (or fact) is being aware of it. Accordingly, 'conscious awareness' and 'consciously aware' are redundancies".
7 To be more precise, they distinguished between consciousness of one's acts and of one's intellect, as the rational part of the soul. See Perler & Schierbaum (2014: 19).
8 See Perler & Schierbaum (2014: 39). Two particularly clear examples of these tendencies can be found in the Aristotelian John Peter Olivi (1248–1298) and Platonist Marsilio Ficino (1433–1499).
9 One reason for neglecting the cognitive access to any "self" is that it is no longer conceived as an immaterial substance, but as a mere psychologically needed "construction" or "projection". This latter conception goes back at least to Hume's conception of the self as a mere "bundle of perceptions".
10 "That to see and feel a thing is to be (perceptually) conscious of it. And the same is true of facts: to see, smell, or feel that P is to be (or to become) aware that P. Hence, (1) S sees (hears, etc.) x (or that P) → S is conscious of x (that P)" (Dretske 1997: 773–774).
11 That I am in a certain mental state is, of course, also a fact. My point in distinguishing between fact-awareness and propositional self-awareness is that fact-awareness does not necessarily involve one's own mental acts, whereas propositional self-awareness does.
12 There are distinct types of "Higher-Order" theories, such as "Higher-Order" Perception (HOP) theory – prominently defended by Armstrong 1968 and Lycan 1996, and "Higher-Order" Thought (HOT) theory, where the latter further divides into the actualist (such as Rosenthal 2005) and the dispositionalist camp (Dennett 1978; Carruthers 1996, 2005). In general, (HOP) says that humans have not only first-order perceptual states, but also second-order perceptual-like states *of* their first-order states yielding (non-but also propositional higher-order representations of the first-order states, whereas (HOT) says that there can be higher-order (propositional) thoughts about the first-order states which are caused by these first-order states. All these HOT theories agree that first-order states become *conscious* by means of higher-order states. The question is whether the medieval "adherents" of (something like) HOT can be taken to be committed to that view as well. I shall try to show that they cannot.
13 Note that the reasons for their disagreement on this point are partly metaphysical. Due to their differing views on the metaphysical structure of the soul, Ockham admits of the possibility of a kind of higher-order perception of one's own act, whereas Chatton rejects this as superfluous. I say more on the metaphysical basis of their disagreement in Schierbaum (2016). In Ockham's view, the sensory and the intellective soul are distinct entities, whereas for Chatton, there is only one human soul. See Chapter 3 of this volume.
14 In this chapter, I assume that none of the authors discussed here held the view that attention takes the form of acts in addition to other cognitive acts, since this would make attention an extra power. Also, this would imply that there could be acts of "bare attention" without anything attended to by means of a cognitive act. I think this would be odd in Ockham's, Chatton's and Suarez's view, given their broadly Aristotelian picture of cognitive powers and their relation to the soul. Rather, attention seems to be a matter of *how* an act is exercised; just as speaking slowly does not require an act of "slowliness" in addition to the act of speaking, seeing with great attention does not require an act of attention in addition to the act of seeing. For further discussion of attention in this context and especially in the context of perception see Brown 2007; Silva & Yrjönsuuri 2014.
15 Ockham, *Ord.* I, prol., q.1, (*OTh* I: 39–42).
16 *Ord.* I, prol., q.1 (*OTh* I: 31).

17 I owe this formulation to Wolfgang Künne. See Künne (1995: 370).
18 Here I neglect the fact that it is at least logically possible for God to replace the thing as an efficient cause. See Ockham's famous discussion of the intuition of non-existents in *Ord.* I, prol., q.1 (*OTh* I: 38–39). For discussion of these "supernaturally induced cases" of intuition see Panaccio 2010 and Brower-Toland 2007.
19 *Quodl.* I, q.13 (*OTh* IX: 73).
20 For discussion of the question of the reliability of the cognitive mechanism see Panaccio & Piché 2010.
21 *Quodl.* V, q. 5 (*OTh* IX: 496). See also Freddoso (1991: 414, n. 18).
22 *Quodl.* I, q.14 (*OTh* IX: 79).
23 *Quodl.* II, q.12 (*OTh* IX: 165).
24 *Quodl.* I, q.14 (*OTh* IX: 80).
25 This becomes relevant in the explanation of how one can judge that *one* is cognizing *oneself* although one does not intuitively grasp one's act *as* one's own.
26 See note 25.
27 See Ockham, *Quaest. Var.*, q. V, (*OTh* VIII: 177).
28 *Quaest. Var.*, q.5 (*OTh* VIII: 177–178), emphasis added.
29 For a discussion of this alleged infinite-regress argument see Brower-Toland 2012, Schierbaum, 2016, Yrjönsuuri 2007a.
30 As Ockham states elsewhere: "I say that attention, a higher or lesser striving, actual tension or relaxation are effected solely by an act of will". *Quaest. Var.*, q.5 (*OTh* VIII: 180).
31 See Ockham *Rep.*II, q.20 (*OTh* V: 438).
32 Ockham emphasizes that one can intellectually intuit everything in the same way in which one can perceive something by one of the five senses. That is, there can be an intellectual intuition of sounds just as there can be intellectual intuitions of colours or odours. See *Rep.* II, qq.12–13 (*OTh* V: 269).
33 See *Quodl.* I, q.14 (*OTh* IX: 81).
34 "Experiences and beliefs are conscious, not because you are conscious of them, but because, so to speak, you are conscious *with* them". Dretske (1997: 785).
35 I leave the following question open: If one is not paying attention to the object of one's seeing *at all*, does it follow that one's seeing is not conscious? For instance, if an act of seeing a dog occurs in Peter, but Peter does not pay attention to the dog at all, does it follow that his seeing is *not* conscious? David Armstrong denies this. See Armstrong (1997: 721–728). Fortunately, I do not have to answer this difficult question for Ockham. All I need to say here is that a subject must pay attention to some degree to the object of his act in order to become aware *of* this act. And certainly those acts accompanied by some degree of attention *are* conscious acts. But of course this does not imply that *only* those acts are conscious.
36 One might object that there are two shifting cases: a shift of attention from (a) the dog to another external thing (say, the cat next to the dog) and from (b) the dog to the act of cognizing the dog. The question then is how one can know that (b) but not (a) involves the shift to an *act* (of oneself). An answer has to start from the following point: In order to shift one's attention away from an object to the vehicle of cognition, one *still* has to cognize the object. However, in shifting one's attention away from a dog to a cat, one does not need to be aware of the dog anymore (I'd like to thank Stephan Schmid for drawing my attention to this difficulty). This difference can help the subject to realize that (b) involves the shift to an act, but not (a).
37 Ockham himself refers to the case of mind-reading angels. See the following note.
38 "One angel acts on another only in the manner of an object, since [the other angel] can be the object of an intuitive or abstractive act of the intellect or of the will". *Rep.* II, q. 16 (*OTh* V: 369).

39 I elaborate further on cases of mind-reading in Schierbaum (2014: 232–240).
40 One could object that willing to become aware of one's act presupposes awareness *of* one's act. This seems to render the account circular. Circularity, however, can be avoided. If one assumes that to actually reflect upon one's act, one has to know in general that one is aware of things by means of acts, then, knowing this and being aware of, say, a dog by seeing it, one can want to focus on *that* very act of seeing by means of which one is aware of the dog. Wanting to focus on that particular act does not imply one's being aware *of* that act (by another act); it only presupposes one's being aware of the *dog*. For a discussion of this point, see Brower-Toland 2014.
41 See above, n. 26.
42 There are different versions of this regress argument in Chatton, *Reportatio*, prol., q. 2, art. 5, 118–119. I discuss the regress argument in more detail in Schierbaum, 2016.
43 *Reportatio*, prol., q. 2, art. 5, 121.
44 In his discussion of the difference between intuition and abstractive cognition on the intellectual level, Chatton explicitly compares intellectual intuition to sense perception of external things and abstractive cognition to imagination. See *Reportatio*, prol., q. 2, art. 3, 102. See Rode (2014: 272) for a presentation of Chatton's account of abstractive cognition.
45 See Ockham, *Ord.* prol., q. 1 (*OTh* I: 31).
46 Chatton, *Reportatio*, prol., q. 2, art. 5, 121. The translation relies heavily on Brower-Toland's; see Brower-Toland 2012.
47 For Chatton's conception of "experience" see again Rode (2014: 268–274).
48 "Experiri non est nisi subiectum vivum recipere suum actum". *Reportatio*, prol., q. 2, art. 5, 121. On this point see also Michon (2007: 133).
49 For a discussion of further problems with Chatton's account see Yrjönsuuri 2007a.
50 Chatton, *Reportatio*, prol., q. 2, art. 5, 125, (emphasis added).
51 Due to my limited aim in this section, I cannot even remotely do justice to Suárez's rich account. For a more extensive and excellent discussion see Perler 2014 and also Leijenhorst 2012 and Rode (2014: 373–395).
52 Suárez develops his theory in *De anima*, a set of questions on Aristotle's *De anima*. Suárez commented on this work while teaching at the University of Segovia (1571–74) and started revising the text late in his life, without ever finishing it. His pupil Balthasar Alvarez was responsible for the final redaction and published it in 1621. See Leijenhorst (2012: 138). In this context, I refer to the new edition: *Commentaria una cum questionibus in libros Aristotelis De anima* (= *CDA*) ed. Salvador Castellote, 3 vols. (Madrid, 1978–1991).
53 Suárez, *CDA*, disp. 6, q. 4, n. 2. The question is "whether any sense can cognize its proper act" ("utrum aliquis sensus possit cognoscere proprium actum").
54 Suárez, *CDA*, disp. 6, q. 4, n. 2, 502.
55 "[V]ision cannot see an act of vision, because this power is determined by its truly bright object; however, an act of vision is a more perfect quality of another kind . . . it is given only with respect to the spiritual power that it can cognize its proper act by means of another act, since the power has a most universal object comprising every object". Suárez, *CDA*, disp. 6, q. 4, n. 4, 506.
56 Suárez makes this more general claim just a little later: "Since every cognition occurs by means of vital attention". Suárez, *CDA*, disp. 6, q. 4, n. 7, 510, (emphasis added).
57 Roughly speaking, *species* are conceived by medieval authors as the formal means or the principle of cognition (*ratio cognoscendi*). According to Aristotelian models of cognition, cognition implies the reception of the form of a thing. Since, however, it is not possible to receive the form itself, a *species* is posited as the vehicle or means of the reception of the form of a thing which results in the cognition of the

thing. For a discussion of the role of species in Suárez's theory of cognition see Spruit (1994: 294–307). See also Chapter 5 of this volume for a further discussion of both intelligible and sensible species and Chapter 8 for a discussion of sensible species.
58 "Recipitur species in oculo quando, ad alia attendens, homo non videt". Suárez, *CDA*, disp. 5, q. 3, n. 1, 340.
59 "Therefore in another way the species is received vitally in the power, as when the soul attends. This attention is not a thing distinct from the soul and its power, but a certain mode of it". Suárez, *CDA*, disp. 5, q. 3, n. 1, 340.
60 Perhaps the "initial" turning to the species by means of attention can be compared to pressing the "play" button.
61 See Rode (2014: 402–404).
62 See again Ockham *Quaest. Var.*, q.5 (*OTh* VIII: 179–180).
63 Suárez, *CDA*, disp. 6, q. 4, n. 7, 510. The production of the cognitive act, as an actualization of the power, is conceived in Aristotelian terms as a change of the power, e.g., the change from mere potentiality to actuality.
64 In medieval semantics it was common to distinguish between the "*actus exercitus*" and the "*actus signatus*". Roughly speaking, the former designates first-order acts whereas the latter designates second-order acts. See Nuchelmans 1988 for discussion of this distinction.
65 Rather, it is intentional insofar as it is directed at its external object.
66 Most recently, Perler has argued that this awareness of one's act is necessarily non-intentional. See Perler 2014. See also Leijenhorst (2012: 142–4). In my view, its being pre-reflexive is not yet sufficient to exclude its being intentional in some improper sense. Suárez at least refers to the perceptual act as the improper object of awareness in the quoted passage. Of course, it is far from clear what exactly "intentional in some improper sense" amounts to.

Bibliography

Primary sources

Augustinus, A. *De trinitate* (= *De trin.*): (Bücher VIII–XI, XIV–XV, Anhang: Buch V); lateinisch – deutsch. J. Kreuzer (trans. introd. & ed.). Hamburg: Meiner, 2001.

Chatton, Walter. *Reportatio et Lectura super Sententias: Collatio ad Librum Primum et Prologus* (= *Reportatio*). J. C. Wey (ed.). Toronto: Pontifical Institute 1989.

William of Ockham. *Ordinatio: Scriptum in Librum Primum Sententiarum, prologus et distinctio prima* (= *Ord.*). In *Opera Theologica*, S. Brown & G. Gál (eds). St. Bonaventure: The Franciscan Institute, 1967.

———. *Ordinatio. Scriptum in Librum Primum Sententiarum, distinctiones II–III* (= *Ord.*). In *Opera Theologica* II, S. Brown & G. Gál (eds). St. Bonaventure: The Franciscan Institute, 1970.

———. *Quodlibeta Septem* (= *Quodl.*). In *Opera Theologica* IX, J. C. Wey (ed.). St. Bonaventure: The Franciscan Institute, 1980.

———. *Reportatio: Quaestiones in Librum Secundum Sententiarum* (= *Rep.*). *Opera Theologica* V, G. Gál & R. Wood (eds). St. Bonaventure: The Franciscan Institute, 1981.

———. *Quaestiones Variae* (= *Quaest. Var.*). In *Opera Theologica* VIII, G. Etzkorn & F. E. Kelley & J. W. Wey (eds). St. Bonaventure: The Franciscan Institute, 1984.

Suárez, Francisco. *Commentaria una cum questionibus in libros Aristotelis De anima* (= *CDA*), 3 vols. S. Castellote (ed.). Madrid: Editorial Labor, 1978–1991.

———. *Disputationes metaphysicae* (= *Disp. metaph.*). In *Opera omnia* 25, Ch. Berton (ed.). Hildesheim: Olms, 1965 = 1866.

Secondary sources

Armstrong, D. 1968. *A Materialist Theory of the Mind*. London: Routledge.

———. 1997. "What Is Consciousness?" In *The Nature of Consciousness – Philosophical Debates*, N. Block, O. Flanagan & G. Güzeldere (eds), 721–728. Cambridge, MA: MIT Press.

Brower-Toland, S. 2007. "Intuition, Externalism, and Direct Reference in Ockham". *History of Philosophy Quarterly* **24**: 317–336.

———. 2012. "Medieval Approaches to Consciousness: Ockham and Chatton". *Philosophers' Imprint* **12**(17).

———. 2014. "William Ockham on the Scope and Limits of Consciousness". *Vivarium* **52**(3): 197–219.

Brown, D. 2007. "Augustine and Descartes on the Function of Attention in Perceptual Awareness". In *Consciousness: From Perception to Reflection in the History of Philosophy*, S. Heinämaa, V. Lähteenmäki & P. Remes (eds), 153–175. Dordrecht, The Netherlands: Springer.

Carruthers, P. 1996. *Language, Thought and Consciousness*. Cambridge: Cambridge University Press.

———. 2005. *Consciousness: Essays From a Higher-Order Perspective*. Oxford: Oxford University Press.

Chalmers, D. 1995. "Facing Up to the Problem of Consciousness". *Journal of Consciousness Studies* **2**(3): 200–219.

Dennett, D. 1978. "Toward a Cognitive Theory of Consciousness". In *Perception and Cognition: Issues in the Foundations of Psychology*, C. Savage (ed.), 201–228. Minneapolis: University of Minnesota Press.

De Libera, A. 2010. *Archéologie du sujet: Naissance du sujet*. Paris: Vrin.

Dretske, F. 1997. "Conscious Experience". In *The Nature of Consciousness – Philosophical Debates*, N. Block, O. Flanagan & G. Güzeldere (eds), 773–788. Cambridge, MA: MIT Press.

Freddoso, A. 1991. *William of Ockham: Quodlibetal Questions*, vol. 2. New Haven: Yale University Press.

Güzeldere, G. 1997. "Approaching Consciousness". In *The Nature of Consciousness – Philosophical Debates*, N. Block, O. Flanagan & G. Güzeldere (eds), 1–67. Cambridge, MA: MIT Press.

Kriegel, U. 2004. "Consciousness and Self-Consciousness". *Monist* **87**: 182–205.

Künne, W. 1995. "Some Varieties of Thinking: Reflections on Meinong and Fodor". In *Meinong und die Gegenstandstheorie*, R. Haller (ed.), *Grazer Philosophische Studien* **50**: 365–395.

Leijenhorst, C. 2012. "Suárez on Self-Awareness". In *The Philosophy of Francisco Suárez*, B. Hill & H. Lagerlund (eds), 137–153. Oxford, New York: OUP.

Lycan, W. 1996. *Consciousness and Experience*. Cambridge, MA: MIT Press.

McCord Adams, M. 1987. *William Ockham*, 2 vols. Notre Dame: University of Notre Dame Press.

Michon, C. 2007. "Ego intelligo (lapidem). Deux conceptions de la réflexion au Moyen Age". In *Généalogies du sujet: De saint Anselm à Malebranche*, O. Boulnois (ed.), 113–150. Paris: Vrin.
Nagel, Th. 1974. "What It Is Like to Be a Bat". *The Philosophical Review* **83**(4): 435–450.
Normore, C. 2012. "Ockham on Being". In *Categories of Being: Essays on Metaphysics and Logic*, L. Haaparanta & H. Koskinen (eds), 78–98. Oxford, New York: OUP.
Nuchelmans, G. 1988. "The Distinction *actus exercitus/actus significatus* in Medieval Semantics". In *Meaning and Inference in Medieval Philosophy: Studies in Memory of Jan Pinborg*, N. Kretzmann (ed.), 57–90. Dordrecht, The Netherlands: Springer.
Panaccio, C. 2004. *Ockham on Concepts*. Aldershot: Ashgate.
———. 2010. "Intuition and Causality: Ockham's Externalism Revisited". In *Later Medieval Perspectives on Intentionality*, Fabrizio Amerini (ed.), *Quaestio* **10**: 241–254.
Panaccio, C. & Piché, D. 2010. "Ockham's Reliabilism and the Intuition of Non-Existents". In *Rethinking the History of Skepticism: The Missing Medieval Background*, H. Lagerlund (ed.), 97–118. Leiden: Brill.
Pasnau, R. 1997a. *Theories of Cognition in the Later Middle Ages*. Cambridge, New York: Cambridge University Press.
———. 1997b. "Olivi on the Metaphysics of the Soul". *Medieval Philosophy and Theology* **6**: 109–132.
Perler, D. 2010. "Ockham über die Seele und ihre Teile". *Recherches de théologie et philosophie médiévales* **77**: 329–366.
———. 2014. "Suárez on Consciousness". *Vivarium* **52**(3): 261–286.
Perler, D. & Schierbaum, S. 2014. *Selbstbezug und Selbstwissen – Texte zu einer mittelalterlichen Debatte*. Frankfurt: Klostermann.
Rode, Chr. 2014. "*Zugänge zum Selbst. Innere Erfahrung in Spätmittelalter und Früher Neuzeit*". Habilitationsschrift: Rheinische Friedrich-Wilhelms-Universität Bonn.
Rosenthal, D. 2005. *Consciousness and Mind*. Oxford: Oxford University Press.
———. 2014. "Ockham on the Possibility of Self-Knowledge: Knowing Acts Without Knowing Subjects". *Vivarium* **52**(3): 220–240.
Schierbaum, S. 2016. "Chatton's Critique of Ockham's Conception of Intuitive Cognition". In *Responses to Ockham*, Ch. Rode (ed.), 15–46. Leiden: Brill.
Silva, J. F. 2012. *Robert Kilwardby on the Human Soul: Plurality of Forms and Censorship in the Thirteenth Century*. Leiden: Brill.
Silva, J. F. & Yrjönsuuri, M. (eds). 2014. *Active Perception in the History of Philosophy: From Plato to Modern Philosophy*. Dordrecht, The Netherlands: Springer.
Spruit, L. 1994. *Species Intelligibilis: From Perception to Knowledge*, vol. 2. Leiden: Brill.
Yrjönsuuri, M. 2006. "Types of Self-Awareness in Medieval Thought". In *Mind and Modality: Studies in the History of Philosophy in Honour of Simo Knuuttila*, V. Hirvonen, T. J. Holopainen & M. Touminen (eds), 153–169. Leiden: Brill.
———. 2007a. "The Structure of Self-Consciousness: A Fourteenth-Century Debate". In *Consciousness: From Perception to Refletcion in the History of Philosophy*, S. Heinämaa, V. Lähteenmäki & P. Remes (eds), 141–152. Dordrecht, The Netherlands: Springer.
———. 2007b. "The Soul as an Entity". In *Forming the Mind: Essays on the Internal Senses and the Mind/Body-Problem From Avicenna to the Medieval Enlightenment*, H. Lagerlund (ed.), 59–92. Dordrecht, The Netherlands: Springer.

7

DEBATES ABOUT THE WILL AND ITS FREEDOM

Sydney Penner

1 Introduction

As in recent debates about free will, medieval and Renaissance discussions of the will and its freedom focused on whether being free is compatible with determinism. A determinist threat was perceived in several places. Perhaps God's infallible foreknowledge of all propositions concerning the future, necessary or contingent, determines our choices. Call that "theological determinism". Perhaps the heavens determine all events in the sublunary world. Call that "astral determinism". Or perhaps our intellectual judgements about how good and bad our various options are determine our choices. Call that "intellectual determinism". Additional kinds of determinism could be identified.

Each kind of determinism raises different issues, permits different responses, and makes different arguments salient, but each kind was widely taken seriously and widely viewed as posing at least a *prima facie* threat to free will. For a volume on the philosophy of mind, the most interesting discussions are the ones concerning intellectual determinism since they address not only the question of the will's freedom but also further questions about the psychological economy, especially about the relationship between intellect and will. Hence, this chapter will focus on intellectual determinism. The section on Ḥasdai Crescas is the one notable exception. Crescas is primarily motivated by concerns about theological determinism; he does, however, make several apt arguments for a general causal determinism, and given a typical medieval psychology, one might think intellectual determinism a consequence.

Even with discussions of theological and astral determinisms largely set aside, it is still impossible to do justice to the myriad discussions of free will in the historical period in question. The question is of intrinsic importance and was tied up with key religious and political events. Many figures from many and varied intellectual traditions weighed in. Rather than trying to provide encyclopaedic coverage of this panoply, the strategy adopted here is simply to select four sophisticated thinkers to represent something of the diversity of views found in the period.[1] Although the present selection omits significant authors and views, my four chosen figures provide some sense of the range of views in play in late medieval and Renaissance discussions in Europe: Ockham represents a radical voluntarism; Buridan, an intellectualism (albeit in fairly disguised form); Crescas, a compatibilism that leaves only a minimal sort of freedom; and Suárez, a moderate voluntarism.[2]

Despite discussing the figures in chronological order and ending with Suárez's moderate position, I do not intend to suggest a historical story of a battle between two opposing views culminating in Suárez's grand synthesis. It is true that he is something of a synthesizer, but with respect to the issue at hand there were many moderate voluntarists long before Suárez. I have made no attempt to impose a narrative arc on what is actually a messy story of continual disagreement. The relative predominance of various views may have shifted to some degree, but the more salient fact is that the same disputes and fundamentally similar positions can be found throughout the period. Although I do not offer a historical narrative in this chapter, I do, nevertheless, briefly discuss several significant historical events that are worth keeping in mind when looking at accounts of free will.

2 Psychological framework

In recent discussions concerning the problem of free will, some views that attribute libertarian freedom (that is, a freedom that is incompatible with determinism) to human beings are characterized as views that endorse agent-causation. The picture is one according to which most causation that occurs in the world involves events causing subsequent events (all of which might happen deterministically), but where human free actions are caused by human agents rather than by prior events. In other words, although most events are caused by prior events, some events are caused by persisting substances, namely human beings. Obvious questions then follow about how this agent-causation is supposed to fit into the broader picture.

The figures discussed in this chapter would have found this framework alien. On their view, inspired by Aristotle, all causation is agent-causation in the sense that all effects are caused by agents, that is, by substances and their powers. A human being builds a house and thereby is the cause of the house being built. Likewise, fire warms the water in the pot above it and thereby is the cause of the water being heated. The human and the fire have different kinds of capacities, but they are both agents.

But medieval philosophers do not take this commitment to ubiquitous agent-causation to settle the question of free will. Having freedom was not part of the notion of being an agent. It was generally agreed that at least some agents act necessarily once the requisite conditions for acting are in place (e.g., the water is adjacent to the fire, there is no insulating barrier between them, and so forth). But perhaps not all agents act necessarily in that manner. That is the important question: not whether some effects are caused by agents rather than by events, but whether some agents act freely rather than necessarily.[3]

The figures discussed in this chapter also agree that human beings have a rational soul. But this claim should not be taken to imply anything about whether the rational soul is one part of a human soul also comprised of other parts such as nutritive and sensitive parts or whether the rational soul is a separate soul in its own right or even whether the rational soul has a faculty or capacity for understanding – namely the intellect – and a faculty for willing – namely the will.[4] There is some agreement about these matters, at least on the surface. As a matter of fact, there were active disputes about whether these faculties are really identical to the soul or distinct from it and whether the faculties are really distinct from each other or really identical and only conceptually distinct (see Chapter 3). But even Ockham, who thinks the will is only conceptually distinct from the intellect, still takes this conceptual distinction to be useful and develops his psychological theories in terms of the intellect and will.

Our concern is with the will. It is typically characterized as the rational appetite, that is, the desiring faculty of the rational part of the soul. The will, however, is not the only appetite a human has. Rather, it is the appetite of the *rational* soul or the *rational* part of the soul. The sensitive part of the soul, for example, might bring its own appetites to bear and figure in the explanation why a given action was performed.

One way to get a better sense of the nature of the will is to look at what sorts of acts are characteristic of it. The most obvious one is choice. The will chooses between different courses of action. As the story common to the figures in this chapter goes, when one deliberates about what to do, the intellect presents different options to the will. This is necessary, since the will by itself is blind. Once intellect has presented the different options and judged of their respective merits, the will chooses one, which then typically leads the agent to perform the actions that accord with the chosen course. Choice is, in fact, the act that receives the lion's share of attention. But it is by no means the only act attributed to the will. Love, desire, intention, and enjoyment (that is, enjoyment of a willed good once it has been attained) are also attributed to the will.[5] These are, of course, all acts that involve the will's objects. The will loves and desires a variety of good things, chooses and intends some of them, and enjoys them should it be fortunate enough to attain the chosen and intended goods.

Since our primary concern is with the will's freedom, our primary concern will also be with choice, since it is in making choices that the will's putative freedom would be exercised.

3 The Condemnation of 1277

To better understand the philosophical currents regarding the issue of the will's freedom, it will be helpful to begin with an event that occurred slightly before the period examined in this volume. The sudden influx of previously lost Aristotelian texts in the twelfth and thirteenth centuries excited much scholarly attention in the Latin West. Some of the attention was enthusiastic – after all, here was a sophisticated philosophical picture ranging over a wide array of issues – but some was more wary. A variety of Aristotelian positions were or at least seemed incompatible with Christian doctrine. Unsurprisingly, then, the thirteenth century saw a series of battles between those more enthusiastic about Aristotelian philosophy and those more concerned with defending Christian doctrine from this pagan threat.

One salvo came in 1277 when, at the behest of Pope John XXI, Stephen Tempier, the Bishop of Paris, issued a condemnation of 219 or 220 propositions that a commission of 16 theologians had purportedly drawn from a number of suspect writings. Tempier was concerned that some scholars, especially in the faculty of arts, were giving serious consideration to a variety of positions contrary to the Catholic faith, supporting them by appeal to "gentile" writings, and then failing adequately to refute those erroneous positions. Consequently, in order to save those who might hear such things and be led into error, Tempier forbade the teaching of the condemned propositions and excommunicated all who in any way taught or defended them or even just listened to them.

The condemned propositions deal with a wide range of topics from the unicity of the intellect (whose late medieval reception is discussed in Chapter 4) to the eternity of the world to astral determinism to the killing of irrational animals. Most relevant for present purposes, a number of the condemned propositions seem to limit human freedom in some way or other. Propositions stating that the will is moved by heavenly bodies, that the will follows appetite, and that the will submits to the intellect's judgements are all condemned as undermining the human freedom essential for moral responsibility (Wippel 1995: 255–261, 2002: 70).

There is very little consensus about the Condemnation of 1277.[6] Scholars disagree, for example, about who the targets of the condemnation were (especially whether Thomas Aquinas was a target), and they disagree about how much of an effect these condemnations had on subsequent philosophical work. With respect to our topic, it appears that voluntarist accounts that emphasized human freedom became more prevalent after the condemnations. Since certain accounts that in modern terms might be labelled determinist or compatibilist accounts were clearly condemned, one might attribute this rise in voluntarist accounts to the constraints imposed by Tempier's condemnations. Certainly, some who subsequently defended voluntarist accounts appealed explicitly to the condemnations in support of their own views. On the other hand, perhaps the condemnations merely captured the sentiments of a philosophical trend already underway. Perhaps dissatisfaction with intellectualist accounts was already increasing for independent philosophical reasons. It seems safe to say, however, that the 1277 Parisian condemnations helped create an environment hospitable to accounts emphasizing the libertarian freedom of the human will, at least for those working within its orbit of influence.[7]

4 William of Ockham (c. 1288–1347)

One of the most striking fourteenth-century advocates of the will's primacy and freedom is William of Ockham.[8] The Franciscan order of which he was a part was known for emphasizing the will and its freedom, but Ockham went significantly beyond the more standard Franciscan views and certainly went well beyond anything demanded by the Condemnation of 1277.

In keeping with voluntarist themes, Ockham declares the will to be more noble than the intellect and not to be determined by the latter. These claims need to be examined carefully to be understood, since at an ontological level Ockham does not think that the soul and its faculties are really distinct.[9] As he puts it: "I say that the faculties of the soul that we are speaking of in the case under discussion, namely, intellect and will . . . are really the same as each other and with the essence of the soul."[10] Ockham both emphasizes the will's freedom from the intellect more than most medieval philosophers and takes the minority position that the distinction between the soul's faculties or powers is merely conceptual (on the latter point, see Chapter 3, section 2.1, of this volume). Holding those two positions might sound paradoxical. But a resolution is ready to hand. On Ockham's view, the terms "intellect" and "will" both have the same signification in that both signify the soul, but they have different connotations. The former connotes the soul insofar as it can understand and the latter insofar as it can will, and those acts are really distinct.[11] So to say that the will is not determined by the intellect is simply a shorter way of saying that those acts that we characterize as the will's acts (e.g., choices) are not determined by those acts that we characterize as the intellect's acts (e.g., cognitions).

For example, suppose Mary promised her friend Sarah that she would help her move into her new apartment, but on the day of the move, Mary discovers that there will be a concert at the same time, featuring her favourite cello concerto. She thinks about her options and judges that, while there is something to be said for breaking her promise (she would really enjoy a live performance of the cello concerto, especially given that it has been several years since she last had the pleasure), nevertheless, the better thing to do would be to keep her promise and help her friend. That judgement is an intellectual act. Does it constitute or determine a choice to go help her friend? Not on Ockham's view. He thinks that Mary is still free to help or not to help her friend. She can still choose the pleasure of the concert, despite having to go against her better judgement in doing so.

Nor is the will otherwise determined:

> As for the first article, it should be noted that what I am calling freedom is the power by which I can indifferently and contingently posit diverse things, in such a way that I am both able to cause and able not to cause the same effect when there is no difference anywhere else outside that power.[12]

This text helps explain just what is distinctive about the will's freedom. Ockham frequently describes the will as having a power for opposites. The significance of that description might not immediately be obvious. Are not many powers like that? Someone with the power of vision, for example, can both see red and not see red (when looking at a blue sky, for example). A cat has the power to eat mice and not to eat mice. But a cat is not free, and vision is not a free power. On Ockham's view, the circumstances under which a cat is able to eat mice are different than the conditions under which it is able not to eat mice. Non-free powers may have a capacity for opposites in some sense, but only if they themselves are affected in different ways (they are not indifferent, as Ockham would say). When there are red roses in front of my eyes, my vision allows me to see red, but not when my eyes are only presented with a blue sky. The will, however, is altogether different. It is free to choose for or against a course of action even once all the other conditions are present and accounted for.

The only kind of necessity in willing that Ockham allows is a necessity that is conditional on a prior willing. On the assumption that I will to go to Grand Manan Island and that the only way to get there is by boat, we might say that my willing to go to the island necessarily leads to my willing to take a boat. But willing to take a boat is not strictly necessary, since I am always free to cease willing to go to Grand Manan Island (Osborne 2012: 439).

All that has been said so far is compatible with saying that the will is fundamentally oriented to the good. On such a view the will is constrained to some degree in its willing. It necessarily wills something perceived as good, but perhaps is still left free with respect to a wide range of options, namely all those that are perceived as good. Ockham goes further, however, and suggests that one can even will something evil without viewing it as good and can nill (that is, will against the good) without seeing it as connected to evil in any way.[13] Augustine famously struggles to explain why he stole pears as a youth, given that he had no need for them as food (1998: 28–34).[14] He considers the possibility that he simply wanted to steal the pears precisely because doing so would be wicked, but he finds such an explanation incredible. Surely there must have been some good he was pursuing, even if only an inferior one! Ockham does not think that any good need be found to explain such actions. Perhaps Augustine simply wanted to steal.

Ockham suggests that there is a way of reading the traditional claim that the good is the will's object or that the will can only will good that is compatible with his account. The term "good" can be understood in two ways. In one sense, the good is just what can be willed. Understood that way, it is true that the will can only will good, but it is a trivial truth. On the other hand, "good" can also be understood as designating something in one of the three traditional classes of goods: the fine (*honestum*), the useful, and the pleasurable. If we understand "good" in this way, then Ockham insists that a rational agent is free to will a bad thing even though it neither is nor appears to be good in any of these three ways and is free to will against such a good even if it neither is nor appears to be bad in any of the corresponding ways.[15]

In particular, Ockham argues that one can will to be unhappy. By this he does not simply mean that one can mistakenly pursue false goods that will in fact lead to unhappiness. Nobody denies that could happen. Instead, Ockham makes the much more striking claim that people are free to will unhappiness knowingly.

He cites several cases in support of his claim. One case is that of an unbeliever who does not think there is an afterlife let alone any rewards to be had in such an afterlife and yet sacrifices his life for the common good. The other case is that of a person who commits suicide, thereby precluding happiness. These cases were frequently discussed, of course, and medieval theologians who thought that the will always pursues the good had standard accounts to give of how an agent pursuing happiness might come to sacrifice her life or commit suicide. But Ockham rejects those explanations and takes these cases to support his contention that one can fail to will happiness or even will unhappiness. Ockham also argues that there are cases where people sin knowing perfectly well that doing so will lead to unhappiness and amounts to choosing unhappiness (Osborne 2012: 448–455).

What grounds do we have for thinking that we possess this sort of radically free power? Ockham is sceptical about demonstrating by argument that the will is free:

> [T]he thesis in question cannot be proved by any argument, since every argument meant to prove it will assume something that is just as unknown as, or more unknown than, the conclusion. Nevertheless, the thesis can be known evidently through experience, since a human being experiences that, no matter how much reason dictates a given thing, the will is still able to will that thing or not to will it or to will against it.[16]

In his view, arguments for the freedom of our will necessarily end up begging the question. He thinks, however, that introspective experience can show us that we are free. I can deliberate at length about what to do, canvass all the reasons for and against each option, and carefully judge the relative goodness of each. Yet there is still a moment of choice, and at that moment, my will is free and undetermined. I am free to will what I judged best or to will against it. I am even free to will against all the good options and pursue something that I know perfectly well to be bad and lacking in any redeeming good. And, Ockham thinks, I can know from experience that I am free in this way at the moment of choice.

5 Jean Buridan (c. 1300–after 1358)

While some scholastics were happy to subscribe to the prevalent voluntarist spirit, whether in an extreme form such as Ockham's or in a more moderate form, others were not. The fourteenth-century Parisian arts master Jean Buridan often defends positions similar to Ockham's but not when it comes to the will and its relation to intellectual acts.[17] Buridan's position, however, has to be interpreted with care, since much of what he says appears on the surface to be in keeping with voluntarism. He himself claims to be offering a "middle opinion" between voluntarism and intellectualism.[18]

Early in his extended discussion of the will in his commentary on Aristotle's *Nicomachean Ethics*, Buridan defines voluntary agents as agents that "can, with everything else disposed in the same way, freely determine themselves to each opposite."[19] This, of course, sounds similar to what Ockham says. Furthermore, Buridan also makes heavy use of a threefold division of which voluntarists are fond: in relation to a given object, an agent can will it, nill it, or not-will it. The last term is sometimes used as a negation of the first, in which case it includes nilling. That is, I can not-will an object either by nilling it or by simply lacking an act of willing. But "not-willing" can also be used more strictly to refer just to those cases where an agent neither wills nor nills, and thus a proper threefold division results. In Buridan's case the third alternative is typically cast as deferring. That is, in addition to willing or nilling, a voluntary agent can defer or hold off, and neither will nor nill. That we are free in this way, he thinks, anyone can experience for themselves.[20]

Such voluntarist-sounding strands have suggested to some scholars that Buridan accepts voluntarism, albeit in a more moderate form than Ockham's. There are other strands, however, and I take Zupko (1995) and Pironet (2001) to have argued convincingly that Buridan is better read as an intellectualist.[21] I shall follow their reading. A number of strands may be pointed to that suggest a more intellectualist account. First, Buridan sees the will as both a passive and an active faculty. Its passive acts flow necessarily from the intellect's judgements. By presenting an object as good, the intellect generates a kind of pleasure or agreement in the will towards the object, while by presenting an object as bad it generates a kind of displeasure or disagreement. If an object is presented as having both good and bad aspects, both kinds of receptive acts follow. These receptive acts are causally necessary, albeit not sufficient, for the active acts of willing, nilling, and deferring.[22] Second, Buridan does not think that the will can act against the deliverances of reason as such. If an object is presented as absolutely good, the agent necessarily comes to will it. If an object is presented as wholly bad, the agent necessarily comes to nill it. Those, of course, would be extraordinary cases. But even in cases where objects are presented as having a mixture of good and bad aspects, if one object is presented as better than another, the will cannot choose the lesser good, although it can defer.[23] Third, Buridan makes it clear that the reason the will has been given this freedom to defer is in order to allow fallible creatures like us to make more reasonable decisions. Sometimes what initially appears good turns out to be bad on closer inspection. Sometimes what appears bad turns out to lead to good. Our capacity to defer allows us to make a closer inspection, as needed. So deferment is not intended as a means to allow the will to go against intellect, but as a mechanism to allow the intellect to go back and look harder.[24]

While these three strands are certainly of a more intellectualist bent, they are, strictly speaking, compatible with the fundamental voluntarist claim that will is not always determined by intellect. The matter now hinges on how one understands deferral. If the will's deferral amounted to the will picking an option that the intellect deems less good than another option, a capacity for deferral would conflict with intellectualist accounts. On the other hand, if deferral only comes at the recommendation of the intellect, then the deferment in no way threatens the intellectualist claim that the intellect ultimately determines the will. Buridan, it turns out, is not entirely forthcoming about exactly how the psychological process surrounding deferment works. But Zupko makes a strong case that Buridan says enough to imply that the only way the will can defer is if the intellect has judged that doing so would be good (1995: 91–94). Deferment in order to deliberate further is no exception to the general rule that one can only will what the intellect has presented as good. It is evident from experience that agents do sometimes return to the drawing board to investigate their options further, so what Buridan is acknowledging with the capacity for deferral is simply what any reasonably sophisticated intellectualist will acknowledge (even if he himself presents deferment as providing the middle road between voluntarism and intellectualism). Sometimes a particular judgement or set of judgements does not result in willing or nilling the options presented; sometimes the agent decides to deliberate further. But on the intellectualist view that decision will itself need to be based on a judgement. However many iterations that process may involve, on Buridan's intellectualist view the sequence will bottom out in a judgement.

Given that the first occasion for hearing Buridan's name typically arises in discussions of Buridan's ass, I should say something about the choice between two equally good options. As it happens, the infamous ass between two equally attractive piles of hay cannot be found in Buridan's writings. He does, however, talk about humans and dogs faced with equally attractive options. In the case of human beings, he seems to depart somewhat from a straightforward intellectualist account and grants that the will can opt for one of two options judged equally good. He notes, however, that this would be difficult to prove by reason and so is better taken on faith (Rescher 2005: 18–22).[25]

Why did Buridan borrow so much voluntarist language for a fundamentally intellectualist account? He was well aware of the 1277 Paris condemnations and explicitly attempts to show that he is not violating them. One may suppose, then, that at least part of the motivation for expressing his views the way he does was to avoid falling afoul of the condemnations (Pironet 2001: 213–219; Zupko 1995: 98–99).

6 Ḥasdai Crescas (c. 1340–1410/11)

In the fourteenth century, Ḥasdai Crescas, a leading rabbinic figure in the Iberian Jewish community, vigorously critiqued the Aristotelian philosophy, which, thanks to Maimonides, was prevalent not only in Christian scholasticism but also in Jewish philosophy.[26] In his view, Aristotelian philosophy undermined crucial aspects of the Jewish tradition and therefore ought to be resisted. As previously mentioned, the 1277 Parisian condemnations also sprang from the fear that Aristotelianism was undermining a religious tradition. On the issue of the will's freedom, however, Crescas went in the opposite direction, arguing for a universal determinism without making any exception for human choice. Crescas, of course, felt no need to heed the Parisian condemnations.

Debates about free will became a central issue in Jewish thought in the fourteenth century, probably due in part to Christian scholastic influence and perhaps also to impetus received from complicated entanglements with the Inquisition and Christian and Jewish polemics (Pines 1967; Rudavsky 2003; Sirat 1990: esp. 308–322). The standard context for these debates was concern about the compatibility of human free will and divine omniscience – in particular, divine foreknowledge of future contingents. Although I have focused on discussions about the psychological economy of the intellect and will, concern about divine foreknowledge and human free will is prevalent in the Christian tradition as well, having already received an influential formulation in the fifth book of Boethius's *The Consolation of Philosophy*. There are many ways of spelling out the details, but the basic concern is that God's omniscience implies that, for any future state of affairs, God infallibly knows that the state of affairs will come about, and so that state of affairs cannot fail to come about, since if it did not then God's foreknowledge would be falsified contrary to the assumption of his omniscience. But if all future states of affairs cannot fail to come about, that is, if all future states of affairs are necessitated, then there is no room for human free choice. An agent has no control over the antecedent conditions and consequently has no control over the state of affairs they necessitate.[27]

A wide range of responses have been offered to this issue. Most philosophers and theologians, both Christian and Jewish, have opted for stratagems designed to leave divine foreknowledge and human free will compatible. Some, however, have conceded that initial appearances are correct and that they really are incompatible. Such incompatibilists can then take one of two tacks. One is to give up divine omniscience or at least to carefully constrain our understanding of it. In the Jewish tradition, this option finds a prominent representative in Gersonides (1288–1344). Gersonides argues that when it comes to any future contingent state of affairs, God knows that the state of affairs may or may not be actualized, but God does not know which of two contrary states of affairs will be actualized. Gersonides's motivation precisely is to safeguard contingency in the world and thus allow for human free choice. This is clearly an incompatibilist proposal insofar as Gersonides denies that God knows which future contingent states of affairs will be actualized. It should be noted, however, that he does not take himself to have sacrificed divine omniscience, since he does not think that it belongs to omniscience or to divine perfection to know things as they are not. Since a future contingent state of affairs is merely possible, God's omniscience only requires knowing that it is possible (Rudavsky 1983, 1985).

The other incompatibilist tack is to preserve divine foreknowledge but to deny human free will. One might charge Crescas with going this route; he certainly has no use for Gersonides's account, though it should be noted that he identifies himself as a compatibilist. In fact, he opens the second treatise of *The Light of the Lord* by identifying six cornerstones of the Torah or six pillars "upon which the House of God is established" and one of those six is choice.[28] Commandments do not apply to those whose actions are under coercion or compulsion, so the commandments of the Law make sense only if human beings can choose to follow the law. Crescas also grants that this requires contingency.[29] As we will see, however, his compatibilism turns on carefully circumscribed notions of free choice and contingency (cf. Sirat 1990: 367).[30]

The guiding question of the relevant section is whether "the nature of the possible exists."[31] Adopting the scholastic method, Crescas first presents a series of arguments for an affirmative answer, then a series of arguments for a negative answer, before finally offering his own resolution of the issue. It should be noted that Crescas uses the term "possible" for that "which may be or may not be."[32] Readers who find it odd to say that the necessary is not possible may wish to think in terms of contingency instead.

Two of the arguments that Crescas presents for the conclusion that the possible exists are versions of the notorious laziness objection that goes back to ancient responses to Stoicism. If everything is necessitated, then there is no reason for effort and diligence. If everything is necessitated, then the commandments and prohibitions of the Torah are pointless. He also presents the claim that we can tell from experience that our wills are free. We do not feel compelled; at the moment of choice, we experience ourselves as able to will and able not to will. Another argument he presents starts from the premise that it is unjust to reward and punish necessitated actions. Reward and punishment of human action are prominent features of the Torah, however, so human actions must be possible, i.e., not necessitated. Crescas presents several other arguments as well, but these are the ones of greatest interest for present purposes.[33]

Turning to the arguments for the negative answer, the main impetus comes from considerations of causality and from the doctrine of divine foreknowledge. Regarding the latter point, Crescas vehemently opposes the Gersonidean position and argues at length earlier in the work that God's omniscience extends to all particulars and to knowledge of which future contingents will obtain.[34] With that incompatibilist route closed off, one might then conclude that God's foreknowledge precludes human freedom.[35] The first of the causal arguments relies on the premises (i) that all generable and corruptible things must have causes; (ii) that causal connections are necessary connections (that is, the effect is necessarily brought about if the cause obtains); (iii) that all causes must have prior causes until one reaches the First Being; and (iv) that the First Being is a necessarily existing being. Hence, necessity flows from the First Being through a chain of necessary connections to any given effect.[36] The second causal argument, while couched in different terms, makes a similar point. The third argument takes the premise that nothing can bring itself from potentiality to actuality and applies it to the will. For the will to move itself would require either that the will bring itself to actuality from potentiality (violating the premise) or that a prior willing bring this willing into actuality (thereby launching an infinite regress, unless one of the prior willings was caused by an external object). Consequently, any actual willing must trace back to an external object that caused it.[37] Finally, Crescas invites his readers to consider a thought experiment. Imagine "two people in identical situations, with identical temperaments, identical characteristics, and [an] identical relation to a particular thing."[38] It is not obvious that his libertarian opponents would give the desired answer, but Crescas deems it inconceivable for one of these two people to choose one way and the other to choose the other way. After all, there is *ex hypothesi* nothing that could explain the difference in choice.[39] All of these arguments lead to the conclusion that the possible has no place; everything actual is necessary.

Having presented the arguments for and against the existence of possibility, Crescas proposes to resolve the issue by making a distinction between the modality of things in themselves and of things with respect to their causes.[40] With this distinction in place, there is logical space for something to be (i) necessary in itself, (ii) not necessary in itself but necessary with respect to its causes, or (iii) neither necessary in itself nor necessary with respect to its causes. According to Crescas, however, the last class is empty; there are no things that are necessary in either way. God is necessary in himself, but most things fall into the second class, as do human volitions. Considered in itself, there is nothing about my will that necessitates it choosing to raise my hand or not to raise my hand. But my choice will not come about without a cause. With respect to that cause, my will is necessitated. Being necessary in one way and not in another way is not unique to human agency. In fact, Crescas himself uses the example of copper developing a green patina or verdigris.[41] There is nothing about copper in itself that necessitates verdigris, so in that sense verdigris is possible. But once the relevant causes are in place, the verdigris is necessitated. In other words, verdigris is possible in itself but necessary with respect to its causes, just as human volitions are.

Although Crescas presents his resolution as a *via media*, his position is clearly more in keeping with the arguments against the existence of possibility than with the arguments for it, and someone who made such arguments for possibility would probably be unhappy with his resolution. The text also makes it obvious that Crescas is more sympathetic to the arguments against possibility, since he responds at greater length to the arguments for possibility and offers harsher criticism. For example, he charges some with begging the question, including the argument from experience. The determinist is proposing that we have wills whose choices are caused but without any feeling of compulsion; to respond that we know we are free because we feel free begs the question.[42]

In response to the laziness objections, he makes the equally classic response: if the effects were necessary in themselves, then effort, diligence, commandments, and so forth would be futile.[43] But effects in general and our volitions and actions in particular are not necessary in themselves. Rather, they are necessary with respect to their causes. So those causes are, of course, not irrelevant to the effects. Commandments, for example, could be one of the causes leading to an effect. If part of the causal chain leading to Noah building an ark is God commanding him to do so, then God's command is not futile. In fact, Noah's action depends on the command in the same way that effects normally depend on their causes.

Punishments and rewards can, of course, serve the same purpose of helping to cause some actions rather than others. But is it just? Here Crescas suggests that rewards and punishments are necessitated by our actions just as effects are necessitated by causes. Causal consequences are not evaluated as just or unjust. It is not unjust for someone who sticks her hand in fire to be burned, since that is simply the causal consequence of doing so.[44]

This response might seem to suggest that any action, whether coerced or not, may be punished. Crescas recognizes the concern,[45] but nevertheless thinks it important to distinguish between actions that are caused "without felt compulsion" and actions that are caused "with felt compulsion." The former are caused via the will and so properly involve volitions, whereas the latter are not voluntary. This distinction is straightforward enough and is a standard fixture in accounts arguing that free choice is compatible with determinism. There is an obvious difference between getting an agent to do something by causing her to want to do it versus compelling her to do it despite her not wanting to do it. Furthermore, in principle one could obviously argue that rewards and punishments are just in the case of voluntary actions but not in the case of involuntary or coerced actions. It is less clear, however, on what basis Crescas can declare rewards and punishments just in one case but not the other. He himself notes that getting burned is not unjust even if one comes too close to a fire involuntarily.[46] It is difficult to discern a fully satisfactory response to this question in Crescas – partly because he immediately turns his attention away from the general question to the more particular question how it can be just to punish people for false beliefs about the Torah, given that beliefs are not voluntary. The answer to the more particular question is to say that rewards and punishments are not so much for the beliefs themselves but for the voluntary desires and pleasures accompanying them. But that still leaves the general question. Here the view seems to be that the causal consequences, namely the rewards and punishments, are in fact caused by the soul's volitions. Hence, when those volitions are not present in the case of involuntary actions, the rewards and punishments do not apply.[47]

Before moving on, it is worth noting that there is also an esoteric element in Crescas's account. He acknowledges that publicizing the true view about the will "is dangerous to the masses."[48] If people are told that their actions are necessitated, morality will suffer because most people will fail to see that the laziness objections are unsound and that divine punishment for their misdeeds is still just.

7 Francisco Suárez (1548–1617)

In the later medieval Christian tradition, theologians and philosophers generally give more robust accounts of the will's freedom or at least frame their theories carefully to avoid suspicions of denying the freedom of the will. That caution is thrown to the wind in the upheavals of the Reformation. Magisterial Protestant Reformers such as Martin Luther and John Calvin are adamant that attributing any robust free will to humans fails to account adequately for the utter corruption that resulted from sin and the necessity of divine grace. Luther, in particular, is reacting in part to the Ockhamist legacy as passed down through the fifteenth-century German scholastic Gabriel Biel (Biechler 1970). Luther's dismissals of free will, however, need to be interpreted with some caution both because he clearly assumes a libertarian understanding of free will and because he has a penchant for making intemperate statements in the heat of battle (perhaps he would, for example, concede that we have a sort of compatibilist freedom that is sufficient for moral responsibility). Many of these Reformation discussions, e.g., the famous dispute between Luther and Erasmus (Rupp & Watson 1969), help make vivid what is at stake between rival accounts of the will but are less philosophically sophisticated than many earlier treatments. Still, the Protestant Reformers may fairly be credited with helping make freedom of the will one of the dominant issues of the sixteenth century (see Penner 2017) and making at least some quarters more hospitable for accounts that either deny the will's freedom altogether or reanalyze the will's freedom as a voluntariness compatible with being necessitated by prior causes.

Towards the end of the century, the same issues came under fierce dispute within Roman Catholic circles in what is sometimes known as the *De auxiliis* controversy after the papal tribunal convened to resolve the matter (ending in a stalemate). The history is complex, but a key event occurred in 1588 with the publication of Luis de Molina's aptly titled work *The Harmony of Free Will with the Gift of Grace, Divine Foreknowledge, Providence, Predestination, and Reprobation*. Molina insisted that an adequate account of human agency and moral responsibility requires attributing libertarian freedom to the human will. As Molina puts it: "that agent is called free which, once all the requisites for acting have been posited, is able to act and able not to act, or is able to do one thing in such a way that it is also able to do some contrary."[49] He further asserts that his theory of middle knowledge allows us to reconcile this kind of human freedom with divine foreknowledge, providence, and predestination. His opponents were unimpressed. A fellow Spanish theologian, the Dominican Domingo Bañez, led an effort to have the Spanish Inquisition place Molina's work on the list of prohibited books. Molina's fellow Jesuits rushed to his defence, charging Bañez with falling into the same heresy as Luther and Calvin by denying human beings any responsibility for their salvation, while Bañez and his Dominican allies charged Molina and his fellow Jesuits with falling into the Pelagian heresy of granting human beings the ability to choose what is good without the aid of divine grace.

Participants in this dispute wrote a prodigious amount of work, and even a summary of the various positions would make this chapter too long. As a result, I shall focus solely on the account offered by the broadly Molinist Francisco Suárez (1548–1617). His view was widely influential, representative of the views within the Jesuit order, and moderate in the sense of falling between Protestant and Dominican views on the one hand and the radically voluntarist views of Ockham and Biel on the other. Even treating Suárez's views comprehensively is impossible here.[50] His works include extensive discussions of the divine will, angelic will, of human free will in relation to theological concerns such as divine foreknowledge, providence, and grace, and of human free will in relation to the intellect. I shall focus on the last topic, which receives its most sophisticated treatment in the context of Suárez's extensive account of efficient causation in the *Metaphysical Disputations*.

On Suárez's general picture of causation, efficient causation and final causation are intimately connected in that neither efficient causes nor final causes can exercise their causality without the other. The way this plays out in the case of choice is that the agent efficiently causes choice via the relevant power, namely the will, in response to an object presented as good, this object being the final cause. But first comes an act of love for that object. That love cannot actually be elicited by the final cause unless the will efficiently causes it, and it cannot be efficiently caused by the will unless the final cause elicits it. The efficient cause and final cause have to concur for the act of love to be produced. This is the sense in which the efficient causal aspect and final causal aspect are mutually interdependent. Or, as Suárez sometimes likes to put it, there is a "mutual causality" between final and efficient causes.[51] Intellect is crucially involved because the will is blind. So a potential end or final cause must be presented to the will by intellect. Once an object has been cognized, the will can respond to the object with one of its characteristic acts, e.g., choice.[52]

With respect to freedom, Suárez's account can be seen as a balancing act between attributing sufficient freedom to the will to ground moral responsibility and attributing sufficient responsiveness to reasons to justify counting the will as a rational appetite. Like Molina, Suárez thinks our moral practices presuppose libertarian freedom. For non-rational causes, Suárez agrees with Crescas that there are necessary connections between causes and effects, at least once all the prerequisites for causation are in place. Fire by itself may not necessarily heat water (for example, if the fire is far away from the water), but once all the prerequisites such as proximity and absence of impediments are in place, the fire necessarily heats the water. But Suárez by no means agrees that this model also applies in the case of our wills. He argues at length that human agents are free in the sense of being able both to act and not to act even once all the prerequisites for acting are posited.[53]

Initially Suárez says that it is obvious from experience that we have this freedom, though he then notes precisely the sorts of objections that a compatibilist such as Crescas would make, namely that even if we were determined, we would feel as if we were operating freely if our actions were determined by a causal chain passing through our judgements and will rather than our actions being coerced against our will. Suárez then concedes that perhaps the argument from experience is not as evident as one might have hoped. There is still room for an "obstinate person" to raise difficulties. Still, Suárez thinks that our experience of being able to resist rewards and punishments provides at least some experiential evidence for thinking that we have this sort of freedom.[54] He also argues that it would be impious to suggest that our wicked actions were necessitated by God.

Hence, we have to be free to allow for the needed breaks in the chain of necessitation. It would, he notes, be especially outrageous to suggest that God necessitates our wicked actions and then punishes us for them.[55] Furthermore, Suárez argues that our practices of praise and blame presuppose freedom. He notes that people get indignant when they suffer an injustice, but not if the agent cannot help inflicting the injustice because she lacks the relevant mental capacities to act freely. Rather, people are blamed and punished if it is thought that they were free to do otherwise.[56]

Suárez thinks this freedom comes in via the will since the intellect's judgements cannot be directly free. He is indeed happy to allow for doxastic voluntarism, but he stresses the latter half of that term. There are, in fact, cases where we are free to judge one way or another way, but that is precisely because we can *will* to judge one way or another way. Were it not for the willing, the intellect would not be free in that way. Suárez is also willing to grant that judgements about what is good sometimes determine an agent's choices. Psychological processes can be complex. But since the intellect is not directly free, its freedom ultimately traces back to a free act of will on pain of an infinite regress (Penner 2013: 18–26).

There are several sorts of cases where Suárez thinks it quite clear that the will is free to accept or reject an object presented by the intellect. He seems to think that in ordinary cases we simply judge an object to be good and make no comparative judgements that it is better than or inferior to some other object. Furthermore, the judgement is typically not that the object *must* be pursued but simply that it is good enough. Such a judgement is sufficient for the will to be able to choose the object but does not necessitate its choice. The will could also refrain from choosing it.[57] Sometimes there are judgements that are comparative yet inconclusive either because both objects are judged equally good or because one object is judged better in one respect while the other object is judged better in another respect (for example, judging that eating another helping of dessert would be more pleasurable but not eating it would be better for health). In such cases he also thinks it clear that the will is left free. The more difficult case is where an agent judges that one option is better overall than another option. Buridan, one may recall, denied that the will can then choose the option that is less good. Suárez, on the other hand, concludes that the will can still choose that option, a conclusion motivated in part by his desire to safeguard God's freedom, since some of the other options rely on epistemic limitations not present in the case of God. He does, however, seem less confident about the case of choosing a lesser good.[58]

But because he wants to safeguard the will's status as the appetite responsive to reasons, Suárez is not willing to attribute as radical a freedom as Ockham suggested. On Suárez's view, only the intellect enables an agent to choose an object presented to it as good.[59] The will cannot choose just anything. It can only choose something if there is a reason to choose it. The result is that for any choice a human agent makes, there is an answer to the question why that choice was made: because the chosen option appeared good. If I choose to eat a second helping of dessert and am asked why I did so, there is a ready answer: because it tastes good, and so eating it is pleasurable.

As with any libertarian account of freedom, note that the explanation only goes so far. At some point, if I am asked why I chose this good *rather* than that good, no reason can be provided. I chose to eat a second helping of dessert because doing so promised pleasure, but if I am asked why I chose short-term pleasure over long-term health, both objects that I recognize as good, I may not have anything to say. I simply did. There is always something to be said about why an agent chose as she did, but there is sometimes no answer to the contrastive question why she chose this good rather than that good. Someone like Crescas will, of course, be unsatisfied. The consequence of Suárez's position, after all, is the one that Crescas finds inconceivable, namely that two identical agents in identical scenarios could choose differently such that there is no cause that explains their differing choices. Of course, Suárez would in turn be incredulous to learn that for Crescas human acts of willing are no less determined than verdigris developing on copper.[60]

Notes

1 I am keenly aware of how many figures, including well-known ones, I am passing over. In a few cases, it seems to me that well-known contributions to free will discussions do not warrant the level of regard they have received. But in most cases, their neglect in this chapter is simply a result of space not permitting a satisfying discussion. It would be an easy matter to provide the names of dozens of figures who merit inclusion. Some sense of the range of figures that might have been discussed can be found in Marenbon (2012).
2 All of these terms are used in a variety of ways, but in the present chapter, intellectualism is the view that the will is determined by the intellect and voluntarism the view that the will is not so determined. Compatibilism is the view that freedom is compatible with determinism and incompatibilism that it is not compatible. Intellectualists are often compatibilists and voluntarists often incompatibilists, but those positions need not be so allied. For example, one could hold the view that the intellect's judgements determine the will's choices but that the judgements themselves are free in an incompatibilist sense or that agents simply are not free.
3 A question could be raised about how deep this difference between event-causation and agent-causation goes. Perhaps the agent-causal expressions employed by medieval philosophers could readily be translated into event-causal expressions more in keeping with recent philosophical idioms. Answering that question is not necessary for present purposes. We can merely proceed on the understanding that the framework within which medieval philosophers operate is one according to which the world is populated by substances and those substances have powers whereby they act, whereby they cause effects. If this can be translated readily into event-causal language, then little harm should result from using agent-causal language. If the difference goes deeper, then agent-causal language will appropriately represent the late medieval and Renaissance discussions that are the focus of this chapter.
4 Given that Aristotle has no explicit notion of the will, one might find it surprising that the medieval Aristotelians are all so assured of there being such a faculty.
5 One systematic discussion of the different acts of the will from the end of our period of concern can be found in Francisco Suárez's *De voluntario et involuntario* (1856–1878: 241–271).

6 A sense of the state of the literature can be found by consulting Aertsen et al. (2001); Normore (1995); Piché (1999); and Wippel (1995, 2002).
7 For example, there is no reason to think that the Jewish Ḥasdai Crescas to be discussed later felt especially constrained by the condemnations of a Catholic bishop. It is also worth noting that, after Aquinas was canonized, some of the condemnations were retracted in 1325 insofar as they were in tension with Aquinas's views (Wippel 1995: 239).
8 For an introduction to Ockham's life and intellectual context, see Courtenay (1999). My discussion of Ockham's account of the will has been very much influenced by a recent and excellent paper by Osborne (2012).
9 For more on this issue, see King 2008 and Perler 2013.
10 Ockham, *Rep.* II, q. 20 (*OTh V*: 435). All translations are mine unless a translation is cited.
11 *Rep.* II, q. 20 (*OTh* V: 435 & 444).
12 *QQ* I, q. 16 (p. 75).
13 *QV* q. 8 (*QTh* VIII: 442–445).
14 *Confessions* II.iv.9–x.18.
15 *QV* q. 8 (*QTh* VIII: 442–445).
16 *QQ* q. 16 (pp. 75–76).
17 He does agree with Ockham that the will and intellect are not distinct faculties in reality.
18 *QNE* III, q. 4 (p. 175).
19 *QNE* III, q. 1 (p. 152).
20 *QNE* III, q. 3 (p. 168).
21 I will cite Zupko (1995) but the same content, as well as additional material, can also be found in Chapter 15 of his (2003).
22 *QNE* III, q. 3 (p. 168). See also Zupko (1995: 80–82).
23 *QNE* III, q. 4 (p. 175). Cf. Pironet (2001: 202–204).
24 *QNE* III, q. 3 (p. 169). See also Zupko (1995: 88–91).
25 My thanks to Martin Klein for reminding me of Rescher's discussion of Buridan's ass.
26 For an introduction to Crescas, see Sadik (2014).
27 A good introduction to the issue can be found in Zagzebski (2011).
28 *Light* II, intro. (p. 192).
29 *Light* II.5, intro. (p. 216).
30 There are passages in Crescas's text that at least at first glance seem in tension with the determinist line. Some scholars suggest that these passages were incorporated from later marginal notations, notations that may represent Crescas's evolving views or may not be by Crescas at all. This is not the place to pursue more subtle matters of interpretation. See the discussion in Sadik (2014: §§ 2.4 and 5). For the present work, I will simply present the prominent determinist strand without worrying about the passages that might pull in a different direction.
31 *Light* II.5 (pp. 216–235). A helpful treatment of Crescas's views on choice can be found in Feldman (1984).
32 *Light* II.1.1 (p. 195).
33 *Light* II.5.1 (pp. 217–218).
34 *Light* II.1 (pp. 192–216).
35 *Light* II.5.2 (p. 220).
36 Ibid. (p. 219).
37 Ibid. (pp. 219–220).
38 Ibid. (p. 220).
39 Feldman offers an illuminating discussion of Crescas's causal arguments (1984: 19–22).

40 *Light* II.5.3 (pp. 221–227).
41 *Light* II.5.3 (pp. 223–224).
42 Ibid. (p. 221).
43 Ibid. (pp. 222–223).
44 Ibid. (p. 223).
45 *Light* II.5.5 (p. 229).
46 *Light* II.5.3 (p. 223).
47 *Light* II.5.5 (p. 231).
48 *Light* II.5.3 (p. 224).
49 *Concordia* ad q. 14, art. 13, disp. 2.
50 Any brief treatment of Suárez will necessarily leave something to be desired since the interest in late scholastics such as him usually focuses not so much on the basic outlines of their positions – their basic positions have usually been held before by others – but in the extraordinary detail with which they develop their positions. More detail can be found in Penner (2013).
51 *DM* 27.2.7–14.
52 *DM* 23.7.
53 *DM* 19.2. Note that *DM* 17–19 are available in translation in *On Efficient Causality*.
54 *DM* 19.2.12–15.
55 *DM* 19.2.16.
56 Ibid.
57 *DM* 19.6.10–14.
58 *DM* 19.6.13.
59 *DM* 23.5.
60 My thanks to the participants in the conference "Late Medieval and Renaissance Accounts of the Mind" for valuable comments on this chapter. Sabrina Ebbersmeyer, Dominik Perler, and Stephan Schmid provided especially valuable feedback.

Bibliography

Primary sources

Augustine. *Confessions*. H. Chadwick (trans.). Oxford: Oxford University Press, 1998.
Boethius. *The Consolation of Philosophy*. V. Watts (trans.), rev. ed. London: Penguin Books 1999.
Buridan, Jean. *Quaestiones in decem libros Ethicorum Aristotelis ad Nicomachum* (= *QNE*). Oxoniae: Excudebat L. L. Impensis Hen. Cripps, Ed. Forrest, Hen. Curtayne, & Ioh. Wilmot, 1637.
Crescas, Ḥasdai. *The Light of the Lord* (= *Light*). In *Medieval Jewish Philosophical Writings*, C. Manekin (ed.), 192–235. Cambridge: Cambridge University Press, 2007.
Molina, Luis de. *Liberi arbitrii cum gratiae donis, divina praescientia, providentia, praedestinatione et reprobatione concordia* (= *Concordia*). Antwerp: Joachim Trognaesius, 1595.
———. *On Divine Foreknowledge: Part IV of the Concordia*. A. J. Freddoso (trans.). Ithaca: Cornell University Press, 1988.
Suárez, Francisco. *De voluntario et involuntario*, M. André & C. Berton (eds). In *Opera Omnia* 4. Paris: Ludovicus Vivès, 1856.
———. *Disputationes Metaphysicae* (= *DM*). In *Opera Omnia*, M. André & C. Berton (eds), 25–26. Paris: Ludovicus Vivès, 1861.

———. *On Efficient Causality: Metaphysical Disputations 17, 18, and 19*. A. J. Freddoso (trans.). New Haven: Yale University Press, 1994.
William of Ockham. *Quaestiones Variae* (= *QV*). In *Opera Theologica* VIII, G. Etzkorn, F. E. Kelley, & J. C. Wey (eds). St. Bonaventure: The Franciscan Institute, 1984.
———. *Reportatio* (= *Rep.*). In *Opera Theologica* V, G. Gál & R. Wood (eds). St. Bonaventure: The Franciscan Institute, 1985.
———. *Quodlibetal Questions* (= *QQ*). A. J. Freddoso & F. E. Kelley (trans.). New Haven: Yale University Press, 1991.

Secondary sources

Aertsen, J. A., Emery Jr., K. & Speer, A. (eds). 2001. *Nach der Verurteilung von 1277: Philosophie und Theologie an der Universität von Paris im letzten Viertel des 13. Jahrhunderts: Studien und Texte*. Berlin: de Gruyter.
Biechler, J. E. 1970. "Gabriel Biel on *Liberum Arbitrium*: Prelude to Luther's *De Servo Arbitrio*." *The Thomist* **23**: 114–127.
Courtenay, W. J. 1999. "The Academic and Intellectual Worlds of Ockham." In *The Cambridge Companion to Ockham*, P. V. Spade (ed.), 17–30. Cambridge: Cambridge University Press.
Feldman, S. 1984. "A Debate Concerning Determinism in Late Medieval Jewish Philosophy." *Proceedings of the American Academy for Jewish Research* **51**: 15–54.
King, P. 2008. "The Inner Cathedral: Mental Architecture in High Scholasticism." *Vivarium* **46**: 253–274.
Marenbon, J. 2012. "Late Medieval Philosophy? Renaissance Philosophy?" In *The Oxford Handbook of Medieval Philosophy*, J. Marenbon (ed.), 220–244. Oxford: Oxford University Press.
Normore, C. G. 1995. "Who Was Condemned in 1277?" *The Modern Schoolman* **72**: 273–281.
Osborne, T. M. 2012. "William of Ockham on the Freedom of the Will and Happiness." *American Catholic Philosophical Quarterly* **86**(3): 435–456.
Penner, S. 2013. "Free and Rational: Suárez on the Will." *Archiv für Geschichte der Philosophie* **95**(1): 1–35.
———. 2017. "Free Will." In *The Routledge Companion to Sixteenth Century Philosophy*, H. Lagerlund & B. Hill (eds), 493–515. New York: Routledge.
Perler, D. 2013. "What are Faculties of the Soul? Descartes and His Scholastic Background." In *Continuity and Innovation in Medieval and Early Modern Philosophy*, J. Marenbon (ed.), 9–38. Oxford: Oxford University Press.
Piché, D. 1999. *La condamnation parisienne de 1277: nouvelle édition du texte latin: traduction, introduction et commentaires*. Paris: Vrin.
Pines, S. 1967. "Scholasticism After Thomas Aquinas and the Teachings of Ḥasdai Crescas and his Predecessors." *Proceedings of the Israel Academy of Sciences and Humanities* **1**(10): 1–101.
Pironet, F. 2001. "The Notion of 'Non Velle' in Buridan's Ethics." In *The Metaphysics and Natural Philosophy of John Buridan*, J. M. M. H. Thijssen & J. Zupko (eds), 199–219. Leiden: Brill.
Rescher, Nicholas. 2005. "Choice Without Preference: The Problem of 'Buridan's Ass.'" In *Scholastic Meditations*, Nicholas Rescher (ed.), 1–48. Washington, DC: Catholic University of America Press.

Rudavsky, T. 1983. "Divine Omniscience and Future Contingents in Gersonides." *Journal of the History of Philosophy* **21**(4): 513–536.

———. 1985. "Divine Omniscience, Contingency and Prophecy." In *Divine Omniscience and Omnipotence in Medieval Philosophy*, T. Rudavsky (ed.), 161–181. Dordrecht, The Netherlands: D. Reidel.

———. 2003. "The Impact of Scholasticism upon Jewish Philosophy in the Fourteenth and Fifteenth Centuries." In *The Cambridge Companion to Medieval Jewish Philosophy*, D. H. Frank & O. Leaman (eds), 345–370. Cambridge: Cambridge University Press.

Rupp, E. G. & Watson, S. 1969. *Luther and Erasmus: Free Will and Salvation*. Philadelphia: The Westminster Press.

Sadik, S. 2014. "Hasdai Crescas." In *The Stanford Encyclopedia of Philosophy*, Spring 2014 Edition, E. N. Zalta (ed.). http://plato.stanford.edu/archives/spr2014/entries/crescas/.

Sirat, C. 1990. *A History of Jewish Philosophy in the Middle Ages*. Cambridge: Cambridge University Press.

Wippel, J. F. 1995. "Thomas Aquinas and the Condemnation of 1277." *The Modern Schoolman* **72**: 233–272.

———. 2002. "The Parisian Condemnations of 1270 and 1277." In *A Companion to Philosophy in the Middle Ages*, J. J. E. Gracia & T. B. Noone (eds), 65–73. Malden: Blackwell Pub.

Zagzebski, L. "Foreknowledge and Free Will." In *The Stanford Encyclopedia of Philosophy*, Fall 2011 Edition, E. N. Zalta (ed.). http://plato.stanford.edu/archives/fall2011/entries/free-will-foreknowledge/.

Zupko, J. 1995. "Freedom of Choice in Buridan's Moral Psychology." *Mediaeval Studies* **57**: 75–99.

———. 2003. *John Buridan: Portrait of a Fourteenth-Century Arts Master*. Notre Dame: University of Notre Dame Press.

8

LATE SCHOLASTIC DEBATES ABOUT EXTERNAL AND INTERNAL SENSES

In the direction of Francisco Suárez (1548–1617)

Daniel Heider

1 Introduction

A typical methodological feature of scholastic philosophy is its focus on solving problems shared by various philosophical schools and traditions from different historical periods.[1] Besides universals, which at a certain time epitomized scholastic philosophy, a persistent issue in late Medieval and Renaissance philosophy happened to be the question of the efficient causes of sensory cognitive acts having intentional content. The issue is far from restricted to that period, though. Sensation can be seen either as (passively) mirroring sensibles that exist extramentally (the mirror metaphor) or as actively searching for an object, much like a headlight searching for something in the darkness (the lamp metaphor).[2] Both approaches can be taken as two different "answers" to the two main criteria of a "successful" theory of perception, criteria that are generally embraced by all present-day analytical philosophers engaging in research on perception. While the first touchstone constitutes the epistemological test, the second is connected with the phenomenological requirement. Accordingly, a viable philosophical theory of perception is supposed to explain both the fact that a veridical visual experience yields a piece of information about the extramental world (the epistemological criterion) and the fact that sensory experience is the paradigmatic example of a conscious experience (the phenomenological criterion). As William Fish (2010: 2) notes, both criteria are not easy to accommodate in a single theory. Considering the dichotomy of cognitive activism and cognitive passivism it may be said that, while the receptivist account of perception can easily accommodate the epistemological standard, it has difficulties satisfying the phenomenological demand; the activist account neatly fulfils the phenomenological criterion, but is at a disadvantage when it comes to meeting the epistemological standard.

The question of the efficient causes of sensory perception partly overlaps with another issue: How can something extramental become part of our consciousness?[3]

As is well known, replies to this enquiry in the broadly conceived Peripatetic tradition oscillate between two extremes; some assume actively efficacious sensibles and essentially receptive powers, while others endorse significantly spontaneous faculties and widely inert sensibles. The articulation of this issue in terms of material objects and (animated) cognitive acts also makes clear why this problem came to be stated in terms of "the issue of ascendant (upward) causality". How can an ontologically less perfect (material) sensible produce something ontologically more perfect, i.e., an (animate) cognitive act?

In this chapter I intend to present the answers to the abovementioned causal question given by those authors in the late Middle Ages and the Renaissance who, as recent literature confirms,[4] can be considered representative and standing in a systematic connection. Even though I focus predominantly on the issue of the cognitive acts of the external senses, in the case of Francisco Suárez, I will also include a treatment of the sensible species (likeness)[5] of the internal sense.[6] A major stimulus to this dispute in the late Middle Ages came from the theory of the agent sense contrived by the Latin Averroist John of Jandun (ca. 1285–1328). Jandun defended the provocative claim that, for Averroes and Aristotle, sensation is not primarily a receptive process, in which a power receives sensible species, as an initial, impartial reading seems to evince, but rather an active process enacted in successive steps by different sensory powers, namely the agent sense (*sensus agens*) and the passive sense (*sensus passivus*).[7] This theory, later identified with *the* Averroist teaching, became a challenge not only for late medieval authors immediately following Jandun but also for Renaissance authors including Suárez. Jandun's theory soon became the target of a systematic critique. No doubt the most extensive criticism was formulated by the Renaissance Aristotelian Agostino Nifo (1469/70–1538) in his treatise *De sensu agente* (1497). The theories of both Jandun and Nifo became an important point of reference (and critique) for Suárez in his *Commentaria una cum quaestionibus in libros Aristotelis De anima* (1621).

Although Jandun's theory of the agent sense represents a significant doctrinal shift in the late scholastic treatment of the efficient causes of sensory operation,[8] it is far from being the origin of the debate. Jandun's intention was to defend Averroist Aristotelianism. With respect to this point of departure, I will start with a brief prologue concerning the historical background given by Aristotle's statements in *De anima* and by Averroes's comments on the text suggesting the existence of an external mover, the main function of which is to "lift up" sensible things (less perfect entities) to the level of intentions, i.e., of (the more perfect) "entities" capable of intentionally affecting the sensory power.[9]

Two preliminary methodological notes are in order, however. First, even though not all of the abovementioned authors distinguish between the issue of the production of *species sensibilis* and that of the sensory cognitive act (e.g., Nifo), for the sake of orderliness I will keep these two questions separate.[10] Second, I will not concern myself with all the nuances of the later authors' arguments against the opinions of their predecessors. I aim to present Latin Averroism as the historical "spawn" of Suárez's elaboration, i.e., as the background against which the Jesuit distinguishes between the issue of the origin of sensible species and that of sensation on the level of external senses,[11] and between the enquiry concerning the production of the sensible species in the external senses and in the internal sense. A historian of early modern scholasticism must not ignore the fact that although Suárez is a non-secular philosopher, or with respect to his *Opera omnia* a theologian rather than a philosopher, and although he primarily refers to authors such as Augustine, Aquinas or Scotus, he has a good knowledge of Averroist doctrines such as those of Jandun or Nifo. In other words, I would like to show that a full understanding of Suárez's general theory of sensation, which constitutes the *terminus ad quem* of the chapter, cannot be attained without taking into account the tradition of Latin Averroism.[12]

2 Aristotle and Averroes

The dominant interpretation of Aristotle's theory of sensation is receptivism.[13] Sensation is conceived by Aristotle as a kind of accidental change (*alteratio, immutatio*). As with every change, an active and a potential component must be present. As Aristotle says in *De anima* II.5, "sensation consists ... in being moved and acted upon" (416b33–34). Unlike the internal senses, the external senses can only experience sensation in the presence of sensibles, i.e., sensible qualities such as colours, sounds, odours and tastes. By analogy to physical changes such as fire heating water in a pot, where fire represents the active and water the (purely) passive potency, the sensibles correspond to the active potency and the sensory power to the receptive potency. Provided that external factors do not prevent sensation from being realized, e.g., in the case of vision the medium is transparent and the power is in contact with the sensible by means of a sensible species, sensation is triggered as soon as a sensible is situated within the cognitive range of a percipient. Aristotle likens sensation to wax receiving the impression of a gold signet ring without the gold, i.e., to receiving the form of a signet ring without its matter (424a18–22). Naturally, wax cannot take the impression of a signet ring without receiving the impression from an immediate agent, namely from a gold signet ring. Similarly, a sensible is an agent that brings – or as the scholastics would say, "reduces" – the sensory power from potency to act. The sensory power, the passive potency, cannot reduce itself from potency to act. That requires the activity of an extrinsic agent. Aristotle formulates this view concisely: "The activity of the sensible object and of the sensation is one and the same" (425b25–26). If the activity of the sensible object implies sensation, the only function remaining for the sensory power is that of reception.

Even though sensible objects seem to be capable of affecting the cognitive sensory power on their own by producing and multiplying the sensible intentional species in the medium, Aristotle appears to suggest a complementary agent. In his *De anima* III.4, when treating the relationship between sensing and thinking, he mentions a structural analogy between sensing and thinking: "as the sensitive is to the sensible, so must mind be to the thinkable" (429a17–18). However, we know that for the Stagirite the mind is related to the thinkable in a twofold way, due to there being two intellects. The agent intellect is the power of transforming sensibles or potential intelligibles, namely phantasms, into actual intelligibles, which can later be received by the (immaterial) potential intellect. As an immaterial power, the potential intellect receives only actual intelligibles. Unlike Platonic intelligibles, which exist *in actu* extramentally, actual intelligibles according to Aristotle need to be produced by the illuminating activity of the agent intellect, which prepares these intelligibles for the potential intellect, the only function of which – at least in the process of simple apprehension – is to receive actual intelligibles. Now, if we are to take Aristotle's proposed similarity between thought and sensation seriously, we must say that sensation involves two powers, too: an active potency or some extrinsic mover reducing potential sensibles to actual sensibles and a passive sense, which receives actual sensibles.

In his *Commentarium magnum in Aristotelis De anima*, Averroes seems to detect precisely this active agent of sensation. Averroes makes clear that sensibles, as material sensible forms, cannot intentionally affect the sensory power. Sensing a green colour does not turn us green. It is clear that a change in sensation cannot be of the same type as corporeal change. Averroes underlines that sensibles can act on powers only as intentions, never as material sensibles (Averroes *CMDA* 223). But how do these sensible things turn into intentions? How do they acquire intentional being, which they seem to have not only in the organs but in the medium itself? In his commentary on *De anima* II.5, Averroes says:

> And one can say that sensibles do not move the senses in the way they exist outside the soul, for they move the senses insofar as they are intentions, since in matter they are not intentions in act but in potency. And one cannot say that this difference occurs by virtue of the difference of subject such that intentions come to be on account of spiritual matter which is the sense, not on account of an external mover. It is better to think that the cause of the diversity of matter is the diversity of forms and not that the diversity of matter is the cause of the diversity of forms. Since it is so, it is necessary to posit an external motor in senses different from sensibles, as was necessary in the case of the intellect. It has been seen, therefore, that if we concede that the diversity of forms is the cause of the diversity of matter, then it will be necessary that the mover be external. But Aristotle was silent about this because it is hidden in the case of sensation and apparent in the case of the intellect.
>
> (*CMDA* 221)

Even though, according to Averroes, Aristotle did not speak explicitly about an external mover in the case of the senses, that does not mean he did not take such a mover into account. Although in comparison to the agent intellect this agent is not as apparent, that does not mean it does not exist. Since sensibles cannot immediately affect sensory powers, we need an ontological "elevator" to "lift up" material sensibles to the level of sensible intentions. It cannot be said that sensibles become intentions by virtue of the subject or the "substrate" that receives them, since form does not exist for the sake of matter but vice versa. Moreover, Averroes indicates that the emission of stimuli from sensibles must be assisted by the mover, which is not inherent to the perceiver's soul. Only an external mover can secure the reduction of potential sensibles to actual sensibles. Only the assistance of some external (higher) agent can explain how an ontologically lower entity, i.e., a sensible thing, can alter an ontologically higher one, i.e., a cognitive power.

3 John of Jandun on the *sensus agens*

Although Jandun makes clear that we have to consider an agent that bridges two hierarchically different planes, he does not find this *agens* in the field of the production of sensible species but within the process of the formation of the act of perception.[14] If we assume that the sensible form is visible *per se*, it must be the sensible alone that produces sensible intentions, without any extrinsic assistance. As Jandun states, the sensible form can be conceived not only as the material form but also as an essence that does not comprise matter. And it is only *qua* essence that it can cause the intentional species both in the medium (air, water, etc.) and in the pertinent organ (Pattin 1988: 226).

Reception of a sensible species is for Jandun far from being identical with a perceptual act. Before presenting his arguments for an affirmative reply to the question whether the agent sense is necessary in the case of a cognitive act, Jandun proposes four *fundamenta* of his theory (Pattin 1988: 128–131) in *Sophisma de sensu agente*. First, everything that is received in a subject depends on an effective principle. A passive potency always presupposes an active potency that reduces the passive faculty to an act. Second, that being is nobler whose proper operation is nobler. If it generally holds that an operation is the goal of the subject of that operation, one can recognize the perfection of the subject of an operation through knowledge of the perfection of its operation. Third, producing an effect is *simpliciter* more perfect than receiving an effect. Activity is nobler than passivity, and a more perfect being is more active than less perfect beings. While separated substances stand higher on "the ontological ladder" because they are active in moving heavenly bodies, prime matter is the least noble being because it is pure (inactive) potency. Fourth, as regards sensory cognition, the sensible species is not more perfect than the cognitive power. The sensible species of the colour red is not more perfect than the visual power, and the species of the sound of a flute is not more perfect than the auditory faculty. One of Jandun's main reasons for this ordering of powers and sensible species consists in the fact that the cognitive act is animated, whereas a sensible species is of a corporeal nature.

Leaving aside the arguments for the doctrine of the agent sense that are based on the activity of the internal senses, namely that the cogitative power, common sense and memory are all essentially active powers that judge, distinguish and discourse in the field of particular intentions (Pattin 1988: 226), one of Jandun's main arguments for the theory of the agent sense can be labelled "from the elimination of alternatives" (*ibid.*, 227). Obviously, sensation must have its own immediate efficient principle. If this is not the agent sense, then it must be one of the following: 1) the soul, 2) the extramental sensible, 3) the passive sense or 4) the sensible species. Concerning the first option, Jandun claims that the soul cannot be the immediate principle of the production of sensory operation since like every Aristotelian he argues that the soul becomes active only by means of sensory powers. As for the second option, Jandun shows that the sensible, being an entity less perfect than the cognitive power and an entity removed from the power, can in no way be the immediate cause of the perceptive act. As regards the passive sense, the passive potency cannot be the immediate principle of a cognitive act since the same power cannot be simultaneously passive and active in the same regard. Finally, if the efficient cause of sensation were sensible species, they would have to be more perfect than the cognitive power since activity is nobler than passivity. And this is not the case.

The only tenable option thus seems to be that sensation is efficiently caused by the agent sense. When describing the mechanism of sensation, Jandun asserts that the first actualization consists in the passive sense receiving a determination from the sensible species emitted (without any "lifter") by the sensible. This reception is a mere disposing reception, which is not yet sensation proper. According to Jandun, sensation proper consists in the second act, which is received in the passive sense. While discussing visual perception, Jandun stresses that the eye is a corporeal potency, which puts it on the same ontological level as an inanimate medium, such as illuminated air. When disposed by the sensible species, the agent sense, as the *agens perficiens*, produces the act of sensation (*ibid.*, 159–160).[15] This act of sensation, identified by Jandun with Averroes's notion of *intentio*,[16] is later received in the passive sense. So for Jandun the cognitive faculty is not the agent sense but only the passive sense. However, vis-à-vis the abovementioned third *fundamentum* we encounter the following problem: If the cognitive faculty is the passive sense and if passivity is less perfect than activity, then we have to conclude that the cognitive power is less perfect than a non-cognitive power, which is, to say the least, a problematic claim. Jandun's reply, typical of his overall strategy for making his exposition consistent with Aristotle's *dicta*, is to distinguish the qualified sense (*secundum quid*) of sense and the non-qualified sense (*simpliciter*). Even though with respect to cognition (i.e., *secundum quid*) it is true that the agent sense is less perfect than the cognitive passive sense, absolutely speaking (*simpliciter*), i.e., with respect to the very substance of the power, the agent sense is more perfect that the passive sense (Pattin 1988: 232).

When explaining away the Stagirite's receptivism, the Latin Averroist underlines the specific historical context of *De anima*, which was in Aristotle's days determined by the dominant doctrine of extramission, according to which visual perception, at least in its first stage, is based on the primordial emanation of the intraocular fire toward the sensibles and the medium of sensation.[17] On Jandun's reading, when Aristotle emphasizes the reception of forms, he does so just to counterbalance this prevalent (activist) approach. Consequently, we must assume that what is only briefly indicated in Aristotle, i.e., cognitive activism, must be taken as seriously into account as the numerous passages manifesting the receptivist approach. Aristotle's silence about the *sensus agens* is far from implying his denial of this power (Pattin 1988: 163).

4 Agostino Nifo on the origin of the sensible species

As already said, Jandun's theory of the agent sense was sharply criticized by Agostino Nifo.[18] Nifo's central programme in his *De sensu agente*, which belongs to his early Averroist period,[19] was to deliver an authentic interpretation of the doctrine of Averroes, devoid of Jandun's misinterpretation. The brief treatise is a systematic and differentiated attack at Jandun's thesis. In presenting this treatise I pursue two goals. First, I intend to present what I consider to be Nifo's main argument against Jandun's theory of the agent sense; second, I aim to bring in Nifo's theory of the origin of the sensible species, which is supposed to replace the theoretical work that Jandun has assigned to the agent sense.

Nifo's crucial argument, recurring throughout the treatise, is based on cognitive receptivism.[20] Cognition is nothing but assimilation to a cognizable object. The mere possession of the sensible species representing the sensible object is all we actually need for sensation. Sensation is the perfect representation of an object to the pertinent cognitive power. There is no doubt that this representation can come through without the operation of the agent sense. The organ or the power informed by the sensible species is actually all we need to obtain an act of perception. According to Nifo, for Aristotle and Averroes the only agent in the production of sensation is the sensible species. Consequently, only a passive role remains for the sensory power. The existence of the agent sense can in no way be substantiated by Aristotle's *corpus*. In fact, Aristotle nowhere mentions it. As Nifo states, the species and sensation must be taken "as really one and the same entity" (Nifo *DSA* 127a). Consequently, an act of perception merely consists in the acquisition of a sensible species. Contrary to what was later proposed by Suárez (*IDA* 5, 3, 2), a cognitive sensory act ceases to be an independent ontological "unit".

When focusing on the issue of uplifting the sensible form to the level of sensible acts or species, the question according to Nifo is how the less perfect sensible thing can cause the more perfect sensible intention or act. Nifo makes clear that Jandun was mistaken in thinking that Averroes left the question of this "elevator" unanswered. On the contrary, Averroes was quite sure that there is an external mover of sensible forms that reduces them to sensibles in acts. The only problem is to determine the nature of this mover and how it actually operates (*DSA* 128a).

According to Nifo, a perfect understanding of Averroes's opinion must be based on three assumptions, which are related to three factors inherent in each natural change on the part of an agent. The first is the form of the agent; the second is the matter, in which the natural form exists, since if the physical change is an individual transformation, then the existence of matter is necessary; the third element is the universal agent in virtue of which all particular agents are made operative. All these factors are indispensable in the case of sensation as well. For Nifo it is clear that the universal agent is the prime mover or God, who is ultimately responsible for all particular movements. The situation is not different with regard to the origination of intelligible species, which he at least co-causes. While the sensible is the proximate and instrumental cause, the prime mover is the remote and principle cause. Since the universal agent (God) cannot be the cause of particular effects, such as the apprehension of this or that shade of blue, Nifo asserts that this particular causation, which is connected with the particular formal content in the given sensation, is provided by the concrete sensible form. The prime mover is the principle cause of the spirituality of the sensible species. Without being uplifted by the prime mover the sensible forms could not intentionally affect the cognitive powers. There is no need for the agent sense advocated by Jandun since the immediate and *per se* efficient cause of sensation is the sensible form *qua* the instrument of the prime mover (*DSA* 128b–129a).

5 Suárez's theory of sensory cognition

The theories of Jandun and Nifo mentioned above both find their main reference point in Suárez's complex elaboration of the issue of sensory cognition.[21] While Suárez considers Jandun's theory in the context of the formation of an act of sensory perception, he refers to the doctrines of Nifo in his treatise on the production of sensible species.[22] Allowing for a third issue, namely that of the efficient cause of the sensible species of the internal sense, we arrive at three topics that have to be presented in relation to Suárez's general doctrine of the efficient causes of sensory knowledge.[23]

5.1 Production and ontology of the sensible species

How does Suárez evaluate Nifo's approach in the context of the production of the sensible species? It may be said that Suárez's appraisal is thoroughly negative. The Jesuit categorically denies all conceptions that appeal to non-naturalistic sources (*IDA* 6.2.3). Dismissing this theory leads Suárez to conclude that sensible species are fully caused by the sensible objects themselves (*IDA* 6.2.6). However, is this "naturalizing" statement not in conflict with the abovementioned upshot of the passage from Averroes, according to which the less perfect cannot bring about the more perfect? Suárez does not think so. In order to fully understand his reply, we must become familiar with the Jesuit's ontology of the sensible species.

Suárez makes clear that ontologically speaking the sensible species is nothing but an accident of quality inhering either in the medium or in the sensory organ (*IDA* 5.2.2). In the natural order, sensible species are essentially dependent upon sensibles in both their being and becoming. In order to actualize the sensory power, sensible species do not need to be substances. Consequently, if they are accidents, the manner of their union with the power can also be merely accidental (*IDA* 5.2.4). The union of the sensible species and the power cannot result, as e.g., Cajetan claimed, in a type of unity that is tighter than the substantial unity of form and matter, in which a new thing (a *tertium quid*), i.e., the material composite of form and matter, is produced. In the case of cognition no such *tertium quid* is established since the cognitive power is ultimately assimilated, thus becoming identical with the cognized thing (Caietan 2000: 57). For Suárez, on the other hand, the mode of union of the sensible species and the cognitive power does not differ from the aggregative union of any accident and substance (*IDA* 5.2.5).

Still, the sensible species are not of the same order and kind as the sensible accidents that emit them (*IDA* 5.2.8). As Suárez says, these species are only traces (*vestigia*) of their emitting objects (*IDA* 6.2.6). They are only non-sensed, virtual representations in need of further cognitive processing and perfecting (*IDA* 5.2.6) before full-blown sensation can be established. Their subtlety, their invisibility, in fact, to which they owe their transmittability through the medium, is not a consequence of their immateriality since, contrary to the *species intelligibilis*, they are material and extended. If they are received in material and extended power, they must be material and extended (*IDA* 5.2.17).

Suárez's emphasis on the accidental and material aspects of the sensible species does not mean that the sensible species cease to function as formal similitudes (*similitudines formales*) of their sensibles (*IDA* 5.2.21). The representative aspect pertains to their "essence", since ontologically speaking they belong to the kind of quality called disposition, and consequently their basic function is to dispose the cognitive power to elicit an act of perception, and to accomplish this, species need to be representational entities (*IDA* 5.2.23). Importantly, the representative aspect of the sensible species is for Suárez *realiter* identical with the so-called entitative aspect. Contrary to Aquinas and some Thomists,[24] Suárez denies a real distinction between these two aspects (*IDA* 5.2.24). And it was only a real distinction like this that enabled Cajetan to speak about the "tighter than substantial union" of the cognitive power and the cognized thing.

Against this ontological backdrop we can also see why Suárez easily dispenses with the assistance of more perfect natures, such as separated substances, in his account of the production of sensible species. As a material trace of a sensible object, a sensible species not only is less perfect than a sensible object but also requires further cognitive elaboration in order to become a perfect or second-act representation of the sensible.

5.2 The efficient causes of a sensory cognitive act of the external senses

The abovementioned character of the *species sensibilis* goes a long way towards characterizing Suárez's stance on the issue of the efficient causes of sensation. Suárez rejects two versions of cognitive passivism by appealing to the material and "incomplete" nature of sensible species and emphasizing the vital character of mental operations, including cognitive ones. If the sensible species were the total efficient cause of sensation, the cognitive act would cease to be the vital operation since it would originate in an external agent. He also rejects a weaker form of receptivism that claims that the efficient cause is the cognitive power informed by the sensible species, whereas the *ratio agendi* of the cognitive act is the sensible species, analogous to hot water heating up the immediate surroundings, where the immediate agent of the heating is not the water as such but its accident of heat (*IDA* 5.4.4). The basic principle underlying Suárez's arguments against these opinions, which he associates with the names of Aquinas and Nifo, is Jandun's assumption that the sensible species cannot efficiently and immediately concur in the production of sensation. On the assumption, presumably shared by Jandun, that sensible species are material in character, a sensible species, as a less perfect (inanimate) entity, cannot efficiently produce a more perfect (animate) quality, namely a cognitive act. Moreover, if a sensible species were the *ratio agendi*, its reception would necessarily entail the elicitation of a cognitive act. But that contradicts experience, since if we are not attentive, we do not perceive, despite being informed by the myriad of species (*IDA* 5.4.5).

Suárez's criticism of Jandun concerns above all his theory of the real distinction between the agent and the passive sense.[25] The Jesuit adduces two arguments against this doctrine. First, by analogy to his critique of receptivist conceptions, Suárez states that if Jandun's theory were true, we would have to admit two really distinct powers, one of which, the agent sense, is productive of the act of sensation, while the other, the passive sense, is actually cognitive. That would violate the immanent character of the cognitive operation, however. Its immanent character requires that the act remain in the very same power by which it has been elicited. Hence, such an act cannot be received in a potency that is really distinct from the potency producing the act, even if it resides in the same substance. Second, Jandun's doctrine leaves open which of these two potencies will actually be cognitive. Will it be the power that produces a cognitive act, or the one that receives it?[26] Suárez makes clear that neither of these alternatives can hold. The cognitive power cannot be a passive sense since cognition is a vital operation. A cognitive act must intrinsically include an active component. The cognitive power cannot be the *sensus agens* either. In consonance with his Aristotelianism, Suárez declares the necessity of the power's extrinsic determination by the sensible. If cognition involves both the assimilation to a cognized thing and its cognitive expression or articulation, the cognitive power can only be determined by receiving a sensible species. Suárez's evaluation of Jandun's theory is thus unambiguous: *Agere* and *recipere* cannot be separated in the way that they are attributed to two different powers. Cognition is formed by one and the same power, which is both passive and active (*IDA* 5.4.2).[27]

In accordance with his reply to Jandun, in which he considers the integral principle of the formation of the cognitive act, Suárez affirms both the activity of the cognitive power and the sensible species. His conciliatory conclusion is formulated as follows: "The integral principle of the cognitive act is the power informed by the intentional species" (*IDA* 5.4.15). However, isn't this formulation, which Cees Leijenhorst characterizes as identical to that of Cajetan (Leijenhorst 2007: 256),[28] at odds with the abovementioned assumption that a sensible species, being less perfect, cannot immediately concur in the production of a cognitive act? Shouldn't Suárez rather conclude that a sensible species does not efficiently concur in the formation of a cognitive act and, consequently, that the only efficiency pertains to the cognitive power? Shouldn't Suárez embrace precisely this extremely activist conception, which Leen Spruit describes as mirroring the *Zeitgeist* of Renaissance philosophy?[29]

The brilliance of Suárez's solution is that he is not forced to accept this somewhat extreme opinion. In his reply to the argument that a sensible species cannot concur in the production of a cognitive act, an argument formulated about three centuries before Suárez by Henry of Ghent (ca. 1217–1293), whose theory he presents as the position of radical activism,[30] the Jesuit starts from the basic assumption that a cognitive act is a more perfect entity than an intentional or sensible species. Suárez begins his reply with the following three negations, which he shares with Henry. He claims that a less perfect thing, a sensible species, cannot concur in the production of a more perfect thing, a cognitive act, neither i) as the immediate total cause (strong receptivism), nor ii) as the principle cause complemented by the cognitive power (weaker receptivism), nor iii) as the total instrumental cause (sic!). On my reading, this last denial shows that Suárez differs not only from Aquinas and the Thomists, but also from Scotus, whose theory states that an act of cognition occurs on the basis of the coordination of two partial causes, namely the cognitive power and the intentional species, where the cognitive power constitutes the principle and the sensible species the instrumental cause.[31] The originality of Suárez's thesis consists in his claim that the intentional species does not constitute the total instrumental cause but only instrumentally co-produces the total instrumental cause in concert with the other partial instrumental cause, i.e., the cognitive power. Only in conjunction do these two partial instrumental causes constitute the total instrumental cause. And the latter, importantly, is operated by the principle cause, which, as Suárez says, is the attentive soul.[32] Accordingly, Suárez solves the abovementioned problem of ascendant causality by means of this causal distribution, in which one can discern traces of Augustinianism in its reliance on the direct agency of the soul. If not only a material species but also the animate power is part of the integral instrumental cause of a sensory act (a claim that coheres with Suárez's view that the *species sensibilis* is not received purely mechanistically in the corporeal organ but in the animate power), then the instrumental cause can well be considered to be more perfect than the cognitive act, or at least equally perfect. Consequently, this instrumental cause, in fact, comprises both indispensable components. One is the more perfect part, the animate power, which is not accountable for the representation of the sensible thing, while the second is the less perfect, the sensible species, which provides the cognitive act with the representation or the intentional content. While the first component gives entitative perfection to the cognitive act, the second provides it with representational content. And although a sensible species does not achieve the perfection of a cognitive act, the animate power clearly does (*IDA* 5.4.16). To sum up, it may be said that Suárez's abovementioned conciliatory conclusion (*IDA* 5.4.15) can be stated more precisely as: "The integral principle producing sensory cognition is the power informed by the species, *and the soul of the percipient*".[33]

5.3 The principles of the sensible species of the internal sense

Since the validity of Suárez's exposition hinges not only on the cognitive acts of the external senses but also on the cognitive operation of the internal sense and intellection,[34] the only remaining question to be answered is the one concerning the efficient principles of the non-complex sensed species (*species sensatae*) of the internal sense of fantasy.[35] As with the issue of the *species sensibilis* of the external senses, Suárez's theory of the internal sense seeks to avoid any problematic instance of upward causality.

First of all, Suárez shows that the sensible species of the internal sense, or the imaginative species (*species imaginativa*), cannot be efficiently caused by the sensible species of the external senses. Imaginative species cannot be brought about by visual species since the former are more perfect than the latter. Imaginative species are more perfect because fantasy and its manifold acts are more perfect than the external senses and their operations. While the being and becoming of sensible species of the external senses naturally depend on an existent extramental object, this is not the case with imaginative species. Moreover, if the visual species of, say, Peter caused the imaginative species of Peter in a fantasy, it would follow that whenever the external sense receives the species of Peter, the internal sense necessarily receives the same species. However, that is not the case. As a counterexample Suárez adduces the phenomenon of "dead reception" of a sensible species, e.g., the reception of a species in the state of ecstasy or apoplexy. In these states the cognitive power simply does not elicit a cognitive act, regardless of how strongly the external senses are affected by the sensible species. If the external senses are not reduced to the second act and remain in the first act, the internal sense cannot be affected. Without reduction to the second act we cannot imagine the object whose species we have received via the external sense. Experience supports the view that we can receive the imaginative species in the fantasy only if it has been previously cognized by the external sense, in other words, only if the pertinent species was reduced to the second act by the external sense (*IDA* 6.2.9).

Consequently, if the sensed species of the internal sense cannot be produced by the sensible species emitted by the sensible object, the remaining possibility, which Suárez considered probable, seems to be that the imaginative species is caused by the external sense through a cognitive act. At first sight, this sentence seems to cohere with Suárez's theory of the end-product of the cognitive act of the external senses or the *species expressa*.[36] This probable tenet can be confirmed by the following phenomenological fact: The more we pay attention to the affected external senses the more the sensible object imprints its sensible species on the internal sense (*IDA* 6.2.10). However, this opinion also faces an objection that an imaginative species specifically (ontologically) differs not only from a *species sensibilis* of the external senses but also from a cognitive act of the external senses (*IDA* 6.2.11). As specifically different and "located" in the higher faculty, it will be more perfect than a cognitive act of the external senses. Considering the requirement of upward causality, even actually seeing Peter cannot cause the reception of the imaginative species of Peter, as otherwise the being and conservation of an imaginative species would be fully dependent on external sensation and the fantasy would thus be limited only to the perception of the sensibles *hic et nunc*. In reply to this objection Suárez concedes that, if we compare the first acts of the powers with each other and do the same with the second acts, then we will see that the sensible species and the cognitive act of the internal sense truly are more perfect than the counterparts of the external senses. However, Suárez asserts that comparing the first act of the internal sense with the second act of the external senses reveals that the act of the external sense, as a second act and as a vital operation, is more perfect than the *species imaginativa*. As regards the (abstractive) independence of the imaginative species from the cognitive act of the external sense, Suárez notes that it is the result of the character of the form and the subject that is the internal sense. He argues that this independence cannot be violated by this causality. External sensation imprints a perfect likeness on the internal sense (the product of the second act) and precisely this perfect likeness is consequently received in the interior sense, whose dispositions make it capable of conserving these imaginative species even in the absence of the sensible (*IDA* 6.2.12).

Nevertheless, Suárez's statement about the causal efficiency of external sensation with regard to the sensible species of the internal sense is not his final word. The Jesuit is far from attributing the true *causal* agency to the cognitive act of the external sense. In the last conclusion he comes up with the following non-causal claim: "It is probable that these interior species result in the internal sense through its own activity, and not through the efficiency of something exterior" (*IDA* 6.2.13). Again, with an appeal to the immanent character of the cognitive act, Suárez claims that, in principle, an act of cognition cannot (transitively) cause a distinct quality that would be "localized" in a (really) distinct faculty.[37] As said above, for Suárez the terminus of the cognitive act cannot be really distinct from the act. The terminus of a cognitive operation is the cognitive operation itself.

However, if external sensation does not, strictly speaking, cause the internal species, how is this imaginative species actually generated? We seem to have exhausted all possible candidates. In answering this question Suárez refers to the attentive and conscious soul, which is also responsible for the production of cognitive acts of the external senses as we have seen above. Even though an act of cognition by a lower faculty cannot directly cause a quality in a higher power, this mediation can proceed indirectly. In line with his Aristotelian commitments,

Suárez is indeed eager to remark that it is the sensory power (which is really distinct from the soul) that perceives by means of its act.[38] But in connection with the efficient causes of a cognitive act the Jesuit states that the principal agency of the cognitive act pertains to the attentive soul. It is the soul that perceives or, more precisely, is aware of its operations.[39] And since the soul, as the principle of unity, is the common root of all its vital operations, it can well be aware of all its activities. This awareness allows it to coordinate all the vital activities occurring in the different powers of the animate subject. The soul not only perceives these activities, but also produces the sensible species in the interior sense. Unlike the sensible species of the external senses, which are produced from outside by the sensibles, the sensible species of the internal sense are caused by the soul (*IDA* 6.2.13).

However, given that the soul ultimately produces the imaginative species, what is the function of external sensation, which, according to the previous conclusion, was considered to be a causal agent? Much like in the treatise on the efficient causes of intellection, where Suárez states that phantasms are quasi – *exempla* for the intellect and its "depiction" (*IDA* 9.2.12), it may be said that in the context of the cognition of the internal sense the second acts of the external senses likewise do not figure as efficient causes but only as quasi-exemplars. The substantial, efficient influx of the soul in the powers and their operations in the form of overall awareness is a sufficient guarantee of what is called the harmony or sympathy of powers.[40] If the soul by means of the visual power perceives Peter, the same soul immediately produces a likeness of Peter in the fantasy.[41] Moreover, as Suárez says, fantasy then proceeds to the second act since at the moment it receives the sensible species, no obstacle can in fact prevent it from eliciting the cognitive act (*IDA* 8.1.17).

In the conclusion Suárez somewhat obscurely states that, unlike in the external senses, in the internal sense it is necessary to consider the agent sense (*IDA* 6.2.16). In the case of the imaginative species we need a "lifter" of the sensible species of the external senses. Adriaan Pattin refers to this position with the slightly pejorative label "eclectic" (Pattin 1988: 420). He finds that, while Suárez rejects the agent sense in the case of the production of the sensible species of the external senses, he admits this active potency when analyzing the production of the imaginative species. Two reasons should make us reluctant to embrace Pattin's negative evaluation unreservedly. First, provided that the theory of the *sensus agens*, represented by Jandun's teaching, is essentially connected (at least for Suárez) with the real distinction between the passive and the active sense, this doctrine of the agent sense can hardly be ascribed to the Jesuit. Much like in the treatise on the nature of the distinction between the agent and potential intellect, in which Suárez refers to Nifo (*IDA* 9.8.18), the two senses are only conceptually distinct for Suárez.[42] Second, the agent sense in the context of the internal sense does not seem to be a power really distinct from the soul. Rather, the agent sense is much more an abbreviation for the soul's mediating activity.

6 Conclusion

Considering its Late Medieval and Renaissance roots, Suárez's theory of sensory cognition, its *Fragestellung* and its main theoretical assumptions can be seen as having been formed by the Averroist challenge, which was no doubt originally influenced by the Neoplatonic tradition of positing a psychological or cosmological device that "elevates" the sensibles or the material sensible species to the level of (immaterial) intentional species or (animate) cognitive sensory acts. This historical context shows that Suárez's cognitive psychology cannot be fully appreciated solely in the context of the strictly non-secular Aristotelianism represented by the names of Aquinas, Scotus, etc. Even though Suárez's theory of the efficient causes of sensation comes close to that of Scotus, it cannot be identified with it.[43] This "anchorage" in the tradition of Late Medieval and Renaissance Latin Averroism, represented by John of Jandun, together with a marked tendency towards Augustinian philosophy, which often surfaces in the ocean of the Jesuit's Peripatetic philosophy,[44] together make Suárez's theory similar in significant respects to some medieval philosophers not mentioned above (especially Peter John Olivi, ca. 1248–1298)[45] and significantly different from the cognitive passivism of Aquinas and his followers. Comparing Suárez's theory with that of Thomism clearly reveals that his teaching, strongly motivated by the abovementioned phenomenological "test", represents a significant historical shift from cognitive passivism,[46] which dominated in the 13th century (with the important exception of Olivi), to cognitive activism, which reflected the *Zeitgeist* of Renaissance philosophy. Although in this respect Suárez's cognitive psychology deviates from cognitive passivism his doctrine still must be considered as deeply embedded in the traditional Aristotelian – scholastic philosophy, thus satisfying the aforesaid epistemological criterion, and as essentially different from that of the early modern classics such as Descartes. Despite the Jesuit's "naturalization" of the sensible species, manifest in his denial of the *Deus ex machina* in the form of "causae incognitae", Suárez's philosophy of mind employs ontological items such as sensible species or powers distinct from the soul, which were rejected and ridiculed by early modern philosophers and scientists including Descartes.[47]

Notes

1 This chapter is a result of research funded by the Czech Science Foundation as project GA ČR 14–37038G "Between Renaissance and Baroque: Philosophy and Knowledge in the Czech Lands within the Wider European Context".
2 For these metaphors see Abrams 1953.
3 For accounts of consciousness see Chapter 6 of this volume.
4 I have in mind especially Pattin (1974–1975, 1988), Leijenhorst (2007, 2014: 168–175) and to some extent MacClintock (1956: 10–50).
5 I will not delve into the exposition of terms such as sensible likeness (species, form), which are standard items in the scholastic account of sensory cognition. For an

introduction to the theory of cognition in general, including an explanation of the term *species intentionalis*, see Chapter 5 of this volume.

6   I use the term "internal sense" in the singular since Suárez reduces the plurality of internal senses to a single sense, namely the fantasy (see Suárez, *IDA*, disp. 8, q. 1). As regards Suárez's reduction of the internal senses to a single faculty, see South 2001b.

7   For a transcription of Jandun's three main texts on the issue of *sensus agens* see Pattin (1988: 111–234).

8   For Jandun's *new* reading of Averroes, see Brenet (2014: 161–164).

9   For this interpretation see Brenet (2014: 147–160).

10 For a strict distinction between these two questions in Renaissance philosophy see Kennedy (1966).

11 This distinction seems to have first been explicitly advocated by Scotus. As regards Scotistic influence both on Jandun, see Brenet (2014: 161), and on Suárez, see Leijenhorst (2014: 172). Below, contra Leijenhorst, I shall argue that the affinity of Suárez's theory to that of Scotus is not absolute, however.

12 By that, of course, I do not want to deny the role of other historical influences, both positive and negative. As regards the significance of Durandus's theory of intentional species for Suárez, see Tellkamp 2012.

13 For this interpretation see, *inter alia*, Knuuttila 2008.

14 Jandun deals with the issue of *sensus agens* in three different treatises, namely in *Sophisma de sensu agente*, dated 1310; in *Tractatus de sensu agente*, in which he replies to 24 arguments of his main opponent, Bartholomew of Bruggs (ca. 1286–1356); and in *Quaestio de sensu agente*, i.e., in the 16th question of the second book of *De anima* in his *Super libros Aristotelis De anima* published around 1318. For these texts see Pattin (1988: 118–234).

15 Note that the agent sense is multiplied in number according to the number of external senses (Pattin 1988: 230), which are really (or at least formally) distinct from the agent sense (*ibid.*, 234), and have the same organ as the passive sense (*ibid.*, 231).

16 As Brenet notes, this interpretation obviously "descends from Averroes" (Brenet 2014: 161).

17 As regards the theories of intramission (related, in general, to the pure reception of the stimuli coming from sensibles) and extramission in connection with the theory of vision in ancient philosophy, see Lindberg (1976: 1–17).

18 For an analysis of Nifo's *De sensu agente* see Mahoney 1971. As Nifo remarks, the text was finished in 1495, and rather than *De sensu agente*, it should have been titled *Tractatum de Errore Joannis de Sensu Agente* (Nifo 1517: 129a). The treatise was first published in Venice in 1497 as the last part of Nifo's *In librum Destructio Destructionum Averrois commentationes*. I make use of the second (also Venetian) edition from 1517.

19 Concerning the two periods in Nifo's philosophical career see Leen Spruit's "Introduction" in Nifo (2011: 12–13).

20 There are also other kinds of arguments taken from Jandun himself, which are later "deconstructed" by Nifo.

21 This section on Suárez is based almost exclusively on his *Commentaria una cum quaestionibus in libros Aristotelis De anima*, published in 1621, even though the text had already been written in the early 1570s when the Jesuit was teaching at the University of Segovia.

22 Nifo's theory is also dealt with as examples of reduction of the cognitive act to the sensory power informed by the species (see *IDA* 5.3.1).

23 An exposition of Suárez's theory, especially in comparison with Aquinas, can be found in South (2001a) – external sensation, and South (2001b) – internal sensation. For an exposition of Suárez's theory in the context of the non-causal theory of vitals acts based on the sympathy of powers rooted in the common soul, see the recent titles by Knuuttila (2014a: 261–266, 2014b: 309–327) and Perler (2014: 279–284).

24 Concerning this real distinction in Aquinas see *ScG*, lib. 3, cap. 51, n. 4. For an explicit statement about the real distinction of both aspects see Ioannes a Sancto Thoma (*CPT*, vol. 3: 102ff).
25 Admittedly, Suárez's evaluation, as in other cases, does not fully correspond to the *litera* of Jandun's text, where he repeatedly states that the two powers differ only "ratione formali" (see Pattin 1988: 152, 234).
26 We have seen that for Jandun it was the passive potency.
27 Not incidentally, the same also holds for the agent and potential intellect (*IDA* 9.8.18).
28 That is also why Leijenhorst does not consider Suárez's critique of Cajetan as the "arch – receptivist" to be fully competent (Leijenhorst 2007: 255–256).
29 This conclusion was formulated by Jacobo Zabarella (1533–1589). On Zabarella's theory of sensory cognition see South (2002) and Leijenhorst (2014); on the activist *Zeitgeist* of Renaissance philosophy see Spruit (2008).
30 Even though Suárez seems to present Henry's theory as refusing *en bloc* the intentional species in the cognitive mechanism, in his *Quodlibet* 4, q. 7, Gandavensis dismisses the intelligible species only in the case of self-cognition and cognition of God. For Suárez's brief exposition of Henry's theory see *IDA* 5.4.8. For Henry's partial refusal of intentional species, see Tachau (1988: 28–39).
31 Scotus (*Ordin.* 1, d 3, p 3, q 2, 326): "as the superior cause is determined to its activity by the concurrence of the particular inferior cause. . ., so the intellect, being the superior and indefinite cause, is determined to this object by the concurrence of the particular determined cause . . . by the concurrence of this species". On "the mixture" of cognitive activism and cognitive passivism in the cognitive theory of the Subtle Doctor see also Chabada (2005).
32 Therefore, I cannot fully agree with C. Leijenhorst's view that Suárez's model of sense perception is identical with that of Scotus (Leijenhorst 2014: 172). When exposing Scotus's theory Leijenhorst conceives the cognitive power and the sensible species to be two concurring partial causes that form one total or integral cause. Even though this statement corresponds to what Suárez literally says in *IDA* 5.4.15, it does not square with the qualification adduced in the paragraph below (*IDA* 5.4.16). There, Suárez explicitly states that these two concurring partial causes constitute the total *instrumental* cause and not the total cause *simpliciter*.
33 The soul is not the per se (direct) principal principle of acting quod, i.e., it is not that which operates but only the principal principle quo of acting, i.e., the principle of operating (*principium operandi*). The main principle quod of acting is the composite of body and soul (for this specification see *DM* 17.2.7, 586).
34 The exposition is presented in the 5th disputation, entitled "De potentiis cognoscitivis in *communi*" [italics, D. H.].
35 I leave aside the issue of the so-called non-sensed species (*species insensata*), conceived by Aquinas (*QDV*, q. 25, a. 2c), not by Suárez (*IDA* 6.2.15), as a special kind of sensible species received in the internal sense, called *vis aestimativa* (in humans, *vis cogitativa*), representing, e.g., the non-sensed quality of danger or desirability, and the complex species composed of sensed species (*species compositae ex sensatis*), e.g., a golden mountain.
36 Unlike Aquinas and some other Thomists, Suárez argues for the existence of expressed species in all the cognitive acts, not excepting the operation of the external senses. Production obtains not for the sake of having the representations of absent objects, but from the intrinsic nature of a cognitive act as such (*IDA* 5, 5, 9). For Suárez's theory of the terminus of the cognitive act (*species expressa*) being really identical with this act, which, again, is a claim hardly attributable to Aquinas and his followers, see *IDA* 5, 4.
37 For Suárez the two faculties are really distinct from each other and from the soul (see *IDA* 3.1.7). For Suárez's theory of the "parts" of the soul see Chapter 3 of this volume.

38 In this Suárez also differs from St. Augustine who highlights the identity of the soul with the cognitive acts: "And it is a certain image of the Trinity, mind and its cognition, which is its offspring and its word and the third is love, and these three are connected in one substance" (Augustine, *De Trin.*, lib. 9, n. 18).
39 In his clear exposition of the various forms of consciousness in Suárez's cognitive psychology, Dominik Perler speaks about "the first-order non-intentional consciousness", which is an experience present in every perceptual act (Perler 2014: 269–273). As regards this form of consciousness in Suárez, see also Chapter 6 of this volume.
40 As regards the substantial (efficient) influx of the (substantial form) soul in the vital operations see also Suárez (*DM* 18.5.2, 628). On the originality of this theory of the sympathy of powers and its impact on Suárez's psychology in general see Ludwig 1929, old but still unequalled.
41 This is also why Suárez holds the primary object of intellectual cognition to be material singulars, and not universal quiddities (see *IDA* 9.3.15).
42 For a similar claim about the conceptual distinction of the agent and passive components in the internal senses see also Nifo (*DSA* 129a).
43 Of course, this claim would require a detailed analysis of Scotus's theory, which cannot be provided in this chapter.
44 For instance, the following quotation from Augustine's *De Mus.* (l. 6, c. 5, n. 10) illustrates the similarity to Suárez's position: "it seems to me that when the soul senses in the body, it does not receive any form of something else, but it is active toward its affects . . . and that is what is called to sense".
45 For their similarity see Spruit (1995: 306).
46 As Simmons 1998 notes, in the Jesuit philosophy of the 16th century this cognitive activism was far from being limited to Suárez.
47 As is well known, for Descartes in the first phase of *sensatio* nothing else occurs than the purely mechanistic affection of the sensory organs receiving the figural configurations of particles of light, which are emitted and reflected by extramental objects. As for the literal reading of the analogy of perception with the reception of the form of a seal in wax, see Descartes (1996, AT X: 412).

My thanks are due above all to Stephan Schmid for his very useful comment on the draft of this chapter. I am also grateful to Sydney Penner for his references to Suárez's treatment of the instrumental cause and to Joshua Crone for his excellent proofreading.

Bibliography

Primary sources

Aristotle. *On the Soul, Parva naturalia, On Breath* (= *De anima*). In *Loeb Classical Library*, W. S. Hett (trans.). Cambridge, MA: Harvard University Press, 2000.

Augustine. *De Musica* (= *De Mus*). In *Patrologia cursus completus*, vol. 32, J. P. Migne (ed.). Paris: Gamier, 1844–1904.

———. *De Trinitate* (= *De Trin*). In *Patrologia cursus completus*, vol. 42, J. P. Migne (ed.). Paris: Gamier, 1844–1904.

Averroes. *Commentarium magnum in Aristotelis 'De anima' libros* (= *CMDA*). F. S. Crawford (ed.). Cambridge, MA: The Medieval Academy of America, 1953.

Descartes, R. *Regulae ad directionem ingenii*. In *Oeuvres de Descartes* (= AT), vol. 10, C. Adam & P. Tannery (eds). Paris: Vrin, 1996.

Henricus de Gandavo. *Quodlibeta IV*. G. A. Wilson & G. J. Etzkorn (eds). Leuven: Leuven University Press, 2011.

Ioannes a S. Thoma. *Cursus philosophicus Thomisticus* (= *CPT*), vol. 3. Hildesheim, Zürich, New York: Georg Olms Verlag, 2000.
Ioannes Duns Scotus. *Ordinatio. Liber primus. Distinctio tertia* (= *Ordin.*). In *Opera omnia*, vol. 3. Civitas Vaticana: Typis polyglottis Vaticanis, 1954.
Nifo, A. *De sensu agente* (= *DSA*). In *In librum Destructio Destructionum Averrois commentationes*, 124–129. Venetiis: Ottaviano Scoto, 1517.
———. *De intellectu*. L. Spruit (ed.). Leiden: Brill, 2011.
Thomas de Aquino. *Quaestiones Disputatae de Veritate* (= *QDV*). 2011a. www.corpus thomisticum.org/qdv25.html (accessed October 2014).
———. *Summa contra Gentiles* (= *ScG*). 2011b. www.corpusthomisticum.org/scg3001.html (accessed October 2014).
Suárez, F. *Disputationes metaphysicae* (= *DM*). Hildesheim: Georg Olms Verlag, 1965.
———. *Commentaria una cum quaestionibus in libros Aristotelis De anima* (= *IDA*), 3 vols. S. Castellote (ed.). Madrid, 1978–1991. www.salvadorcastellote.com/investiga cion.htm (accessed October 2014).
Thomas de Vio Caietan. *In libros Aristotelis de Anima*. Compluti: Apud Ferdinandum Ramirez, 1583.
———. *Summa totius theologiae S. Thomae de Aquino cum commentariis*. Hildesheim, Zürich, New York: Georg Olms Verlag, 2000.

Secondary sources

Abrams, M. H. 1953. *The Mirror and the Lamp: Romantic Theory and the Critical Tradition*. Oxford: Oxford University Press.
Brenet, J.-B. 2014. "Agent Sense in Averroes and Latin Averroism". In *Active Perception in the History of Philosophy*, J. F. Silva & M. Yrjönsuuri (eds), 147–166. Dordrecht, The Netherlands: Springer.
Chabada, M. 2005. *Cognitio intuitiva et abstractiva: Die ontologische Implikationen der Erkenntnislehre des Johannes Duns Scotus mit Gegenüberstellung zu Aristoteles und I. Kant*. Mönchengladbach: B. Kühlen Verlag.
Fish, W. 2010. *Philosophy of Perception: A Contemporary Introduction*. London, New York: Routledge.
Heider, D. 2016. "Francisco de Toledo, Francisco Suárez, Manuel de Góis and Antonio Rubio on the Activity and Passivity of the External Senses". In *Cognitive Psychology in Early Jesuit Scholasticism*, D. Heider (ed.), 38–66. Neunkirchen-Seelscheid: Editiones Scholasticae.
Kennedy, L. A. 1966. "Sylvester of Ferrara and the Agent Sense". *The New Scholasticism* **40**(4): 464–477.
Knuuttila, S. 2008. "Aristotle's Theory of Perception and Medieval Aristotelianism". In *Theories of Perception in Medieval and Early Modern Philosophy*, S. Knuuttila & P. Kärkkäinen (eds), 1–22. Dordrecht, The Netherlands: Springer.
———. 2014a. "The Connexions between Vital Acts in Suárez's Psychology". In *Suárez's Metaphysics in Its Historical and Systematic Context*, L. Novák (ed.), 259–274. Berlin: de Gruyter.
———. 2014b. "Suárez's Psychology". In *A Companion to Francisco Suárez*, V. M. Salas & R. Fastiggi (eds), 192–220. Leiden: Brill.

Leijenhorst, C. 2007. "Cajetan and Suarez on Agent Sense: Metaphysics and Epistemology in Late Aristotelian Thought". In *Forming the Mind: Essays on the Internal Senses and the Mind/Body Problem From Avicenna to the Medical Enlightenment*, H. Lagerlund (ed.), 237–262. Dordrecht, The Netherlands: Springer.

———. 2014. "Active Perception From Nicholas of Cusa to Thomas Hobbes". In *Active Perception in the History of Philosophy*, J. F. Silva & M. Yrjönsuuri (eds), 167–185. Dordrecht, The Netherlands: Springer.

Lindberg, D. C. 1976. *Theories of Vision From Al-kindi to Kepler*. Chicago: The University of Chicago Press.

Ludwig, J. 1929. *Das akausale Zusammenwirken (sympathia) der Seelenvermögen in der Erkenntnislehre des Suárez*. München: Karl Ludwig.

MacClintock, S. 1956. *Perversity and Error: Studies on the "Averroist" John of Jandun*. Bloomington: Indiana University Press.

Mahoney, E. P. 1971. "Agostino Nifo's De Sensu Agente". *Archiv für Geschichte der Philosophie* **53**: 119–142.

Pattin, A. 1974–1975. "Pour l'histoire du sens agent au Moyen Âge". *Bulletin de philosophie médiévale* **16–17**: 100–113.

———. 1988. *Pour l'historie du sens agent. La controverse entre Barthélemy de Bruges et Jean de Jandun. Ses antécédents et son évolution*. Leuven: Leuven University Press.

Perler, D. 2014. "Suárez on Consciousness". *Vivarium* **52**(3–4): 261–286.

Simmons, A. 1998. "Descartes and the Jesuits on the Efficient Cause of Sensation". In *Meeting of the Minds: The Relations Between Medieval and Classical Modern European Philosophy*, S. F. Brown (ed.), 63–76. Turnhout: Brepols.

Spruit, L. 1995. *Species Intelligibilis. From Perception to Knowledge. Volume Two: Renaissance Controversies, Later Scholasticism, and the Elimination of the Intelligible Species in Modern Philosophy*. Leiden: Brill.

———. 2008. "Renaissance Views of Active Perception". In *Theories of Perception in Medieval and Early Modern Philosophy*, Knuuttila, S. & P. Kärkkäinen (eds), 203–224. Dordrecht, The Netherlands: Springer.

South, J. B. 2001a. "Suárez and the Problem of External Sensation". *Medieval Philosophy and Theology* **10**(2): 217–240.

———. 2001b. "Francisco Suárez on Imagination". *Vivarium* **39**(1): 119–158.

———. 2002. "Zabarella and the Intentionality of Sensation". *Rivista di storia della filosofia* **1**: 5–25.

Tachau, K. H. 1988. *Vision and Certitude in the Age of Ockham: Optics, Epistemology and the Foundations of Semantics*. Leiden: Brill.

Tellkamp, J. A. 2012. "Francisco Suárez on the Intentional Species". *Quaestio* **12**: 3–23.

9

RENAISSANCE THEORIES OF THE PASSIONS

Embodied minds

Sabrina Ebbersmeyer

1 Introduction: an alternative approach to the mind

When considering influential theories of mind between the middle ages and the early modern period, two stand out as particularly significant: the Aristotelian theory of the soul as the form of a human body and the Cartesian theory of the human mind as a non-material entity (*res cogitans*) that shares no attributes with the material world (*res extensa*). During the Renaissance, however, several philosophers remained critical of the Aristotelian conception without endorsing the mechanistic approach, which reduced the human mind to an insulated, non-extended unit surrounded by a material world ruled by the laws of matter in motion. Rather they took up a view that seems antipodal to this approach; inspired by classical sources, especially from the Platonic, Stoic, and medical traditions, philosophers such as Ficino (1433–1499), Cardano (1501–1576), Telesio (1508–1588), Patrizi (1529–1597), Bruno (1548–1600), and Campanella (1568–1639) understood the human mind as an integral part of a cosmological structure, in which mind (or spirit or soul) could be found everywhere.

Although these philosophers developed different theories of the world and the mind, they shared the basic assumption that the human mind is not something exceptional and singular in nature, but rather part of a complex cosmos in which mental forces and structures are found on various levels. This position is expressed, for instance, by Giordano Bruno, when he states that "one finds spirit (*spirto*) in all things and there is no such tiny body that has not enough of it to be living."[1] This position could aptly be termed "panpsychism," especially given that another Renaissance philosopher, Francesco Patrizi, used the term (*pampsychia*) for the first time in order to denote a conception of the world in which soul is ubiquitous.[2]

Obviously, this position has some serious consequences for the understanding of the human mind and of the surrounding world. To start with the latter, the material world is not regarded merely as inert, extended matter, but as an organic unity, in which principles of life (sensation, growth, etc.) are found everywhere and on every level. In this sense, the cosmos can be considered as a living organism endowed with a soul (*anima mundi*)[3] and sometimes with a world spirit.[4] This opens up the possibility that the world as a whole has a spiritual dimension which the human mind can communicate with.

With regard to the human mind, the emphasis lies not so much on the *difference* between the human mind and the rest of nature (including its own body for that matter), but on the various ways the human mind is *similar to* and *part of* the rest of nature. The human mind is understood as (1) embodied and (2) embedded in its surroundings[5]: (1) It is acknowledged that the human mind is deeply united with and enwrapped in its physical body. Here the concept of the spirit (*spiritus*, *pneuma*), prominent in medical traditions, becomes increasingly significant, for the spirit can account for the mutual interaction between mind and body; it is subtle enough to have an impact on our perceptions and thoughts and corporeal enough to affect and be affected by our body.[6] The spirit was understood as an instrument of the soul, but sometimes it even replaced the soul.[7] (2) In addition, the human mind is not understood as an isolated entity that stands opposed to the rest of nature just contemplating and measuring its environment, but rather as an integral part of the whole of nature, to which it is similar and related in various ways.

In this conception of the human mind as embodied and embedded, it is not so much the mind's capacity for abstract thinking or its ability to detect indubitable truth that is of most interest, but rather its capacity to *feel*. Being in a passionate state no longer appears frightening, nor does it necessarily entail forfeiting the ability to think rationally. Instead, passions provide us with a certain kind of knowledge. Firstly and fundamentally they teach us what is good and bad for the preservation and perfection of the living organism. At the same time, we learn something about the external world through our emotional responses, namely about its structure and its relation to us. Additionally, passions are important routes by which external influences come to bear on our minds. A change of climate, diet, or even, as Bruno holds, certain gemstones can generate "new affects and passion in the soul, not just in the body."[8] Accordingly, knowing about our affective reactions to external circumstances can enable us to manipulate our minds.

In the following, I will outline how the passions were understood within this broader conception of the mind by three well-known philosophers of the Renaissance, namely Marsilio Ficino (1433–1499), Bernardino Telesio (1508–1588), and Tommaso Campanella (1568–1639).[9] It goes without saying that this is not the place to give a comprehensive account of their complex philosophies. Rather I will emphasize certain aspects of their thought that could be taken to support the thesis that within the framework of "panpsychism" the understanding and evaluation of the passions changes: The passions are no longer opposed to thinking or the rational life, rather they are understood as appropriate reactions to how we perceive the world, reactions that teach us something about ourselves and the surrounding world. This was no minor current in the course of Renaissance thought, and it is well worth integrating into our map of the history of the philosophy of mind.

2 Ficino on love and melancholy

In the works of Marsilio Ficino, two passions stand out as particularly relevant: love (*amor*) and melancholy (*melancholia*). Whereas love is one of the central topics in Ficino's earlier works, especially in his *Commentary* on Plato's *Symposium*, melancholy becomes relevant in Ficino's later work on medicine, his *De vita libri tres* (*Three Books on Life*). Although Ficino's attitude towards these passions differs (he encourages and exhorts us to love, but he tries to cure melancholy), they still share some common features. Firstly, both passions reveal that we are related to the surrounding world in various ways, be it love or melancholy. And secondly, they illustrate, although in different ways, that our emotional dispositions are important for and relevant to our intellectual life and endeavors.

2.1 Ficino's approach

Today's interpreters often find Ficino's works difficult to understand. In his writings he relates to and combines different discourses, such as metaphysical speculation and medical analysis, without making these shifts explicit. This is no coincidence or oversight, but the expression of a philosophical program. Ficino explains his attitude in a letter to his friend Francesco Musano:[10]

> Do not be surprised, Francesco, that we combine medicine and the lyre with the study of theology. Since you are dedicated to philosophy, you must remember that within us nature has bonded body and spirit with the soul. The body is indeed healed by the remedies of medicine; but spirit, which is the airy vapour of our blood and the link between body and soul, is tempered and nourished by airy smells, by sounds, and by song. Finally, the soul, as it is divine, is purified by the divine mysteries of theology. In nature a union is made from soul, body and spirit. To the Egyptian priests medicine, music and the mysteries were one and the same study. Would that we could master this natural and Egyptian art as successfully as we tenaciously and wholeheartedly apply ourselves to it!

Analyzing, separating, distinguishing, and dissolving complicated entities into isolated and manageable units in order to obtain clear and indubitable knowledge of certain parts of reality – this philosophical program, which achieved paradigmatic significance with Descartes and still characterizes our scientific perspective today, is the exact opposite of Ficino's intellectual approach. Ficino emphasizes instead the *connections* between heterogeneous discourses; relates disparate traditions back to common sources; and argues that theoretical issues and practical concerns, medical therapies and artistic activity, philosophical speculation and religious worship, man's self-knowledge, and his interest in exploring nature – all these are interconnected and interwoven through a variety of relations, so that one cannot study successfully in one field without understanding the others.

According to Ficino, the world is a complex unity whose parts are internally related to each other. In order to understand one thing, the best approach is to know as much as possible from very different angles and perspectives and to recognize its diverse relations to other parts of reality.[11] This is particularly true of the concept of love, which has cosmological, astrological, medical, metaphysical, ethical, religious, and magical aspects. Love is related to the human soul, but also to the human body, to the stars in the sky but also to the sublunary elements. In order to understand these relations, one has to look for analogies, mediations, and similitudes. Before I outline Ficino's concept of love and melancholy, I will take a brief look at the underlying ontological assumptions, which will help explain, why love in particular occupies such a central position in Ficino's thought.

2.2 Ontological assumptions

With reference to Plotinus, Ficino distinguishes various stages of being,[12] namely mind (*mens*), soul (*anima*), nature (*natura*), and matter (*materia*), as four different hierarchical stages of the cosmos, all of which tend back to god (*deus*) or the one (*unum*) as the beloved (*DA* 208–210). There is one and the same "circle, from God to the world and from the world to God" (*DA* 134).

The world we live in is constituted by these different stages and is understood as a complex artwork created by an artist. As all the parts of this world derive from one common source, they all share common features and bear similarities to one another. Its nature is best understood in analogy to the animal: "The parts of this world, like the parts of a single animal, all hanging from one author, are joined to each other by the mutuality of one nature" (*DA* 119).[13]

Understood as a large animal, the world is assigned a soul by Ficinio: the so-called "world soul" (*anima mundi*).[14] In *De amore* he gives two arguments for this. The first stems from the concept of perfection[15]: Why should parts of the world (e.g., animals) have a soul, but not the whole, which is more perfect than its parts? (*DA* 184) The other is commonly called the genetic argument[16]: If animals have life, then the elements from which they are generated and which give them life, namely earth and water, should be endowed with life as well (*ibid.*).

When it comes to the human being, Ficino does more than just reiterate the well-known Platonic (and Christian) dualism of soul and body; he refers to a tri-partition of man. With reference to the medical tradition, in which the concept of the *spiritus* played a prominent role, he positions the spirit between body and soul (*DA* 189).[17] The spirit is understood as the "chariot of the soul" (*currus animae*) and as its instrument (*DA* 196; 194). It links the soul to its body, by perceiving the forces of the soul and transmitting them to the body, and vice versa, thus enabling the mental and the bodily realm to interact. Following the medical tradition, Ficino calls the spirit a "very thin and clear vapor" (*vapor tenuissimus et perlucidus*; *DA*

189). Although the soul is clearly understood as distinct from the body, it still remains deeply linked to the body through the spirit. Insofar as the soul is "present to the spirit in every part" (*DA* 189), it is extended throughout the body.

2.3 *Love as* copula mundi

Love reveals its full meaning in Ficino's thought against the backdrop just outlined above. The most important aspect of love is its relational and communicational power; as all parts of the cosmos belong together and share a common nature, they are related to and strive for each other, that is, they share a common attraction: love (*DA* 200).[18] This mutual love (*mutua caritas*) is the binding force within the cosmos and can be called a "perpetual knot" (*nodus perpetuus*) and a "binder of the universe" (*copula mundi*) (*DA* 152). What this implies becomes clear in a passage from Pseudo-Dionysius Areopagita[19] cited by Ficino:

> Whether divine, angelic, spiritual, animal, or natural, we mean by love a certain joining and uniting force which moves even the higher to care for the lower, brings equals into mutual intercourse with each other, and finally, admonishes the inferior to devote themselves to the higher and stronger.
>
> (*DA* 149)

Personal love, that is, the love between two humans, is also understood within this ontological framework. This kind of love is just a particular instance of the general tendency that is found everywhere in the cosmos, a tendency leading towards the beautiful and back to the divine origin. We love someone as a "part of the world order" (*DA* 171), and we are attracted to another person because we perceive her or him as beautiful. Ficino is standing on Platonic grounds when he argues that what humans truly love is the beautiful, which is a divine attribute.[20] Beauty is understood as something incorporeal (*DA* 167), a splendor (*DA* 169), a spiritual gift (*DA* 173) that we can perceive through our minds, eyes, and ears.

In humans, love has different layers due to the complexity of human nature. The *soul* strives for the beloved, but also for the image of the beloved person stored in the imagination. If this image corresponds to the innate concept of humankind (*humani generis ratio*), this correspondence causes love in the soul. But because we also have a *body* and a *spirit* we are more than just souls. Our bodily nature tends to a more corporeal unification and our spirit, too, is attracted to the beloved person. As a result, it flies over to her or him and evaporates (*DA* 194–195), thereby rendering the lover melancholic. However, the true lover knows how to overcome the attraction to a single human being and uses his or her love as a means to reveal the true structure and meaning of the world:

> They are most skilful, and most wise of all, and they so philosophize that they prudently advance through the forms of bodies as though through

some kind of track, or scent, and by means of these they skilfully track down the holy beauty of the soul and divinity; and hunting thus wisely, they happily catch their quarry.

(*DA* 198)

Thus, for humans love is not just a binding force, which relates humans to the surrounding world; love can also serve as a means for intellectual development and personal perfection.

2.4 Melancholy and the spirit

De vita libri tres (*Three Books on Life*) is one of Ficino's most successful works,[21] especially the third book, *De vita coelitus comparanda* (*On Obtaining Life from the Heavens*), which contains Ficino's highly influential explanation of magic.[22] *De vita* is a medical advisory specifically for those working with their mind and brain, that is, intellectuals. Just as runners take care of their legs and athletes tend to their arms, so intellectuals should look after the organs that are particularly relevant to their activities, namely the brain, heart, liver, and stomach (*DV* 110), but first and foremost, they should take care of their spirit. Following the medical tradition, Ficino describes the spirit as a fine vapor of blood generated by the heat of the heart. Traditionally, the spirit is responsible for mediating between soul and body. The brain needs the spirit in order to process internal and external perceptions. What is more, the spirit is also important for the activity of reason (*ratio*): "the blood subserves the spirit; the spirit, the senses; and finally, the senses, reason" (*ibid.*). Ficino stresses that the ability to think is largely conditioned by the nature of the spirit: "Thus, undoubtedly the contemplation is usually as good as is the compliance of the sense; the sense is as good as is the spirit" (*ibid.*).

For intellectuals, this results in a particular occupational disease, as we might call it today. For the scholar consumes too much spirit during frequent and intense reflection. The spirit is distilled from the blood, which as a consequence becomes thick, dry and black. To the physician it is immediately clear that these are the symptoms of melancholy: "All these things characteristically make the spirit melancholy and the soul sad and fearful" (*DV* 115). This is particularly true for the philosopher.[23]

Now, this disease can be cured by absorbing more spirit than one consumes. This is possible, according to Ficino, because the spirit in us has a counterpart in outward nature, namely the world spirit (*spiritus mundi*). In analogy to the medical spirits, which serve as a link between the bodily functions and the mental functions of the human being, Ficino assumes a cosmic spirit. It is needed in order to communicate the life of the soul to the coarser bodies:

Therefore, between the tangible and partly transient body of the world and its very soul, whose nature is very far from its body, there exists everywhere a spirit, just as there is between the soul and body in us, assuming that life everywhere is always communicated by a soul to a grosser body.

(*DV* 255)

The world spirit is described as "a very tenuous body, as if now it were soul and not body, and now body and not soul" (*DV* 257). The four elements are generated from this world spirit, so that everything found in nature is endowed with the world spirit. We can absorb this spirit through our own spirit, because it is similar to it. And we can make our own spirit more akin to it by means of certain practices, for example, by purging our own spirit from beclouding vapors through medicines, by exposing it to luminous things, by rendering it more rarefied, and finally by exposing it to the influences of the celestial bodies, in particular of the sun (*DV* 259). "And so from this spirit, acting as a mediator in us, the celestial gifts located mainly in it will overflow not only to our body but also to our mind" (*ibid.*).

Ficino goes on to explain in great detail that we can restore the spirit in us by absorbing the life-spending spirit of the world, for example, through the rays of the sun and the constellation of the planets and fixed stars, through things that capture the celestial influence eminently, e.g., images and figures, and through stones, herbs, spices, and music. The most powerful means of affecting the human spirit is music, especially song, as it can actually cure certain mental and physical diseases.[24] Toward the end of the third book Ficino once again addresses the intellectuals, as they have to take particular care of their spirit. He advises them to nourish their spirit with four things: wine, the odor of wine, song and sound, and finally light (*DV* 379).

According to Ficino, melancholy is an emotional disposition that renders us sad and fearful. This disposition can be cured by realizing that the state of our soul can be changed through changes in our bodily and spiritual constitution. In fact, our spiritual constitution is changed and transformed constantly through the constellation of the stars, the climate, the light, diet, music etc. The reason he gives for this interaction is the *similarity* between our own spiritual nature and the spiritual nature of the universe. We are related to the surrounding world in various ways, although we are not always aware of this.

To sum up, emotional dispositions are understood in relation to the tripartition of the human being. Insofar as we are rational beings, our love or melancholy can be caused by certain beliefs. But insofar as we are corporeal and spiritual beings, there are other things that can influence our emotional disposition: It might be that our bodily constitution renders us fearful. And finally, as spiritual beings, the surrounding world has some impact on our emotional disposition. In order to transform certain emotional dispositions, we have to learn about the influences and expose ourselves to them according to our own needs.

3 Telesio: pan-sensation and human passions

Roughly a hundred years after Ficino, another Italian philosopher, Bernadino Telesio, presented a new philosophy of nature, in which some elements that figured prominently in Ficino, became central as well. Firstly, there was the idea that the world is not constituted by mere matter, but features sentient characters on every level. And secondly, there was the concept of spirit as a subtle corporeal substance that can account for living processes in animated beings. And as in Ficino's philosophy, the passions gain special attention, though for different reasons.

Telesio, however, follows his own agenda, which differs greatly from Ficino's.[25] He can hardly be described as a Platonic philosopher, and his main intention is to present a new philosophy of nature, which would cure the defects he observed in the Aristotelian account of nature. Thus, his style of argument is much more systematic and coherent than Ficino's. He is not interested in hidden relations between man and nature and tries to give a coherent account of nature based on a few principles. In the following I will briefly outline (1) Telesio's conception of universal sensation, (2) the function and meaning of the spirit, and (3) the role of the passions in his argumentation for a theory of the human soul.[26]

3.1 The universality of the sensations of pleasure and pain

Right at the beginning of his work, after having proclaimed his intention to be led in his investigation by "nature" and "sensation" (*sensus*) rather than to construct arbitrary rational assumptions about the world, Telesio introduces the first principles of nature, namely heat and cold, as two antagonistic active forces, and matter as the passive principle.[27] The whole of nature, Telesio states, is constituted by these forces, which act and react upon each other. However, in order to explain why the antagonistic forces heat and cold do not annihilate each other, Telesio refers to an assumption that is of great significance for his understanding of nature and for the composition of his work: Telesio holds that the fundamental forces heat and cold are both endowed with a sense (*sensus*) through which they can perceive their own passions and the actions and forces of the other. Through this capacity for sensing, the principal forces and all things in nature that evolve from their conflict are able to pursue what helps sustain their nature and to avoid what corrupts it. The sensation of a being's own actions and those similar to them that support and preserve the respective force, is described by Telesio as "pleasant" (*perblandus*), while the sensation of the contrary force, through which it decays, is described as "extremely troublesome" (*maxime molestus*) (*DRN* I, 64–66). Accordingly, perceiving things as pleasant or troublesome in relation to their impact on the preservation of the perceiving subject is an ability common to all natural things, not only animated beings.[28]

3.2 The spirit

Although the ability to perceive pleasure and pain is ubiquitous in nature, it is more developed in animated beings due to their more complex composition.[29] Animated beings are composed of various things, such as flesh, nerves, bones, and spirit (*DRN* II, 224–226). The spirit is understood as a subtle, corporeal substance, whose main portion resides in the ventricles of the brain and that is distributed throughout the body in varying proportions via the nervous system.[30] The concept of spirit is of great importance in Telesio's work. It is equated with "the soul that is evolved from the semen" (*anima e semine educta*) and replaces the Aristotelian conception of the soul as a form of the body (*forma corporis*). While the term "spirit" was already prominent in the medical tradition, Telesio breaks with this tradition, insofar as he understands the spirit not as an intermediary between body and soul or as an instrument of the soul, but as the soul itself.

It is the spirit, which is responsible for an animated being's ability to perceive. Telesio explains in great detail what sensation in animated beings really is and how it works. Since the spirit is understood as a corporeal substance, what the spirit senses while affected by different things is the alteration of its own bodily constitution. So in the end it all comes down to the alteration of different parts of the spirit. The spirit can either be squeezed or pushed apart, and these changes constitute the basis of all sensations. As Telesio writes, "There is no doubt that the sense is nothing else than the sense of expansion and compression of itself and not of any other thing."[31] Through this ability to perceive its own alteration, that is, its expansion and compression, the spirit is also able to perceive the various things that cause these alterations. "At any rate it is clear that the spirit perceives (*sentire*) the forces and actions of the things and the incitements of the air, because the spirit itself is inflicted, changed and moved by them." (*DRN* III, 4). So the sense is defined as the perception of the spirit's own alteration caused by the actions of various things:

> After all it remains that the sense (*sensus*) is the perception (*perceptio*) of the actions of the things, of the incitements of the air, of its own passions, of its own changing and of its own movements and particularly of the latter. For it perceives the former, because it perceives being afflicted, changed and moved by them.
>
> (*DRN* III, 6)

However, these affections are not neutral. They affect the spirit in one of two ways: The alterations of the spirit's own movements give rise to either pleasure or pain. As long as the broadening or compression of the spirit is moderate and gentle, the spirit is affected by pleasure. But if the forces of the things that affect the spirit are no longer moderate and gentle, but increase and become stronger or come nearer they are perceived by the spirit with great pain (*summo dolore*) and as great evil (*summo malo*; *DRN* II, 4). In addition, pleasure and pain is not only a matter of quantity, but also of quality; if the external forces that affect the spirit are similar to it, support its nature, or bring it back to its own disposition, they produce pleasure (*voluptas*). If, on the contrary, they are dissimilar and destroy the spirit or remove the body and the spirit from their respective nature and disposition they produce pain (*dolor*; *DRN* III, 12). So pleasure and pain indicate the state of the spirit in relation to its preservation or destruction respectively: "At any rate it is obvious that pleasure is the sensation of preservation, pain on the contrary is the sensation of destruction."[32]

What then is the nature of the spirit that is either supported or diminished by what the spirit perceives? According to Telesio, the nature of the spirit is movement.[33] It is characterized as "the most mobile" (*summe mobilis*).[34] Thus, the spirit feels pleasure through being affected by sensible things, whenever they stimulate it to move. For movement is the proper operation of the spirit.[35]

Telesio does not appeal to the concept of the spirit in order to bridge two different ontological realms, that is, soul and body. This is because he sees no need for a specific immaterial soul, as everything can be explained by matter, heat, and cold. Rather the spirit helps explain the more complex attributes of animated beings.

3.3 Human passions as the touchstone for Telesio's theory of the spirit

The passions play a crucial role when Telesio justifies his conception of the soul as spirit and refutes the Aristotelian doctrine of the soul as the form of the body (*forma corporis*) in book five of *De rerum natura*.[36] In this context, Telesio refers several times to certain passions in order to provide evidence for his view that the soul (spirit)[37] is distinct from the body but nevertheless corporeal. Indeed, the passions serve as one of the main pieces of evidence for Telesio's claim that the soul has to be understood as a unitary corporeal substance spread throughout the body and concentrated in the brain. In making this claim, he explicitly disagrees with Aristotle and his followers, who took the soul to be an incorporeal form of the body or of its parts:

> Finally, all that which occurs to animals during the various affections (*affectiones*) of the soul demonstrates clearly that the soul evolved from the semen is neither the form of the whole body nor of its parts. For, if this were the case, one could not reasonably explain their cause.
> (*DRN* II: 385)

The passions serve as a touchstone for any theory about body and soul, as they contain both certain states of the soul and certain states of the body, which are intimately related to each other.

In fact, Telesio's reference to the passions or "affections" in the passage quoted above serves two purposes. First, Telesio refers to the passions in order to argue for his conception of the soul as a unitary spirit which is spread throughout the body but which is nevertheless moved by its principal portion residing in the brain. Let's illustrate this rationale by considering a person under the influence of a passion. When the whole spirit of this person is agitated by joy (*laetitia*), fear (*timor*), or any other strong passion (*affectio*), the pulse accelerates as if the person faced a bad thing that has to be removed. And this happens despite the fact that there isn't anything touching the respective portion of the spirit, which is the only portion capable of producing such bodily alteration (*DRN* II, 294). It is the mere thought of something joyful or fearful that causes the body to change. How can this be explained? According to Telesio, this happens because the single portions of the spirit distributed throughout the body are connected with each other and with the main portion residing in the brain. This portion also contains the memories of past events (*DRN* II, 274–276). So when something happens that resembles any previous event, the central portion of the spirit remembers what should be done on such an occasion and the respective portions of the spirit are moved according to the will (*arbitrium*) of the central portion of the spirit (*DRN* II, 292).

Second, and more important, Telesio refers to the passions in order to provide evidence of the corporeal nature of the soul and the intimate relation between body and soul. It sometimes happens that the spirit decays under the influence of a strong passion, such as sadness (*tristitia*), fear (*timor*), joy (*laetitia*), or rage (*iracundia*). According to Telesio, this cannot be explained if one assumes that the soul is the form of the body:

> It is even less intelligible that an incorporeal substance decays because it perceives good or bad things affecting others, or that the body, in which it exists, changes through its perception.
>
> (*DRN* II, 376)

If the soul is incorporeal, why should it be destroyed by what it perceives, especially if what it perceives is good or evil only for others, such as our parents for instance? And how could the body be affected and changed through what the incorporeal soul perceives? If one assumes instead a corporeal spirit, it is possible to give a reasonable explanation for these cases. Telesio's argument runs as follows: The spirit desires primarily its self-preservation and becomes sad (*tristatur*) when it encounters things that are contrary to this goal. If these things become so strong that the spirit can no longer cope with them, it constricts all its portions to the principal seat, where it becomes compressed and can eventually decay, when it is no longer able to sustain the basic functions (like respiration or circulation) of the body in which it resides (*DRN* II, 376). While the spirit perishes by sadness or fear when compressed in the brain, it perishes by joy and rage when its principle portion bursts out to the external parts of the body, grows coarse, and finally decays.[38]

In addition, the spirit can also be affected by the nature and disposition of the body, because it derives from the same humors and from the same blood (*DRN* II, 416–418), as can clearly be seen in the case of long lasting passions:

> "And in all alienations of the soul," says the same Galen, "when fear or sadness endure, one has to judge that black bile is the cause, from which a dark and fuliginous exhalation moves up to the spirit."
>
> (*DRN* II, 418)

Telesio refers to Galen when arguing that bodily humors influence the condition of the spirit by means of black bile.[39] In doing so, he makes use of arguments developed in the medical tradition in order to refute the Aristotelian doctrine of the soul and to replace it with his theory of a corporeal spirit.[40] According to Telesio, the Aristotelian conception of the soul as either the form of the whole body or the form of its different parts cannot yield a satisfactory explanation for how body and soul are affected while under the influence of a strong passion. The concept of the spirit, by contrast, can account for this. As we have seen, the expansion and compression of the spirit can cause serious alterations to the body, such as disrupting the respiratory organs. The physiological alterations resulting from the influence of strong passions clearly show the unity of the spirit and the close and intimate relation between spirit and body; the spirit is not divided into different parts, nor is it an incorporeal substance. Rather, it has to be understood as a complex and subtle net distributed throughout the body via the nervous system with its principal portion in the brain.

According to Telesio's conception, the passions are not opposed to reason or to a rational way of life. The passions are neither attributed to an irrational part of the soul engaged in combat with its rational part, as in Aristotle,[41] nor are they attributed to the struggle between body and soul, as in Descartes. Rather, they are ascribed to the unitary spirit of a complex living being which seeks to preserve itself by means of diverse operations such as sensing, thinking, feeling, and acting. From the viewpoint of the living organism, the capacities for thinking and for feeling emotions do not contradict each other, but operate complementarily.

4 Campanella: magic and the passions

In his work *Del senso delle cose e della magia* (*On the sense of things and on magic*),[42] Tommaso Campanella takes up many of the elements we have already discussed. However, he pursues his own interests and presents an amalgamation of Telesian and Ficinian thought. He explicitly cites Telesio as an influence, admits to sharing many of his views, and refers to him as his main inspiration.[43] At the same time, he shares many of Ficino's interests and insights.[44] The result is a natural philosophy based on the concept of universal sensation with magical elements (stressing the interrelation between the spirit of humans and the world spirit and investigating how thoughts and actions can be manipulated through the passions).[45] He is much more interested than Telesio in the relation between the human spirit and the world spirit and how the former can be changed and manipulated. In the following, I will give an outline of (1) how Campanella takes up the Telesian understanding of nature and transforms it according to his own agenda, (2) what role the spirit (both the world spirit and the individual spirits of human beings) play in communication, and (3) why the passions figure so prominently into his explanation of the effectiveness of magic.

4.1 The ubiquity of sensation and the world as a living animal

Campanella shares with Telesio the basic assumption that everything in nature is endowed with "sensation" (*sentimento, senso*). Although Campanella is highly influenced by Telesio and shares many of his basic assumptions, his approach and focus are different and he ends up with different explanations for the phenomena he examines. At the very beginning of his work, he presents the genetic argument we have already encountered in Ficino, although Campanella's version is more elaborate. According to Campanella, everyone agrees that animals have sensations. But this capacity cannot emerge from nothing (*ex nihilo fit nihil*). In particular it cannot emerge from elements that do not have sensation. Consequently, the elements that constitute the animal, and hence all of nature, must have sense already (*DS* 3). Campanella is arguing against atomism (targeting Lucretius, Democritus, and Epicurus), when he states that heat and cold which are "active powers" (*virtù agente*) could not emerge from merely passive atoms (*DS* 8).

Following Telesio, Campanella explains that the purpose of sensation is to perceive what is conducive and destructive to the sentient being. As sense is the ability to register how an event affects one's own preservation, it is called a passion (*passione*) or rather the perception of a passion (*percettione di passione*). There are two types of passions. If what is perceived contributes to one's own preservation, then it is perceived as pleasant (*piacevole*). If it is destructive, then it is perceived as painful (*dolorosa*): "Therefore the sense is the perception of a passion, which one resists and fights, if it is destructive and painful, and which one applauds, follows and loves, if it is pleasant and preservative." (*DS* 12) Contrary to Aristotle's view, perception does not arise through information, Campanella argues, but rather through mutation (*immutazione*).

Unlike Telesio but in accordance with Ficino, Campanella assumes that the world is a living organism endowed with a soul and a spirit, its spirit being the sky, its coarse body the earth, its blood the sea, and its mind the world soul (*DS* 120). "The world, thus, is all sense, life and soul and body" (*DS* 235). Although the air is full of spiritual beings (*cose spirituali*), we cannot see them. "They pass us before the winds and the air and we don't see them; much less do we see the angels and demons, of which the world is plenteous" (*DS* 130). The air (*aria*) that we breathe and that surrounds us is part of the sky and therefore has spirit and sense perception; it "perceives and consents without organs" (*DS* 135).

4.2 Communication and interaction between spirits

According to Campanella, there is a close connection between the spirit of the world, which is found in the sky, and the spirit found in human beings. Following Telesio, Campanella does not understand the human spirit as the instrument of the soul, but as the soul itself. The spirit is hot, mobile, and subtle and is responsible for all the functions traditionally attributed to the sensitive soul, including remembering, imagining, and thinking. It is precisely the passions that provide evidence for the assumption that, contrary to Aristotle, "the sensitive soul is not incorporeal and impassible, but a very subtle and fleeting body" (*DS* 43). However, Campanella also assumes that humans, unlike animals, are endowed with a divine mind. But not even this mind is completely separated from the body. It is rather "wrapped in the spirit and acts and suffers with it" (*DS* 115).

Our own spirit, which is of an airy nature, cannot touch other spirits directly. It can only communicate with other particular spirits through the world spirit found in the air. "Therefore, the air is like the common soul, which helps all and through which all communicate, as Pliny remarks" (*DS* 136).[46] This helps to explain why one can perceive (*sentire*) what someone else is thinking (*pensare*). As thought (*pensare*) is the movement of the spirit, which is transmitted to the air, some "very sagacious, ardent spirits" can perceive instantly what another person is thinking. This also provides an explanation for how one is able to perceive the mood of another person without understanding her. Thinking is the movement of the spirit, which is communicated to the air. The air receives not only the movement but also the affect. Specific words have, in addition to their meaning, an impact through the way they move the spirit. We perceive these movements, but do not understand them:

> [A]nd if there were between us no sounds arranged to signify, every one would perceive the other through the affect impressed in the air, as can be seen in he who cries or laughs or sings, even though he were of a foreign nation, we get to know what he suffers.
>
> (*DS* 136)

Sometimes we can perceive what a crying person is feeling, not because we cognize and evaluate the bodily signs of an emotion, but because our spirit is affected by the common spirit that is altered by the spirit of the crying person. This also explains why words can affect us more fundamentally and independently of their meaning, so that they are capable of arousing anger (*ira*) in war or devotion (*pietà*) in the church. In addition, the air can have a certain constitution or quality that affects the spirit. And thus the air, if it is serene and pure, renders us cheerful and happy or, if it is disturbed and polluted, sad and melancholic (*DS* 136).

4.3 How to generate and manipulate the passions through magic

The fourth book of Campanella's *De senso* is dedicated to magic and magical practices.[47] According to Campanella, magicians investigate "the occult things of god and nature" and engage in miraculous operations, insofar as they apply their knowledge of occult things for the use of humans (*DS* 163). Campanella distinguishes "natural magic" (*magia naturale*) from "divine magic" on the one hand and from "diabolic magic" on the other. Whereas there is little to know about divine magic, as it depends entirely on god and his grace, diabolic magic is based on the art of the devil and is directed towards harming human beings.

Natural magic, by contrast, occupies a middle position between the two and can be applied for the use and benefit of mankind.

With reference to Pliny,[48] Campanella distinguishes three types of natural magic: (i) religion, whose task is to purge the soul and to instill trust, fear, and reverence in the soul; (ii) medicine, which enables us to know the hidden powers and capacities of certain herbs, stones, metals, and their sympathies and antipathies towards each other and ourselves, so that we can use them; and (iii) finally astrology, which reveals to us the right time to act, as the constellations of the fixed stars, the planets, and the moon and the sun "are the cause of the power and mutations of all things" (*DS* 164). Natural magic can be used as a tool to influence human beings without them being aware of it. This is because the magician works not directly on their mind, but on their spirit.

When it comes to understanding and applying magical knowledge about the hidden qualities and connections of things, the passions become particularly important, as they indicate how the spirit is affected by certain features of the surrounding world. Chapter 6 of *De sensu* is devoted to the "natural affects that the magician incites in order to achieve his effect" (*DS* 177). The principle affects are pleasure (*voluttà*) and pain (*dolore*), that is, the sense of a present good or evil; love (*amore*) and hate (*odio*), which are tendencies towards something good or bad; and hope (*speranza*) and fear (*timore*), which are directed towards an absent good or bad thing. Trust (*fiducia*) is the sense of a thing we are convinced is good, while distrust (*diffidenza*) is its contrary. Faith (*fede*) is called the mother of trust. Campanella mentions even imagination (*imaginazione*) as one of the various ways the spirit is affected: True imagination occurs when the spirit conceives something as it really is, while false imagination is when the spirit is fixed and cannot move otherwise.[49]

All these affects can be evoked through magical practices: "He who knows how to generate all these effects in man, through herbs, actions, and other appropriate things, can be called a magician" (*DS* 177). For Campanella there are many ways by which a magician can generate these emotional responses. All these ways of generating and changing affects, however, follow one universal rule.

> Because preservation is the highest good, and destruction the highest evil, that incident generates more delight, joy, hope and faith, that preserves more or disposes more towards preservation; and that induces more pain, hate, sadness, distrust and incredulity, that destroys more or prevents preservation to greater extent.
>
> (*DS* 200)

On account of this, food, air, and freedom, which are – among other things – all similar to the spirit and support its nature, are experienced as pleasurable, whereas the opposed things are painful.

Campanella goes on to explain how certain kinds of food have an impact on the spirit and consequently generate certain passions, such as courage, love, hate, anger. He also expands his survey to include the effects of herbs and minerals. The natural world is full of these hidden causes; one simply has to investigate the properties carefully and look for similarities between them. "He who is going to philosophize about colours, smells, tastes, figures, actions, the property and consistency of the things, will find infinite secrets for all his purposes" (*DS* 204). Sounds and words in particular have a magical force:

> Because sounds have a magical force that moves the spirit to diverse affects according to their variety: the rough sounds of trumpets and drums incite war and anger; the soft and slow of the lute inspires love; the catchy and meaningful sounds of the church arouse pity.
>
> (*DS* 211)

The generation of certain passions is also crucial in medicine. Campanella agrees with Avicenna,[50] that confidence in a good physician cures the sick, "because the spirit, believing that healing is taking place, is affected by health and gains power over the illness, since trust is half of the power" (*DS* 212).

So what is Campanella's affective magic? Human affects display the constitution of the spirit; they indicate in what sense certain features of the surrounding world affect us, whether they support or constrain us. The magician knows how the spirit is affected by climate, diet, colors, music, and many other things and qualities in the surrounding world, and thus he knows what affects they generate. He is therefore able to generate certain affects in others and so to manipulate them according to his own purposes. These can be honorable, as in the case of medicine mentioned above. But influencing people's emotions might also be risky and have serious consequences for society, as Campanella is well aware, when he comments on the impact of music: "today this is proved by the Lutherans, who changed religion with it" (*DS* 211).

5 Conclusion

The intention of this chapter was to present an alternative conception of the human mind, one that was prominent during the Renaissance and that viewed the mind as embodied and extended. As I hope has become plain, this embodied conception of the mind also changed the conception of the passions. The philosophers discussed in this chapter, Ficino, Telesio, and Campanella, shared the view that the passions are not dysfunctions of the mind, but indispensable means to engage with the surrounding world. In different ways and with different emphasis, the passions reveal how we are related to and part of the world that surrounds us.

Ficino understands the surrounding world as a living organism endowed with a world soul. All parts of the world are internally related through love and tend back to their common origin. He describes the human being as tripartite, with a body, spirit, and soul, thus easing the strict dualism of the Platonic and Christian tradition by emphasizing a mediating entity, which adopts certain features of both the soul and the body. Human love can thus have different outlooks: *The soul* might realize the true meaning of love, namely the beautiful, and thus be led back to our divine origin. But our body and our bodily spirit react to the same person in different ways, as they tend to a more corporeal unification with the beloved person. The spirit then evaporates and might cause melancholy in the lover. The human being is seen as related in various ways to the surrounding world. This becomes particularly relevant when analyzing the emotional state of the intellectual, which is described as melancholic. Ficino offers some help by explicitly assuming, in analogy to the bodily spirit in human beings, a world spirit that can be absorbed through medicine, music, and astrological and magical practices.

Telesio does not think of the cosmos as an ensouled animal, but as a dynamic entity endowed with sensation (*sensus*). This dynamic is ruled by the principle of self-preservation. Telesio does not assume non-extended souls, but only corporeal spirits. The spirit is not understood as a mere instrument of the soul; rather it is identified with the soul. It is constituted by the first powers, that is, by the greatest amount of heat and the smallest amount of matter. Human passions serve as a touchstone for any theory of the mind, as they display bodily and mental features. According to Telesio, human passions are not opposed to rational conduct, nor are they attributed to an irrational part of the soul. The passions are understood in the framework of the living organism, which is capable of sensing, thinking, being affected and acting, all of which serve the purpose of self-preservation.

Campanella combines elements of Telesio's and Ficino's philosophies. He holds with Telesio that sense is to be found everywhere in nature. And like Ficino, he holds that the world has to be understood as a living organism. Campanella displays a great interest in the ways different parts of the surrounding world are able to communicate with each other, a phenomenon made possible through the ubiquitous presence of spirit. When it comes to human beings, Campanella is particularly interested in the ways humans can use the hidden properties and relations of all beings for their own purposes through magical knowledge. Here the passions become prominent because they are produced by the spirit and thus can be manipulated once we know the conditions under which the spirit gives rise to them.

With the triumph of the mechanistic paradigm and the implementation of the modern scientific worldview, the conception of the mind investigated in this chapter became more and more marginalized. Although some elements of this thought found their way into the works of philosophers like Francis Bacon[51] or Leibniz – who actually tried to re-introduce the term of force into his conception of substance and proclaimed perception and appetition as the main properties of substances as such[52] – and although it underwent a revival in the philosophies of the so-called "Cambridge Platonists" – especially in Ralph Cudworth's notion of "plastic nature," Henry More's conception of "the spirit of nature," and in Anne Conway's spiritual ontology[53] – this approach still became increasingly insignificant. In recent times, however, with a growing interest in the bodily and environmental conditions of cognition and assisted by philosophical criticism of the concept of emergentism, universal panpsychism seems to be regaining ground as a philosophically tenable position.[54]

Notes

1 Giordano Bruno, "De la causa, principio et uno," *Dialoghi italiani* 1958: I 242.
2 Francisco Patrizi, "Pampsychia," *Nova de universis philosophia*, tomus III, Ferrara 1591, Lib IV, 49–59; esp. 52v. For a recent discussion of panpsychism see Skrbina 2005 and 2009 as well as Seager & Allen-Hermanson 2015. In this chapter I use the term "panpsychism" in a very broad sense, encompassing theories in which the concepts "soul," "spirit," or "sense" are fundamental.
3 As already Plato suggested in his *Timaeus* 29e-37c. For the debate on the world soul, see Schlette 1993.
4 The concept of a world spirit (*pneuma*) is of Stoic origin (*cf.* Diogenes Laertius 47O; Philo 47P; Alex. Aph. 48C, all in Long & Sedley 1987), see Verbeke 1945. The concept became important in Ficino's and Campanella's philosophies, as we will see below.
5 For more recent debates on embodiment and embeddedness see Varela et al. 1991 and Clark & Chalmers 1998.
6 "Spirit" is a sparkling concept with a great variety of meaning, see Fattori & Bianchi 1984 and Göttler & Neuber 2007. For the medical tradition see for instance Burnett & Jacquart 1994 and Gill 2008.
7 See below the different understandings of the human spirit in Ficino and Telesio.
8 Giordano Bruno, "De la causa, principio et uno," *Dialoghi italiani* 1958: I 243.
9 Naturally, there were also other important traditions in which the passions were reconsidered during the Renaissance; concerning the humanist tradition see Ebbersmeyer 2013a and Chapter 12 of this volume; concerning the late-scholastic tradition see Knuuttila 2012 and also Chapter 12 of this volume.
10 Ficino, *Lettere* ed. Gentile 92; trans. *Letters* I: 39.
11 For more on Ficino's "holistic approach" to philosophical questions see the Introduction and Chapter 1 of this volume.
12 The exact labelling and number of the stages vary in Ficino's work, *cf. Theologia platonica* I. 1–6, where he distinguishes "body," "quality," "soul," "mind," and "God." See also Introduction and Chapter 1 of this volume.
13 See Plotinus, *Enn.* IV.4. 31–43.
14 On the world soul see also *PTh* IV. 1.
15 The concept of perfection is crucial to Ficino's thought; it describes his way of thinking: "In any genus we must ascend from the imperfect things to the perfect since the perfect naturally come first" (*PTh* I.5: 69).
16 For the history of the argument and its role in current debates on panpsychism, see Seager & Allen-Hermanson 2010.
17 In *De amore* Ficino sometimes uses the singular and sometimes the plural form of "spirit."
18 This common attraction in nature is, according to Ficino, also the foundation for true magic. Thus, all magic consists in love (*DA* 199–200). As we will see below, this understanding of magic is taken up and elaborated by Campanella.
19 *De divinis nominibus*, IV.15.
20 For a more detailed account of the Platonic background in Ficino's concept of love, see Ebbersmeyer 2012.
21 Between the *editio princeps* in 1489 and the year 1647, there were about thirty printed editions and during the 16th century it was translated into German, French, and Italian.
22 On Ficino's magic see Walker 1958 and more recently Copenhaver 2007 and 2015.

23 The connection between melancholy and philosophy goes back to Aristotle, who asks in *Problemata* XXX, 1: "Why is it that all those men who have become extraordinary in philosophy, politics, poetry, or the arts are obviously melancholic [. . .]?" Aristotle, *Problems*, p. 277."
24 Concerning musical therapy in Ficino see Voss 1992.
25 I have explored this agenda more extensively in Ebbersmeyer (forthcoming), from which I have adopted parts of the following section.
26 I am not going to analyze the ethical implications of Telesio's theory of the passions, which are found in the ninth book of his *De rerum natura* (= *DRN*); for more detail see Ebbersmeyer (forthcoming).
27 *DRN* I, 4. For Telesio's concept of matter see Schuhmann 1990; who also discusses possible sources for Telesio's understanding of heat and cold as incorporeal active forces.
28 See also *DRN* III, 338.
29 For the distinction between human and animal passions in Telesio see Ebbersmeyer 2013b.
30 See *DRN* II 268–284. On this point see also *DRN* II, 358.
31 *DRN* III, 18; see also II, 254.
32 *DRN* III, 10. See also III, 340.
33 The relation between spirit and movement derives from the substance of the spirit. The spirit is composed of the greatest amount of heat, and the nature of heat is to be mobile (see *DRN* I, 40–44). Although the spirit does not consist entirely of heat, it has subtility (*tenuitas*) and therefore abhors immobility and compression. See *DRN* II, 476–478.
34 *DRN* II, 324 and III, 6
35 See *DRN* III, 16. See also *DRN* II, 258.
36 In the same book Telesio also introduces the concept of a divine soul which is infused in men by god and which is united to the corporeal spirit as its form (see *DRN* II, 210–222). There is a long debate among scholars about how to interpret these statements. While some argue with valid arguments for the claim that Telesio introduced this divine soul as "a compromise" in order to be spared from prosecution for his thesis (see especially Bondì 1993), others admit that Telesio might have had some objective reason to introduce it (see for instance Schuhmann (1988: 116–117)). Pupo 1999 gives a survey of the history of the interpretation of this topic. For present purposes this problem can be put aside, as Telesio does not refer to the divine soul in order to explain the passions.
37 In general, Telesio uses the term "*spiritus*," but sometimes he also uses the term "*anima*" with the attribute "*e semine educta*." As he states in *DRN* III, 17, the spirit is "the substance of the animal soul evolved from the semen."
38 *DNR* II, 376–378. See also *DNR* II, 384–388.
39 In referring to Galen Telesio joins an important late medieval tradition that defended their views about the mind with reference to medical data. For more on this tradition see Chapter 2 of this volume.
40 Telesio does not hesitate to criticize Galen, too, when he takes him to be wrong. In his treatise *Quod animal universum ab unica animae substantia gubernator. Contra Galenum*, Telesio refers to the affects (such as fear, rage, sadness, joy, shame, sorrow) in order to argue against the tripartition of the soul held by Galen, following Plato and Hippocrates. See Bernardino Telesio, *Quod animal universum*, ed. L. de Franco, 188–288, see esp. ch. 21–35, 241–281.
41 See Telesio's critique of Aristotle's distinction between a rational and an irrational part of the soul (*EN* 1102b14–21) in *DRN* III, 426–432. For the moral implications of this view of combatting passions see Chapter 12 of this volume.
42 The book was originally written in Italian in 1604, but it was the Latin version, that was finally published in 1620 and which was reprinted several times.

43 See esp. Campanella's *Philosophia sensibus demonstrata* (1591). Concerning the differences between Telesio's and Campanella's approach to nature, see Lerner 2007.
44 On Ficino's influence on Campanella, see Walker 1958 and, more recently, Giglioni 2013.
45 On the concepts of sense, spirit, and natural magic in Campanella's *Del senso*, see Ernst (2010: 114–127).
46 Campanella refers to Pliny, *Nat. Hist.*, II. 10, here.
47 In 1590 Campanella made the acquaintance of Giambattista della Porta, author of the famous *Magiae naturalis sive de miraculis rerum naturalium* (1558). On Campanella's magic, see also Ernst 2010.
48 Pliny, *Natural History* XXX.i–ii.
49 Although we don't count imagination usually as a passion, Campanella counts it as such with good reasons, because (a) the imagination depends on the spirit and can, in this sense, be regarded as an "affection" of the spirit, and because (b) the imagination is one of the central features that is manipulated through magical practices.
50 Germana Ernst refers to Pietro d'Abano as the one who made this dictum famous (in his *Conciliator*, diff. Cxxv); see *DS* 212, *note*.
51 See Walker 1958: 199–202.
52 See Leibniz *Principes de la nature et de la grace fondés en raison* § 2; *Monadologie* § 15.
53 Cudworth, *The True Intellectual System of the Universe* (1678); More, *Enchiridion Metaphysicum* (1671); Conway, *The principles of the most ancient and modern philosophy* (1692). For the context, see Popkin 1990 and Rogers et al. 1997.
54 See Nagel 1979 or, more recently, Strawson 2006.

Bibliography

Primary sources

Aristotle. *De anima*. R. D. Hicks (trans.). Cambridge, UK: Cambridge University Press, 1907.

———. *Problems*, volume II: Books 20–38. Rhetoric to Alexander, trans. by W. S. Hett and H. Rackham, Harvard: Harvard University Press (Loeb Classical Library), 2011.

Bruni, Giordano. *Dialoghi italiani*. In *Opere italiani*, 2 vols, G. Aquilecchia & N. Ordine (eds). Torino: UTET, 2002.

Campanella, Tomasso. *Philosophia sensibus demonstrata*. L. De Franco (ed.), Naples: Vivarium, 1992.

———. *Del senso delle cose e della magia* (= *DS*). G. Ernst (ed.). Bari: Laterza, 2007.

Conway, Anne. *The Principles of the Most Ancient and Modern Philosophy*, A. P. Coudert & T. Corse (eds). Cambridge, MA: Cambridge University Press, 1996 [1692].

Cudworth, Ralph. *The True Intellectual System of the Universe*. London: Printed for Robert Royston, 1678 (RP Stuttgart-Bad Cannstadt: Frommann 1964) [1678].

Della Porta, Giambattista. *Magiae naturalis sive de miraculis rerum naturalium*. Naples: Matthias Cancer, 1558.

Descartes, René. *The Philosophical Writings of Descartes*. J. Cottingham, R. Stoothoff & D. Murdoch (eds). Cambridge, MA: Cambridge University Press, 1985.

Ficino, Marsilio. *Commentary on Plato's Symposium* (= *DA*). S. R. Jayne (trans.). Columbia: The University of Missouri, 1944.

———. *Three Books on Life*. C. V. Kaske & J. R. Clarke (eds). Binghamton: Center for Medieval and Early Renaissance Studies, 1989.

———. *Lettere I. Epistolarum familiarum liber I*. S. Gentile (ed.). Florence: Olschki, 1990.

———. *Platonic Theology* (= *PTh*), 6 vols. M. J. B. Allen & J. Hankins (trans. & eds). Cambridge, MA: Harvard University Press, 2001–2006.

———. *Commentaire sur 'Le banquet' de Platon, 'De l'amour'*. P. Laurens (ed.). Paris: Les Belles Lettres, 2002.

———. *The Letters of Marsilio Ficino*, 8 vols. (Translated from Latin by members of the Language Department of the School of Economic Science, London). London: Shepheard-Walwyn, 1975–2009.

Leibniz, Gottfried Wilhelm. *Sämtliche Schriften und Briefe*. Akademie der Wissenschaften (ed.). Darmstadt and Berlin: Akademie Verlag, 1923–.

———. *Philosophical Essays*. R. Ariew & D. Garber (trans. & eds). Indianapolis: Hacket, 1989.

More, Henry. *Opera Omnia*. London, 1675–1679, 3 vols. Reprint: Hildesheim: Olms, 1966.

———. *Enchiridion Metaphysicum*. London: Typis E. Flesher; Prostat apud Guilielmum Morden, 1671. In *Opera Omnia* t. II,1. (Engl.: *Henry More's Manual of metaphysics* [1679], Alexander Jacob (trans.). Reprint: Hildesheim: Olms, 1995).

Patrizi, Francesco. *Nova de universis philosophiae*. Ferrara: Mamarellus, 1591.

Telesio, Bernardino. *De rerum natura iuxta propria principia* (=*DRN*), 3 vols. L. de Franco (ed. & ital. trans.). Cosenza: Casa del Libro, 1965, 1974; Florence: La Nuova Italia, 1976.

———. "Quod animal universum". In *Varii de naturalibus rebus libelli*, L. de Franco (ed.). Florence: La Nuova Italia Ed., 1981.

Secondary sources

Bondì, R. 1993. "'Spiritus' e 'anima' in Bernardino Telesio". *Giornale critico della filosofia italiana* **72**: 405–417.

Burnett, Ch. & Jacquart, D. (eds). 1994. *Constantine the African and 'Alī ibn al-'Abbās al-Maǧūs: The Pantegni and Related Texts*. Leiden: Brill.

Clark, A., & Chalmers, D. 1998. "The Extended Mind". *Analysis* **58**: 10–23.

Copenhaver, B. 1984. "Scholastic Philosophy and Renaissance Magic in the 'De vita' of Marsilio Ficino". *Renaissance Quarterly* **37**: 523–554.

———. 2007. "How to Do Magic, and Why Philosophical Prescriptions". In *The Cambridge Companion to Renaissance Philosophy*, J. Hankins (ed.), 137–170. Cambridge: Cambridge University Press.

———. 2015. *Magic in Western Culture: From Antiquity to the Enlightenment*. Cambridge, MA: Cambridge University Press.

Ebbersmeyer, S. 2012. "The Philosopher as a Lover: Renaissance Debates on Platonic 'Eros'". See Shapiro & Pickavé (2012), 133–155.

———. 2013a. "Passions for This Life in Renaissance Philosophy". In *Rethinking Virtue, Reforming Society: New Directions in Renaissance Ethics, 1400–1600*, S. Ebbersmeyer & D. A. Lines (eds), 193–213. Turnhout: Brepols.

———. 2013b. "Do Humans Feel Differently? Telesio on the Affective Nature of Men and Animals". In *The Debate of the Soul of Animals in Renaissance Philosophy*, C. Muratori (ed.), 97–111. Pisa, Rome: Fabrizio Serra Editore.

———. Forthcoming. "Telesio's Vitalistic Conception of the Passions". In *Sense, Affect and Self-Preservation in Bernardino Telesio (1509–1588)*, G. Giglioni & J. Kraye (eds). Dordrecht, The Netherlands: Springer.

Ernst, G. 2010. *Tommaso Campanella: The Book and the Body of Nature*. D. Marshall (trans.). Dordrecht, The Netherlands: Springer.

Fattori, M. & Bianchi, L. M. (eds). 1984. *Spiritus*. IV Colloquio Internazionale del Lessico Intellettuale Europeo. Rome: Edizioni dell'Ateneo.

Giglioni, G. 2013. "Heavenly Negotiations in Ficino's 'De vita coelitus comparanda' and Their Place in Campanella's 'Metaphysica'". *Bruniana & Campanelliana* 19(1): 33–46.

Gill, Christopher. 2008. "Die antike medizinische Tradition: Die körperliche Basis emotionaler Dispositionen". In *Klassische Emotionstheorien*, H. Landweer & U. Renz (eds), 95–120. Berlin: de Gruyter.

Göttler, Ch. & Neuber, W. (eds). 2007. *Spirits Unseen: The Representation of Subtle Bodies in Early Modern European Culture*. Leiden: Brill.

Knuuttila, S. 2012. "Sixteenth-Century Discussions of the Passions of the Will". See Shapiro & Pickavé (2012), 116–132.

Lerner, M. P. 2007. "Telesio et Campanella: de la nature 'iuxta propria principia' à la nature 'instrumentum dei'". *Bruniana & Campanelliana* 13(1): 79–97.

Long, A. A. & Sedley, D. N. 1987. *The Hellenistic Philosophers. Vol. 1: Translations of the Principal Sources and Philosophical Commentary*. Cambridge, MA: Cambridge University Press.

Nagel, T. 1979. "Panpsychism". In *Mortal Questions*, 181–195. Cambridge: Cambridge University Press.

Popkin, R. H. 1990. "The Spiritualistic Cosmologies of Henry More and Anne Conway". In *Henry More (1614–1687) Tercentenary Studies*, S. Hutton (ed.), 97–114. Dordrecht, The Netherlands: Springer.

Pupo, S. 1999. *L'anima immortale in Telesio: Per una storia delle interpretazioni*. Cosenza: Pellegrini.

Rogers, G. A. J., Vienne, J. M. & Zarka, Y. C. (eds). 1997. *The Cambridge Platonists in Philosophical Context*. Dordrecht, The Netherlands: Springer.

Schlette, H. R. 1993. *Weltseele: Geschichte und Hermeneutik*. Frankfurt/M: Knecht.

Schuhmann, K. 1988. "Hobbes and Telesio". *Hobbes Studies* 1: 109–133.

———. 1990. "Telesio's Concept of Matter". In: *Atti del convegno internazionale di studi su Bernardino Telesio*, 115–134. Cosenza: Accad. Cosentina.

Seager, W. & Allen-Hermanson, S. 2015. "Panpsychism". In *The Stanford Encyclopedia of Philosophy*, Fall 2015 Edition, Edward N. Zalta (ed.). http://plato.stanford.edu/archives/fall2015/entries/panpsychism/.

Shapiro, L. & Pickavé, M. (eds). 2012. *Emotions and Cognitive Life in Medieval and Early Modern Philosophy*. Oxford: Oxford University Press.

Skrbina, D. 2005. *Panpsychism in the West*. Cambridge, MA: MIT Press.

———. (ed.). 2009. *Mind That Abides: Panpsychism in the New Millennium*. Amsterdam: John Benjamins.

Strawson, G. 2006. "Realistic Monism: Why Physicalism Entails Panpsychism". *Journal of Consciousness Studies* 13: 3–31.

Varela, F. J., Thompson, E. & Rosch, E. 1991. *The Embodied Mind*. Cambridge, MA: MIT Press.

Verbeke, G. 1945. *L'évolution de la doctrine du pneuma du stoicism à S. Augustine*. Paris: Desclée De Brouwer.

Voss, A. 1992. "The Natural Magic of Marsilio Ficino". *Historical Dance* 3: 25–30.

Walker, D. P. 1958. *Spiritual and Demonic Magic From Ficino to Campanella*. London: Warburg Institute.

10

DUALISM AND THE MIND-BODY PROBLEM

*Sander W. de Boer**

It is not easy to precisely state the nature of the mind-body problem, which is part of the reason why it is such a difficult problem in the first place (McGinn 1989). Still, it seems immediately evident that there is such a problem, since, as Jaegwon Kim (1996: 9) nicely puts it, the mind-body problem is "at bottom . . . the problem of accounting for the place of mind in a world that is essentially physical". Surely the mind at least *seems to be* something entirely different from the physical objects we see around us. Minds are capable of conscious thought, whereas physical objects are not. These, at least, are the terms in which René Descartes (1596–1650) put the distinction. This led him to conclude that mind and body are entirely different kinds of substances, a view we would now label substance dualism.[1] It will be useful to note the key elements that set up the mind-body problem as it derives from the Cartesian dualistic view of the world:

1   Mind and body are two ontologically distinct kinds of entities, each with its own functions, and "the whole nature of the mind consists in the fact that it thinks, while the whole nature of the body consists in its being an extended thing" (*CSM* II 248).
2   Bodies are able to exist and function without minds (as shown by non-human animals), and vice versa (as proven by the *cogito* argument).
3   Any interaction between body and mind is therefore a puzzle that needs to be explained.

It may be, of course, that after a detailed analysis we are able to account for the mind in purely physical terms, in which case Cartesian dualism would turn out to be wrong. But it is hard to imagine how any philosopher could fail to see that the relation between the conscious mind and the unconscious body is a fundamental problem that needs to be addressed.

At first sight, tracing this theme in the late medieval and Renaissance period seems relatively easy, since it contains several philosophers who have been labelled dualists. Henrik Lagerlund (2004, 2011), for instance, has argued that we find dualistic positions as early as the fourteenth century, for instance, in John Buridan (c. 1300–c. 1360). More recently, Jeffrey Brower (2014: 259–278) has maintained that if we are to apply one of our contemporary labels to Thomas Aquinas's (1224–1274/5) *sui generis* philosophy of mind, then we should opt for dualism.[2] Moreover, the outlines of Plato's dualistic views on mind and body were well known in this period. Surprisingly, however, medieval philosophers paid little if any attention to the mind-body problem. Peter King (2007) has even argued that the mind-body problem simply did not exist in the Middle Ages and that, importantly, it could not even be formulated in the terms used by medieval philosophers.[3] All this suggests that it may have been possible to be a dualist without taking the mind-body problem seriously. But if this is so, then it would seem that such dualism is markedly different from Cartesian substance dualism. This should not surprise us. The metaphysical frameworks in which pre-modern discussions on mind and body were situated are very different from that of the mechanistic philosophy in which the Cartesian problem arose.

This chapter will explore some medieval and Renaissance approaches to the mind-body relation that have been linked to either dualism or the mind-body problem. It consists of three parts, each of which considers a different metaphysical framework. The first parts deals with late-thirteenth- and fourteenth-century Aristotelian approaches. Taking Thomas Aquinas as a starting point, it will explore some criticisms of his view as presented by William of Ockham (c. 1287–1347) and John Buridan. The second part deals with approaches that took their main inspiration from the Platonic traditions, especially that of Marsilio Ficino (1433–1499). The third and final part addresses the anti-Aristotelian views of Bernardino Telesio (1509–1588).

1 Aristotelian approaches

Up to at least the early seventeenth century, the dominant metaphysical framework was an Aristotelian one, and the borders between the mental and the physical were drawn differently than they are now. These different borders make it difficult, at times even impossible, to accurately render medieval views on the mind-body relation in contemporary terms. Notably, medieval philosophers tended to talk about soul rather than mind, taking their cue from Aristotle's ground-breaking work on philosophical psychology *De anima* (*On the Soul*). When they did use the term mind (*mens*), they described it as being merely a part of soul, namely its rational part (*anima rationalis*). Descartes targets this Aristotelian tradition directly in his reply to the objections against his *Mediations* formulated by Pierre Gassendi (1592–1655):

> Thus, primitive man probably did not distinguish between, on the one hand, the principle by which we are nourished and grow and accomplish without any thought all the other operations which we have in common with the brutes, and, on the other hand, the principle in virtue of which we think. He therefore used the single term 'soul' to apply to both; . . . I,

by contrast . . . have said that the term 'soul', when it is used to refer to both these principles, is ambiguous.

(*CSM* II, 246)

If Descartes is right, we seem to be better off ignoring the whole Aristotelian tradition. The term 'soul', as used by Aristotelian philosophers, indeed covered not only all forms of cognition, but every manifestation of life, including nutrition, growth and even the generation of offspring. But were the Aristotelians really as confused as Descartes suggests? Hardly.[4] The broad extension of 'soul' should instead be explained in terms of one of the most intriguing features of Aristotelian psychology, namely the two aspects ascribed to the soul. The soul is viewed not only as a mind, but also as a substantial form (Pasnau 2012).[5] Following Aristotle, Aquinas describes all living bodies, ranging from plants to human beings, as informed by souls. This brings us to the first reason why the mind-body problem is difficult to formulate: Aristotle's definition of the soul as "substance *qua* form of a natural body which has life potentially" (*DA* II.1, 412a18–19) implies that the soul is essentially embodied and that the body in question should be described in terms of its having a certain soul. When combined with Aquinas's position that substances only have a single substantial form, the difficulty increases, because now, strictly speaking, it does not even make sense to talk about the soulless bodies of living human beings as one thing, and their souls as another.

> It is necessary to say that it is one and the same substantial form by which this individual thing is a particular or substance, and by which it is a body and an animated body, and so on. . . . It should not be understood, therefore . . . as if body were constituted by one form that makes it be a body and the soul is added to it, making it a living body. But rather it should be understood that it is by the soul that it exists, that it is a body, and that it is a living body.
>
> (*SentDeA*, II.1: 71)

In terms of Aquinas's metaphysical framework it is relatively easy to formulate a mind-soul problem (Pasnau 2007).[6] That is, we can question how exactly the mind part of soul relates to its other parts. But it is very difficult to even formulate a mind-body problem. This is because Aquinas argues consistently for the radical position that souls, like all other substantial forms, not only provide a specific type of being to the substance they inform, but account for the substance's very existence. Not only do we need to appeal to souls in our description of the bodies of living things, but these bodies cannot possibly exist in the absence of soul.[7]

There is a second reason why the mind-body problem is difficult to even formulate in Aristotelian terms. The mind-body problem as we know it, is the problem of how to account for the presence of consciousness in a material world. Since the perception of colours, tastes, smells and sounds is part of the realm of consciousness, all sense perception falls under the mind part of the mind-body distinction. Of course there must be some physical cause that is responsible for stimulating the relevant regions of the brain, but conscious perception itself is part of the life of the mind. Late medieval philosophers, by contrast, drew a different distinction, namely between activities that can only be exercised in and through a body and those that can be exercised without. The question whether the perception of colours, smells and tastes are mental or physical phenomena therefore translates into the question whether these processes are essentially embodied or whether they could, in principle, also be performed by disembodied souls. Like most late medieval philosophers (though not all, as we will see), Aquinas places perception unambiguously under the heading of embodied activities. Perception, he argues, is the activity of an ensouled body and not something that the soul could carry out on its own, even if it turns out that (part of) it could be separated from the body.

At this point we might object that Aquinas's discussion of perception is flawed. We might agree with him that perception is an embodied process, in the sense that the physical changes in the eye, the optic nerve and the brain are what cause our being conscious of colours, for instance. But surely our being conscious is something other than these physical states of the body. If Aquinas is writing about activities of the senses and about sensations as if they were the same, this means either that he is a proto-physicalist who fails to defend his position or that his account is hopelessly ambiguous. Aquinas, in turn, would likely be puzzled by this objection, assuming we even managed to make clear what we meant. As Watson (1966) and King (2007) have convincingly shown, there is no clear equivalent for our term 'sensations' as the conscious by-product of sense perceptions in either ancient or medieval philosophy. The term was "introduced into philosophy precisely to make it possible to speak of a conscious state without committing oneself as to the nature or even existence of external stimuli" (Watson 1966: 101). If we tried to render our objection into a language Aquinas could understand by using the Latin terms '*sensatio*' and '*sensus*', all we would have achieved is pointing out the difference between the activity of the sense organs and the organs themselves. The whole idea of 'raw feels' is alien to the Aristotelian tradition, because the division between the conscious realm of the mental and the unconscious realm of the physical is not yet in place. It was considered a basic, empirically established fact that part of the physical world is alive and that part of the living physical world is endowed with the ability to sense. Put in Aristotelian terms, physical things are perfectly capable of many forms of cognition; all that is required is that they be informed by the right soul.

There is one cognitive phenomenon that Aquinas and his contemporaries thought is not embodied in this way, namely abstract thought.[8] For this reason, medieval philosophers tend to argue for some distinction between an immaterial intellect and an embodied soul. But this distinction could be fleshed out in several ways, and according to Aquinas, the required immateriality of the intellect should not be spelled out in terms of its being a separate substance (similar to Descartes' mind) but instead in terms of its being a power of the embodied soul that does not, *qua* exercise of its function, rely on any bodily organ.

Aquinas's optimistic view of the possibility of giving a unified account of the whole range of human activities in terms of a single soul that informs our body was, however, not shared by all of his contemporaries. Some even perceived the tension between an immaterial intellect and an embodied soul inherent in this approach as bordering on a contradiction. One of these critics was William of Ockham.[9]

One of Ockham's arguments against Aquinas's position is that we ascribe an entirely different range of properties to our intellect than to the remainder of our soul. We talk about the intellective soul as being immaterial and non-extended, whereas we call the sensitive soul material and extended (*Quodlibetal Questions*, II.10, 134). Taken on its own, this argument is hardly conclusive, but Ockham's other arguments are more difficult to refute. One of these reads as follows:

> It is impossible that contraries should exist simultaneously in the same subject. But an act of desiring something and an act of spurning that same thing are contraries in the same subject. Therefore, if they exist simultaneously in reality, they do not exist in the same subject. But it is manifest that they exist simultaneously in a human being, since a human being spurns by his intellective appetite the very same thing he desires by his sensitive appetite.
> (*Quodlibetal Questions*, II.10: 132–133)

Any description of our psychological life should be able to account for conflicting desires that arise simultaneously concerning *one and the same object*. One may have a strong desire to eat an entire cake, while simultaneously wanting to stick to one's diet and not a have single bite. This specific type of inner conflict, Ockham argues, can only be explained in terms of the two competing desires inhering in two different subjects: the first in the sensitive and the second in the intellective soul. The possibility that both inhere in the same soul would imply that contraries can be present simultaneously in the same subject. But just as it is impossible for the same object to be both (completely) black and (completely) white, it is impossible for the same soul to desire and reject the same object.

The most relevant argument for present purposes concerns sensation. Aquinas argued that acts of sensation belong to the ensouled body and that the subject in which these act inhere is the sensitive organ. This was a common analysis of sensation. John Duns Scotus (1265/66–1308), for instance, argued for the same point (*Quodlibetal Questions*, 9: 227). But Ockham takes a different view. Acts of sensation, he writes, inhere principally in the sensitive soul alone.[10] This view has immediate repercussions for his analysis of soul and body. Suppose, Ockham argues, the sensitive soul were but a metaphysical part of the intellective soul (as

Aquinas argued). This would imply that this single soul could still have acts of sensation once it has been separated from our body, because:

> [I]f (i) a sensation exists subjectively in the intellective soul and (ii) God is able to conserve every accident in its subject in the absence of everything else, then it follows that he is able to conserve a sensation in a separated soul – which is absurd.
> (*Quodlibetal Questions*, II.10: 134)

If there were no real distinction between the sensitive and intellective soul, then God, being omnipotent, would be able to produce sensations in a disembodied human soul. The most noteworthy element of this passage is its structure. The argument is a *reductio ad absurdum*. That is, Ockham rejects as absurd the idea that a disembodied soul could have sensations. The logical possibility of disembodied sensation alone, which follows from the assumption of a single soul, is enough to conclude that we must have two souls: a mortal sensitive soul, on the one hand, and an immortal intellective soul, on the other. This also implies that, despite Ockham's point about the sensitive soul being the principle subject of acts of sensation, sensation is for him an essentially embodied phenomenon. This is because the sensitive soul only exists as the form of the body, in contrast to the intellective soul, which can also exist on its own after death.

Ockham's arguments address the mind-soul problem and conclude that the mind must be a substantial form of its own. But Ockham does more than just introduce a real distinction between two souls. He also gives the body itself a more independent status, by arguing that the body can, at least to some extent, be described without reference to any soul. In Ockham's terms, a human being consists of three substantial forms, which are ordered hierarchically (*Quodlibetal Questions* II.11). The first of these, the form of the body, endows the body with its own non-living existence. The second, the sensitive soul, endows the body with all its vital functions up to and including sensation, and functions as the subject of our sensations and our sensitive desires. The last, the intellective soul, introduces the capacity for abstract thought and free will and functions as the subject of our thoughts and our intellectual desires. When the body dies, the first two forms corrupt with it, whereas the immaterial and intellective soul remains.

Ockham's position seems to be as close to dualism as we can reasonably expect to come in Aristotelian terms. Not surprisingly, then, he has often been labelled a dualist.[11] But this label is misleading without the following qualifications. First, Ockham describes the intellect as one of the *substantial forms* of the human body, similar to the way he describes the sensitive soul. That is, he considers the intellective soul to be that which together with the body's other forms accounts for the human body's unity, structure and functions. Granted, his emphasis on the immateriality of this form raises questions about how the form-matter relation comes about in this unique case, but Ockham is adamant that the intellective soul is a constitutive metaphysical part of the human animal (*Quodlibetal Questions*

II.10). The second, and related, qualification is that Ockham's 'dualism' arises within the specifically Aristotelian mind-soul problem, in which the debate is occasioned by the difference between operations that are exercised within or through a certain part of the body and those that are not. The complete absence of any mind-body problem in terms of the relation between consciousness and the physical world became apparent from his analysis of sensation. Like Aquinas, though with a different underlying metaphysics, Ockham ascribes sensation to the ensouled body, not to the intellect; indeed, he takes the impossibility of disembodied sensation as establishing the real distinction between our two souls in the first place.

Another fourteenth-century philosopher whose name often comes up in discussions about dualism in the Middle Ages is John Buridan. Like virtually all medieval philosophers, Buridan is convinced that the human soul survives the corruption of the body. And like Aquinas, Buridan argues for the position that there is but one soul in a human being and that, moreover, this soul is its only substantial form. But there is a crucial difference between Buridan's and Aquinas's accounts of the soul-body relation. In contrast to Aquinas, Buridan accepts the main principle through which Ockham arrived at his two souls, namely that the intellectual soul of a human being has a completely different structure than the sensitive soul of a brute animal. Human souls are indivisible, unextended and hence incorruptible, whereas animal souls are divisible, extended and therefore subject to corruption. Because he postulates only a single soul in a human being, Buridan concludes that every operation of the human soul, including perception, is itself unextended and indivisible since it inheres in an indivisible form.

Whereas Aquinas and Ockham view human and animal perception as taking place in roughly the same way, Buridan regards human perception as radically different from animal perception, since the former is an unextended and indivisible act on account of its inhering in an indivisible soul. But given this analysis, there seems to be nothing stopping us from formulating our mind-body problem in Buridan's terms, especially given the way Buridan summarizes the difficulties in accounting for human perception:

> Truly, this is a very difficult problem indeed if we assume in man a single soul. For this soul has to be intellective and indivisible, not extended by some extension of matter or of its subject. And then this unextended soul is the sensitive and vegetative soul as well. How, therefore, since sensation is taken to be extended with the extension of the organ and matter, can it be inherent in an indivisible subject, and, as it were, brought forth from its potency? ... And I respond that this certainly is miraculous, *for the human soul inheres in a miraculous and supernatural manner in the extended human body*, not extended, nor brought forth from the potency of the matter in which it inheres, and yet it inheres in the whole body and in its every part.
>
> (Buridan, *QdA*, II.9: 138, my emphasis)[12]

Passages such as this illustrate why it is at least tempting to read Buridan as defending a soul-body dualism. Granted, like Ockham, Buridan continues to call the human soul the form of the body. But Buridan faces difficulties that Ockham could avoid by appealing to a human sensitive soul, which functions as a normal form of the body. On Ockham's view that sensations are due to the material sensitive soul, which is distinct from the immaterial rational soul, the mind/soul-body problem does not arise in the first place (even though it gives rise to a mind-soul problem). Buridan's case, however, is more complex, since he can only appeal to a single immaterial soul. Insofar as he argues that human sense perception is radically different from animal sense perception, because human perception inheres in an immaterial, unextended soul whereas animal sensation inheres in a material, extended soul, he certainly seems to be moving in the direction of a human soul-body dualism.[13] And it is tempting to read Buridan's comment about the supernatural inherence of the human soul as confirmation of a dualistic view. But in a rarely cited passage, Buridan cautions the reader not to misunderstand the meaning of indivisibility in question:

> The intellective soul is not indivisible as something having a position in the continuum, as it would be imagined about a point, but in such a manner that it is indifferently in every part of the body, no matter how extended.
>
> (*QdA* II.9: 139)

That is, the indivisibility of the human soul does not mean that it is somehow placed outside the body, or even that it is connected to the body only at a single point, but that there is no part of the body where the soul is not present in its entirety. Given that this description of the intellective soul is found in many medieval authors, Aquinas included, we should hesitate to label Buridan a human soul-body dualist on account of his emphasis on the immateriality of the soul alone.[14]

More importantly, the reason why human sensation poses special difficulties for Buridan is not that its connection to the body cannot be explained. Instead the difficulty is this: Buridan too is convinced that sensation is embodied, and if sensation inheres in extended matter, acts of sensation must be extended like matter is. But like so many Aristotelians, Buridan is equally convinced that sensation does not inhere in matter alone, but also in the soul. In his words:

> [N]either matter without the soul, nor the soul without matter would sense, since sensation is not sufficiently brought forth from the potency of either, unless God would miraculously want to preserve sensation without the subject from the potency of which it was brought forth.
>
> (*QdA* II.9: 142)

In the case of animal souls, this double inherence poses no special difficulties. But in the case of the human soul, one of the two subjects which the extended sensation inheres in is itself indivisible. And how can something extended inhere in something indivisible? This is the puzzle Buridan wrestles with. Even this difficulty need not be insurmountable, though, since Buridan himself points out that the presence of the whole indivisible soul in each and every part of the body might explain at least in part how it could receive extended sensations. This is because every part of the matter in which the extended sensation inheres is also informed by the whole indivisible soul (Buridan, *QdA* II.9: 139).

With these qualifications in place, applying the label 'dualist' to Buridan arguably tends to obscure more than it illuminates. His view is puzzling, to be sure, but does not seem to have been intended as a mind-body dualism, or even a human soul-body dualism. Buridan's emphasis is always on the unity of soul and body, which results from their relation as form to matter. This is precisely why Buridan faces the same difficulties in accounting for vegetative life functions such as digestion; here too his emphasis on the immateriality of the human soul forces him to admit a radical difference from such functions in other animals (*QdA* III.17, 293).[15] But undeniably, the way in which Buridan and Ockham framed their respective discussions on soul and mind to some extent paved the way for later dualistic views.[16] And the next critical step in that direction was taken as early as the fourteenth century.

Adam Wodeham, one of Ockham's students, challenged Ockham's argument based on sensation. This argument (quoted above, p. 212) started from the premise that acts of sensation inhere in the soul and then appealed to the absurdity of disembodied sensation to conclude that we must have two souls. Wodeham accepts the premise. He writes that an act of sensation is "a spiritual form that is non-extended, just as its subject is non-extended" (*Lectura*, prologue, q. 1, par. 15). But he fails to see why disembodied sensation is an *a priori* absurdity. And if it is not absurd, then there is no reason to conclude that we must have two souls. So Wodeham draws two conclusions: (i) a single human soul suffices, and (ii) it must be possible, at least in principle, for sensation to take place in this soul even when disembodied (*Lectura*, Prologue, q. 1, par. 15). Wodeham is no dualist; he agrees with Aristotle that our single human soul is the form of our body (*Lectura*, Prologue, q. 1, par. 5). Yet allowing for the logical possibility of disembodied sensation is a crucial step in making mind-body dualism possible. And Wodeham is not the only one taking this step. Similar points are raised in Gregory of Rimini, and, as we will see in the next section, in Peter John Olivi.[17] Although this shift is as yet underexplored in the scholarly literature, these authors are hard to reconcile with Peter King's explanation for the absence of a medieval mind-body problem, namely that all philosophers in the period view sensation as an essentially bodily phenomenon.

2 Platonic approaches

Ultimately, the Aristotelian, biologically oriented conception of the soul and its functions, as further developed in the later Middle Ages, tends to emphasize the unity of soul and body, even though by the fourteenth century several cracks had appeared in this model. A more promising hunting ground for dualism, therefore, is the Platonic tradition. Few of Plato's texts were available in the Latin West prior to the second half of the fifteenth century, but his dualistic approach to the soul-body relation had already become well known in the Middle Ages through other sources, especially the works of St. Augustine (354–430). Although the details of Augustine's own views on the relation between soul and body are hard to pin down, there is undeniably a strong emphasis on the self-sufficiency of soul, which was not lost on medieval philosophers. This emphasis was reinforced by the widely read pseudo-Augustinian treatise *On Spirit and Soul*, which defined the human soul not as a form but as "an intellectual spirit which is rational, always living, always moving, and capable of willing good and evil" (788–789).

Because Augustine was highly regarded throughout the Middle Ages, his views pulled philosophers towards a more dualistic conception of soul and body. In the authors discussed in the previous section, this pull was offset by Aristotle's emphasis on the unity of the human being. But in some cases, the combination of Aristotle and Augustine led to concessions that were fundamentally at odds with the basic Aristotelian tenets outlined in the previous section. One of the more extreme cases was Peter John Olivi (1248–1298), who made it clear on many occasions that he cared little for the authority of Aristotle and preferred to follow Augustine instead. While staying within a basically Aristotelian framework, he modified the approach to soul and body to such an extent that one could wonder if his version of the human soul still functions as the form of the body, leading Juhana Toivanen (2013: 194) to label his views as "close-to-dualistic anthropology".[18]

Olivi's model of the soul-body relation is complex. He argues that we have but one soul constituted by its various powers, which he labels its "partial forms",[19] and like all substantial forms, this soul informs some kind of matter. Olivi rejects, however, the model in which this matter is understood in purely bodily terms. Instead he argues for a two-tier model, in which there are two different types of matter. First and foremost, our whole soul informs a so-called "spiritual matter". In contrast to normal matter, spiritual matter is unextended and indivisible. A substance that is metaphysically composed of form and spiritual matter therefore is not spatially extended, which is why this type of matter was invoked by many medieval philosophers to account for the metaphysical structure of angels. But human beings are clearly different from angels. This difference is spelled out in terms of the second type of matter also informed by our soul, namely normal corporeal matter. At this point we might ask what the net result of this analysis is, apart from a more complex metaphysics. The answer is found in the different relation of our soul to these two types of matter. Whereas the vegetative and sensitive parts of our soul inform both types of matter simultaneously, the intellective part informs only spiritual matter.

The dual inherence of the soul is key to understanding Olivi's position. Due to the lower parts of soul informing both types of matter simultaneously, human beings are rightly described as soul-body unities. Yet due to the intellective part informing spiritual matter only, our soul is also a spiritual substance on its own, although only in a qualified sense because of the relation of the other parts of soul to corporeal matter:

> Although the rational soul has spiritual matter, it should not be said to be a complete substance but an incomplete one, because it also has an essential relation to the human body just like a form has to its matter.[20]

As Toivanen (2013: 38–42) rightly argues, Olivi is not a substance dualist in a strict sense. In all contexts, Olivi argues that our soul is incomplete without our body. And he continues to discuss the soul within a hylomorphist framework. But all this notwithstanding, there is a remarkably strong emphasis on the soul's ability to exist and function without the body, to such an extent "that he can be considered as coming close to substance dualism" (Toivanen 2013: 22), so close, in fact, that it stretches the matter-form framework to its limits or, arguably, even exceeds them. Indeed, Olivi introduced the whole framework of two types of matter to allow for more independence of the soul. Again, this can be traced clearly in his account of perception. As we would expect, Olivi argues for the possibility of disembodied sensation and does so much more strongly than Wodeham and Rimini mentioned above.[21] But even in his analysis of embodied sensation, Olivi minimizes the role of the body. Rather than analyzing perception as a (mostly) passive process in which the senses undergo changes brought about by the perceived object, Olivi emphasizes the activity of our soul in perception. Without denying that perception involves bodily changes, he ultimately argues that such changes do not constitute perception. Rather perception consists in an activity of the soul itself, by which it turns to and apprehends objects. According to Olivi, "we intimately experience that these acts in us proceed from ourselves and that we truly exercise them" (II *Sent.* q. 58: 463–464).[22]

Had Olivi's account been taken seriously as a possible candidate for the soul-body relation, the history of philosophical psychology would have been markedly different. But other views prevailed. The Council of Vienne, which was held in 1311/12, issued a famous decree stating that it is heretical to deny that the human soul is *per se* the substantial form of the body. This decree, which seems to have been phrased with Olivi's views specifically in mind, pushed philosophers to stress the unity of human beings, rather than the distinction between soul and body. Due to his views being censored, Olivi had, for better or worse, little further impact on the debates on the relation between soul and body.

The next century, however, brought with it a strong revival of Platonism, which put even the very basic foundations of the Aristotelian approach to the soul into question. One of the leading philosophers in this movement was Marsilio Ficino. In his *magnum opus* titled *Platonic Theology. Or on the Immortality of the Soul* (early 1470s), Ficino gives a detailed description of the ontological status of the soul and its relationship to the body. His description starts from a Neoplatonic metaphysics, in which reality is described in terms of layers which emanate from one another, and in which each layer is more changeable, more complex and hence less perfect than the preceding one. The *Platonic Theology* describes five such metaphysical layers, with God at the top, material body at the bottom and soul occupying the central, middle position, making it "the mirror of things divine, the life of things mortal, the bond joining the two" (*PT* III.2: 237).[23]

Soul is the nexus that binds the spiritual and material realms and therefore shares in the properties of both. Because of this unique position, Ficino argues, its ontological status has often been misunderstood, not just in the past, but also in his own time by the dominant, Aristotelian approach to psychology, whose advocates he describes elsewhere as follows:

> The entire world is occupied by the Aristotelians who are mostly divided into two sects: those who follow Alexander and those who follow Averroes. The former take our intellect to be mortal and the latter contend that it is one. Both equally destroy all religion from the foundation.[24]

As a characterization of the general Aristotelian approach to the relation between mind and body, this is hardly fair. But it is true that philosophers had become increasingly aware of the tensions present in the Aristotelian approach, an awareness that would culminate in Pietro Pomponazzi's treatise on the immortality of the soul (1516) a few decades later.[25] These tensions derive from the combination of the soul's status as the form of the body and the assumed immateriality and immortality of the rational soul. The solution once proposed by Alexander of Aphrodias (*fl.* 200) came close to materialism; it turned the rational soul into a bodily, extended form, which will corrupt once the whole living being corrupts, just as all other forms do. Averroes's (1126–1198) solution went in the opposite direction; he turned the rational soul into an immaterial, unique and divine substance shared by all humankind, thus saving its immateriality at the cost of making it a supra-individual entity. The merits and demerits of these solutions had long been debated in the Aristotelian tradition and were at times put forward as either the solution our natural reason will arrive at when unaided by faith, or as the correct interpretation of Aristotle, or both.

Ficino's own position is more subtle than the criticism voiced in the quote above would suggest. Taking up a theme found in earlier Neoplatonists, he refers to a basic underlying harmony between the views of Plato and Aristotle. Although this is to a large extent a rhetorical strategy, and although the Neoplatonic framework is by far the dominant one, there are many clear traces of the Aristotelian tradition in the *Platonic Theology*.[26] The result of this blend is a view that aims to avoid two extremes: (1) turning soul and body into two completely distinct substances, both of which can also exist without the other, and (2) reducing the soul to its embodied state.

Ficino describes our rational soul as "life that of its own nature gives life to bodies" and as that which "knows itself and divine and natural things" (*PT* III.2:

247).[27] This rational soul is also our only soul, and through its various powers, it is responsible for all vital functions, from vegetation to intellectual thought:

> Thus through the lowest of its powers it [i.e., the rational soul] is the form of matter, through the next lowest it is the form of composite body, through the third it is the form of plants, through the fourth it is the form of an animate creature, or rather the form of the [other three] forms. As a result the rational soul does more than the other forms to form bodies, since it forms them through more powers, and it forms them more purely.
>
> (*PT* XV.4: 57)

On the surface, there is almost nothing in this passage that an Aristotelian would have disagreed with; the soul is called a form, it is assigned several powers and it is deemed responsible for all vital operations. But despite the Aristotelian terminology, Ficino's underlying metaphysics is one in which the soul is a substance in its own right that occupies a higher layer of reality than the body (Kristeller 1940: 325–326). The terminology of forms and powers in the quote above hides that the connection between soul and body is not straightforwardly that of (Aristotelian) form and (Aristotelian) matter. The differences come to the fore when Ficino argues that the connection between soul and body cannot be direct, since the two are too different from one another to relate directly. In other words, Ficino faces a soul-body problem that is generated by their radically different ontological status. Their relation must therefore be mediated by a third entity that shares in the characteristics of both:

> As true philosophy teaches us, the soul, since it is most pure, is linked to this gross and earthy body, which is so different from it, only by means of a superlatively fine, transparent, diminutive body which we call the spirit. It is generated by the hearts heat out of the finest part of the blood and thence spread through the whole body. . . . Initially it [i.e., the soul] gives life and movement to the spirit and makes it vital and then uses it to control and move the body. Anything from the body that presses into this spirit the soul immediately perceives since it is present there. This act of perception we call sense.
>
> (*PT* VII.6: 235)

The connection between soul and body is mediated by the spirit, which Ficino describes as a very subtle type of matter, so subtle, indeed, that it borders on the spiritual.[28] This spirit serves as a sort of intermediate 'body' or 'vehicle' for the soul and allows it to become one with the body. Importantly, the spirit also accounts for perception, which shows that even in this model, perception is still an essentially embodied phenomenon. The soul depends entirely on its relation with spirit for its perception of the external world, which means that there can be no disembodied perception (Corrias 2012: 95).

The importance of an intermediate entity between soul and body is reinforced by Ficino's references to two additional 'vehicles', which are even more subtle and less material than the spirit and which, in contrast to the spirit, remain with the soul after it has left the body.[29] Although the details of these other vehicles are mostly irrelevant for understanding how the soul functions in this life, they immediately show that Ficino's position is much more complex than soul-body dualism. Even when the soul leaves the body and casts off the spirit, it will continue to be embodied in some qualified sense on account of the continuing presence of these other two 'vehicles', which explains why Ficino is able to speak of an immortal animal and not just of an immortal soul:

> The immortal animal is composed of a soul and a celestial body, but the mortal animal of an elemental body besides.
>
> (*Phaedrus*: 121)

But how does Ficino view the corporeal body, to which the soul is connected through the spirit? Is it an independent substance with its own activities? Throughout the *Platonic theology*, Ficino argues for a qualified no to this last question. Material bodies in general, he writes, occupy the lowest of the five metaphysical layers and, therefore, possess the least amount of causal power. Such bodies are nothing but extended matter and are entirely passive when taken on their own. They are active only on account of the presence of various qualities, which constitute the metaphysical layer between soul and matter. But even the activity of such bodily qualities, Ficino argues, is 'limited' and 'crippled'. Whatever stronger causal power these qualities and their bodies exhibit derives from the next higher metaphysical level, that is, from soul (*PT* I.3: 16).[30] Ficino puts it even more strongly than this when he writes that the qualities depend on the existence of soul for their very being (*PT* I.3: 14, 25). This downplaying of the causal role of the body and its qualities is understandable given his Neoplatonic metaphysical framework. In this model of a layered reality, the lower levels ultimately derive everything from the higher ones, including their very being (Kristeller 1940: 139–141).

Whatever a body does, indeed its very existence, ultimately depends on the presence of soul, which shares its life-giving act with the body. Without soul, there can be no body in any interesting sense of the word. For Ficino, there simply is no independent material world that could, let alone should, be studied in abstraction from the soul, just as in the final analysis soul itself cannot be studied in abstraction from the metaphysical layers that exist above it. At the same time, Ficino's references to the immortal animal and the different vehicles of the soul show that our soul is always embodied to some extent. The result is a complex, 'embodied' soul-body dualism, in which the soul's interaction with our corporeal body is mediated by spirit, itself generated by the body.

3 The Italian naturalists

The last tradition to be mentioned in this chapter goes in the opposite direction to Ficino. Rather than prioritizing the soul over the material world, it tries to make the soul a part of the material world. For this reason, the tradition has often been labelled naturalist.[31]

The Italian philosopher Bernardino Telesio was well acquainted with Aristotelian analyses of soul and body, which continued to dominate philosophical psychology in the sixteenth century. He was especially familiar with Pomponazzi's views, having studied with him at the University of Padua (Boenke 2005: 126–139). But there is little in this tradition that he values, since in his view Aristotelian philosophy is both inconsistent and contradicts what we perceive by our senses (*DRN*, epistle dedicatory: 18). To remedy this defect, Telesio advocates and develops a new philosophy based entirely on sense perception, for which he was highly regarded by philosophers such as René Descartes and Francis Bacon, the latter of whom praised him as the "first of the moderns" (Schuhmann 1988: 110).

Telesio was among the first to develop a complete alternative to the Aristotelian account, in which the entire hylomorphist framework was discarded. That is, he rejected not only the position that souls are forms of bodies, but even the existence of substantial forms in general. In Telesio's view, the world consists instead of completely passive, underlying matter and two active qualities that inhere in it: heat and cold. The first of these qualities is exemplified by the sun, the second by the earth (*DRN* I.1). The presence of different proportions and degrees of these qualities gives rise to the various things, properties and operations we encounter in nature (Schuhmann 2004). Moreover, since the two qualities are described as antagonists engaged in a perpetual struggle, their presence and interaction also account for all change.

Like all material objects, the human body is constituted out of matter imbued with a certain appropriate proportion of the two qualities. But how is this body related to the soul? Here a comparison with Ficino is useful. Like Ficino, Telesio describes the soul-body relation in terms of the spirit. But the two philosophers use this term in very different ways. For Ficino, as seen above, spirit is the subtle material vehicle for the immaterial soul, by means of which it can relate to the material body. Telesio, by contrast, completely identifies soul with spirit. Souls are neither Aristotelian forms, nor Ficinian immaterial substances, but material entities located within bodies. Importantly, it does not matter whether we are referring to the soul of a brute animal or that of a human being. Both are material, and, consequently, between the two there is only a difference of degree:

> If it has been proved that in the spirit derived from the seed is the substance of the soul of other animals, one cannot doubt that it is the same in humans as well, in a more noble form, and it is surely not of a different

nature and does not have very different capabilities. We see that humans are constituted by the same things as other animals, and that they have the same capabilities and even the same organs for feeding and reproduction.
(*DRN* V.3)[32]

The spirit consists of a very refined type of heat and is located in our body's nervous system, especially in the brain. Being so distributed, the spirit is able to influence and be influenced by all parts of the body, with the part of spirit that is present in the brain functioning as the main coordinating part (Spruit 1997: 133–135). To emphasize the difference from the Aristotelian account of soul, Telesio writes that the spirit is present in the body as a sailor is present in a ship (*DRN* IV.19: 124). At the same time, Telesio's spirit gives rise to all the operations that Aristotle had ascribed to soul. This functional relation between spirit and body can be made more precise by focusing once again on sensation.

Telesio describes sensation as the spirit's reaction to external stimuli, namely to external objects touching our senses. When this contact occurs, the spirit is passively set in motion through changes in our sense organs. The process is, however, more than just passive; the spirit also actively responds to how it is set in motion by expanding or contracting, depending on whether the sensation is agreeable or disagreeable (*DRN* VII.1: 160–162).[33] And most importantly, in doing so it is aware of how it reacts. In Telesio's own words, "when the spirit is affected, in being so affected it senses" (*DRN* VII.9: 34). This conception of spirit as an "active and self-organizing system" has been characterized as the main innovation in Telesio's philosophical psychology (Spruit 1997). And it was influential. Telesio's account of spirit was, for instance, taken up by Francis Bacon and also seems to have had an impact on Hobbes.[34]

It is one thing to give an account of sensation in material terms. Although no Aristotelian philosopher could have agreed with it, nor could Ficino, they could at least relate to the idea that sensation has to be an embodied phenomenon. But what about the functions traditionally ascribed to our intellect? Aristotelians and Ficino alike had described rational thought as a unique phenomenon that somehow transcends our body and is therefore fundamentally different from sensation. Here too, Telesio turns away from the traditional analyses. Instead of emphasizing the differences between sensation and intellectual thought, he describes both in similar terms. According to him, abstract thought in no way constitutes a noteworthy class of cognitive acts on its own, but should be conceived of as merely an extension of regular sense perception (Boenke 2005: 154–158). And given that spirit is present in human beings and animals, Telesio argues, both are necessarily endowed with rationality (*DRN* VIII.14, 226–232). To be sure, there are different degrees of spirit. The one found in human beings is the most subtle, which allows for much more effective use of the cognitive abilities we share with other animals (*DRN* VIII.14). But the difference between human beings and other animals is in this respect merely gradual.

Telesio's materialistic conception of soul in terms of spirit is easily misunderstood, and it is important to emphasize some of the differences with contemporary materialism. First, although Telesio's spirit is material, it is neither inert nor passive, but inherently active. Second, the spirit does not coincide with our body, but is located in our body, namely in the nerves and the brain. Although the spirit is fully material, there is therefore a spirit-body dualism. This dualism is a key element of Telesio's philosophy of mind. But there is another, more significant difference with contemporary materialism, related to a second type of dualism.

To the surprise of his readers, both today and in his own time, Telesio reintroduces the concept of an immaterial rational soul at the final stages of his analysis. Human beings, he writes, are unique in that they have both a spirit and a divinely infused rational soul, which he calls "the form of the body and especially of the spirit" in clear reference to Aristotle's definition (*DRN* VIII.15: 232). The reasons he presents for introducing this immaterial soul are our capacity to direct our thoughts to the non-material, especially God, and our having a free will, unlike any other animal (*DRN* VIII.15: 238). This unexpected turn has been much debated. Is it merely an insincere concession to Church authorities? Or was he really convinced that our experience presents us with phenomena that cannot be accounted for without an immortal soul?

Whatever Telesio's reason for postulating an immortal soul in addition to the bodily spirit, his focus remains on the unity of the whole living being rather than on the duality of mind and body (Boenke 2005: 169). Still, Telesio's view certainly comes closer than any of the other frameworks discussed above to anticipating the dualism associated with the Early Modern mind-body problem. One needs only to conceive the material world in mechanistic terms to end up with Cartesian dualism and its familiar mind-body problem. But we should keep in mind that taking this final step would mean approaching nature in a fundamentally different way than Telesio does. Although he describes the world in general and bodies in particular as if they were machines of some sort, he ultimately conceives of the world in vitalistic terms (Leijenhorst 2010: 176). This vitalistic approach is even clearer in one of Telesio's early followers, Tommaso Campanella (1568–1639), who further developed Telesio's observation that some form of sensation must always be present on the level of the two basic active qualities (*DRN* I.6).[35] According to both philosophers, sensation cannot be a feature of spirit alone, even though it is the most developed there.

In conclusion, let us briefly return to the key elements that set up the mind-body problem mentioned at the beginning. The Aristotelian hylomorphic framework proved to be highly resilient to this problem, although it generated mind-soul problems. It did not allow for the thesis that "the whole nature of the body consists in its being an extended thing" and consequently tended to analyze sensation as a phenomenon that should be ascribed to living bodies rather than immaterial minds, which left little room for a dualist approach. But the fourteenth-century stress on the immateriality of the human soul caused the first cracks to appear in this model, especially when philosophers started seriously considering the possibility of disembodied perception. Ficino's metaphysics, by contrast, left more room for a dualist approach from the start, which is precisely why the nature of the interaction between soul and body became an important theme for him. But on closer analysis, Ficino's soul turned out to be embodied to some extent even when it loses its relation to our earthly body, which resulted in a complex 'embodied' soul-body dualism. Not even the Italian naturalists were dualists in terms of these key elements, since they not only proposed a vitalistic analysis of body but also rejected the view that "the whole nature of the mind consists in the fact that it thinks", relegating almost all cognition to the bodily spirit instead. It is not until the seventeenth century that the material world begins to be conceived in fully mechanistic terms, at which point Cartesian dualism and Hobbesian materialism became viable positions.

Notes

* Research for this paper was made possible by a grant (275-20-034) from the Netherlands Organisation for Scientific Research (NWO).
1. Descartes' considered view is, however, much more nuanced than his assertion that mind and body are two distinct substances has often been taken to imply. See, for instance, Chapter 3 on Descartes in volume 4.
2. Brower also argues, rightly, that in the final analysis Aquinas's position cannot be fully captured in terms of any of the three labels he considers: materialism, dualism and trialism.
3. The paper is an extension of Watson (1966), who argued that there was no mind-body problem in ancient Greek philosophy.
4. Pasnau (2007: 4) comments that the passage is "remarkable above all for its implausibility".
5. See the Introduction to this volume.
6. See the Introduction to this volume.
7. For a detailed analysis of Aquinas's philosophical psychology see Pasnau (2002). For Aquinas's view of the soul in relation to fourteenth-century accounts, see De Boer (2013).
8. Here they followed Aristotle's tentative suggestion that "some [parts of soul] may be separable because they are not the actualities of any body at all" (*De anima* II.1, 413a6–7).
9. The arguments are discussed in Adams (1987: II: 654–661).
10. The reason why Ockham claims that the soul is the principle subject of sensations is not that he thinks that sensations are special entities, but that accidents in general cannot be metaphysically more complex than the subject they inhere in (*Reportatio* III, q. 3, a. 2, 118–119).
11. See, for instance, Michael (2003: 147–172).
12. For discussion, see Zupko (2003: 180). All Buridan translations have been taken from a draft of the forthcoming new edition of his commentary on *De anima* (see http://buridanica.org/). The page numbers refer to Peter Sobol's edition, which was the only published edition at the moment of writing.
13. Henrik Lagerlund (2004), for instance, argued that we should call Buridan a strong dualist for this reason.
14. Interestingly, this type of presence of an indivisible human soul in the body was appealed to by hylomorphists and dualists alike. See Rozemond (2003).
15. See Zupko (2008: 178–182)
16. Lagerlund (2011) argued that their analyses of the relation between efficient and final causality generates another variant of mind-body problems. I will not discuss that perspective here.

17 For Rimini, see Chapter 5 of this volume.
18 See also Pasnau (1997).
19 Toivanen (2013: 91–97).
20 Olivi, *Sent.* II, q. 16: 352. Translated in Toivanen (2013: 40).
21 Toivanen (2013: 213–222).
22 Translation and detailed discussion in Adriaenssen (2013: 39–83).
23 The details and the number of layers, however, vary throughout his works. See Allen (1982) and Kristeller (1940: 106–108).
24 From the preface of Ficino's translation of Plotinus. Translated in Knuuttila & Sihvola (2014: 31).
25 See Chapter 8 of this volume.
26 For a nuanced account of Ficino's relation to Plato and Aristotle, see Monfasani (2002: 189–196).
27 Ficino also ascribes souls to the different cosmological spheres, such as that of the earth.
28 See Walker (1958: 3–11). Being the son of a physician, and having received medical training himself, Ficino was undoubtedly well acquainted with the medical tradition from which the term derives.
29 For a detailed discussion of the soul's vehicles, see Corrias (2012).
30 Ficino is not merely talking about the human rational soul here, but also and especially about a world soul.
31 For an important qualification of this naturalism in the main exponent, Telesio, see Kessler (1997: 142).
32 Translated in Knuuttila & Sihvola (2014: 32).
33 A similar account is given for the rise and presence of emotions. See Ebbersmeyer (2013) and Chapter 9 of this volume.
34 Walker (1984: 287–288); Schuhmann (1988).
35 For Telesio's observation, see Boenke (2005: 178) and Ebbersmeyer (2013: 99).

Bibliography

Primary sources

Aristotle, *De anima*. J. A. Smith (trans.). In *The Complete Works of Aristotle*, J. Barnes (ed.). Princeton: Princeton University Press, 1984.

Bernardino Telesio. *De rerum natura iuxta propria principia libri XI*, 3 vols. L. De Franco (ed. & transl.), I–II: Cosenza: Casa del Libro, 1965, 1974, III: Firenze: La Nuova Italia, 1976.

Descartes, Rene. *The Philosophical Writings of Descartes*, vol. II. (= *CSM* II). J. Cottingham, R. Stoothoff & D. Murdoch (trans.). Cambridge: Cambridge University Press, 1984.

John Buridan. *Quaestiones de anima, liber secundus [ultima lectura]* (= *QdA*). In *John Buridan on the Soul and Sensation: An Edition of Book II of His Commentary on Aristotle's Book of the Soul With an Introduction and a Translation of Question 18 on Sensible Species, P. Sobol*. PhD Thesis, Indiana University, 1984.

———. *Quaestiones de anima, liber tertius [ultima lectura]* (= *QdA*). In *John Buridan's Philosophy of Mind: An Edition of Book III of his "Questions on Aristotle's De anima" (Third redaction), With Commentary and Critical and Interpretative Essays, J. Zupko*. PhD Thesis, Cornell University, 1989 (2 vols).

John Duns Scotus. *Quodlibetal Questions*. In *God and Creatures: The Quodlibetal Questions*, A. B. Wolter & F. Alluntis (eds). Washington, DC: The Catholic University of America Press, 1975.
Marsilio Ficino. *Platonic Theology* (= *PT*), 6 vols. M. J. B. Allen & J. Hankins (trans. & eds). Cambridge, MA: Harvard University Press, 2001–2006.
———. *Commentaries on Plato. Vol I: Phaedrus and Ion*, M. J. B. Allen (trans. & ed.). Cambridge, MA: Harvard University Press, 2008.
Peter John Olivi. *Quaestiones in secundum librum Sententiarum* (= *Sent*), 3 vols. B. Jansen (ed.). Florence: Collegium S. Bonaventurae, 1922–1926.
Plato, *Phaedo*. G. M. A. Grube (trans.). In *Complete Works*, J. M. Cooper (ed.). Indianapolis: Hackett, 1997.
Ps.-Augustine. *Liber de spiritu et anima*. In *Patrologiae cursus completus, Series Latina* 40. J. P. Migne (ed.). Paris: Migne, 1845.
Thomas Aquinas. *In duodecim libros Metaphysicorum Aristotelis expositio*. M.-R. Cathala & R. M. Spiazzi (eds). Torino: Marietti, 1950.
———. *Sentencia libri De anima* (= *SentDeA*). R.-A. Gauthier (ed.). Rome: Commissio Leonina, 1984 (*Opera omnia* **45**(1)).
———. *The Treatise on Human Nature: Summa Theologiae 1a 75–89*. R. Pasnau (ed. & trans. Indianapolis: Hackett Publishing, 2002.
William of Ockham. *Quaestiones in Librum Tertium Sententiarum* (= *Reportatio*). F. E. Kelley & G. I. Etzkorn (eds). St. Bonaventure: St. Bonaventure University, 1982 (*Opera theologica* **6**).
———. *Quodlibetal Questions*, 2 vols. A. J. Freddoso & F. E. Kelley (eds & trans.). New Haven: Yale University Press, 1991.

Secondary sources

Adriaenssen, H. T. 2013. *Knowledge and the Veil of Representation: A Comparison of Late-Medieval and Early-Modern Critiques of Species and Ideas*. PhD Dissertation, University of Groningen.
Allen, M. J. B. 1982. "Ficino's Theory of the Five Substances and the Neoplatonists' *Parmenides*". *Journal of Medieval and Renaissance Studies* **12**: 19–44.
Boenke, M. 2005. *Körper, Spiritus, Geist: Psychologie vor Descartes*. München: Wilhelm Fink.
Brower, J. E. 2014. *Aquinas's Ontology of the Material World: Change, Hylomorphism, & Material Objects*. Oxford: Oxford University Press.
Corrias, A. 2012. "Imagination and Memory in Marsilio Ficino's Theory of the Vehicles of the Soul". *The International Journal of the Platonic Tradition* **6**: 81–114.
Cranefield, P. F. 1970. "On the Origin of the Phrase Nihil est in intellectu quod non prius fuerit in sensu". *Journal of the History of Medicine and Allied Sciences* **25**(1): 77–80.
De Boer, S. W. 2013. *The Science of the Soul: A Study of the Transformations of the scientia de anima, c. 1260–c. 1360*. Leuven: Leuven University Press.
Ebbersmeyer, S. 2013. "Do Human Beings Feel Differently? Telesio on the Affective Nature of Man and Animals". In *The Animal Soul and the Human Mind: Renaissance Debates*, C. Muratori (ed.), 97–111. Pisa: Fabrizio Serra.
Kessler, E. 1997. "Method in the Aristotelian Tradition: Taking a Second Look". In *Method and Order in Renaissance Philosophy of Nature: The Aristotle Commentary Tradition*, D. A. Di Liscia, E. Kessler & C. Methuen (eds), 113–142. Aldershot: Ashgate.

Kim, J. 1996. *Philosophy of Mind*. Boulder: Westview Press.
King, P. 2007. "Why Isn't the Mind-body Problem Medieval?". In *Forming the Mind: Essays on the Internal Senses and the Mind/Body Problem From Avicenna to the Medical Enlightenment*, H. Lagerlund (ed.), 187–205. Dordrecht, The Netherlands: Springer.
Knuuttila, S. & Sihvola, J. (eds). 2014. *Sourcebook for the History of the Philosophy of Mind: Philosophical Psychology From Plato to Kant*. Dordrecht, The Netherlands: Springer.
Lagerlund, H. 2004. "John Buridan and the Problems of Dualism in the Early Fourteenth Century". *Journal of the History of Philosophy* **42**(4): 369–387.
———. 2011. "The Unity of Efficient and Final Causality: The Mind/Body Problem Reconsidered". *British Journal for the History of Philosophy* **19**(4): 587–603.
Leijenhorst, C. 2010. "Bernardino Telesio (1509–1588): New Fundamental Principles of Nature". In *Philosophers of the Renaissance*, R. Blum (ed.), 169–180. Washington, DC: The Catholic University of America Press.
McCord Adams, M. 1987. *William Ockham*, 2 vols. Notre Dame: University of Notre Dame Press.
McGinn, C. 1989. "Can We Solve the Mind-body Problem?". *Mind*, New Series **98**(391): 349–366.
Michael, E. 2003. "Renaissance Theories of Body, Soul, and Mind". In *Psyche and Soma: Physicians and Metaphysicians on the Mind-Body Problem From Antiquity to Enlightenment*, J. N. Wright & P. Potter (eds), 147–172. Oxford: Oxford University Press.
Monfasani, J. 2002. "Marsilio Ficino and the Plato-Aristotle Controversy". In *Marsilio Ficino: His Theology, His Philosophy, His Legacy*, M. J. B. Allen & V. Rees (eds), 179–202. Leiden: Brill.
Pasnau, R. 1997. "Olivi on the Metaphysics of Soul". *Medieval Philosophy and Theology* **6**: 109–132.
———. 2002. *Thomas Aquinas on Human Nature: A Philosophical Study of the Summa theologiae 1a 75–89*. Cambridge: Cambridge University Press.
———. 2007. "The Mind-Soul Problem". In *Mind, Cognition and Representation: The Tradition of Commentaries on Aristotle's De anima*, P. J. J. M. Bakker & J. M. M. H. Thijssen (eds), 3–19. Aldershot: Ashgate.
———. 2012. "Mind and Hylomorphism". In *The Oxford Handbook of Medieval Philosophy*, J. Marenbon (ed.), 486–504. Oxford: Oxford University Press.
Rozemond, M. 2003. "Descartes on Mind-Body Union and Holenmerism". *Philosophical Topics* **31**: 343–367.
Schuhmann, K. 1988. "Hobbes and Telesio". *Hobbes Studies* **1**: 109–133.
———. [1990] 2004. "Telesio's Concept of Matter". In *Selected Papers on Renaissance Philosophy and on Thomas Hobbes*, P. Steenbakkers & C. Leijenhorst (eds), 99–116. Dordrecht, The Netherlands: Kluwer.
Spruit, L. 1997. "Telesio's Reform of the Philosophy of Mind". *Bruniana & Campanelliana* **3**: 123–143.
Toivanen, J. 2013. *Perception and the Internal Senses: Peter of John Olivi on the Cognitive Functions of the Sensitive Soul*. Leiden: Brill.
Walker, D. P. 1958. *Spiritual and Demonic Magic From Ficino to Campanella*. London: Warburg Institute.
———. 1984. "Medical Spirits in Philosophy and Theology From Ficino to Newton". In *Arts du spectacle et histoire des idées: Recueil offert en hommage à Jean Jacquot*, J.-M. Vaccaro (ed.), 287–300. Tours: Centre d'Études Supérieures de la Renaissance.

Watson, W. I. 1966. "Why Isn't the Mind-body Problem Ancient?". In *Mind, Matter, and Method. Essays in Philosophy and Science in Honor of Herbert Feigl*, P. K. Feyerabend & G. Maxwell (eds), 92–102. Minneapolis: University of Minnesota Press.

Zupko, J. 2003. *John Buridan: Portrait of a Fourteenth-Century Arts Master*. Notre Dame: University of Notre Dame Press.

———. 2008. "Horse Sense and Human Sense: The Heterogeneity of Sense Perception in Buridan's Philosophical Psychology". In *Theories of Perception in Medieval and Early Modern Philosophy*, S. Knuuttila & P. Kärkkäinen (eds), 171–186. Dordrecht, The Netherlands: Springer.

11

THE IMMORTALITY OF THE SOUL

Lorenzo Casini

1 Introduction

The question of the immortality of the human soul was one of the most hotly debated philosophical issues of the late fifteenth and early sixteenth century. These disputes were fought in the context of general agreement on a number of basic issues that from the point of view of contemporary philosophy of mind might appear implausible and antiquated. However, the picture that emerges from these discussions is one of philosophers hard at work trying to understand and illuminate aspects of our mental life that still today are considered obscure and problematic. A substantial part of these debates concerned fundamental questions in the philosophy of mind, such as the relation of mental phenomena to the physical body. These problems were discussed not only in relation to metaphysics and Christian theology, but also, as we shall see, from the point of view of epistemology.[1]

These controversies did not arise without historical antecedents. Prior to the medieval reception of Aristotle's *De anima*, Latin Christian thought was heavily influenced by Augustine, and the doctrine of the immortality of the soul was more or less taken for granted. In this tradition, there was a clear tendency to identify the human being with the soul, which was conceived as a spiritual substance using a body, but capable of an independent existence. However, during the second half of the twelfth century, the question of the immortality of the soul started to spark philosophical interest.[2] Among the factors that spurred medieval thinkers to give more attention to the theme of immortality was a set of problems generated by the gradual assimilation of ancient philosophical texts that had been rediscovered and were becoming available in Latin translations. One of the results of the diffusion of Aristotle's work was an increase in the number of questions concerning the relation of the soul to the body. Medieval philosophers had to reconcile the traditional idea of the soul as an independent substance with the Aristotelian theory of the soul as the form of the body.[3]

One of the basic problems became whether the soul can be simultaneously a separate substance and the form of the body. It was not until Thomas Aquinas (1225–1274) that the problem received a precise formulation: how to account for the genuine unity of man and at the same time save the self-subsistent reality of the soul.[4] Aquinas maintained that the soul is by its very nature the form of the body. But even though the soul is not a substance, it is a self-subsistent being, capable of existing apart from the body. In Aquinas's view, the very essence of the human soul consists in its being a substantial form that has self-subsistence because it can function independently of the body.[5]

Following Aquinas, many philosophers and theologians strongly affirmed that reason could demonstrate the immortality of the soul. Not everyone was convinced, however. John Duns Scotus (c. 1266–1308), arguing against Aquinas, held that philosophy provides probable but not conclusive arguments for the immortality of the soul. William of Ockham (c. 1287–1347) was more forthright and denied that philosophy could prove the immortality of the soul.[6]

The problem that contributed most significantly to the increase in writings devoted to this issue was related to the interpretation of Aristotle's account of the intellect. In the extremely condensed chapter 5 of book III of *De anima*, Aristotle distinguishes two sorts of intellect: the "passive" or "possible" intellect, and what became known to later commentators as the "agent" or "active" intellect. The former is described as the matter of thought, because it becomes all things, and hence is perishable. The latter, on the other hand, makes everything, and since it is separable, unaffected and unmixed, it is also immortal and eternal.[7] The brevity and obscurity of Aristotle's account generated a number of questions concerning the nature of the intellect and its relation to an individual human being. Two of the most influential interpretations of Aristotle's view became those of Alexander of Aphrodisias (*fl. c.* AD 200) and Averroes (1126–1198).

2 The influence of Alexander of Aphrodisias and Averroes on late medieval and Renaissance psychology

Alexander of Aphrodisias's interpretation of Aristotle's views on the intellect is his most influential and controversial doctrine. He identifies the potential or material intellect with the human intellect. The active intellect, on the other hand, he considers an external substance acting upon the individual soul, a force that is ultimately to be identified with the divine intellect. When our intellect apprehends the divine intellect, it becomes identical with it and so immortal. This, however, does not entail any individual immortality. On the contrary, since the human soul is educed from a mixture of bodily elements, it is perishable and cannot exist apart from the body.[8]

Throughout the Late Middle Ages, the name of Alexander was primarily associated with the doctrine of the mortality of the soul, which Aquinas and many others severely criticized. The first medieval thinker who defended Alexander's theory of the soul is John Buridan (*c.* 1300–after 1358).[9] The influence of Alexander can also be discerned in several of Buridan's followers, such as Marsilius of Inghen (1330–1396), Blasius of Parma (d. 1416), Lawrence of Lindores (d. 1437) and Nicholas of Amsterdam (d. 1460).[10] In his *Quaestiones de anima*, Blasius states that inasmuch as the human soul has no operation independent from the body, there are no grounds for arguing that it can survive the death of the body. In 1396, as a consequence of his denial of the demonstrability of the immortality of the soul, Blasius was summoned before the bishop of Pavia. He was compelled to retract his controversial view and was reprimanded for his remarks against the Christian faith.[11] The impact of Alexander's position on the sixteenth-century debate owes much to Girolamo Donato's Latin translation of his *De anima*, which was printed in 1495, and to Pietro Pomponazzi's (1462–1525) presentation of Alexander's interpretation as the true Aristotelian position.

The Arabic philosopher Averroes had an even bigger impact on late medieval and Renaissance thought. Averroes agreed with Alexander that there is a distinction to be made between the active and the material intellect, but he maintained that the latter is not perishable. In his view, the material intellect cannot be corporeal like the other faculties of the soul, since it can receive all material forms as intelligible thoughts, and this is only possible if it is initially free from all such forms. Therefore, it must be incorporeal and cannot be subject to decay. Moreover, since the material intellect is not a power of something corporeal, it must be numerically one for all individuals. Since multiplication in accordance with the number of individuals is inconceivable without the presence of matter, there cannot be more than one material intellect.[12]

Averroes's position was never taken lightly, and opposition to it arose as early as the mid-thirteenth century. Between 1260 and 1277, however, there was a doctrinal movement in Paris that embraced the Averroist interpretation of the intellective soul and held that there is only one intellect for all mankind. The most celebrated representative of this movement was Siger of Brabant (*c.* 1240–*c.* 1284).[13] The views adopted by him and other masters of the faculty of arts at the University of Paris, such as Boethius of Dacia (*fl. c.* 1275), were condemned by the bishop of Paris, Etienne Tempier, in 1270 and 1277.[14] Despite these condemnations, by the end of the century there was a growing interest in Averroes's interpretation of Aristotle's philosophy among Masters of Arts in Paris.[15] And at the beginning of the fourteenth century the doctrine of the unity of the intellect was openly supported by John of Jandun (d. 1328).[16]

Together with Siger of Brabant, John of Jandun played a key role in the transmission of Averroism from Northern Europe to Renaissance Italy. Throughout the first half of the fourteenth century the main centre of Averroist philosophy was the arts faculty of the University of Bologna, where Taddeo da Parma (*fl. c.* 1320) and several others adopted the thesis that there is only one intellect for all human beings.[17] From the beginning of the fifteenth century the hotbed of Averroism became the University of Padua, where many Aristotelians expended much of their philosophical energy on explicating the texts of Averroes and discussing the writings of Siger of Brabant and John of Jandun.[18] Gasparo Contarini (1483–1542) wrote in his *De immortalitate animae* (1518) that during his days at the University of Padua almost everyone appeared to accept Averroes's doctrine of the unity of the intellect.[19]

Among the defenders of that doctrine we find Paul of Venice (1369/1372–1429), Niccolò Tignosi (1402–1474), Elijah del Medigo (1458–1493) and Alessandro Achillini (1463–1512).[20] In his early career, Nicoletto Vernia (d. 1499) was a strict follower of Averroes and denied that personal immortality could be demonstrated philosophically. The same position can also be discerned in the early writings of his student Agostino Nifo (c. 1469–1538). In 1489, the bishop of Padua, Pietro Barozzi, promulgated a decree forbidding any further public discussion of the Averroist doctrine of the unity of the intellect and compelled Vernia to recant. Vernia and Nifo went from being loyal followers of Averroes as the best guide to Aristotle to becoming careful students of the Greek commentators, and in their later thought, they attacked Averroes as a misleading interpreter of Aristotle and came to hold that personal immortality could, in fact, be demonstrated.[21]

3 Marsilio Ficino and Renaissance Platonism

Disillusioned by the perilous disputes of the scholastics, several fifteenth-century humanists and theologians turned to Platonism. For many of these authors, the problem of the immortality of the soul was closely associated with the concept of the dignity of man and man's similarity to God.[22] Around 1460, the humanist Pier Candido Decembrio (1399–1477) composed his *De immortalitate humani animi*, which exhibits a general tendency to emphasize the agreement between the Christian and the Platonic doctrines of the soul and of its immortality.[23]

The most important figure arguing against the secular Aristotelians was Marsilio Ficino (1433–1499), who launched a thorough campaign for the demonstrability of the immortality of the soul. In his pursuit of a pious philosophy, he took up the task of defending the Christian faith from the threat posed by the influence of Alexander's and Averroes's commentaries. First in a famous letter and then again in the preface to his translation of Plotinus's *Enneads*, Ficino specifically condemned contemporary Aristotelians on the grounds that they were all Averroists or Alexandrians who denied the immortality of the soul:

> For the entire world is in the hands of the Aristotelians, who are divided into two sects: those who follow Alexander of Aphrodisias, and those who follow Averroes. The former think that our rational soul is mortal; while the latter contend that there is only one such soul. Both equally destroy all religion from the foundation.[24]

Ficino devoted the *Theologia platonica de immortalitate animorum* (1482), his most important and extensive work, to the doctrine of the immortality of the soul.[25] Throughout the eighteen books that comprise it he provides a multitude of arguments: "firstly by general arguments, secondly by specific proofs, thirdly by signs, and lastly by resolving questions". Many of these arguments presuppose the central place of the soul within creation and the first four books are devoted to a systematic account of the hierarchy of reality. In a fivefold scheme, partly indebted to Proclus, the soul occupies the middle place in the chain of being and is described as "the link that holds all nature together". The higher essences are God and angel (i.e., the Neo-platonic *nous*), while the lower are body and quality (I.1.3).[26]

Ficino's two main arguments, which are repeated in different forms throughout the treatise, are based on the concept of natural desire and on the principle of affinity. Losing no time, Ficino maintains in the opening lines of the first book that if the human soul were not immortal, then "no animal would be more miserable than man" (I.1.1). In his view, the primary end of human existence is to ascend to a spiritual union with God. However, in this life the fulfilment of this natural desire is only partial and transitory. A satisfactory realization of it seems to require an afterlife. Otherwise all our efforts would be completely hopeless. Since nothing in nature is in vain, a natural desire must at some point reach its goal. Thus, Ficino concludes that the natural desire for the knowledge and enjoyment of God must be fulfilled in a future life.[27]

The other mainstay of Ficino's defence of the immortality of the soul is represented by arguments from affinity. This line of argument, which goes back to Plato's *Phaedo* and appears in a number of different versions, stresses the correspondence between incorporeal entities and the soul. According to Ficino, there is a necessary affinity between the soul and the intelligible entities it contemplates. Since the intelligible entities that constitute the objects of thought are eternal and immutable, the soul that conceives them must be likewise eternal and immortal in its essence.[28]

Many of Ficino's arguments aim at refuting alternative views. At the beginning of book VI, he provides an inventory of the views of various philosophers concerning the human soul. These can, according to him, be reduced to five. The first four consist in different forms of materialism, such as the views of ancient atomists and Stoics (VI.1.2–6). Although Alexander of Aphrodisias is not mentioned in this section, it might be the case that Ficino regarded his position as an expression of the fourth form of materialism, according to which the soul depends on the nature of the body "in one of two ways: either the body's complexion has produced it, or else, though the complexion has not produced it, yet the progenitor of it, whoever he may be, has led it forth from the potentiality, from the vitals, of matter" (VI.1.6).[29] According to the fifth view, by contrast, the human soul is

> something divine, that is, something indivisible, wholly present to every part of the body and produced by an incorporeal creator such that it depends only on the power of that agent, not on the inchoate foundation or capacity or kindling of matter.

This is the teaching of Plato and the other ancient theologians, which Aristotle for the most part follows (VI.1.7).

Accordingly, a sizeable portion of the following books is devoted to arguments against materialistic views of the soul, especially those of Epicurus and Lucretius.

Ficino's extensive criticism of materialism reveals his appreciation of its persuasive power, and it would seem that he considered the menace posed by materialism as even greater than the threat from secular Aristotelianism, which dominated the Italian universities at the time.[30] Ficino was the first philosopher of the Renaissance to make a serious study of Lucretius. In his youth, he wrote a small commentary on *De rerum natura*, which did not circulate and was later destroyed. However, his preoccupation with materialism derived not only from his study of Epicureanism, but also from his own conception of the human soul.[31]

According to Ficino, the rational soul, on account of its intermediate nature, looks in two directions like Janus (XVI.5.5). Since it shares some of its qualities with both God and matter, the soul "by a natural instinct ... ascends to the higher and descends to the lower" (III.2.2). Thus, the soul is generally afflicted with a certain confusion concerning what is real and good. One expression of this confusion is represented by the soul's natural tendency to conceive of itself in material terms. Ficino often presents the soul as naturally informing a body while it has one, but not depending essentially on the body.[32] According to him, the soul operates in three ways: It acts in the body through the vegetative power, which the Platonists call nature; it acts through the body by means of the external and internal senses; and it acts through itself by means of the intellective power (VI.2.2).[33] In other words, the soul needs the co-operation of the body for parts of its activity, but in its intellectual and volitional functions it is independent of it.

Ficino maintains that materialism is a "vulgar error born from habitual intercourse with the body" (VI.2.11). In his view, those who suppose that the soul is corporeal are forced into this opinion by custom. They rely on the judgement of the senses and cannot think of the soul as being incorporeal and divine. He therefore initiates his refutation of materialism with a hortatory chapter "whose purpose is to dispel that wretched lack of trust which completely seduces the rational soul of the vulgar from acknowledging the realm of the spirits" (VI.2.21). In attempting to refute materialistic views of the soul, Ficino quotes extensively from his translation of the allegory of the cave from the seventh book of Plato's *Republic* (VI.2.14–15), and provides his own version of Avicenna's (980–1037) famous argument of the so-called "flying man".[34] In this thought experiment, which aims at proving the independence of the soul from the body, we are asked to imagine "a man instantly created by God". He is "made fully mature but so disposed that he apprehends nothing through any of his five senses". Ficino argues that a man in this condition would have the essence of his soul present to his mind, but would not be able to attribute any sensual properties to his soul (VI.2.11).

The last part of the treatise is devoted to resolving a number of questions related to the immortality of the soul. The fifteenth book, which consists entirely of a series of arguments against Averroes's doctrine of the unity of the intellect, examines the following question: "Is there one intellect for all men?". The first chapter deals with a summary of Averroes's view.[35] According to Ficino, Averroes draws three conclusions from the fact that the intellect is not mixed with any material and mortal nature:

> The first is that intellect is not body, is not composed, that is, of matter and form; the second, that intellect is not a quality divisible along with body or in any way dependent on body; the third, that intellect is not a form such that it can perfect, give life to, and govern body, and adhere to body such that a single composite results from matter and from the intellect's substance, a composite whose being is one.
>
> (XV.1.3)

Ficino accepts the first two, but rejects the third. In his view, Averroes's major fault was to deny that "the intellect's substance can be the form perfecting body, can be its life-giving act" (XV.1.3).

Ficino therefore spends much of the book targeting the idea that the intellect is not the substantial form of the body. According to him, "the soul of man is incorporeal yet also something which belongs to a body" (XV.7.11). One should not "suppose it absurd for a rational substance to be joined to matter, since the order of nature cannot be preserved in any other way" (XV.4.4). Later on, he remarks:

> To confute the many fallacious arguments with which the Averroists obstinately strive to trap the Platonists, we must remember that it is not over and beyond nature for the human soul to be joined with the body; but that it is natural for this eternal soul to be joined to an eternal and heavenly body forever but only for a limited time to the temporal and earthly body.
>
> (XV.12.2)

At the end of book XV, Ficino suggests that by taking from Averroes the doctrine that the material intellect is immortal and combining it with Alexander's belief that each person has such an intellect one can prove the truth of the Platonic and Christian doctrine of the immortality of the individual soul (XV.19.11).

4 Pietro Pomponazzi and the bull *Apostolici regiminis*

In December 1513, the eighth session of the Fifth Lateran Council issued the bull *Apostolici regiminis*, which declared that the soul is the immortal and individually infused form of the human body. The decree, which might have been the result of the wide impact that Renaissance Platonism had on contemporary theology, was principally a reaction to the influence of the commentaries of Alexander of Aphrodisias and Averroes.[36] Two of the "extremely pernicious errors" that the Lateran Council wanted to condemn and reject concerned the claim that, "at least according to philosophy", the rational soul "is mortal, or only one among all human beings".³⁷ As we have seen, this was not the first time that an Italian religious authority had intervened in these issues.

The Lateran Council, however, also issued the unprecedented request that philosophers not only "apply themselves to the full extent of their energies" to refute principles or conclusions "known to deviate from the true faith – as in the assertion of the soul's mortality or of there being only one soul" – but also "devote their every effort to clarify ... the truth of the Christian religion".³⁸ This demand had long-range consequences for the development of philosophical psychology. Before the Lateran Council, as we have seen, philosophers could support the doctrine of the immortality of the soul by referring to faith, but after 1513 this strategy was ruled out, and for nearly two centuries individual immortality was viewed as a critical and pressing philosophical problem.³⁹

One of the only two delegates to the Lateran Council who voted against ordering philosophers to endeavour to vindicate the Christian belief in the immortality of the soul was the head of the Dominican order Tommaso de Vio (1469–1534), also known as Cajetan. In his *Commentaria in Primam Parte Summae Theologiae* (1508), he had maintained that the immortality of the human soul was demonstrable and accepted Aquinas's argument that the soul must be immaterial and subsistent. But in his *Commentaria in De anima Aristotelis* (1509), he changed his view, denying that the immortality of the soul could be philosophically demonstrated and arguing that it is a doctrine that must be accepted simply by faith, a position that he held for the rest of his life.⁴⁰ Cajetan's new position, which resulted in his dissent at the Lateran Council, provoked a reaction from a number of fellow Dominicans, such as his former teacher Valentino da Camerino (1438–1515).⁴¹

The debate reached its peak a few years after the publication of the Lateran decree, when Pomponazzi published his *De immortalitate animae* (1516).⁴² At the beginning and end of the treatise, Pomponazzi maintains that the doctrine of the immortality of the soul must be accepted as revealed truth. All contrary conclusions, being based on fallible human reason, are merely probable. In the philosophic core of the treatise, however, he deals with the immortality of the soul strictly in philosophical terms.

The starting point of Pomponazzi's investigation is the theme of the mid-point occupied by the human being: "Man is clearly not of simple but of multiple, not of certain but of ambiguous nature, and he is to be placed as a mean between mortal and immortal things" (M, 6; H, 282).⁴³ For, the human being assumes mortality in performing the functions of the vegetative and the sensitive soul, which cannot be performed without a bodily instrument. However, in knowing and willing – operations that are held to be performed without any bodily instrument, and to prove that the rational soul is immaterial and separable from the body – the human being is considered immortal. Therefore, the human being is neither unqualifiedly mortal nor unqualifiedly immortal, but instead embraces both natures. Thus, the problem consists in explaining human nature without violating the principle of contradiction. In other words, how can mortality and immortality, which are opposites, be affirmed of the same thing at the same time (M, 8; H, 283)?

Pomponazzi systematically outlines six alternatives that can be adopted in order to explain the intermediate character of human nature. His taxonomy consists of two major subdivisions, with three options under each. To begin with, we must assume either one and the same nature, which is at once mortal and immortal, or two different natures, one of which is mortal and the other immortal. If the first position is taken, i.e., that through one and the same nature the human being is both mortal and immortal, it is impossible for this same nature to be unqualifiedly mortal and immortal, since it is not possible to affirm opposites of the same thing, unless both belong to it relatively, i.e., only in a certain way, or one belongs relatively and the other without qualification (M, 10; H, 283f.).[44] Therefore, according to this position, human nature will be either unqualifiedly immortal and relatively mortal; or, vice versa, unqualifiedly mortal but relatively immortal; or it will be relatively both mortal and immortal. The last possibility, however, is not taken into consideration, since no one, Pomponazzi claims, has ever maintained that the same thing is equally mortal and immortal (M, 10 & 12; H, 284).

The second position, i.e., that a human being has two different natures, can also be understood in three ways. Either the number of mortal and immortal natures will be the same as the number of individuals; or there will be only one immortal nature for all individuals, while the mortal one will be distributed and multiplied among individuals; or, conversely, the immortal nature will be multiplied, but the mortal will be common to all. This last possibility, however, is also dropped, since Pomponazzi again claims that no one has ever held this position. Consequently, there remain four different positions (M, 10 & 12; H, 283f.).

The first view discussed by Pomponazzi is the one according to which a human being consists of two different natures: an immortal soul that is one in number and a mortal soul that is distributed and multiplied in each individual. He attributes this view to Averroes (M, 12; H, 285).[45] In Pomponazzi's assessment, Averroes's opinion, which he describes as "widely held in our time and by almost all taken to be that of Aristotle", is not only false, but also unintelligible, monstrous and quite foreign to Aristotle. Regarding the philosophical validity of Averroes's doctrine of the unity of the intellect, he maintains that Aquinas's critique is so lucid and subtle that it leaves nothing unrefuted (M, 14 & 16; H, 286).[46] And so rather than reiterate Aquinas's refutation, he devotes the rest of the chapter to attacking Averroes's interpretation of Aristotle. His lengthy discussion focuses on Averroes's opinion that, according to Aristotle, the intellect performs certain operations entirely independently of the body. In Pomponazzi's view, however, Aristotle never held that position because he thought that the intellect can only know things on the basis of phantasms.

The following chapters deal with the view that the intellective soul is distinct in existence from the sensitive soul, but corresponds to it in number. According to Pomponazzi, this opinion maintains that the soul is related to a human being either as a mover to what is moved, or as form to matter. The former view he ascribes to Plato, pointing to a passage from *Alcibiades I* where a human being is described as a soul using a body (129c – e). Once again, Pomponazzi refers to the criticism put forward by Aquinas, which he says is based on abundant and clear arguments. He also remarks that if the human being were not composed of form and matter, but rather of a mover and a thing which is moved, soul and body would have no greater unity than an ox and a cart. Against the latter view, Pomponazzi maintains that to posit a plurality of substantial forms in the same composite seems foreign both to Aristotle and to many Peripatetics. Moreover, this opinion also seems to contradict experience. If I feel pain, which is a function of the sensitive soul, and at the same time think of the medical causes of the pain in order to remove it, which cannot be done save by the intellect, then how can the essence by which I feel be different from that by which I think? For then we could say that two men joined together have common thoughts, which is ridiculous (M, 42; H, 298).

Having discussed the views of those who conceive the human soul in terms of two different natures, Pomponazzi turns to the Thomist position, which he summarizes in five propositions:

> First, that the intellective and the sensitive in man are the same in existence. Secondly, that this soul is truly and unqualifiedly immortal, while relatively mortal. Thirdly, that such a soul is truly the form of man and not only as it were the mover. Fourthly, that this same soul corresponds in number to the number of individuals. Fifthly, that a soul of this kind begins its existence with the body but that it comes from without and is produced by God alone, not indeed by generation, but by creation; however, it does not cease to be with the body, but is perpetual from that time on.
>
> (M, 46; H, 300)

Pomponazzi points out that there can be no doubt as to the truth of the Thomist position, since canonical Scripture must be preferred to human reasoning and experience. The gist of his analysis, however, is that Aquinas cannot prove immortality on the basis of reason, nor can he remain in accord with Aristotle (M, 52; H, 302f.).[47]

> Pomponazzi's argument is based on a passage in *De anima* in which Aristotle writes that "there seems to be no case in which the soul can act or be acted upon without involving the body.... Thinking seems the most probable exception; but if this too proves to be a form of imagination or to be impossible without imagination, it too requires a body as a condition of its existence."[48]

In order to defend the self-subsistent nature of the intellect, Aquinas made a distinction between the sense faculties' dependence on the body and the intellect's. The senses depend on the body not only for their object, but also because they cannot operate without a bodily organ. For intellectual operations, on the other hand, the body is necessary only as an object and not as an organ.[49]

However, Pomponazzi does not think that this distinction succeeds in saving the intellect from corruption. Arguing from the Aristotelian text, he maintains that proof of the intellect's ability to survive the death of the body must be found in an activity of the intellect which functions without any dependence on the body: "Hence for knowing that the soul is separable it is necessary that it should neither need the body as subject, nor as object, at least in some operation" (M, 58; H, 305).[50] In other words, in order to prove the immortality of the soul, it is not sufficient to point to an activity of the intellect that is not carried out by a corporeal organ. What is required is rather an activity of the intellect that is not dependent on any operation carried out by corporeal organs.

In Pomponazzi's view, no such activity can be found, since the highest activity of the intellect, the attainment of universals in cognition, is always mediated by sense impression:

> But although the human intellect, as has been considered, does not use quantity in knowing, nevertheless, since it is joined to sense, it cannot be released entirely from matter and quantity, since it never knows without a phantasm, as Aristotle says in *De anima* III: 'The soul does not know at all without a phantasm.' Hence it thus needs the body as object. Nor can it know a universal unqualifiedly but always sees the universal in the singular, as everyone can observe in himself.
>
> (M, 90 & 92; H, 319)

Thus, even the highest power of intellection is always directly linked to and sustained by the sensitive powers, which, in turn, are dependent on the vegetative powers.[51] Since, as all sources agree, the sensitive and vegetative powers decay and perish, the intellect, although immaterial in itself, must perish with them. The soul in its entirety, therefore, dies with the body.

Pomponazzi's treatise immediately aroused violent opposition, especially from the theologians of the Dominican order. Pope Leo X issued a warning, demanding him to bring his position in line with the decree of the Fifth Lateran Council. Public attacks were accompanied by a spate of books written against him.[52] Although the intention of Pomponazzi's opponents was to demolish his arguments, for the most part, they produced mere polemics. As Kessler has pointed out, for "Pomponazzi's opponents the case was lost. The result of the whole affair . . . amounted to a total failure of the 1513 decree".[53]

5 Conclusion

After these events, the debate on the immortality of the human soul developed along different lines. Natural philosophers generally felt free to pursue their investigations of the soul on their own terms.[54] Averroes's theory of the unity of the intellect continued to find support among natural philosophers. In 1521, Luca Prassicio (d. 1533) published *Quaestio de immortalitate anime intellective secundum mentem Aristotelis a nemine verius quam ab Averroi interpretati*, which has been described as one of the most outspoken attempts to defend Averroes during the Renaissance.⁵⁵ Others argued that Alexander of Aphrodisias provided the most accurate interpretation of Aristotle's view and that the most probable conclusion, in terms of philosophy, is that the rational soul is mortal. In 1551, Simone Porzio (1496–1554) published *De mente humana*, which deals with the interpretation of Aristotle's account of the intellect. The starting point of Porzio's investigation, which is heavily influenced by Alexander of Aphrodisias, is a philological analysis of the key term *entelecheia*, from which Porzio concludes that the soul is the individual and corruptible form of the human body.⁵⁶

There were also authors who carried Ficino's syncretism further and attempted to combine pagan philosophy with the Christian tradition. In *De perenni philosophia* (1540), Agostino Steuco (1497–1548) attempted to establish a fundamental harmony between pagan philosophy and Christian theology, arguing that reason and revelation, which both flow from God, necessarily lead to the same conclusion. In book IX, which is devoted to the creation of man and the immortality of the soul, he quotes selected passages from Aristotle, along with Simplicius's commentary on *De anima*, in order to show that Aristotle held the individual soul to be immortal.⁵⁷

Many Christian philosophers continued to follow Aquinas and insisted on the mutual concord of Aristotle and Christian faith. Exemplary in this regard is the branch of Scholasticism that developed on the Iberian Peninsula during the sixteenth century. However, these thinkers faced problems concerning the coherence of the Thomist claim that the intellective soul can function independently of the body. Pomponazzi had forcefully argued that the operations of the intellect could not be independent of the sensitive soul, since the intellective soul depends for its operation on the phantasms produced by the sensitive soul.⁵⁸

If one had to defend the immortality of the soul on the grounds that the intellect has operations that do not depend at all on the senses, some sort of dualism seems to have represented the most promising route as a response to Pomponazzi's arguments. A strategy of this kind can be discerned in the solution that the Jesuit Francisco Suárez (1548–1617) gave to the problem in his commentary on *De anima*, which is based on lectures delivered in the 1570s but was not published until 1621. In order to provide an account of the intellect that could preserve immortality, Suárez waved aside the idea of a causal connection, even an instrumental one, between the operation of the imagination and the operation of the intellect. Instead he argued that the production of intelligible species is concomitant with the operation of the imagination, but causally unconnected with it.⁵⁹

A rather interesting development is represented by a number of philosophers who maintained not only that each human being has two entirely separate souls, but also that one of these souls is material.⁶⁰ For example, in *De rerum natura iuxta propria principia*, whose definitive version was published in 1586, Bernardino Telesio (1509–1588) identifies the human soul with an extremely subtle material substance called *spiritus*, which is educed from the seed, flows through the nervous system and has its main seat in the brain. In addition to the *spiritus*, however, there is also an immaterial and immortal soul infused by God, which Telesio defines as "the form of the *spiritus*".[61] A similar view was advocated by Francis Bacon (1561–1626) and Tommaso Campanella (1568–1639), who were both influenced by Telesio.[62]

The novelty of this approach is perhaps not so much that it eventually promoted a view according to which the mind is a spiritual thinking substance, but rather that it contributed to the gradual elimination of material forms, i.e., forms that are wholly dependent on matter, with the effect that the term "soul" came to be used exclusively in connection with the human mind. For the Aristotelians, there was in fact much more to the soul, but on this new view, operations such as nutrition and locomotion could be accounted for in purely physiological terms. By eliminating those features of the human soul that, on the Aristotelian view, implied its dependence on the body, some of the difficulties which had concerned Aristotelians for over four centuries were decisively overcome.[63]

Notes

1 See Blum 2007 and 2012.
2 See Vanni Rovighi 1936, Pluta 1986 and especially Oguejiofor 1995.
3 See Dales 1995.
4 See Bazán 1997.
5 See, e.g., Thomas Aquinas, *Summa theologiae*, I, q. 75, art. 2. For a discussion of Aquinas's argument, see Owens 1987 and Cross 1997. For some general accounts of Aquinas's views on the human soul, see Kenny 1993, Kretzmann 1993 and Pasnau 2002.
6 See John Duns Scotus, *Opus oxoniense*, IV, dist. 43, q. 2, and William of Ockham, *Quodlibeta septem*, I, q. 10. By the middle of the fifteenth century, however, a number of Scotists started to repudiate the fideism of their master and argued that the immortality of the soul could be demonstrated philosophically. See Offelli (1954: 18–28), Poppi 1962 and 1964, as well as Di Napoli (1963: 194f.).
7 For more on this distinction, see Chapters 5 and 8 of this volume.
8 See Sharples (1987: esp. 1202–1214). For Alexander's doctrine of the soul and its fortune, see also Kessler 2011.
9 Although Buridan maintained that Alexander's doctrine is the one that most conforms to natural reason, he ultimately accepted the position held by faith. His apparent ambivalence has recently generated a debate on whether he was sincere about the truth of the opinion of faith. See Pluta 2002 and Zupko 2004.
10 See Pluta 1993, 1996 and 2007, as well as Dewender & Pluta 1997.
11 See Maier (1949: 279–299) and Federici-Vescovini (1974: 19–25).
12 For helpful expositions of Averroes's position, see Leaman (1988: 82–116), Davidson (1992: 220–356) and Hyman 1999.
13 On Siger of Brabant, see Van Steenberghen 1977, Putallaz & Imbach 1997, Petagine (2004: 111–165 and 211–241) and Bazán 2005.
14 For a discussion of Bishop Tempier's condemnations, see Chapter 7 of this volume, and, more extensively, Thijssen 1997 and Bianchi 1998.
15 See Kuksewicz 1994.
16 See MacClintock (1956: 51–68), Pacchi 1959, Mahoney 1987, Brenet 2003, and Chapter 4 of this volume.

17 See Kuksewicz (1968: 315–452), Iorio (1991: 83–104), Sorge 2001 and Hasse 2007.
18 See Nardi 1945 and Mahoney 1991.
19 See Lucchetta (1979: 116) and Pine (1986: 131).
20 See Bland 1995, as well as Hasse 2004a and 2004b.
21 See Poppi 1964, Mahoney 1970 and 1976, and Kessler 1994.
22 See Garin (1961: 93–126) and Di Napoli (1963: 51–120).
23 See Kristeller 1966.
24 Ficino (1959: I, 872 and II, 1537). Translation quoted from Kraye (2000: 2.12). For a critical discussion of the historical existence of two organized schools of thought among Renaissance Aristotelians, see Kristeller 1990b.
25 All quotations are taken from Ficino (2001–2006). References are to its book, chapter and paragraph numbers.
26 For an account of Ficino's basic ontology, see the introduction to this volume and, more extensively, Allen 1982. Proclus's scheme was influential among Renaissance Aristotelians, too. See Mahoney (1982: 173–176 and 275–282).
27 A typical example of this argument can be found in book XIV, chapter 2. Cf. also Ficino (1948). Ficino was inspired by Augustine, who had argued that since satisfactory happiness is not possible in this life, there must be an everlasting future life in which to satisfy this natural desire. See Augustine, *De trinitate* XIII.8.11. For the influence of Augustine on Ficino, see Tarabochia Canavero (1978). Different versions of this argument were also discussed by several medieval philosophers. According to Aquinas, for example, the fact that everything that has an intellect naturally desires to exist forever indicates that the intellective soul is incorruptible, since a natural desire cannot be in vain. See Thomas Aquinas, *Summa theologiae*, I, q. 75, 6c. For the influence of Aquinas on Ficino, see Collins (1974).
28 See, e.g., book XI, chapter 1.
29 Alexander of Aphrodisias is only mentioned a few times in the treatise (see XV.1.2, XV.11.10, XV.12.10 and XV.19.11). The reason might be, as Blum has suggested, "that Ficino saw the materialist implications of Alexander's interpretation of Aristotle more clearly, and more dangerously, expressed in Epicurianism, a constant target of his treatise". See Blum (2007: 217). Cf. also Di Napoli (1963: 134).
30 For the influence of Lucretius on Florentine humanists during the fifteenth century, see Brown (2010). Ficino was targeted by the eccentric poet Luigi Pulci (1432–1484), who was known for his intolerance of intellectual speculation and contempt for religion. In his sonnets, Pulci ridiculed the learned discussions on the immortality of the soul describing the afterlife as nothing else but "a dark abyss" and the soul as "no more than a pine nut in hot white bread". See Lebano (1974).
31 See Hankins 2011 and 2013, as well as Snyder 2011.
32 On the dignity of the human body, see X.2.10–12.
33 Cf. Augustine, *De quantitate animae*, XXXIII.70–72.
34 The label "flying man" is not Avicenna's. In this famous argument, the reader is asked to imagine herself suspended in a void in such a state that all forms of sensible perception are impossible. The thought experiment is designed to show that a subject deprived of all sensory experience can still affirm the existence of his own self. On Avicenna's psychology and its influence on the Latin west, see Davidson (1992), Gutas (1998) and Hasse (2000).
35 Brian Copenhaver has argued that Ficino's account is not derived from any of Averroes's own works, but from arguments made against Averroes by Aquinas in the *Summa contra gentiles*. See Copenhaver (2009).
36 The bull was issued by Pope Leo X, who was the son of Ficino's patron Lorenzo de' Medici and personally close both to Ficino's intellectual heir Francesco Cattani da Diacceto (1466–1522) and to Giles of Viterbo (1469–1532), the general of the

Augustinian order, who was an enthusiastic defender and proponent of Platonic philosophy, as well as an outspoken critic of the Averroists in Padua. See Monfasani 1993 and Kraye 2000.
37 Tanner (1990: I, 605). See also Offelli 1955, Gilbert 1967 and Constant 2002.
38 Tanner (1990: I, 606).
39 In the preface to the *Meditations on First Philosophy* (1641), René Descartes (1596–1650) explicitly related his endeavour to the Renaissance debate, presenting himself as faithfully undertaking the commission given to Christian philosophers by the Fifth Lateran Council.
40 See Manzanedo 1999.
41 See Tavuzzi 1994.
42 For the reader's convenience, I shall give references both to the Latin text edited by Mojsisch (henceforth M) in Pomponazzi 1990 and the revised English translation of Hay II (henceforth H) in Pomponazzi 1948.
43 For a discussion of this theme in Pomponazzi and Ficino, see Kristeller 1990a and Suarez-Nani 1995. For a survey of the influence of Platonic and Neo-platonic sources on Pomponazzi, see Kristeller 1983.
44 Cf. Aristotle, *Metaphysics* IV.6, 1011b20–22.
45 The opinion that each human being has two entirely separate souls was often identified with Averroes, and many medieval pluralists cited him in support of their own view. Moreover, several thinkers, such as John of Jandun and Paul of Venice, developed a distinctive pluralistic account, unifying pluralism with Averroes's doctrine of the unity of the intellect. See MacClintock (1956: 58–64), Kuksewicz 1983, Michael 1992 and Brenet 2008. See also Chapter 4 of this volume.
46 For Pomponazzi's use of Aquinas's views and arguments in *De immortalitate animae*, see Petagine 2010.
47 See also Treloar 1990.
48 Aristotle, *De anima*, 403a6–10.
49 Cf. Thomas Aquinas, *Summa theologiae*, I, q. 75, art. 2, ad 3.
50 It has been argued that in pointing out that the intellect does not require the body as subject but does require it as object, Pomponazzi uses the very same terminology as some of Buridan's followers, such as Marsilius of Inghen and Nicholas of Amsterdam. See Pluta 1993 and 2007.
51 For Pomponazzi's views on our knowledge of universals, see Chapter 5 of this volume.
52 These include Contarini's *De immortalitate animae adversus Petrum Pomponatium* (1518), Nifo's *De immortalitate animae libellus adversus Petrum Pomponatium Mantovanum* (1518) and Crisostomo Javelli's (1470–1538) *Solutiones rationum animae mortalitatem probantium* (1519). In his *Apologia* (1518) Pomponazzi replied to Contarini, and in the *Defensorium* (1519), which was printed together with Javelli's treatise, he answered Nifo. Although these works are more elaborate and diffuse than the original treatise, they do not alter Pomponazzi's basic position. A scathing attack also came from the Dominican theologian Bartolomeo Spina (1475–1546), who wrote two books against Pomponazzi, the most important being *Tutela veritatis de immortalitate animae contra Petrum Pomponatium Mantovanum* (1519), as well as from the Augustinian friar Ambrogio Fiandino (c. 1467–1532), whose diatribe was published in dialogue form as *De animorum immortalitate* (1519). For detailed accounts of the controversy, see Gilson 1961, Di Napoli (1963: 265–338) and Pine (1986: 124–234).
53 See Kessler (1988: 507).
54 See Di Napoli (1963: 339–388) and Kessler (1988: 518–534).
55 See Hasse (2004a: 141–144).
56 For a discussion of Porzio's *De mente humana*, see Facca 1992 and Del Soldato (2010: 101–126).

57 On Steuco, see Crociata 1987 and Muccillo 1996.
58 For a discussion of these difficulties, see Fowler (1999: 67–113).
59 Suárez (1978–1991: I: 162–248). See also South 2012 and Chapter 5 of this volume.
60 See Park (1988: 483f.).
61 See Pupo 1999. For the Aristotelian background of Telesio's theory, see Spruit 1992.
62 See, e.g., Wallace (1967: 23–39) and Ernst 1993.
63 For a discussion of the problem of how the mind relates to the soul, see Pasnau 2007. For the influence of the pluralistic view on early modern philosophy of mind, see Michael 1998 and 2000.

Bibliography

Primary sources

Aristotle. 1984. *The Complete Works of Aristotle: The Revised Oxford Translation*, 2 vols. Barnes, J. (ed.). Princeton: Princeton University Press.
Ficino, M. 1948. *Five Questions Concerning the Mind*. J. L. Burroughs (trans.). In *The Renaissance Philosophy of Man*, E. Cassirer et al. (eds), 193–212. Chicago: The University of Chicago Press.
———. [1576] 1959. *Opera omnia*, 2 vols. Turin: Bottega d'Erasmo.
———. 2001–2006. *Platonic Theology*. M. J. B. Allen & J. Hankins (ed. and transl.), 6 vols. Cambridge, MA: Harvard University Press.
Pomponazzi, P. 1948. *On the Immortality of the Soul*. W. H. Hay II (trans.). In *The Renaissance Philosophy of Man*, E. Cassirer et al. (eds), 280–381. Chicago: The University of Chicago Press.
———. 1990. *Abhandlung über die Unsterblichkeit der Seele*. B. Mojsisch (ed.). Hamburg: Felix Meiner.
Suárez, F. 1978–1991. *Commentaria una cum questionibus in libros Aristotelis De anima*, 3 vols. S. Castellote (ed.). Madrid: Societad de Estudios y Publicaciones (vol. I & II) and Fundación Xavier Zubiri (vol. III).

Secondary sources

Allen, M. J. B. 1982. "Ficino's Theory of the Five Substances and the Neoplatonists' *Parmenides*". *Journal of Medieval and Renaissance Studies* **12**: 19–44.
Bazán, B. C. 1997. "The Human Soul: Form *and* Substance? Thomas Aquinas' Critique of Eclectic Aristotelianism". *Archives d'histoire doctrinale et littéraire du Moyen Age* **64**: 95–126.
———. 2005. "Radical Aristotelianism in the Faculties of Arts: The Case of Siger of Brabant". In *Albertus Magnus und die Anfänge der Aristoteles-Rezeption im lateinischen Mittelalter*, L. Honnefelder et al. (eds), 585–629. Münster: Aschendorff.
Bianchi, L. 1998. "1277: A Turning Point in Medieval Philosophy?". In *Was ist Philosophie im Mittelalter?* J. A. Aertsen & A. Speer (eds), 90–110. Berlin: De Gruyter.
Bland, K. P. 1995. "Elijah Del Medigo, Unicity of Intellect, and Immortality of Soul". *Proceedings of the American Academy for Jewish Research* **61**: 1–22.
Blum, P. R. 2007. "The Immortality of the Soul". In *The Cambridge Companion to Renaissance Philosophy*, J. Hankins (ed.), 211–233. Cambridge: Cambridge University Press.

———. 2012. "The Epistemology of Immortality: Searle, Pomponazzi, and Ficino". *Studia Neoaristotelica* **9**: 85–102.
Brenet, J.-B. 2003. *Transferts du sujet: La noétique d'Averroès selon Jean de Jandun*. Paris: Vrin.
———. 2008. "Ame intellective, âme cogitative: Jean de Jandun et la *duplex forma propria* de l'homme". *Vivarium* **46**: 318–341.
Brown, A. 2010. *The Return of Lucretius to Renaissance Florence*. Cambridge, MA: Harvard University Press.
Collins, A. B. 1974. *The Secular Is Sacred: Platonism and Thomism in Marsilio Ficino's Platonic Theology*. The Hague: Nijhoff.
Constant, E. A. 2002. "A Reinterpretation of the Fifth Lateran Council Decree *Apostolici regiminis* (1513)". *The Sixteenth Century Journal* **33**: 353–379.
Copenhaver, B. 2009. "Ten Arguments in Search of a Philosopher: Averroes and Aquinas in Ficino's *Platonic Theology*". *Vivarium* **47**: 444–479.
Crociata, M. 1987. *Umanesimo e teologia in Agostino Steuco: Neoplatonismo e teologia della creazione nel De perenni philosophia*. Rome: Città Nuova Editrice.
Cross, R. 1997. "Is Aquinas's Proof for the Indestructibility of the Soul Successful?". *British Journal for the History of Philosophy* **5**: 1–20.
Dales, R. C. 1995. *The Problem of the Rational Soul in the Thirteenth Century*. Leiden: Brill.
Davidson, H. A. 1992. *Alfarabi, Avicenna, and Averroes, on Intellect: Their Cosmologies, Theories of the Active Intellect, and Theories of Human Intellect*. Oxford: Oxford University Press.
Del Soldato, Eva. 2010. *Simone Porzio: Un aristotelico tra natura e grazia*. Rome: Edizioni di storia e letteratura.
Dewender, T. & Pluta, O. 1997. "Lawrence of Lindores on Immortality: An Edition With Analysis of Four of His *Quaestiones in Aristotelis libros De Anima*". *Bochumer Philosophisches Jahrbuch für Antike und Mittelalter* **2**: 187–242.
Di Napoli, G. 1963. *L'immortalità dell'anima nel Rinascimento*. Turin: Società Editrice Internazionale.
Ernst, G. 1993. "'Nascosto in ciclopea caverna': Natura e condizione umana in Campanella". In *Il Neoplatonismo nel Rinascimento*, P. Prini (ed.), 65–81. Rome: Istituto della Enciclopedia Italiana.
Facca, D. 1992. "'Humana mens corruptibilis': L'antiaverroismo di Simone Porzio". In *Filosofia, filologia, biologia: Itinerari dell'aristotelismo cinquecentesco*, D. Facca & G. Zanier (eds), 5–104. Rome: Edizioni dell'Ateneo.
Federici-Vescovini, G. 1974. *Le* Quaestiones De anima *di Biagio Pelacani da Parma*. Florence: Olshki.
Fowler, C. F. 1999. *Descartes on the Human Soul: Philosophy and the Demands of Christian Doctrine*. Dordrecht, The Netherlands: Kluwer.
Garin, E. 1961. *La cultura filosofica del Rinascimento italiano: Ricerche e documenti*. Florence: Sansoni.
Gentile, S. 2013. "Ficino, Epicuro e Lucrezio". In *The Rebirth of Platonic Theology*, J. Hankins & F. Meroi (eds), 119–135. Florence: Olschki.
Gilbert, F. 1967. "Cristianesimo, umanesimo e la bolla Apostolici regiminis del 1513". *Rivista storica italiana* **79**: 976–990.
Gilson, E. 1961. "Autour de Pomponazzi: Problématique de l'immortalité de l'âme en Italie au début du XVIe siècle". *Archives d'histoire doctrinale et littéraire du Moyen Age* **28**: 163–279.

Gutas, D. 1998. *Avicenna and the Aristotelian Tradition*. Leiden: Brill.
Hankins, J. 2011. "Monstruous Melancholy: Ficino and the Physiological Causes of Atheism". In *Laus Platonici Philosophi: Marsilio Ficino and his Influence*, S. Clucas et al. (eds), 25–43. Leiden: Brill.
———. 2013. "Ficino's Critique of Lucretius". In *The Rebirth of Platonic Theology*, J. Hankins & F. Meroi (eds), 137–154. Florence: Olschki.
Hasse, D. N. 2000. *Avicenna's De anima in the Latin West: The Formation of a Peripatetic Philosophy of the Soul, 1160–1300*. London: The Warburg Institute.
———. 2004a. "The Attraction of Averroism in the Renaissance: Vernia, Achillini, Prassicio". In *Philosophy, Science and Exegesis in Greek, Arabic and Latin Commentaries*, 2 vols., P. Adamson et al. (eds), II: 131–147. London: Institute of Classical Studies.
———. 2004b. "Aufstieg und Niedergang des Averroismus in der Renaissance: Niccolò Tignosi, Agostino Nifo, Francesco Vimercato". In *"Herbst des Mittelalters?": Fragen zur Bewertung des 14. Und 15. Jahrhunderts*, J. A. Aertsen & M. Pickavé (eds), 447–473. Berlin: De Gruyter.
———. 2007. "*Averroica secta*: Notes on the Formation of Averroist Movements in fourteenth-Century Bologna and Renaissance Italy". In *Averroès et les averroïsmes juif et latin*, J.-B. Brenet (ed.), 307–331. Turnhout: Brepols.
Hyman, A. 1999. "Averroes' Theory of the Intellect and the Ancient Commentators". In *Averroes and the Aristotelian Tradition. Sources, Constitution and Reception of the Philosophy of Ibn Rushd (1126–1198)*, G. Endress & J. A. Aertsen (eds), 188–198. Leiden: Brill.
Iorio, D. A. 1991. *The Aristotelians of Renaissance Italy: A Philosophical Exposition*. Lewinston: The Edwin Mellen Press.
Kenny, A. 1993. *Aquinas on Mind*. London: Routledge.
Kessler, E. 1988. "The Intellective Soul". In *The Cambridge History of Renaissance Philosophy*, C. B. Schmitt et al. (eds), 485–534. Cambridge: Cambridge University Press.
———. 1994. "Nicoletto Vernia oder die Rettung eines Averroisten". In *Averroismus im Mittelalter und in der Renaissance*, F. Niewöhner & L. Sturlese (eds), 269–290. Zürich: Spur.
———. 2011. "Alexander of Aphrodisias and his Doctrine of the Soul: 1400 Years of Lasting Significance". *Early Science and Medicine* **16**: 1–93.
Kraye, J. 2000. "The Immortality of the Soul in the Renaissance: Between Natural Philosophy and Theology". *Signatures* **1**: 2.1–2.24. www.chi.ac.uk/sites/default/files/Signatures_Vol1.pdf (accessed January 2015)
Kretzmann, N. 1993. "Philosophy of Mind". In *The Cambridge Companion to Aquinas*, N. Kretzmann & E. Stump (eds), 128–159. Cambridge: Cambridge University Press.
Kristeller, P. O. 1940. "The Theory of Immortality in Marsilio Ficino". *Journal of the History of Ideas* **1**: 299–319.
———. 1943. *The Philosophy of Marsilio Ficino*. New York: Columbia University Press.
———. 1966. "Pier Candido Decembrio and His Unpublished Treatise on the Immortality of the Soul". In *The Classical Tradition: Literary and Historical Studies in Honor of Harry Caplan*, L. Wallach (ed.), 536–558. Ithaca: Cornell University Press.
———. 1983. *Aristotelismo e sincretismo nel pensiero di Pietro Pomponazzi*. Padua: Antenore.
———. 1990a. "Ficino and Pomponazzi on the Place of Man in the Universe". In his *Renaissance Thought and the Arts*, 102–110. Princeton: Princeton University Press.

———. 1990b. "Paduan Averroism and Alexandrism in the Light of Recent Studies". In his *Renaissance Thought and the Arts*, 111–118. Princeton: Princeton University Press.
Kuksewicz, Z. 1968. *De Siger de Brabant à Jacques de Plaisance: La théorie de l'intellect chez les averroïstes latins des XIIIe et XIVe siècles*. Wroclaw: Ossolineum.
———. 1983. "Paul de Venise et sa théorie de l'âme". In *Aristotelismo veneto e scienza moderna*, 2 vols., L. Olivieri (ed.), I: 297–347. Padua: Antenore.
———. 1994. "The Latin Averroism of the Late Thirteenth Century". In *Averroismus im Mittelalter und in der Renaissance*, F. Niewöhner & L. Sturlese (eds), 101–113. Zürich: Spur.
Leaman, O. 1988. *Averroes and His Philosophy*. Oxford: Oxford University Press.
Lebano, E. A. 1974. "Luigi Pulci and Late Fifteenth-Century Humanism in Florence". *Renaissance Quarterly* **27**: 489–498.
Lucchetta, F. 1979. "Studi recenti sull'averroismo padovano". In *L'averroismo in Italia*, 91–120. Rome: Accademia Nazionale dei Lincei.
MacClintock, S. 1956. *Perversity and Error: Studies on the "Averroist" John of Jandun*. Bloomington: Indiana University Press.
Mahoney, E. P. 1970. "Agostino Nifo's Early Views on Immortality". *Journal of the History of Philosophy* **8**: 451–460.
———. 1976. "Nicoletto Vernia on the Soul and Immortality". In *Philosophy and Humanism: Renaissance Essays in Honor of Paul Oskar Kristeller*, E. P. Mahoney (ed.), 144–163. Leiden: Brill.
———. 1982. "Neoplatonism, the Greek Commentators, and Renaissance Aristotelianism". In *Neoplatonism and Christian Thought*, D. J. O'Meara (ed.), 169–177, 264–282. Albany: State University of New York Press.
———. 1987. "Themes and Problems in the Psychology of John of Jandun". In *Studies in Medieval Philosophy*, J. F. Wippel (ed.), 273–288. Washington, DC: The Catholic University of America Press.
———. 1991. "Nicoletto Vernia's Annotations on John of Jandun's *De anima*". In *Historia Philosophiae Medii Aevi: Studien zur Geschichte der Philosophie des Mittelalters*, 2 vols., B. Mojsisch & O. Pluta (eds), II: 573–593. Amsterdam: Grüner.
Maier, A. 1949. *Die Vorläufer Galileis im 14. Jahrhundert: Studien zur Naturphilosophie der Spätscholastik*. Rome: Edizioni di storia e letteratura.
Manzanedo, M. F. 1999. "La inmortalidad del alma humana según Cayetano". *Angelicum* **76**: 309–340.
Muccillo, M. 1996. *Platonismo, ermetismo e "Prisca teologia": Ricerche di storiografia filosofica rinascimentale*. Florence: Olschki.
Michael, E. 1998. "Descartes and Gassendi on Matter and Mind: From Aristotelian Pluralism to Early Modern Dualism". In *Meetings of the Minds: the Relations between Medieval and Classical Modern European Philosophy*, S.F. Brown (ed.), 141–161. Turnhout: Brepols.
———. 1992. "Averroes and the Plurality of Forms". *Franciscan Studies* **52**: 155–182.
———. 2000. "Renaissance Theories of Body, Soul, and Mind". In *Psyche and Soma: Physicians and Metaphysicians on the Mind-Body Problem from Antiquity to Enlightenment*, J.P. Wright & P. Potter (eds.), 147–172. Oxford: Clarendon Press.
Monfasani, J. 1993. "Aristotelians, Platonists, and the Missing Ockhamists: Philosophical Liberty in Pre-Reformation Italy". *Renaissance Quarterly* **46**: 247–276.
Nardi, B. 1945. *Sigieri di Brabante nel pensiero del Rinascimento Italiano*. Rome: Edizioni italiane.

———. 1955. "Di una nuova edizione del *De immortalitate animae* del Pomponazzi". *Rassegna di filosofia* **4**: 149–174.
Offelli, S. 1954. "Il pensiero del Concilio Lateranense V sulla dimostrabilità razionale dell'immortalità dell'anima umana". *Studia Patavina* **1**: 7–40.
———. 1955. "Il pensiero del Concilio Lateranense V sulla dimostrabilità razionale dell'immortalità dell'anima umana". *Studia Patavina* **2**: 3–17.
Oguejiofor, J. O. 1995. *The Arguments for the Immortality of the Soul in the First Half of the Thirteenth Century*. Leuven: Peeters.
Owens, J. 1987. "Aquinas on the Inseparability of the Soul From Existence". *The New Scholasticism* **61**: 249–270.
Pacchi, A. 1959. "Note sul commento al *De Anima* di Giovanni di Jandun. II: L'unicità dell'intelletto e l'unità della scienza". *Rivista critica di storia della filosofia* **14**: 437–457.
Park, K. 1988. "The Organic Soul". In *The Cambridge History of Renaissance Philosophy*, C.B. Schmitt et al. (eds.), 464–484. Cambridge: Cambridge University Press.
Pasnau, R. 2002. *Thomas Aquinas on Human Nature: A Philosophical Study of Summa theologiae 1a, 75–89*. Cambridge: Cambridge University Press.
———. 2007. "The Mind-Soul Problem". In *Mind, Cognition and Representation: The Tradition of Commentaries on Aristotle's De anima*, P. J. J. M. Bakker & J. M. M. H. Thijssen (eds), 3–19. Aldershot: Ashgate.
Petagine, A. 2004. *Aristotelismo difficile: L'intelletto umano nella prospettiva di Alberto Magno, Tommaso d'Aquino e Sigieri di Brabante*. Milan: Vita e pensiero.
———. 2010. "Come una donna di rara saggezza: Il *De immortalitate animae* di Pietro Pomponazzi e la psicologia di Tommaso d'Aquino". In *Pietro Pomponazzi: Tradizione e dissenso*, M. Sgarbi (ed.), 41–74. Florence: Olschki.
Pine, M. L. 1986. *Pietro Pomponazzi: Radical Philosopher of the Renaissance*. Padua: Antenore.
Pluta, O. 1986. *Kritiker der Unsterblichkeitsdoktrin in Mittelalter und Renaissance*. Amsterdam: Grüner.
———. 1993. "Die Diskussion der Unsterblichkeitsfrage bei Marsilius von Inghen". In *Marsilius von Inghen, Werk und Wirkung*, S. Wielgus (ed.), 119–164. Lublin: Redakcja Wydawnictw KUL.
———. 1996. "Der Alexandrismus an den Universitäten im späten Mittelalter". *Bochumer Philosophisches Jahrbuch für Antike und Mittelalter* **1**: 81–109.
———. 2002. "Persecution and the Art of Writing: The Parisian Statute of April 1, 1272, and Its Philosophical Consequences". In *Chemins de la pensée médiévale: Études offertes à Zénon Kaluza*, P. J. J. M. Bakker (ed.), 563–585. Turnhout: Brepols.
———. 2007. "Materialism in the Philosophy of Mind: Nicholas of Amsterdam's *Quaestiones* De anima". In *Mind, Cognition and Representation: The Tradition of Commentaries on Aristotle's De anima*, P. Bakker & J. M. M. H. Thijssen (eds), 109–126. Aldershot: Ashgate.
Poppi, A. 1962. "Lo scotista patavino Antonio Trombetta (1436–1517)". *Il Santo* **2**: 349–367.
———. 1964. "L'antiaverroismo della scolastica padovana alla fine del secolo XV". *Studia patavina* **11**: 102–124.
Pupo, Spartaco. 1999. *L'anima immortale in Telesio: Per una storia delle interpretazioni*. Cosenza: Pellegrini Editore.

Putallaz, F.-X. & Imbach, R. 1997. *Profession: philosophe. Siger de Brabant*. Paris: Editions du Cerf.
Sharples, R. W. 1987. "Alexander of Aphrodisias: Scholasticism and Innovation". In *Aufstieg und Niedergang der römischen Welt*, II.36.2, W. Haase (ed.), 1176–1243. Berlin: De Gruyter.
Snyder, J. G. 2011. "Marsilio Ficino's Critique of the Lucretian Alternative". *Journal of the History of Ideas* **72**: 165–181.
Sorge, V. 2001. *Profili dell'averroismo Bolognese: Metafisica e scienza in Taddeo da Parma*. Naples: Luciano Editore.
South, J. B. 2012. "Suárez, Immortality, and the Soul's Dependence on the Body". In *The Philosophy of Francisco Suárez*, B. Hill & H. Lagerlund (eds), 121–136. Oxford: Oxford University Press.
Spruit, L. 1992. "Elementi aristotelici e polemica anti-peripatetica nella dottrina dell'anima divina di Telesio". *Verifiche* **21**: 351–370.
Suarez-Nani, T. 1995. "Dignità e finitezza dell'uomo: Alcune riflessioni sul *De immortalitate animae* di Pietro Pomponazzi". *Rivista di storia della filosofia* **50**: 7–30.
Tanner, N. P. (ed.). 1990. *Decrees of the Ecumenical Councils*, 2 vols. London: Sheed and Ward.
Tarabochia Canavero, A. 1978. "S. Agostino nella *Teologia platonica* di Marsilio Ficino". *Rivista di filosofia neo-scolastica* **70**: 626–646.
Tavuzzi, M. 1994. "Valentino da Camerino, O.P. (1438–1515): Teacher and Critic of Cajetan". *Traditio* **49**: 287–316.
Thijssen, J. M. M. H. 1997. "What Really Happened on 7 March 1277? Bishop Tempier's Condemnation and its Institutional Context". In *Texts and Contexts in Ancient and Medieval Science*, E. Sylla & M. McVaugh (eds), 84–114. Leiden: Brill.
Treloar, J. L. 1990. "Pomponazzi's Critique of Aquinas's Arguments for the Immortality of the Soul". *The Thomist* **54**: 453–470.
Vanni Rovighi, S. 1936. *L'immortalità dell'anima nei maestri Francescani del secolo XIII*. Milan: Vita e pensiero.
Van Steenberghen, F. 1977. *Maître Siger de Brabant*. Louvain: Publications universitaires.
Wallace, K. R. 1967. *Francis Bacon on the Nature of Man*. Urbana: University of Illinois Press.
Zupko, J. 2004. "On Buridan's Alleged Alexandrianism: Heterodoxy and Natural Philosophy in Fourteenth-Century Paris". *Vivarium* **42**: 43–57.

12

LATE SCHOLASTICS AND RENAISSANCE HUMANISTS ON THE PASSIONS IN MORAL ACTION

Eileen C. Sweeney

This chapter will consider both scholastic (William of Ockham, 1288–1347, and Francisco Suárez, 1548–1617) and humanist authors (Desiderius Erasmus, 1466–1536; Juan Luis Vives, 1492–1540; and Michel de Montaigne, 1533–1592) on how the passions are related to moral action. I shall trace the way in which these scholastic and Renaissance thinkers shift and in some ways weaken the link between the passions and virtue/morality as it was conceived by ancient and medieval thinkers in the West. In Plato we have either the model of the passions being under the rule of reason in dialogues like the *Republic* and *Gorgias*, or the passions, at least eros, being redirected to higher objects, as in the *Symposium* and *Phaedrus*. And, though there are subtleties, we can say that generally for the Stoics, the path of the sage is a path whose progress is counted in the passions extirpated. For Aristotle the definition of moral virtue is in the moderation of the passions and appetites. Nonetheless, there is a shared sense that the question of ethics is a question of how one deals with the passions, a sense that the passions – whether moderated, directed or renounced – are the defining feature of the moral act for Plato, Aristotle and the Stoics.

In the early Christian tradition, the link between passion and morality is even tighter. Influenced by Stoicism and Gnosticism, early Church fathers such as Cassian and Gregory the Great held that passion equals vice.[1] For Cassian the vices emerge as corruptions of the concupiscible and irascible appetites as seats of the passions.[2] The identification of passion with sin is qualified because of the developing idea of the "will" as a distinct faculty or power, identified neither with reason nor passion. Thus in principle in Augustine and explicitly, for example, in Abelard, it is the will's choice or consent that gives acts their moral character, not the passions that might accompany that choice. Nonetheless, in Augustine, the passions are still the moral problem as they are the manifestations of the will, good or bad.[3]

Thomas Aquinas's so-called "treatise on the passions"[4] understands the passions as neither themselves virtuous nor vicious and treats even seemingly irrational emotional responses as completely explicable, thus distancing passion from any identification with sin. Nonetheless, for Aquinas the moral task is to redirect the passions toward true and lasting good and avoidance of evil, and in that sense, morality is still directly about the state of one's passions, about their objects and direction, about whether they are under the control of reason. Aquinas's account of the passions was well-known up into the modern period; his synthesis of so much of ancient and early Christian thought combined with a detailed analysis of eleven major passions became an important foil against which contrary views were worked out.

As these later scholastic and Renaissance thinkers chip away at the central moral role of the passions found in the ancients and early Medieval thinkers, they show us some of the intermediate steps leading to the very different view of the passions espoused by modern thinkers like Descartes and beyond. The changes to the ancient view on the role of the passions in ethics occur on many different fronts having to do with the analysis of particular passions and the place of passion in the overall psychology in relation to reason and the will. The areas of transformation I will outline are 1) the relationship of the passions to the will and their differentiation from the will, 2) the passions as a matter of physiology and as particular to the individual, 3) the passions as erratic and contradictory and 4) the valuing of the passions not as moral phenomena but as feelings.

Through these transformations, the passions are moved out of their central role in moral virtue from two directions: first, because moral significance is unequivocally given to the will (and its virtues) and, second, because the passions themselves are seen as almost involuntary physical responses, capricious, idiosyncratic and conditioned by individual physiology, climate and circumstance. None of these elements causing the panoply of diverse emotional responses are truly chosen, and hence, they are neither things for which we can be held morally responsible nor are they terribly susceptible to discipline and training, to, in other words, virtuous habituation. Though there are echoes of Platonic, Aristotelian, Stoic and Thomistic positions in thinkers in this period, these thinkers sound these notes within a new and different orchestration, one in which the passions are individual, physical reactions that are valued as expressions of individuality rather than as moral markers.

1 Passions and the will

Even though earlier thinkers in the Christian tradition – Augustine, Abelard, Aquinas – distinguish between passion and the will, Medieval Aristotelianism retains the notion that a fully virtuous act is one in which being virtuous means *wanting* to act virtuously rather than willing against or transcending passion. For Aquinas passions are in themselves morally neutral, but as controlled by reason, they are good: "It belongs to the perfection of the moral good that the passions are controlled by reason," Aquinas notes. Even more, he argues that passions can *increase* the moral goodness of an act:

> Accordingly just as it is better that man should both choose good and do it in his external acts; so also does it belong to the perfection of moral good, that man should be moved to good, not only in respect of his will, but also in respect of his sensitive appetite.
>
> (*STh*. I-II, q. 24, a. 3)

Thus the passions for Aquinas are not obstacles to be ignored or bypassed as merely physiological phenomena nor involuntary psychological states, but are essential constituents of moral value, both controlled and directed by reason such that we not only *do* the right thing, but *want* to do the right thing. Moreover, for Aquinas the passions, located in the sensitive appetite, are the subjects of virtue, which reason rules by "political principle," the same principle by which free men, who have in some respects their own proper will, are ruled. (*STh* I-II, q. 56, a. 4, ad 3; cf. Aristotle, *Politics* I.2, 1254b4).[5]

In *On the Connection of the Virtues*, Ockham outlines five levels of virtuous action, all of which locate the morality of action exclusively in the will and *not* in the passions. Ockham's five levels, first, simply leave out the passions and then define virtue in the higher levels by the degree to which they are in opposition to natural inclinations (or passions). The first degree of virtue is when the will elicits an act in conformity with right reason. The second degree is when one wills according to right reason with the intention never to give up such works for any reason contrary to right reason, not even to avoid death. In the third degree, the will wills the performance of the work solely because it is dictated by right reason. The fourth level is when the will wills that act precisely on account of love of God. The last and fifth level is when the will wills to do or undergo something that naturally exceeds the common human state, contrary to the most basic inclination; this is heroic virtue.[6] The will's action is what defines an act as moral at all levels, and the intensification of the moral act at higher levels is effected solely by an intensification of the will's act in its increasing independence from "natural" inclinations, i.e., passions in the sensitive appetite. Thus, for Ockham, morality is not the control, direction and fulfilment of natural desires/passions redirected toward appropriate objects but the utter transcendence of those passions. But unlike the Stoics, he says nothing about *extirpating* the passions; whether we have passionate feelings or not is irrelevant as long as the will does not act on them.

This view of moral action leads Ockham to conclude that the moral virtues are not in the sensitive appetite (i.e., passions) at all. He argues simply: Since a virtuous habit in the strict sense is sufficient to elicit a praiseworthy/moral act, and nothing other than the will can be the subject and principle of such a habit, there can be no virtue in the sensitive appetite. *Any* act to which a habit in the sensitive appetite inclines us can be evil because of an evil intention of the will, and no act can be virtuous without a concurring will.[7] The habits we have of feeling certain passions are tendencies toward behaviour that is independent of the will, such that whether the passions oppose, support or simply differ from the choice of the will, is utterly irrelevant, morally speaking. The virtues, then, are not in or of the passions of the sensitive appetite but are virtues of the *will* – rationally chosen habitual modes of virtuous action.[8]

Suárez, though active at the end of period covered by this volume, allows us to see how far Ockham has changed the conversation in scholastic circles. Suárez struggles to maintain Thomistic positions on the passions even as he holds a more strongly voluntarist position on the will, i.e., one emphasizing the will's freedom and independence from nature and the passions.[9] Following Ockham, he locates the source of morality exclusively in the will, but, following Aquinas, he recognizes the quasi-natural movement of the sensitive appetite, which is determined to desire the good once apprehended. As we will see, however, even his agreement with Aquinas in the end serves his more voluntarist view, because the passions' quasi-natural direction toward objects is seen as a force contrary to that of the will, but by which the will is never completely compelled. In Aquinas, by contrast, the passions are constituents of virtuous actions. They partake of the fundamental teleology of the human person towards the highest good, both as directed by reason and as having of themselves a fundamental striving toward good and away from evil.

Suárez's allegiance to Aquinas amounts to support of Thomistic claims reinterpreted and placed in a more voluntarist/Ockhamist context. This is evident in his discussion of whether the acts of the sensitive appetite can be impeded, i.e., whether the will can stop an emotional response. Though Suárez wants to recognize the will as the centre of moral action and acknowledge its power to control our acts, come what may, his answer is complex and mixed. First, he answers in the negative: the will and intellect cannot immediately move the sensitive appetite because the imagination of some particular, perceived or remembered, must be present. Second, he says that, if there is an "absolute judgment" that an object is appropriate, that is, if an object once apprehended by the sense is recognized by the appetite as completely, fully desirable, the will cannot command the appetite not to desire or not to obey. Here Suárez attempts to carve out an exception to Ockham's claim, stated above, that the will can choose anything anytime, with or against the passions or any other faculty. The appetite, Suárez says, is a natural power and acts necessarily. In the *real* (rather than imagined or remembered) presence of the object or some material alteration of the body, we cannot simply stop the appetite from responding by command when some perception occurs. Even when an object is not present, an interior motion of the imagination can be "vehement and importunate," making it impossible or at least difficult to resist.

Nonetheless Suárez gives some power to reason and the will over the forces of the passions. Though free choice cannot drive out these passions and intellect and will cannot prevent them, the passions can be moderated by reason and the will. However, even this Aristotelian/Thomistic notion of moderating the passions is understood in a different way by Suárez. Suárez explains that we can moderate a passion when the intellect directs the attention to other things than the object and the passion it arouses, though we cannot stop the actual feeling by a command. *Aristotelian* moderation, by contrast, is achieved not by distracting the mind but by reason informing the passions, by showing the relationship between the proposed object and the life of happiness (*eudaimonia*); in Aristotelian virtue, the response of the passions is moderated to appropriate objects and levels, times and places because this is understood and then *felt* as right.

Suárez does not tarry over moderation but continues the discussion by distinguishing between present and absent objects as making a key difference in the will's ability to impede the appetites. If there is no object present (at least no vehement and importunate one), the will can revoke the imagination and impede the appetite. This is clear because, he argues, the will is the general principle of human acts and is oriented to the universal end of man and whatever is related to that end. The will steers us toward this good, and as long as it keeps that in view (but *only* so long), it has the power to command the sensitive appetite. Thus, if the will perseveres, it is necessarily obeyed because the lower appetite has a natural propensity, even against its own particular inclination, to obey the superior. Suárez describes the process of managing the passions as a kind of advance or attack against opposing appetites.[10] Suárez does invoke something closer to an Aristotelian picture of how the passions may be controlled and directed: Their direction to pursue or avoid certain objects is to be brought under the end of happiness. Nevertheless he claims that it is only possible to affect desire directly when the object is imagined rather than real and present. Moreover, the *way* in which he describes the passions as being directly affected is not very Aristotelian: The will and/or reason "advances" or "attacks" them, resorting to tactics like distraction in the face of a present object. And, of course, as soon as this will ceases, the imagination and appetite revert to their acts.

Suárez continues qualifying and nuancing his answer. He gives the objection from experience, that often we want *not* to desire and are unable to resist. Suárez's response is that when the object of pain or pleasure is present, the will cannot command that there be no pain or take away all repugnance, but the will *can* efficaciously command that it persevere without giving in to the pain. And this command of the will, which does not end the affective response but wills to persist in spite of the pain, *must* be obeyed. If, even with this command, Suárez adds, there is some bodily movement against the command of the will, it is not the appetite successfully opposing the will but a kind of accidental motion from some material change in the body.[11]

The picture we end up with is, on the one hand, the assertion of the will's final victory in which it cannot be opposed, and, on the other, passion as natural appetite made something of an autonomous force against which the will's acts are limited. The will can only distract and/or resist, not the feelings themselves, but only any action toward which they might draw us. Though the will can heroically persevere, it is also strangely detached and helpless, unable to educate, direct and bring the passions into full harmony with the rationally chosen good.

ON THE PASSIONS IN MORAL ACTION

Suárez tries to defend the Aristotelian/Thomistic principle that the passions are subject to political rule by explaining that the appetites can "resist or repel" the will, and the will can be "dragged" to consent, though the will can always win if it perseveres.[12] This account sounds less like political rule than a battle, and the battle is not between *reason* and passion but between the *will* and the passions. Thus Suárez follows the more voluntarist line of making the moderation or control of the passions a function of the will rather than reason.[13]

As Peter King (2002) has noted, another change Suárez makes to Aquinas is that he rejects the distinction between the irascible and concupiscible appetites, a rejection repeated by Descartes. The passions of the irascible appetite are aroused when the good is hard to achieve and the evil hard to avoid. Thus, Aquinas would explain rushing into the fire to save a child not as the will overcoming or resisting the natural appetite but by arguing that one desires something else more than saving the body from the pain of the fire, and this would be an act of the irascible appetite, combating an evil hard to escape, the passion of daring. The irascible appetite allows Aquinas to see the move to resist as still *an appetite for* something. The emphasis, then, remains on what one wants, the *telos* toward the good and away from evil, rather than on delineating such acts as doing by a sheer act of will what one *does not* want.[14] For Suárez persisting when the going gets tough is an act of *will*, and not the act of an irascible passion. Thus the rejection of the irascible appetite is another signal of his voluntarism because it moves the impetus for acting in ways that overcome one passion, for example fear or despair, into the will, whereas for Aquinas acting to defeat evil is motivated by the same desire to avoid evil found in fear but also in the passion of daring to overcome it. Doing away with the irascible appetite thus further disconnects morality and passion because the important ethical acts of resisting evil and pursuing good even when it is hard are turned into acts of the will *against* passion, not *motivated by* an irascible passion. Virtuous acts are therefore contrary to passion rather than consonant with correctly formed passion.

This same voluntarism is apparent when Suárez moves from an account of how the passions interact with reason and the will to the role they play in moral action. Suárez places clear emphasis on the will, arguing that no act can be good or bad without freedom. Thus on the question of whether there can be sin in the sensitive appetite, Suárez argues explicitly against Aquinas and with Ockham, stating that there is only sin in the sensitive appetite "by extrinsic denomination" because sin is really only in malice in the will.[15] There cannot even be venial sin in the appetite itself, because the sensitive appetite is not capable of moral acts (*actus honesti*).[16]

When Suárez discusses the origins of sin in passion, ignorance and malice, he seems to make the category of sins of malice quite broad, narrowing considerably the role of passion in sin. Sins of malice are those committed without ignorance or passion and with full freedom and will.[17] Clearly the point is that insofar as a sin is from passion it is less voluntary and further from being the worst kind of sin, a sin from malice, one which is willed and chosen without any clouds of passion or ignorance to mitigate guilt. Even sins of passion are still understood with will at the centre for Suárez. They originate from a motion of the sensitive appetite dragging the will to consent and "determining freedom." In this type of sin passion must "extort the consent of the will" (*extorquere consensum voluntatis*) in such a way that freedom is diminished.[18] This account stands in contrast to Aristotle's discussion of voluntariness and responsibility where he reduces to absurdity the idea that wrongful acts done from passion are not blameworthy since that is exactly what vice is. (*NE* 1114a3-b17)

The fundamental disengagement of the passions from the moral calculus in Ockham thus had profound effects. One branch, exemplified by Suárez's late scholastic approach, found expression in explicit debates about the freedom of the will and its relationship to passion following or at least forced to contend with Ockham's voluntarism. Another branch continued in discussions of the particular passions once they are no longer seen as forces which can be molded by reason to follow the will and, thus, come to be seen as bodily, individual and chaotic.

2 The passions as physiological and individualized

We can see this new kind of reflection on individual passions as following from the changes in the relationship of the will to the passions. As we have seen in Ockham and Suárez, once the seat of morality moves to the will, independent of the passions, the passions themselves become more a matter of physiology than psychology. This tendency is already present in Ockham's corpus. As I noted above in the earlier *Reportatio*, Ockham argued that the habits in the sensitive appetite were not moral since moral acts are only in the will. In the later *Quodlibets*, Ockham goes further, removing even the likeness between the passions and moral qualities, arguing that there cannot be *any* kind of habit in the sensitive appetite at all, only bodily qualities.[19]

Ockham uses this physiological view of the passions, the view that the passions are merely bodily effects, to sidestep two different elements of Aristotle's ethics: first, that we have a "natural inclination" toward the good, and, second, that this good is defined by our nature as human beings. Even though Aristotle argues that the *virtues* are not in us by nature but only as a capacity, Ockham takes it that Aquinas, presumably because of his strong assertion that the "end" of happiness is part of human nature, does claim that the virtues are in us by nature. Ockham rejects both vice and virtue as natural; they are not natural to human beings as a species nor are they natural to some individuals. He notes only that some have by nature certain "dispositions of the body" which give them "natural" tendencies. He gives examples of the body as having greater heat or cold, or the different "*complexiones*" of the young versus the old.[20] Ockham, then, rejects the Aristotelian/Thomistic view that there is a natural tendency oriented toward virtue, admitting only that there can be certain physical conditions or dispositions we might as individuals be born with or acquire as a result of our physical state. These conditions, however, are individual, "natural" differences in the sensitive appetite or passions, not virtue or vice, since on Ockham's view those are present only in the will.

Aristotle (and Aquinas after him) recognized, of course, the different individual temperaments and noted an important sense in which the virtues as the moderation of the passions are "relative" to the individual. But, first, the main emphasis in Aristotle is on the *common* human nature, with individuality as much less significant, and, second, the "relativity" Aristotle allows does not set different standards for virtue in different individuals but recognizes that different individuals with different temperaments or tendencies would have to take *different* moral steps to reach the *same* excellence of virtue.

The view of the passions as narrowly physical and exhibiting great variation in different individuals appears more prominently in Renaissance humanist thinkers. Erasmus's *Enchiridion* discusses particular passions much more than either Ockham or Suárez. The text is constructed as a moral handbook written for an individual as a kind of guide, drawing a sharp line between the "flesh" as the seat of the passions and the "spirit" as the realm of both reason and the desire for non-material goods. Erasmus places the passions in the body, locating different passions in different parts of the body; anger or boldness is positioned lower than the head, between neck and midriff, while bodily lust is banished like a kind of wild beast to the lower part of the body, "which alone of all the members foments rebellion with obscene movements despite the vain protests of the king."[21] So, though he sees the passions as the enemy in a moral battle and, thus, as morally relevant in ways Ockham does not, Erasmus still distances them from the powers of spirit and conceives of them as an enemy, an almost alien, physical force against which spirit must contend.

To the opposition of spirit and flesh, Erasmus adds the "soul" as a distinct faculty or power, which he describes as morally neutral: "the soul has no charge imputed to it. Whatever is carnal is base, whatever is spiritual is perfect, whatever belongs to the soul as life-giving element is in between and indifferent."[22] Erasmus's soul, like the Freudian ego, stands between and makes a choice between flesh (id) and spirit (superego). The passions are clearly identified with the body as the "flesh" that struggles against "spirit." Though he calls it the soul here, not freedom or free choice, its task is similar, in that it must choose between flesh and spirit, a task which amounts to a kind of struggle against the beastly passions: "the spirit makes us gods, the flesh makes us brute animals. . . . The spirit elevates us to heaven: the flesh drags us down to hell."[23]

While Erasmus in many ways plays a traditional melody on the passions, influenced by the church fathers and the Stoics, he sounds a new note, neither scholastic nor Stoic, in his discussion of the affections as varying in strength and object in different individuals. Though he finds it an "insidious opinion" that some people are unable to control themselves and are constrained to act on their passions, he concedes that the affections are gentle and docile in some people and more violent in others. Some passions or vices seem to accompany different temperaments: lust in the sanguine, anger in the choleric, sluggishness in the phlegmatic and envy and sullenness in the melancholic.[24] They vary with age and gender, and are oddly mixed, as he puts it, in such a way that, "sometimes it happens that nature, squaring the account, as it were, compensates a defect of the mind with other good qualities."[25] One could be chaste, but proud, or combine homicide with sure purpose. Moreover, some vices are neighbours of virtue such that their likeness is dangerous. There is no concession to the view that a little passion or vice can function as the beginning of virtue, yet Erasmus allows that vicious passions can be redirected toward virtue. If the angry man restrains his mind, he can become bold and courageous, solemnity can be turned to gravity, stinginess to thrift, flattering to courtesy. Nonetheless, these are still, albeit milder, "diseases of the mind," and Erasmus warns us against mistaking these vices for virtue. What is new here is the notion of unusual and particular mixtures of passions, some turned to virtue, some to vice; there is no unity of virtue here and thus no sense that all virtuous men look alike.

Following Erasmus, Juan Luis Vives strikes more thoroughly modern notes on the physiology of the passions and their particularity to individuals. What is new in Vives is his less moralistic tone. It is exactly the moral irrelevance of the passions that makes Ockham bypass any lengthy reflection on the individual passions, and Erasmus seems to catalogue almost exclusively the destructive power of the passions. Vives, by contrast, is interested in a huge range of phenomena and examines the passions in great detail. While he sometimes makes moral claims and repeats the systematic organizing principles of the passions worked out by Aquinas, neither morality nor systematization seems to drive his account; what does is rather an interest in the complexity and diversity of the phenomena. While not disputing that we innately desire self-preservation and happiness, he rejects the idea (adhered to by Aquinas) that this general claim can organize or make sense of the plethora of affective responses: "As soon as we descend from these heights into more concrete applications, we often fall into enormous precipices," he observes.[26]

I can only give a few examples of rapid descent to the non-systematic, contingent and idiosyncratic phenomena of the passions. Vives describes motion of the soul arising from changes in the body – sadness from black bile, joy from copious blood gathered around the heart; other movements follow the "commotion of our fantasy bearing some resemblance to an opinion or judgment."[27] Different mixtures of hot, cold, wet and dry and the predominance of some humours over others in different individuals make some affections fit and thus become stronger for an individual and some not, he explains. Further, bodily causes – food, beverages, age, diseases – along with "intense thinking" and studies, and a whole raft of external circumstances (time, season), as well as environmental causes (home, clothing, companions, occupations) and the "character of behaviour" (well-planned, vigorous, difficult, irritating, placid, etc.) all influence and individualize our emotional responses.[28] Vives insists that the Stoic *eupatheia* – equanimity, peace of mind, meekness of character or composure – are not emotions borne of judgment but are "natural and depend on individual disposition."[29] In a very long chapter on love, Vives combines the lofty idea of Platonic love of the beautiful as a reflection of the goodness of the divine with detailed descriptions of the ways in which "warm" and thick blooded people, vs. thin blooded and calm people love with vehemence and perseverance, respectively.[30] Just as whom or what we love and how we love are widely diverse, irritation (*offensio*), Vives's name for the "pain we feel at our first contact with something discordant and harmful" can be caused by a wide variety of things: the sound of a saw, the grunting of a pig, the tearing of a piece of cloth, the cracking of a burning coal.[31] Not only are love and irritation peculiar to individuals, but the differences and incompatibilities are, he says, "almost infinite." "It is almost incredible," Vives notes, "how different are the irritations people have; it is practically impossible to find two people who like the same thing."[32]

While Vives recognizes the incredible diversity of temperaments and conditions resulting in the almost infinite number of likes and dislikes, he is still engaged in psychology, an attempt to understand and explicate human behaviour in its diversity by the conditions and circumstances of the people involved and their environment.[33] His explorations do not, however, aim to unify diverse observations under the single essence; rather they expand out from a simple definition to an exploration of differences and variation.

When we move on to Montaigne, we see that Vives's seriousness of purpose stands in contrast to Montaigne's bemused and thoroughly unsystematic attitude toward the passions. The lack of systematic principles, the lack of any search for or interest in essences of human nature or the emotions, are not accidental but both the motivation for and a product of Montaigne's stated method in his writing. Even though he quotes examples of passion in action from history (mostly ancient sources), he turns to these texts to find not the facts but what is possible, not what is normal but what is "rare and memorable to fit my own turn."[34] On the other hand, unlike the scholastics, who make up examples when they have none from real life, he claims that he would not "dare to alter even the most light and indifferent circumstances."[35] While the scholastics (like Aquinas) are more interested in their overall theory and in constructing or culling examples of the passions to support it, Montaigne implies, his account will be truthful and thus motivated by the phenomena; it will seek out and privilege that which is *un*usual.

Besides noting as a general matter that the various "humours" in different individuals dispose them quite differently to different passions, Montaigne often adds observations about his own proclivities. He is not, he tells the reader, prone to violent grief; he is "naturally of a stubborn apprehension," and while he notes that he endeavours to harden this aspect of his temperament, he does not really put such a strategy forward as generalizable or, indeed, as better than nursing one's passions to greater and great heights.[36] It is a matter of personal choice. While not particularly prone to grief, he is very susceptible to the power of imagination. What he seems to mean by imagination in this passage is empathy; he cannot see another in pain without himself feeling what others are feeling.[37] Such passages testify to Montaigne's conviction that the passions are unsystematizable and rejection of any higher purpose in their proclivities.

Montaigne often begins from a point that sounds Stoic and often he even refers to Stoic views, yet he takes things in a quite different direction. For example, he starts from the Stoic premise that we have the power to choose whether to experience things as pleasurable or painful, but takes this as evidence for our ability to respond in diverse and even perversely subjective ways. If the real painful or pleasurable, good or evil character of the objects forced themselves on us, we would all have the same responses, he observes. We have the same tools, essentially the same bodies with the same capacities. That we have such diverse opinions must be because the soul, not the body, is variable across time and from individual to individual; as utterly autonomous, the soul has the power to decide anything: "the soul is variable into all sorts of forms and subject to herself and to her own empire, all things whatsoever. . . . . There is neither reason, force, nor prescription that can anything prevail against her inclination and choice"; the soul has "many thousands of biases at her disposal."[38] Unlike animals, we have freed ourselves from the governance of moderate nature "to give ourselves up to the rambling liberty of our own fancies."[39]

Though enjoying the peculiarities of his emotions, Montaigne takes care not to elevate or romanticize them, pushing the passions more into the body as involuntary (and not terribly dignified) bodily functions. Montaigne takes as a synecdoche for the life of being subject rather than commander to the imagination the way his sex organ is moved and fails to move at his command, arguing that its vagaries are the norm rather than exception for our bodily parts, as our skin and hair react to fear and desire outside of our commands, as does our digestive system both in hunger and excretion.[40] Though Montaigne ascribes these involuntary motions to the imagination rather than the passions, it is clear that in part what he means by the imagination is our inner experience imbued with attractions and aversions, that is, with our affective responses to situations real or imagined.

3 Passions as chaotic, contradictory and unpredictable

Because the passions are divided so sharply from the will and placed more completely in the body, they also become subject to the variations of the body and its conditions and, hence, less predictable. Ockham argues for such a conclusion on the basis of his voluntarism. According to the *Sentences reportatio*, he maintains that no matter how developed a habit might be, "flesh can always rebel against the spirit." Given two contraries generated by different causes, if one grows stronger than the other and draws near to the first, the second can always overcome the first; "a contrary impeding cause," Ockham writes, "could be so strong as to destroy the whole of that activity and prevent the generation" of the contrary habit.[41] He seems to have in mind the way in which even habitual virtues and vices can be destroyed by a strong, countervailing passion or will. This is an important blow against the theory of virtue as a moral stabilizer, guaranteeing the just acts of the just man. For such stability of character is fairly radically undermined if virtues can be overcome at any moment. But the contrary can also happen, Ockham maintains, just as passion can overcome a virtuous habit in the will, the will can choose anything at any time, whether for or against a sensuous passion or virtuous habit. By contrast, Aristotle's theory of virtue is a theory of formation of the passions, in which they are moderated and directed toward the right objects and in which the virtuous person feels the right passions in the right degree toward the right objects. Even on a Stoic theory of virtue formation, where there is a notion of a first, more violent and involuntary movement of the passions, the virtuous person either does not feel such things or is able to make sure they do not reshape or rather distort judgment in a way that leads to action. Ockham promotes the idea that almost anything can happen to anyone; passion/flesh can always overwhelm the will/spirit, and the will can always override passion or habit.

Ockham goes on to argue that the habits of the sensitive appetite and the acts which result from them are so disjoined from the moral character that those good sensitive appetites, for example, the tendency to eat temperately, are "compatible with any vice in the will whatever," even the one directly contrary to the habit.[42] I can, then, continue to eat moderately from a quasi-habit or bodily quality while *willing* gluttonously and thus sin despite my temperate outward actions.

Thus Ockham describes the same habit in the sensitive appetite, e.g., being skilled in war (*exercitatus in bello*, which is a non-moral version of courage as a kind of habitual response of the passion of daring rather than fear in a war situation), as able to be either virtuous or vicious depending on the intention and end for which it is deployed, i.e., in a just or unjust cause. Ockham's underlying notion is that a disposition in the sensory appetite is just the tendency to respond affectively in a certain way.[43] Fuchs (1952: 95–97) seems to take this to mean that the sensitive dispositions are still *morally* important because they continue to affect action, but the only kind of effect they retain is like the movements of a chicken with its head cut off, that is, the action/passion continues as a kind of automatic reflex but is no longer truly chosen. On Aristotle's model of virtue the habit is not just making war efficiently, having acquired reflexes in the form of bodily dispositions to feel certain passions in certain circumstances, but having the passion to make war or not informed by judgments about how, when, whom and by what means it is just and prudent to fight, what to fear and what not to fear. Ockham makes habit mere behaviour when it is in the sensitive appetite/passions, severing the connection between behaviour and judgment and, thus, transforming the relationship between reason (or the will) and the passions.

Ockham is even willing to disjoin passion not just from morality, but from motivation. Steve McGrade highlighted Ockham's attempt refute the views of Peter Aureole, who simplified Aquinas's organization of the passions around the path of natural motion. Aquinas makes *love*, the inclination toward good, the root of all the passions, desire, the motion toward it and pleasure/joy, rest in the possession of that good. Aureole simply says that love as that which incites desire is a form of pleasure and he posits pleasure as "the beginning as well as the end of all volition and behaviour."[44] The arguments and examples Ockham produces to refute this view try to show that the passions function without pleasure, without, in other words, aiming at the enjoyment of the good achieved or the evil avoided. Ockham gives the example of a man so overcome by sadness that he is incapable of taking pleasure in anything, for example, in scientific knowledge; but even while being unable to enjoy it, a person could love having this knowledge. Similarly, those who are angry desire revenge, even if they believe it to be impossible to achieve, and they will still desire it, though without pleasure, either now or in the future. So, too, Ockham continues, the damned will will things positively but be unable to take pleasure in them, and the blessed will want some things not to be without being saddened by them.[45] Even if we disengage these cases from the particulars of Ockham's criticism of Aureole, what they show is what we have seen elsewhere in Ockham: the disjoining of elements Aquinas had done his best to knit seamlessly together. So, the desired pleasure in union with the good is divorced from love, the inclination toward that good.

If Ockham merely maps out as possibilities the ways in which, in principle, the passions and will may act against habit and stable character, Vives looks at the passions in all their complexity and disorder, colouring in, if you will, the outlines drawn by Ockham. Vives spends a good bit of time explaining the fluctuations of desire, varying with confidence and anxiety, experience and age. "Confidence," he notes, "decreases desire, and fear increases it."[46] He devotes a long chapter to various kinds of love. Its many objects, manifestations and transformations are a result of the fact that everything except God, who is the "good without blemish," "carries something that can be repudiated by a probing judgment or rejected by free will."[47] Imperfect objects, desired by imperfect beings and imperfectly possessed, make for a huge variety of variations and complications. Love can make the brave fearful and the insolent respectful and make us seek pain and adversity, abjection and slavery.[48] We become compassionate after exacting revenge and become more fond of those that suffer injustice.[49] Reverence can turn to fear or love; all emotions, whether anger, envy, hatred or love, lessen feelings of respect.[50] Envy and compassion, though apparent opposites, are found together; people generally inclined to one are inclined to the other.[51] Anger lessens "with games, banquets, merriment, success and prosperity."[52] Anger and envy reinforce hatred.[53] For Noreña (1989: 207), such observations are what makes Vives's work new and important; Vives's point is to show how "emotions fluctuate in intensity, interact with others, change into different emotions either gradually or explosively and form constellations and mixtures that defy naming and definition."

Vives, for all the surprising and unusual combinations of passions he notes, still seeks to bring the passions under moral control; he wants to bring understanding without over-simplification, arguing that their excesses and vagaries cannot be cured by "a single magic panacea," as Noreña (1989: 218) puts it, but only "with a complex and diversified stock of drugs." In Montaigne we lose even this reimagined kind of moral psychology. Montaigne takes the contradictory and even self-defeating phenomena of the passions for the main theme of his reflections, explicitly rejecting any moral purpose for his work. Montaigne rejects the commonplace of writing for moral edification: "I would not give myself the trouble, sworn enemy as I am to obligation, assiduity, or perseverance." There is, Montaigne writes, "nothing so contrary to my style as a continued narrative."[54] Thus he must interrupt the flow to catch his breath and has, in a reversal, accommodated not his writing to the subject but his subject to what he is capable of saying. This description of his method of writing mirrors in many ways his view of the passions. Montaigne asserts the value of the idiosyncrasy of his thoughts and feelings, of a kind of freedom that is neither fully controlled by reason nor yet, when taken off the reins, headed full throttle straight toward sensuality (as Erasmus implies).

For Montaigne, then, the passions are unpredictable responses to what the world throws at us and, thus, may have all kinds of perverse results. Fear sometimes roots us in place like statues and other times sends us into frantic flight without consideration of our real safety. To illustrate this perversity and unpredictability, Montaigne cites the example of Roman soldiers who were caught in a trap and in their fear retreated so ferociously that they cut through the rear lines of the Carthaginians, trapping themselves rather than escaping.[55] The experience of fear can be so awful that it drives some toward death to escape its torments, Montaigne notes, citing multiple examples. Thus fear, which Aquinas explained in terms of its function of alerting us to and saving us from evil, and especially from the greatest evil, death, in Montaigne can itself become an evil greater than the one it is supposed to protect us from. Aquinas works to explain away apparent perversity or randomness in our passions; there are reasons for what we love and fear even when our loves and fears are not based on the real goodness or evil of the objects toward which they are directed, he takes pains to point out. Because our passions make sense, they show themselves susceptible to conversion and redirection. Not so for Montaigne.

In this same vein, Montaigne devotes an essay to the phenomenon of simultaneous, contradictory passions.[56] His example uses the passions at the outermost ends of the spectrum in Aquinas's scheme: joy and sadness. Montaigne cites the cases of departing on a much desired journey but still weeping as we leave our families, of brides happy to marry but clinging to the necks of their mothers. These are the kinds of examples which Aquinas did and would have explained, not as contradictory feelings about the same thing, but as perfectly understandable reactions to distinct objects: good, on the one hand, in the desired journey, and evil, on the other, in separation from loved ones. But Montaigne takes these phenomena as outright contradictory responses. He opines first that they are a result of "diverse humours," some of which are more dominant in some individuals than in others. Thus instead of finding this phenomenon in need of further analysis, he takes it as a basic fact. He also expands beyond these to more perverse examples: how we lament the death of someone we do not wish were alive, and, from his own life, how he abuses his servant yet, equally sincerely, values him as honest and good. Similarly for his wife: We would be wrong to find either coldness or fondness toward her feigned; both are real. Even Nero, we are reminded, despite sending his mother to be drowned, was still filled with horror and pity. The sun's light is not continuous but the new rays follow one another so closely that we perceive them as one continuous light though they are not. "Just so the soul variously and imperceptibly darts out her passions," he concludes.[57]

4 Passions as valued in their own right, not as moral but as feelings

In thinkers influenced by Christian Neo-platonism, love is seen as a positive force which needs only to be directed away from material, temporal things toward the divine and eternal. It is a view that remains and is transformed in Medieval and some Early Modern thinkers. For example, Suárez retains the view expressed by Aquinas that love is the central passion and is an orientation toward the good in some real sense.[58] In discussing the goodness or evil of the passions, he notes that emotions are sometimes good, e.g., anger or sadness in Christ or the Blessed Virgin, and that when the appetite "consents" in good works, "those motions are like fires consenting to virtue." Passions can have good effects, like the fear of pain bringing about mercy, and sadness about sins committed bringing about repentance.[59] Moreover, he repeats Aquinas's view that the Stoics do not really reject the goodness of the passions, so that the Stoics, Aristotle and Aquinas can all agree that the moderate movements of the appetites are not passions but virtues.[60]

Erasmus's *Enchiridion*, motivated by almost Pelagian optimism that human beings can make great strides toward virtue on their own, sets its focus on that moral task so uniformly that, somewhat paradoxically, the text has almost nothing to say about any positive role for the passions. If anything, Erasmus has a stronger view of the passions as inherently dangerous and immoral than the other thinkers considered here do. His language about sin, which he comes close to equating with passion, is focused on its filthiness, contrasted with the purity and cleanliness of a sinless conscience and opposed to the dignity of man.[61]

Erasmus's fellow humanist, Vives, reasserts that older Neoplatonic and Thomistic confidence in love of the good as the underlying force in our affective lives. Nonetheless, Vives understands that while love of the good might be the root of our affective lives, the branches multiply out in many confusing directions. Rather than trying to bring back the diversity of objects and reduce the alchemical mixtures of passions to the simplicity of love of the good and aversion to evil as Aquinas does, Vives seems to value those affective responses in all their diversity. He belittles the Stoic rejection of mercy and compassion, not only because we are more ready to help others when we feel for them in their suffering but also because "bending your soul to the affliction of others" itself alleviates others' pain and suffering. "No help is more welcomed and more efficient," he concludes.[62] Compassion is the effect of the love and attachment human beings have for each other, and to be without it is inhuman.[63] Vives catalogues the varieties and perversities of love as the mainspring of the passions, but most striking of all is his conclusion: "Love created us, perfected us and makes us happy." He is referring not only to the love of the divine but also to its many diversions and permutations and concludes by wondering at "its incredible and inexhaustible strength and mysteriousness."[64] It is an appreciation of all of it, funny, petty, perverse and profound, not a Platonic call toward conversion of loves toward the one, true good. The only blanket condemnation of passion Vives issues is of those that proceed from apparent evil rather than apparent good; these emotions, he says, "brutalise and degrade."[65] A tendency to value the positive emotions, no matter the true value of their objects, turns up later in Descartes' work on the passions, where Descartes notes that despite the ephemeral or mistaken character of our loves and desires, we are better off loving than hating, desiring than fearing. Here the defining moral feature of the passions for Plato, Aristotle and Aquinas drops out: the objects as *truly* goods to be sought or evils to be avoided.

Though Suárez and Vives have negative things to say about the passions and seem to resurrect more Stoic sounding claims about the passions as distortions and their role as morally detrimental, they find some level on which to value them. Montaigne goes further in his interest and appreciation of the passions without making any move to convert them to the true over the apparent good. While, like the Stoics, Montaigne catalogues the less than edifying effects of the passions, unlike the Stoics, he values those feelings as feelings, in all their diversity and perversity, taking a worldly and playful perspective on them. It is clear that Montaigne thinks his own propensities toward certain passions, his sensitivities and proclivities, even when they lead him into nonsensical actions and attitudes, are preferable and more interesting than if he were simply average or moderate or practical in his passions.

Even though, like the Stoics, Montaigne asserts that we have unconditional power over our own happiness, he imagines that Cato could not, as he plucked out his own bowels, have been without any horror and that, moreover, he must have felt pleasure and delight in his own noble action.[66] Virtue for Montaigne is found in a kind of resistance, having strong passions but also heroically resisting them and also getting a different kind of pleasure out of heroic acts: "Let the philosophers say what they will, the thing at which we all aim, even in virtue is pleasure."[67]

5 Conclusion

I have attempted to trace four dimensions along which the relation between the passions and morality was transformed in late Scholasticism and Renaissance thought: the passions as 1) strongly separated from the will and 2) as more exclusively located in the body and lower appetites. Thus the passions are understood more as features of individuals rather than of human nature and, thus, as contingent on individual circumstances and conditions. Because so dependent on individuality they are catalogued 3) as capable of infinite variation and combination, pulling against each other and even against the agents' fundamental sense of good and evil. Lastly, 4) we saw the ways in which what emerges is a sense of tolerance and interest in the passions, valuing feelings, good or bad, as a way of being human and alive.

It is mainly in the scholastic tradition that the line of thought locating moral value and choice in the will takes place, but the effect of this view is to make the passions more exclusively physical and not a matter of choice. This shift, already recognized in a general way in scholastic sources, filters down into the details of particular passions by Renaissance thinkers who follow through, tracing the individual and disordered sequences and combinations of passions unmoored from the will. For Ockham, as I noted, individual passions become of less interest because they are basically irrelevant to morality, while Erasmus and Vives hope to control the passions in a more optimistic plan of moral education. The more definitive break is in Montaigne, whose examination of the passions abandons all pretence of interest in morality or, indeed, anything generalizable about human nature that might serve moral education.

Descartes' *Les Passions de l'Âme* does not just share particular claims with these thinkers but constructs a program for investigating, managing and tolerating the passions that owes a great deal to this period. Descartes places the will as free above the passions as the only thing that is both ours and worth valuing. Though unable to directly arouse or dismiss them, the will is able to master the passions by calling up images and reconfiguring associations, he argues. Though arguably more Stoic than these earlier figures, Descartes, too, ends in a place of tolerance, noting that since we cannot always avoid being deceived about the true good or evil of an object, we should seek the positive emotions of love and joy, avoiding hatred. In the end he finds the passions, even the negative ones, to possess a kind of sweetness, granting to human life a fullness it would lack without them.[68] Though woven into a text whose aim is moral, the passions themselves are not moral, ultimately, as Descartes concludes that wisdom teaches us "to manage [the passions] with such ingenuity, that the evils they cause can be easily borne, and we even derive joy from them all."[69] As the covers of many women's magazines and the pages of many self-help books attest, nothing is more contemporary than such conclusions, emerging in the later Middle Ages and Renaissance and fully expressed in the modern period.

Notes

1 See Vecchio (2009: 49).
2 Cassian, *Conferences*, XXIV, 15, 187. Cited in Vecchio (2009: 49).
3 Vecchio (2009: 47).
4 This is *STh*. I-II, qq. 22–48.
5 As Bonnie Kent shows persuasively, there was debate about the view that there can be virtues of or in the passions of the sensitive appetite in Aquinas's own time and certainly after him. Kent follows the relationship between the passions, habits, virtues and the will through late 13th-century thinkers such as Walter of Bruges, Henry of Ghent, Peter Olivi and Scotus among others and shows definitively that though the shift from Aquinas to Scotus (and even more Ockham who is just beyond the time line of her book) *looks* like "a dramatic turn in the direction of the good will ethic," when the thinkers she considers are added to the time line, many small steps were taken along this line before we get to Ockham (Kent 1995: 243).
6 *Virtues*, a. 2, ll. 116–167.

7 *QQ* II, q. 16, 182. Cf. *STh* I-II, q. 50, a. 3. Aquinas argues that *qua* natural instinct, the sensitive appetite does not have habits, but *qua* commanded by reason it does. It has not only habits but virtues, for Aquinas. *STh* I-II, q. 56, a. 4.
8 Kent (1995: 224–245).
9 For more on the late Medieval distinction between voluntarism and intellectualism see Chapter 7 of this volume.
10 *Pass.*, Tr. 2, Disp. 10, 272.
11 *Pass.*, Tr. 2, Disp. 10, 273.
12 *Pass.*, Tr. 2, Disp. 10, 273.
13 See Kent (1995: 212). Kent points out that Aquinas and Godfrey of Fontaine take the more intellectualist position that reason can order the passions, while Henry of Ghent and other Franciscans "make moderation of passion a function of the will."
14 For an account of how this fits into the larger direction of Aquinas's account of how the passions work, understanding them all as either movement toward the good or away from evil, see Sweeney 1998.
15 *Pass.*, Tr IV Disp. IV, sec. V, 563.
16 *Pass.*, Tr IV Disp. IV, sec. V, 563–564.
17 *Pass.*, Tr IV Disp IV, 550.
18 *Pass.*, Tr IV Disp IV, 550.
19 *QQ* II, q. 16. See Leff (1975: 559).
20 *Rep*. III, a. 12, 396.
21 *Enchiridion*, CWE 43; LB V 14A.
22 *Enchiridion* CWE 52, LB V 19D.
23 *Enchiridion* CWE 52, LB V 19D.
24 *Enchiridion* CWE 44–45, LB V 13E-15A.
25 *Enchiridion* CWE 45, LB V 15A.
26 *DAV* III; M, 422; *N* 2.
27 *DAV* III, M 423, N 3.
28 *DAV* III, M 423, N 3–4.
29 *DAV* III, M 426, N 8.
30 *DAV* III, M 436, N 18.
31 *DAV* III, M 470, 474; N 60, 62.
32 *DAV* III, M 472; N 61.
33 *DAV* III, 105–107.
34 *Essays*, I ch. 20; *Les Essais*, I ch. 21, 104. For more on Montaigne's method see Chapter 1 of this volume.
35 *Essays*, I ch. 20; *Les Essais*, I ch. 21, 104.
36 *Essays*, I ch. 2; *Les Essais*, I ch. 2, 10.
37 *Essays*, I ch. 20; *Les Essais*, I ch. 21, 96.
38 *Essays*, I ch. 40; *Les Essais*, I ch. 14, 57.
39 *Essays*, I ch. 40; *Les Essais*, I ch. 14, 58.
40 *Essays*, I ch. 20; *Les Essais*, I ch. 21, 102–103.
41 *Virtues*, a. 2, ll. 447–468.
42 Ockham, *Virtues*, a. 3, ll. 447–451.
43 Ockham, *Rep*. III, a. 12, 361.
44 McGrade (1981: 712).
45 Ockham, *Rep*. I, 408–411. See these cases as described by McGrade (1981: 712–713).
46 *DAV* III, M 437; N 20.
47 *DAV* III, M 442, N 25.
48 *DAV* III, M 447–448; N 31.
49 *DAV* III, M 454; N 39.
50 *DAV* III, M 456–467; N 42–43.

51 *DAV* III M 489, N 82.
52 *DAV* III M 481; N 73.
53 *DAV* III M 484–485; N 76.
54 *Essays*, I, ch. 20; *Les essais*, I, ch. 21, 106.
55 Montaigne, *Essays*, I, chap 17; *Les essais*, I ch. 18, 76.
56 Montaigne, *Essays*, I, chap 37; *Les essais*, I ch. 38, 233–236.
57 *Essays*, I, ch. 37; *Les essais*, I ch. 38, 235.
58 *Pass.*, Tr. IV, Dist. 1, sec.3, pp. 459.
59 *Pass.*, Tr. IV, Disp. 1, sec.2, 457–458.
60 *Pass.*, Tr. IV, Disp. 1, sec.2, 458.
61 E.g., *Enchiridion* LB V 55A; CWE 111; LB V 56C-57D; CWE 113–114.
62 *DAV*, III N 46.
63 *DAV*, III N 46–47.
64 *DAV*, III N 37.
65 *DAV*, III N 60.
66 *Essays* II, ch. 11; *Les essais*, II, ch. 11, 424.
67 *Essays* I, ch. 19; *Les essais* I, 20, 82.
68 *PA* II, 140, 142; *PA* III, 212.
69 *PA* III, 212.

Bibliography

Primary sources

Cassian, *Conférences*, E. Pichery (ed. and trans.), vol. III (Sources chrétiennes 64). Paris: Editions du Cerf, 1959.

Descartes, René. *Les Passions de l'Âme* (=*PA*). G. Rodis-Lewis (ed.). Paris: Vrin, 1991.

Erasmus, Desiderius. *Enchiridion*. In *Desiderii Erasmi Roterodami opera omnia* (= LB), Jean Le Clerc (ed.). Leiden, 1703–1706; repr. London: Gregg Press, 1962.

———. *Enchiridion*. In *Collected Works of Erasmus* (= CWE), vol. 66, J. W. O'Malley (ed.) & Ch. Fantazzi (trans.). Toronto: University of Toronto Press, 1988.

Juan Luis, Vives. *De anima et vita* (= *DAV*). In *Joannis Ludovici Vives Valentini Opera Omnia* (= *M*), vol. 3, G. Majansio (ed.). Valencia: Montfort, 1782.

———. *The Passions of the Soul: The Third Book of De Anima et Vita* (= *N*). C. G. Noreña (trans.). Lewiston: Edwin Mellen Press, 1990.

Montaigne, Michel de. *Essays of Montaigne* (=*Essays*). Ch. Cotton (trans.) & W. Carew Hazlitt (ed.). London: Reever and Turner, 1877. Digital edition: *Project Gutenburg's the Essays of Montaigne*, released 2006, updated 2012. www.gutenberg.org/files/3600/3600-h/3600-h.htm

———. *Les Essais: Édition Villey-Saulnier* (=*Essais*). Pierre Villey & V. L. Saulnier (eds). Paris: Presses Universitaires de France, 2004.

William of Ockham. *Quaestiones in Librum Primum Sententiarum* (*Reportatio*) (=*Rep.* I). In *Opera theological*, vol. IV, F. E. Kelly & G. Etzkorn (eds). St. Bonaventure: St. Bonaventure University, 1979.

———. *Quodlibetal Questions* (= *QQ*). In *Opera theologica*, vol. IX, J. C. Wey (ed.). St. Bonaventure: St. Bonaventure University, 1980.

———. *Quaestiones in Librum Tertium Sententiarum* (*Reportatio*) (=*Rep*.III). In *Opera theological*, vol. VI, F. E. Kelly & G. Etzkorn (eds). St. Bonaventure: St. Bonaventure University, 1982.

———. *On the Virtues* (=*Virtues*). R. Wood (ed. and trans.). West Lafayette: Purdue University Press, 1997.
Suárez, Francisco. *De actibus, qui vocantur passiones, tum etiam de habitibus, praesertime ac vitiosis* (= *Pass.*). In *Opera Omnia*, vol. 4, M. André (ed.). Paris: Ludovicus Vivès, 1856.

Secondary sources

Fuchs, O. 1952. *The Psychology of Habit According to William of Ockham*. St. Bonaventure: The Franciscan Institute.
Kent, B. 1995. *The Virtues of the Will: The Transformation of Ethics in the Late Thirteenth Century*. Washington, DC: The Catholic University of America Press.
King, P. 2002. "Late Scholastic Theories of the Passions: Controversies in the Thomist Tradition". In *Emotions and Choice From Boethius to Descartes*, H. Lagerlund & M. Yrjönsuuri, 229–258. Dordrecht, The Netherlands: Kluwer.
Leff, G. 1975. *William of Ockham: The Metamorphosis of Scholastic Doctrine*. Manchester: Rowman & Littlefield.
McGrade, A. S. 1981. "Ockham on Enjoyments – Toward an Understand of Fourteenth Century Philosophy and Psychology". *Review of Metaphysics* **34**: 706–728.
Noreña, C. G. 1989. *Juan Luis Vives and the Emotions*. Carbondale: Southern Illinois University Press.
Sweeney, E. C. 1998. "Restructuring Desire: Aquinas, Descartes, and Hobbes on the Passions". In *Meeting of the Minds* (= *Rencontres de Philosophie Medievale* **7**), S. F. Brown (ed.), 219–237. Tournhout: Brepols.
Vecchio, S. 2009. "Passions de l'âme et péchés capitaux: les ambiguïtés de la culture médiévale". In *Laster im Mittelalter; Vices in the Middle Ages*, Ch. Flüeler & M. Rohde (eds), 45–64. Berlin: de Gruyter.

13

RENAISSANCE FACULTATIVE LOGIC AND THE WORKINGS OF THE MIND

The "cognitive turn"

Marco Sgarbi

1 What is facultative logic?

The topic of this chapter is the origin of facultative logic within Renaissance Aristotelianism and its impact on early-modern philosophy of mind. In particular, I want to show how Renaissance Aristotelianism foreshadows some of the conceptions that later historical-philosophical research branded as essentially anti-Aristotelian. For a thorough understanding of the development of modern philosophy it is indispensable to focus on the facultative logic of Renaissance Aristotelians in the final decades of the sixteenth century. It was at this time that a paradigm shift took place, especially in the interpretation of Aristotle's psychology. The shift may not always have been sudden and controversial, but was nonetheless significant within the Aristotelian tradition. In what we could call a "cognitive turn", the subjects of facultative logic became, in opposition to classic Aristotelian logic and syllogistic, concepts rather than terms, judgments rather than propositions, reasonings rather than syllogisms.[1]

The main advancements in the field of facultative logic happened in those centres where there was already a strong Aristotelian tradition, such as in Padua, which provided the model for many sixteenth- and seventeenth-century German and English universities. It was in Padua that logic and psychology joined forces to form the new discipline that we now call facultative logic, which forms the basis for the philosophy of mind that developed at the end of the seventeenth century and throughout the eighteenth. This chapter focuses specifically on the developments of Aristotelianism in the British Isles and in the German territories because it is in these two regions that major advancements in the field of philosophy of mind were to occur, with empiricism on the one side and critical philosophy on the other.

What is facultative logic? James Buickerood characterized it as the science of "the principles of the habituated regulation of the mind in the apprehension of truth and the acquisition of knowledge and properly grounded opinion".[2] There are two important aspects of this definition. First, facultative logic has to do with a "habituated", that is, a consolidated way of using the mind, and investigates its principles. Such a definition, however, leaves open the question of whether this "habituated regulation" is something innate or something that is acquired over time, a topic that will be of particular interest at the end of the Renaissance. The second aspect is that this logic should determine the ways in which the mind acquires knowledge by helping to discover the truth or to form a well-grounded opinion starting from sensible experience. Both these aspects had a profound impact on the advancement of the philosophy of mind in Germany and in England, and it is through their examination that I aim to show the developments of facultative logic for the purpose of establishing a connection between the Renaissance and the early-modern period, an area which is largely *terra incognita* for philosophical-historical research.[3]

In the first part of the chapter we introduce the elements of Aristotelian logic, which will contribute to the origin of facultative logic during the Renaissance. This new kind of logic was elaborated first and foremost by Jacopo Zabarella, who developed a complex theory of habits that characterizes both the nature of logic itself and a "second nature" acquired by the mind. Then we focus on the reception of Zabarella's doctrine of habits by Protestant authors working on the European continent such as Johann Heinrich Alsted and Abraham Calov, who helped establish new disciplines concerning the philosophy of mind, namely hexiology, gnostology and noology. Zabarella's ideas also influenced British Aristotelians, who elaborated a distinctive Aristotelian empirical philosophy of mind, to which I will finally turn in my last section.

2 The Aristotelian tradition and facultative logic

In order to understand the origin of facultative logic within Aristotelianism, one should go directly to the source, that is, to Aristotle. Prior to Aristotle, facultative logic was difficult even to conceive, on the one hand because there was no corresponding concept for "faculty". The term most widely used to define it, δύναμις, meaningfully characterized not so much a capacity as a force or a power,[4] for which at least an "intentional" activity of the subject is necessary. On the other hand, Plato did not provide an elaborated theory of cognitive powers or forces and their objects,[5] "by which human beings are able to do what they are able to do".[6]

Aristotle's first sketch of what in the Renaissance would become facultative logic appears in his treatment of the parts of the soul: vegetative, sensible, rational and locomotive.[7] All these parts have in themselves a characteristic force through which the human being can grow, sense, think and move. Only the rational part of the soul that eminently thinks, however, is a "faculty" properly speaking, because in Aristotle's philosophy of mind, a faculty is characterized by an intentional force of the soul and for this reason sensation, lacking any intentional controllability and being merely passive, cannot be properly conceived as a faculty.[8] Also imagination itself, which mediates knowledge between sensation and understanding, is a blind force, not a faculty, precisely because it does not presuppose any active intervention of the knowing subject. Therefore, for Aristotle facultative logic was concerned with neither sensation nor imagination, but with the natural faculty of the understanding, because only understanding is intentional.

Aristotle develops his facultative logic in *Posterior Analytics*, II.19. Even if sensation is not a genuine faculty, it is nonetheless the starting point of Aristotle's facultative logic,[9] because the first objects of knowledge are always sensibles. Without sensation no knowledge would be possible. Sensibles then rest in the mind in some animals. If they do not rest in the mind of an animal, only sensible knowledge is possible, but if they do, then after various sensations, a kind of "intellectualization" is possible. Memory originates from this kind of sensation, followed by experience. From experience a "general concept" (καθόλου) is formed that rests in the mind. In this way, it is possible to acquire a disposition for scientific knowledge. The mental process, which infers from the various particulars to what is the same in all of them, is a kind of inductive process (ἐπᾰγωγή). This form of induction is a process of notification of knowledge from matter to form, from singular to universal, that can be considered as a kind of reflection, because what is in the world is reflected in the mind through a series of mirrorings: 1) from the external object, sensation produces a sensible copy of itself in the mind; 2) particular sensibles are mirrored in the imagination, forming general images; and 3) images are reflected in the intellect, generating universal intelligible species. At the end of the cognitive process, what was initially particular in the sensation and in the external world becomes a universal concept that reflects the object of experience. By contrast, the mental process that produces knowledge of the product of this induction is called intellection (νοεῖν), which is performed by the understanding, that is, as we shall see, the habit of principles. The process of acquiring and knowing general concepts and principles is therefore twofold. On the one hand, we have the formation of preliminary and rough knowledge, which relies on induction (ἐπᾰγωγή), and on the other hand, we have the actual cognition of the intelligibles (νοεῖν), which is a kind of intuitive and immediate act of grasping what is given and generated by experience.

This kind of actual cognition of immediate first principles, with which every scientific demonstration begins, is qualitatively different from the cognition that follows the conclusions of the demonstration, since there is a passage from a general, indeterminate concept to a determinate, universal concept. In fact, for Aristotle the formation and intellection of general concepts and principles produces only temporary knowledge, which must be proven discursively by means of demonstration before becoming scientific knowledge.

Aristotle's facultative logic is concerned with sensation and memory, on the one hand, and with understanding, on the other. Its goal is to determine how sensible knowledge could become universal, since singular, sensible knowledge itself cannot be considered scientific in Aristotelian terms. It is exactly in dealing with scientific knowledge and the understanding that Aristotle tackles one of the key issues of facultative logic in the construction of the knowing subject, namely the problem of habit. In the *Categories*, Aristotle distinguishes habits from dispositions, in that the former are more stable and durable.[10] Dispositions of the mind, by contrast, are easily removable and change quickly. But if a disposition remains, takes root in the mind and is hard to remove, it becomes a habit.[11] In his *Rhetoric*, Aristotle maintains that a habit gives rise to all the actions that we do because we are used to doing them,[12] and he adds that "habit is something like nature, for the distance between 'often' and 'always' is not great, and nature belongs to the idea of 'always,' habit to that of 'often'".[13] In the *Nicomachean Ethics*, Aristotle characterizes five intellectual habits: 1) art, 2) science, 3) prudence, 4) wisdom and 5) understanding, which should not be confused with the understanding as a natural faculty of the mind.[14] Art and prudence relate to production and action, respectively, whereas the habits involved in facultative logic are science, understanding and wisdom. By "science" (*scientia*) Aristotle means "scientific knowledge", that is, the knowledge of what is known as necessary.[15] This kind of knowledge can only be attained through demonstration, which must be based on true and well-known principles.[16] These principles are provided and discovered by the habit of principles, that is, a form of acquired understanding that supervenes on the natural understanding that the mind already possesses.[17] Instead, wisdom is both understanding and the science of higher things, like causes and principles, because wisdom specifically knows what follows from the principles and the highest truths.[18]

The reciprocal relations between science, understanding and wisdom are elaborated by Aristotle in the final chapters of the *Posterior Analytics*. We have already emphasized how crucial these chapters are to understanding the genesis of facultative logic. According to Aristotle, wisdom is knowledge of true, higher and superior things. Before knowing these things, however, we must know true things in general, that is, we must acquire scientific knowledge. Scientific knowledge is only possible through demonstration, but demonstration is based on principles, and only understanding gives assent to principles, therefore wisdom and scientific knowledge require understanding. Thus, for Aristotle, understanding is the fundamental habit without which neither science nor wisdom are possible, and the Renaissance Aristotelian tradition immediately recognized the importance and significance of this particular habit. Aristotle's conception of habits is crucial because it is the foundation of a preliminary theory of knowing subjectivity. Depending on how these habits develop, two or more subjects can know the same object differently.

In *Metaphysics* II.3, 995a15–30, Aristotle states that it is necessary to be trained in "how" (πος) every type of knowledge must be investigated, and it is absurd to simultaneously seek the knowledge and the method for obtaining it (τρόπος ἐπιστήμης). Τρόπος ἐπιστήμης is a central concept in Aristotle's philosophy of mind. Most of the time, τρόπος means manner or method, but also way, disposition or attitude, and in this specific case, it characterizes the relation between the knowing subject and the knowable object. For Aristotle, τρόπος ἐπιστήμης is the point of view, the perspective that one takes in knowing. For instance, unlike mathematics, material objects do not justify adopting a rigorous τρόπος ἐπιστήμης, because matter is accidental and no scientific knowledge (*scientia*) is possible of accidental things. Every subject matter requires a particular method or mode of knowing. This is particularly clear from Aristotle's example:

> [A] carpenter and a geometrician both try to find a right angle, but in different ways; the former is content with that approximation to it which satisfies the purpose of his work; the latter, being a student of truth, seeks to find its essence or essential attributes.[19]

Both carpenter and geometrician have the same matter of cognition, the right angle, but they investigate and consider it differently according to their different purposes. This shows that knowing subjects can adopt many different standpoints. And as Renaissance Aristotelians clearly recognized, these different standpoints depend on the various habits the knowing subjects have acquired.

As Charles Lohr (1999: 288) has rightly pointed out, the search for the intellectual habits was completely neglected by the Aristotelian tradition before the Italian Renaissance.[20] It was Jacopo Zabarella (1533–1589) who rediscovered their importance.[21] According to Zabarella, habit characterizes both logic as an instrumental discipline and the second nature of the mind. This twofold conception would become a constant in the development of facultative logic among early-modern Aristotelians, as well as in defining the other instrumental disciplines that deal with various habits of the mind (e.g., hexiology, gnostology and noology).

In his commentary to *Posterior Analytics*, Zabarella deals with the two main habits that logic presupposes, namely understanding and science. Understanding is the habit of the cognition of principles, while science is the habit of demonstration.[22] Zabarella states preliminarily that the habit of principles (that is the understanding), like all the other habits, is not innate, but supervenient on the inborn powers of the mind and is acquired by experience. The formation of the habit of principles is described following the above-mentioned passage in *Posterior Analytics* II.19. All knowledge comes from sensation, which is a kind of power of judgment that shows the differences among things. The method that proceeds from sensation to the acquisition of general concepts and principles is called induction.[23] Induction for Zabarella is clearly the means to acquire the habit of understanding, but it is not to be confused with the act of intellection. In fact, induction only makes general concepts and principles cognizable from experience, while intellection knows them in a clear and evident way. Induction is not a process for demonstrating or knowing something unknown from something already known as an intellection, but the "notification" of the thing through itself (*notificatio rei per se ipsam*). It presents sensible knowledge to the understanding and makes its intelligibility possible. Sensible knowledge is therefore prior to any other cognition, but it is not the only kind of knowledge; for Zabarella there is also intellectual knowledge, which is the only knowledge properly speaking.[24] Thus, from Zabarella's standpoint, there is no doubt that all our cognition begins with experience. In fact, our cognitive faculties are awakened by experience through the stimulation of the senses. Still, not all our cognitions arise from experience, since the understanding makes an essential contribution by grounding scientific knowledge, firstly by finding the first principles and secondly by formulating correct reasoning through demonstration. After many similar experiences the mind acquires the habit of principles, which makes it more prompt in acquiring future knowledge.

Zabarella develops his theory of habits of the understanding in particular in his *Liber de tribus praecognitis*, which specifically deals with the conditions under which the mind is able to acquire scientific knowledge. The object of knowledge is twofold according to Zabarella. The first, material part is the *res considerata* (the angle in the case of the carpenter-geometrician), while the second, formal part is the *modus considerandi* (the different ways of looking at the angle). Logic concerns the *modus considerandi*, because it is the only stable and invariable element of the object of knowledge, while the *res considerata* changes with every experience. For instance, we can see many different angles, but the ways in which we look at them are always the same if we are a carpenter or geometrician. It is worth noting that the *modus considerandi* does not only pertain to the object of knowledge. Being the mode of consideration of the *res considerata*, it also characterizes the precondition of the mind for knowing the object given by experience.[25] Logic, which deals with the *modi considerandi*, became for Zabarella an inquiry into the condition of the possibility of cognition in relation to a possible object in general. The condition of the possibility of cognizing an object characterizes what Zabarella calls precognition. Precognition is what determines our initial approach to knowledge, and it cannot be accidental, since otherwise all knowledge, and logic itself, would ultimately be accidental too. This precognition, which precedes the actual cognition of the object of knowledge, is ultimately constituted by the habit of the mind, in particular that of the understanding, which differentiates a geometrician from a carpenter in seeing an angle. Zabarella's facultative logic therefore aims to investigate the formation of the habit, focusing on its interplay with the natural powers of sensation, imagination and understanding.

In the process, he contributed to the rise of Renaissance facultative logic in at least two respects. On the one hand, he emphasized the importance of experience and thereby substantiated the view that all knowledge starts from sensation and proceeds from a form of induction for acquiring the epistemological habits of the mind, that is, for developing the cognitive faculties. On the other, he established that facultative logic should dig deeply into the condition of the possibility of knowing in relation to any possible object of knowledge, and thus engage in an inquiry into the cognitive faculties, their possibilities and their limits. This last aspect was particularly developed by German Protestant authors such as Alsted and Calov.

3 Hexiology, gnostology and noology

Zabarella's facultative logic enjoyed widespread success in the German territories. We can count more than a dozen authors who were working on facultative logic in the seventeenth century, names such as Clemens Timpler (1563–1624), Bartholomäus Keckermann (1571–1608), Johann Heinrich Alsted (1588–1638), Georg Gutke (1589–1634) and Abraham Calov (1612–1686).

The early reception of Zabarella is particularly evident in Alsted's *Philosophia digne restituta* (1612). Alsted's originality in the history of facultative logic lies in his awareness of the autonomy of the science of cognitive faculties and in his invention of a new science called hexiology (from the Greek: ἕξις, habit), which represents both the first systematic theory of habits and a rough draft of a facultative logic. Intellectual habits are defined by Alsted as what arranges the mind in such a way as to make cognition possible.[26] For every habit there is one and only one operation of the mind that corresponds to it. There are many kind of habits, but the most interesting for facultative logic are theoretical habits, "which are those inclined to assent to necessary things",[27] such as understanding, science and wisdom. Understanding is "a contemplative habit which is inclined to assent firmly and evidently to first principles",[28] or also "the habit of principles, that is the intellectual power of determining the assent to firm and self-evident principles".[29] Understanding is necessary because the natural light, "which is the intellectual power itself",[30] is not sufficient to convince us to assent to the first principles. Like Zabarella, Alsted therefore recognizes two kinds of understanding: natural and acquired. Natural understanding is characterized by the act of intellection, which knows intelligible species directly and intuitively, while acquired understanding, which is the real habit, is a kind of second nature that the mind attains through experience and is responsible for the formation and possession of universals, or general principles, rather than their cognition.

By contrast, science is the habit that "is inclined to assent to necessary conclusions knowing the proper causes".[31] The habit of science differs from that of understanding because it concerns true and evident conclusions based on principles. Unlike Aristotle, Alsted states that a science of singular things is possible.[32] According to Aristotle, as previously mentioned, science is only what is universal and necessary, and it is not possible to provide a demonstration of singular or accidental things. Yet, Protestant philosophers like Alsted and Timpler wanted to ensure the scientific character of reasoning and theological conclusions by extending the scientific validity of universal conclusions to individual, historical facts dependent on divine providence, in order to attest to the validity of Scripture.[33] For this reason Alsted supports the idea of the possibility of having scientific knowledge of non-being and of accidental things.[34] Wisdom, finally, is the habit that "is inclined to assent to necessary conclusions, according to first and higher causes".[35] Wisdom is the habit of metaphysics[36] and is also characterized as a "combined habit of understanding and science, that is, the habit of principles and conclusions".[37] Therefore, wisdom exceeds understanding and science in dignity, but it cannot exist without them.

The real rise of facultative logic in Protestant countries can be traced back specifically to the foundation of the new disciplines called "gnostology" and "noology" in the wake of Zabarella's and Alsted's ideas. The first important work on gnostology is Georg Gutke's, *Habitus primorum principiorum seu Intelligentia* (1625), which is based on Alsted's *Hexiologia*, but devoted solely to the "understanding", featuring a re-elaboration of Zabarellean logic. After Gutke, Valentin Fromme (1601–1679) published his *Gnostologia* (1631), which exerted a powerful influence in Northern Germany, especially on Abraham Calov.[38] Calov was the first to elaborate an organic system of sciences that introduced disciplines aimed at investigating the habit of mind, namely *gnostologia* and *noologia*.[39]

Like logic for Zabarella, gnostology for Calov is an instrumental discipline[40] that has to do with the habit of mind responsible for perfectly knowing an object.[41] This habit is something that supervenes on natural cognitive powers and is rooted firmly in the mind.[42] It differs from other habits in that it deals not with principles, like the habit of understanding, nor with necessary things, like science, nor with first causes, like wisdom, but with the simply cognizable.[43] In Calov's words, gnostology is a discipline that concerns the mental habit that deals with the cognizable *qua* cognizable,[44] and thus considers an object's mode of knowing in general. The object of this discipline is the cognizable (*cognoscibile*). Gnostology deals with the second nature of the mind as a habit aimed at improving knowledge according to mental natural powers.[45] Calov states that the cognizable differs from the intelligible, which is "all that is", and encompasses both the somewhat (*aliquid*) and the nothing (*nihil*).[46] He denies the possibility of having knowledge of the intelligible object, because this knowledge goes beyond the human faculties and belongs only to God; indeed, "it is rash to know natural things beyond nature".[47] Calov counts as knowledge only what can correspond to reality. For this reason he states that the cognizable always has a representational ground; it has objective reality,[48] while the intelligible does not:

> [T]he object is a real concept . . . an intelligible (*noema*) is in a broader sense an object, since every object that is is an intelligible, but not every intelligible is an object. In fact, all that can be understood by the understanding is an intelligible, but the object still requires another relation (*relatio*).[49]

For the intelligible to be cognizable it must have a relation to something else; for Calov this something else is an object of experience, that is, a representation in the mind. He draws a distinction between what is cognizable, i.e., representable, and what is thinkable. What is contradictory, he argues, is non-being, which is not, however, pure nothing. Non-being is in the realm of thought and intelligibility, but not in the realm of the cognizable. On the contrary, Calov considers being as the first object of cognition.[50] Quoting Zabarella, Calov says: "the object [of cognition] contains two parts: 1) the thing considered, or the material part; 2) the mode of considering, or the formal part".[51] The cognizable can be considered materially, if it concerns the being of the object itself, or formally, if it concerns the way in which object is considered in the mind. In the former case it represents the relation to the mind and, in a broader sense, the concept. In the latter case, it is what specifies the very general abstractions and transforms the being into the real "first cognizable" (*primum cognitum*).[52] The being as first cognizable is not a mere abstract concept but, as we have seen, always requires a representational ground, that is, an object (*objectum*) in front of the subject (*subjectum*). Calov is rehashing Zabarella's distinction between *res considerata* and *modus considerandi rem*, but what is striking is the significant terminological shift. While Zabarella spoke of a "subject" (*subjectum*) that "has two parts, one is material and is called matter; while the other is form and it is called mode of considering",[53] Calov dealt with an object (*objectum*) in two ways: in terms of subject matter and mode of considering, thus demonstrating a new kind of terminological and philosophical sensitivity. This seems like a mere terminological shift with no substantial theoretical consequences, but in fact it opens the way for the early-modern use of the conceptual pair object-subject, where the object is the thing known in external reality and the subject is the knowing mind. Calov adds that beings are material objects, while their form is the possibility of knowing them (*scibilitas*).[54] Form, Calov states, is a pure function of the mind (*pura mentis functio*),[55] which means that our mode of considering (*modus considerandi*) is a pure function of conceiving, knowing and signifying the matter from different standpoints (*res considerata*). It should be clear that from Calov's standpoint, being coincides with the cognizable so that the various transcendentals of being – that is, the properties beings have *qua* beings – must refer to being as a cognizable. That transcendentals of being refer to a cognizable, that is, to an object of cognition in general, is the radical novelty introduced by Calov, one that would allow the notion of "transcendental" to migrate from metaphysics to facultative logic. Transcendentals are very general concepts that define beings in general (including concepts like perfection, unity, truth, goodness, time, space, necessary-contingent, cause-effect, permanent-succeeding).[56] What is really remarkable in Calov is that a transcendental does not designate a mere being, but a cognizable, and thus characterizes all the essential attributes without which the cognizable would not be an object of cognition. Calov's transcendentals are attributes of an objective reality, of a thing represented in the mind. Even if it is true that a cognizable is always a cognizable for a mind, Calov's transcendentals do not pertain to the knower, as in Immanuel Kant, but to the known object. They are the condition of its possibility of being cognizable.

Calov builds his system of habits around the differences between cognizing (*cognoscere*), understanding (*intelligere*) and knowing (*scire*). *Cognoscere* means to have or to acquire a cognition; *intelligere* means to understand or conceive something directly; *scire* means to know scientifically or apodictically or discursively, by means of causes. These three operations of the mind correspond to three different objects. The cognizable, as we have already seen, always has a representational ground,[57] while the intelligible is directly understood and conceived in the mind, and does not necessarily refer to a real, existing object.[58] The knowable (*scibile* or *contemplabile*) is a particular kind of cognizable that our mind understands by means of the causes.[59] Unlike cognizing, knowing characterizes for Calov the contemplation of necessary being (*ens necessarium*).⁶⁰ The knowable as an object of the habit of science stands between the object of understanding and the object of wisdom. On the one hand, understanding is the habit of the first principles⁶¹ that provides the basis for demonstrating the knowable. On the other hand, however, wisdom is the habit of principles and conclusions⁶² and is not possible without science. Between understanding and wisdom there is another difference: "understanding is the simple and first habit, while wisdom is derived and composed".⁶³ Understanding is simple because it merely consists in assenting to the principles and it is first because it knows the first principles. Wisdom is derived in the sense that it assents to conclusions grounded in principles, and composite because it involves both principles and conclusions.⁶⁴ The science of the mental habit that leads the mind to acquire the first principles of knowledge (*principia cognoscendi*) and demonstration is noology.⁶⁵ Invoking Philip Melanchthon's distinction of the three operations of the mind, that is, simple apprehension, judgment and reasoning, based on the three Aristotelian objects of logic (i.e., concepts, propositions and syllogisms), Calov asserts that simple apprehension is studied by gnostology and concerns the way in which we know sensible and intelligible objects. Noology studies the second operation of the mind, which consists in the union of a predicate with a subject by means of a copula in order to formulate propositions. These propositions result in principles and axioms, which are the proper subject of noology. The *prima principia cognoscendi* are "the most common and known axioms, on which every our cognition, which from nature we can have, depends".⁶⁶ Calov's importance in the history of the philosophy of mind consists in the innovative way in which he embraced and reformulated Renaissance Aristotelianism. In the process, he constructed new disciplines that deal specifically with cognitive faculties and came to exert a powerful influence on Gottfried Wilhelm Leibniz, the German Enlightenment and critical philosophy.⁶⁷

4 British Aristotelians and the new philosophy of mind

The dissemination of Zabarella's works in the British Isles marked the definitive abandonment of humanistic logic⁶⁸ and triggered a new interest in facultative logic, which differs greatly from that developed in Germany in that it emphasizes the empirical process of knowledge. British philosophers at the end of the Renaissance showed great expertise in commenting on and interpreting Aristotelian texts by means of Zabarella's exegesis.⁶⁹ The most important Aristotelian scholar of the period was Griffith Powell (1561–1620). In his *Analysis analyticorum posteriorum sive librorum Aristotelis de Demonstratione* (1594), Powell focuses on particular aspects of Aristotelian facultative logic, highlighting its empiricist emphasis on the importance of sensation and induction as instruments of knowledge. According to Powell, all knowledge is knowledge of causes, by means of which the mind properly knows particulars. If science looks for causes and principles, these are not what is "most knowable by us", but what is "most knowable by nature". What is "most knowable by us", by contrast, is what comes from the senses, that is, sensations, which are always particular. The Aristotelian question is: How can we acquire knowledge of first principles and causes from sensations? According to Powell, there is no innate knowledge of first principles; rather, the mind acquires knowledge of them after a lengthy cognitive process which forms the habit of the understanding. After acquiring this habit the mind is able to grasp the principles immediately. Powell describes the workings of the mind as a process of transition from sensible to intelligible knowledge. He explicitly states that there is no knowledge prior to sensible knowledge, for it is only through the senses that we acquire knowledge. Sensation does not passively receive knowledge from experience, but functions as an active faculty in perceiving sensible things; it is a discriminative force. This activity is only possible for certain animals and it consists in the grasping of the sensible object from corporeal things. If enough sensible species rest in the memory, the memory enables the mind to form general concepts. What is important for Powell is that the memory of experience is possible only through sensation, and it is only through experience that general concepts rest in the mind. For Powell, therefore, the entire cognitive process is based on sensation.[70] This process, which operates in the mind together with sensation and understanding, is a kind of induction,[71] and it is the only way of knowing the first universal principles and causes by means of the understanding or *habitus principiorum*.[72] Powell's commentary refers explicitly to Zabarella's ideas, but simplifies them by considering sensation as the central issue of the doctrine of the method for discovering and acquiring scientific knowledge. Powell's work thus represents a first step towards an empirical epistemology.

The influence of Paduan Aristotelianism in general and Zabarella's facultative logic in particular lasted at least until the mid-seventeenth century, as is evident from John Flavell's (1596–1617) *Tractatus de demonstratione methodicus et polemicus* (1619). The popularity of this textbook was so great that it "hath been taken into the hands of all juniors", such as, for instance, Thomas Hobbes and John Locke.[73] Flavell's facultative logic starts from a strong criticism of the doctrine of innatism. Against the Platonists, Flavell argues that there are no innate ideas or principles in the mind, but that all knowledge comes from sensation, so that the mind continuously acquires new knowledge, leading to the acquisition of the habits of science and of principles. Sensation is therefore the first instrument of scientific knowledge.[74] Without sensation and sensible knowledge, science would be impossible for three reasons. First, all scientific knowledge comes from the conclusions of demonstrations, which depend on the cognition of principles, grounded in turn on induction from sensation. Therefore, no conclusions would be possible without sensible knowledge from sensation. Second, all intellectual knowledge, as Aristotle says, comes from previous knowledge, which itself cannot be intellectual knowledge, as otherwise a vicious circle would result. The knowledge which precedes intellectual knowledge is sensible knowledge. And third, according to Flavell, there is nothing in the intellect that was not first in the senses, and so all intellectual knowledge comes from sensation.[75] Flavell explicitly establishes that without sensation, science would be impossible because

1) intellectual knowledge needs the confirmation of the senses; 2) the mind cannot judge things such as colours, odours and so on without the senses; and 3) the intellectual object, being the result of a process of reflection and induction, always comes from the senses.[76] Sensation provides the matter of knowledge (*res considerata*) through induction, which is the process of the formation of universal concepts and principles by which the mind reasons. All arts and sciences are thus based on experience and induction, from which the mind, after many observations, generates the first principles.[77] Flavell adds that induction cannot directly infer a general conclusion from a singular observation, because the mind gives its assent to principles and universal concepts only after many observations and experiments.[78] In Flavell's facultative logic, observation and experiment became central ways of acquiring scientific knowledge. Principles are conclusions of intellectual knowledge. Flavell emphasizes that the knowledge of principles cannot be reduced to a mere apprehension from experience, as one might expect, but always involves experiments and judgments to test its correctness.[79] Like Zabarella, Flavell views induction not as a process proceeding from the unknown to the known, for in itself induction is not properly a process for discovering new knowledge, but a process that transmits to the intellect the universal aspect of what is apprehended by sensation, which would otherwise be obscure and unknown.[80] Induction, however, plays an essential and ancillary role in the scientific method, which both Flavell and Zabarella view as a regressive, two-step method consisting of an (inductive) inference from an observed effect to its cause, and a subsequent inference from the cause to the effect.[81] As Charles B. Schmitt has observed in Powell and Flavell, a radical change occurred in the field of logic, a shift away from humanistic dialectic towards facultative logic, a "cognitive turn", in other words, which lies at the foundation of British empiricism.[82] Flavell's discussion was more systematic than Powell's and more concerned with the epistemological issues of empiricism, giving an overview of important logical topics that would dominate the debates in the following three or four decades in the British Isles, such as the problem of innatism, the origin of sensation, the role of observations and experiments and the systematization of knowledge.

The most important and influential book on facultative logic in England at the end of the Renaissance, however, was Robert Sanderson's *Logicae artis compendium* (1615). Sanderson's handbook on logic has been said to look "like an excessively psychologistic way to define the subject",[83] namely facultative logic in England. Recalling Zabarella's definition,[84] Sanderson defines logic as an instrumental art that directs the mind in knowing things. He rejects the idea that "logic or dialectic is the theory of disputing".[85] There are three parts of logic, following the tripartition of mental operations leading to scientific knowledge. The first part deals with the apprehension of concepts, the second with the formation of judgments, while the third deals with reasoning and method.[86] The most original part of Sanderson's logic is the third, in which he also introduces new elements in an attempt to elaborate a new theory of knowledge. New knowledge is not discovered through demonstration or the regressive method, which are useful only in verifying the scientific nature of knowledge, but is characterized by a fourfold process culminating in induction. The primary and fundamental means of acquiring new knowledge is sensation, through which the mind comes to know various, singular things. The second means of invention is diligent observation, or *historia*, which connects the various sensible particulars in the mind. The third means is experience, which collects and classifies the various observations and conserves them in such a way that they can be applied to future knowledge. The fourth means is induction, which infers universal conclusions from the abundant collection of experience.[87] For Sanderson induction is a particular kind of argumentation that proceeds from a sufficient enumeration of the particular cases to the formation of universals. It can be of three kinds: 1) perspicuous, clear and distinct, if all enumerated cases are considered; 2) implicit, if only some cases are considered and others assumed to be the same; or 3) not perspicuous, when from only one example it infers a general conclusion.[88] Sanderson particularly emphasizes the extreme utility of induction for discovering first principles and universals of the causes and of all other universal things to be proved: universal principles, causes and truths that constitute the edifice of science. But he also recognizes the intrinsic weakness of induction, in that a single exception or counterexample can overturn its universal conclusions.[89] Exceptions and particular cases must necessarily be considered because they can refute the conclusions, and so must not expunged from the theory. Sanderson thus pays particular attention to the empirical aspect of knowledge, more than any other logician of his time. His account of knowledge, although inspired by Zabarella's conception of induction, shifts radically towards empiricism, focusing on the cognitive process of knowing particulars more than the Stagirite himself ever dared to.

Sanderson's facultative logic represents a decisive step toward an empirical philosophy of mind in which the investigation of syllogism has given way to the examination of the cognitive process of knowledge formation based on sensation and induction. It is hard to overstate the importance of Sanderson's epistemology, since all subsequent logicians considered and discussed his approach. If we consider that his *Compendium* was the standard textbook in British universities, we can understand the wide circulation of his empirical ideas and their impact on several generations of thinkers, who came to conceive facultative logic as an instrument of science in which knowledge was based primarily on experience.

Perhaps the most interesting text of facultative logic is Zachary Coke's *The Art of Logick* (1654).[90] Coke's textbook is heavily indebted to Christopher Airay's *Fasciculus* and Bartholomaeus Keckermann's *Systema systematum*.[91] There is no doubt that Coke's logic was the most complete handbook on facultative logic written in English prior to Locke's *Essay*. Coke's work clearly shows how Aristotelian logic increasingly shifted its focus from a mere consideration of syllogism to a careful examination of the intellect and its functions with respect to the objects of experience. There are three specific elements at the base of Coke's facultative logic: 1) the object of knowledge, defined as all those things present in nature;

2) an innate faculty of the mind, which is the intellect; and 3) a particular disposition through which the intellect is ordered in its operation and which can be either immediate or acquired by knowledge.[92] The order and right arrangement of the intellect depends on logic, which is a directive discipline, that is, one that prepares and structures the operations of the mind and reason in the cognition of things.[93] The mental operations required for cognition are: 1) the understanding and the thoughts of things and 2) the signification of these thoughts. Only logic, among directive disciplines, can correctly direct these two operations.[94] Facultative logic is thus primarily the art of directing the mind in its knowledge, secondarily the art of teaching ways of thinking clearly and judging things distinctly and finally a corrective method for the mind's errors. By directing the thoughts and operations of the mind in knowing things, logic reveals itself to be a true τρόπος ἐπισήμης, to repeat the Aristotelian formula.[95]

More particularly, logic guides our thoughts about everything conceivable according to a rule, in such a way that the mind draws correct conclusions by means of an ordered process and avoids any kind of confusion.[96] Logic plays an important role because the mind, being a natural faculty that consists in bodily humours and temperaments, may be ill-disposed to cognition.[97] Logic can be a corrective of the mind, and for this reason it is important to know the faculties of the mind preliminarily by its properties.[98]

Within this framework Coke devotes a long section to the exposition of epistemological doctrines, the limits of the understanding and the use of logic as a corrective instrument for mental errors. For Coke, the fundamental feature of the mind is that sensible objects are the most knowable to us and only subsequently does the intellect acquire intellectual knowledge. Therefore, all knowledge begins from experience. The second feature is that the intellect cannot understand the specific nature of things in a distinct and ordered way, therefore, to discover the truth, artificial rules are required. Third, the intellect is directed toward thinking about universals, while sensation concerns particulars; this implies the necessity of mediating between these two kinds of knowledge. Fourth, according to Coke, at any given time the intellect is occupied with the thought of only one thing, and this thought, amid a flux of other thoughts, is determined by a temporal order within the mind. Fifth, the object of knowledge must be proportionate to the finite capacities of the mind and to the limit of the intellect. For instance, the infinity of God cannot be comprehended by a finite intellect by means of logic. Coke points out, furthermore, that the intellect can assent to conclusions which are not demonstrated in a necessary way, as with induction, for example. Finally, the instruments of mental operations must be pure, that is, the intellect should not be pathologically affected.[99] This is because logic should help us to prevent possible errors and defects of the intellect. There are three defects of the mind in the realm of epistemology. The first is aberration in the apprehension of things, which means that the mind grasps things incorrectly. The second is obscurity in the nature of things and difficulty in distinguishing their marks and properties. The third is negligence and confusion in the apprehension of things, which means that the mind grasps things correctly but confusedly. Logic provides a cure for all these defects by explaining, testing, ordering and arranging things.[100]

It is important to note, however, that logic is not only "cathartic", according to Coke, that is, its role is not simply to prevent or correct possible errors of the mind. It also focuses on the interplay among the various workings of the mind, in particular on thinking, which is the understanding, insofar as it deals with things in the world.[101] These can be of three kinds. Some are infinite, such as God, and no logical instrument is sufficient to understand them. Others are finite and created. Of these, some are spiritual, imperceptible and understood only with great effort; others are corporeal and known properly by the understanding. This last class is the proper subject of facultative logic.[102]

Coke narrows the field of facultative logic, and therefore of knowledge, to corporeal and physical things alone and defines the limits and boundaries of human understanding. All that goes beyond experience and sensible knowledge is the object of either divine revelation or a confused understanding; distinct knowledge and the correct use of the intellect rely only on sensory experience. The intellect, however, does not act directly on sensible knowledge of particulars, but rather on their conceptual abstractions.[103] The first means by which facultative logic acquires new knowledge is through the senses. The second means is observation, which presupposes the use of the senses; observation, in Coke's definition, is a reflection of the data obtained by the senses. The third means is experience, that is, the collecting of the observations and examples retained in the memory. The final means is induction, the real inventive instrument, which, from the judgment of the senses and from the experience of observations, generates a common universal notion on which the logical instrument can operate.[104] For Coke facultative logic is defined not only by the process of acquiring knowledge, but also by the material on which it operates. This material is twofold: primary and representative or secondary. The latter consists of logical terms, or words, which represent concepts, also called *secundae notiones*. *Primae notiones*, meanwhile, are our concepts of things as they are. *Secundae notiones* do not refer directly to things themselves, but rather to intellectual rules by which the mind can deal distinctly and regularly with things. For Coke, as for Zabarella, *primae notiones*, even if they are concepts, directly concern things as they are. Thus, Coke writes, when someone imposes names, they aim first of all to name the things themselves and only afterwards other concepts. For instance, the word "man" primarily expresses the concept of human nature, and as such it is a *prima notio* or *intentio*, but when we consider the word "man" as a species, or a kind, it becomes a *secunda notio*, which is not derived immediately from the things that constitute human nature, but rather from the intellect's way of conceiving "man".[105] Perhaps the most interesting part of Coke's facultative logic is his idea of method, which brings Zabarella's philosophy of mind very close to that of Locke. Like Zabarella, Coke recognizes two methods: the compositive (synthetic) and resolutive (analytic) method. The compositive method proceeds from the universal to the particular, from the simple to the compound, while the resolutive method proceeds from the effect to the cause, from the compound to the simple.[106] Resolution, Coke adds, is feasible and effective only if we know the process by which the compound was constructed. In other words, only if the mind knows how a thing is constructed can it resolve that thing into its correct parts. Thus, every analytic process begins with the knowledge of a thing to be analyzed, of the thing's construction.[107] This "constructivist" perspective, which is shared by Thomas Hobbes, leads to the corollary, that we cannot know the essence or substance of natural things, because they are not generated by the human mind. By means of resolution it is possible to know only certain qualities of a thing, but not what it truly is. Knowledge of the thing, therefore, depends on the mind's capacity to resolve the object of knowledge into simple and elementary concepts, which usually coincide with what is apprehended by the senses. Coke therefore reaches the Aristotelian conclusion that facultative logic does not deal with things in themselves, but with the elements that make knowledge of things possible. Even if there is an isomorphism between things and *primae notiones*, from a cognitive standpoint, it is impossible to know the essence of things since they are not generated by the mind. Scientific knowledge only concerns mathematical and geometrical truths; in physical matter the mind can acquire scientific knowledge only if the observed effect or "fact" can be reproduced from the causes. In this sense, Coke's facultative logic could only lead to an empirical and experimental approach in which controlled experiments determine the cause of a given effect, a cause which would have remained unknown by analysis alone. In conclusion, Coke represents a move towards a more complex philosophy of mind through the original development of certain suggestions inherent in the facultative logic that English Aristotelianism had originally inherited from Zabarella. He presages issues and problems that are typical of the philosophy of mind of John Locke, Richard Burthogge and David Hume.[108]

5 Conclusion

A melting pot of philosophies and philosophical trends, almost all of which were destined to disappear in the following century, the Renaissance was without doubt a controversial age. It has often been said that early-modern philosophy arose in opposition to the philosophy of the Renaissance, to Aristotelianism in particular, which is thought to represent a conservative and static kind of thought that was incapable of responding to the needs of the modern world. Historiography loves clear-cut contrasts and grand oppositions and generally shuns the various shades of grey. Moments of rupture and contradiction are easier to handle than continuity and periods of hardly perceptible transformation, yet it is not always possible to accurately capture the movement of a thought through history. The cases I have mentioned here, albeit briefly, show that Aristotelianism did not vanish with the advent of modern philosophy, but was in fact receptive to new developments and problems, and this allowed it to be changed and transformed from within. Internal changes within Aristotelianism were varied because the stimuli that the Aristotelians received were different. In Germany, three new disciplines – hexiology, gnostology and noology – emerged within Aristotelianism. In themselves they were instrumental habits for the other sciences, but most of all they dealt with the habits that the mind acquires over time in the exercise of its cognitive faculties. The peculiar aspect of the German thinkers of this period is their insightful investigation of the condition of the possibility of knowledge, an investigation based on examining the formation and use of these habits of the mind. Their works make it possible to identify different objects of knowledge according to the various ways of knowing and to engage in a preliminary and a priori critique of the boundaries of the mind's faculties. In England, on the other hand, a peculiar Aristotelianism emerged that focused on the problem of sensible knowledge and the empirical approach. It is no coincidence, therefore, that this movement led to British empiricism. Both philosophical movements, in Germany and in England, represent a decisive cognitive turn of Aristotelian logic in favour of the construction of a new philosophy of mind.

With its investigation of the workings of the mind, Renaissance Aristotelianism therefore represents an important starting point, a *palaestra rationis* for the facultative logic of the next two centuries: a movement that demands reassessment in the overall history of the philosophy of mind.

Notes

1. Cf. Falkenstein & Easton (1997: 1).
2. Buickerood (1985: 163).
3. So the lamentable lack of knowledge of the history of philosophy even extends beyond the years 1300 to 1600, as Schmid has mentioned in the introduction to this volume.
4. For a prehistory of the concept of δύναμις, Cf. von Staden 1999.
5. Cf. Plato, *Republic*, 477 D7–E3.
6. Plato, *Republic*, 477 C1. Cf. Smith 2000.
7. See Chapter 3 of this volume.
8. Aristotle, *DA*, II.5, 417 b 242–245.
9. Aristotle, *PostAn*, II.19, 99b35.
10. Cf. Aristotle, *Cat.*, I.8, 8b27–29.
11. Cf. *Cat.* I.8, 9a1–4.
12. Cf. Aristotle, *Rhet*. I.10, 1369b6.
13. *Rhet*. I.11, 1370a4–7.
14. Cf. Aristotle, *NE* VI.3, 1139b16–17.
15. Cf. *NE* VI.3, 1139b20–21.
16. Cf. *NE* VI.3, 1139b33–34.
17. Cf. *NE* VI.6, 1141a6–8.
18. Cf. Aristotle, *NE* VI.7, 1141b1–2, and 1141a18–20.
19. Aristotle, *NE* I.7, 1098a25–35. Cf. Pozzo 1998.
20. Cf. Lohr (1999: 288).
21. Cf. Sgarbi 2012a; Sgarbi 2013.
22. Cf. Zabarella, *OL*, 1262f.
23. *OL*, 1266c.
24. *OL*, 1282f – 1283a.
25. Cf. *OL*, 502e. Cf. Pozzo (1998: 157–158).
26. Cf. Alsted, *PDR*, 254.

27 *PDR*, 260.
28 *PDR*, 260.
29 *PDR*, 261.
30 *PDR*, 261.
31 *PDR*, 268.
32 *PDR*, 274.
33 Cf. Lohr (1999: 292).
34 *PDR*, 274.
35 *PDR*, 277.
36 Cf. *PDR*, 277.
37 *PDR*, 278.
38 Cf. Wundt (1945: 242–257).
39 Cf. Wundt (1939: 242–254); Sparn (2001: 582–585).
40 Cf. Calov, *MD*, 1.
41 Cf. *MD*, 1.
42 Cf. *MD*, 1–2. In the *Gnostologia*, Calov defines the habit as "firm quality rooted in the mind for the perfection of the cognition of the object". Cf. *MD*, 29.
43 Cf. *MD*, 2.
44 *MD*, 1.
45 *MD*, 1.
46 Cf. Timpler, *MSM*, 38.
47 Calov, *SP*, 10.
48 *SP*, 10.
49 *MD*, 25.
50 Cf. *MD*, 183.
51 *MD*, 26.
52 Cf. *MD*, 183.
53 *OL*, 502e. On this shift cf. Pozzo 2003; Pozzo 2004; Pozzo 2012.
54 *MD*, 28.
55 *MD*, 28–29.
56 Cf. *SP*, 198.
57 *MD*, 10.
58 *MD*, 10.
59 *MD*, 47–48.
60 Cf. *MD*, 48.
61 *MD*, 51.
62 *MD*, 51.
63 *MD*, 54–55.
64 Cf. *MD*, 55.
65 *MD*, 38.
66 *MD*, 38.
67 Cf. Sgarbi 2010.
68 Cf. Jardine 1988.
69 Cf. Sgarbi 2013.
70 Cf. Powell, *APP*, 338–339.
71 Cf. *APP*, 340.
72 Cf. *APP*, 340.
73 Wood (1817, vol. 2: 207).
74 Cf. Flavell, *TDMP*, b. 2, 107–108.
75 Cf. *TDMP*, 108–109.
76 Cf. *TDMP*, 109.
77 Cf. *TDMP*, 48.

78 Cf. *TDMP*, 48–49.
79 Cf. *TDMP*, 49.
80 Cf. *TDMP*, 51.
81 On regress cf. Jardine (1988: 686–693).
82 Cf. Schmitt (1983: 36).
83 Trentman (1976: 192).
84 Cf. Sanderson, *LAC*, 1.
85 Howell 1961, 304.
86 Cf. *LAC*, 2–3.
87 Cf. *LAC*, 226–227.
88 Cf. *LAC*, 151.
89 Cf. *LAC*, 152.
90 Some have raised doubts about the authorship of the work by attributing it to the theologian Henry Ainsworth (1569–1622). Cf. Measell 1977; Measell 1978.
91 On Keckermann's influence on Coke, cf. (Serjeantson 1999: 207).
92 Cf. Coke, *AL*, 1.
93 Cf. *AL*, 2.
94 Cf. *AL*, 2–3.
95 Cf. *AL*, 3.
96 Cf. *AL*, 8.
97 Cf. *AL*, 8.
98 Cf. *AL*, 4.
99 Cf. *AL*, 5. Cf. Keckermann, *SS*, 67.
100 Cf. *AL*, 5. Cf. *SS*, 68.
101 Cf. *AL*, 3.
102 Cf. *AL*, 6–7.
103 See page XXX below for a characterization of this distinction.
104 Cf. *AL*, 6–7.
105 Cf. *AL*, 11–12.
106 Cf. *AL*, 187.
107 Cf. *AL*, 217.
108 Cf. Ayers 2005; Sgarbi 2012b.

Bibliography

Primary sources

Alsted, Johann Heinrich. *Philosophia digne restituta* (= *PDR*). Herborn: Corvinus, 1612.
Aristotle, *Complete Works*, 2 vols. J. Barnes (ed.). Princeton: Princeton University Press, 1984.
———. *Categories* (= Cat.). See *Complete Works*, vol. 1.
———. *Posterior Analytics* (= *PostAn*). See *Complete Works*, vol. 1.
———. *Nicomachean Ethics* (= *NE*). See *Complete Works*, vol. 2.
———. *Rhetoric* (= *Rhet*.). See *Complete Works*, vol. 2.
———. *On the Soul* (= *DA*). See *Complete Works*, vol. 1.
Calov, Abraham. *Metaphysica divina* (= *MD*). Rostock: Hallervord, 1640.
———. *Scripta philosophica* (= *SP*). Lübeck: Wilden, 1651.
Coke, Zachary. *The Art of Logick or the Entire Body of Logick in English* (= *AL*). London: White, 1654.

Flavell, John. *Tractatus de demonstratione methodicus et polemicus* (= *TDMP*). Oxford: Lichfield-Short, 1619.
Keckermann, Bartholomäus. *Systema Systematum* (= *SS*). Hanau: Heirs of Wilhelm Antonius, 1613.
Powell, Griffin. *Analysis analyticorum posteriorum* (= *AAP*). Oxford: Barnes, 1595.
Sanderson, Robert. *Logicae artis compendium* (= *LAC*). Oxford: Barnes, 1615.
Timpler, Clemens. *Metaphysicae systema methodicum* (= *MSM*). Marburg: Ketzel, 1607.
Zabarella, Jacopo. *Opera logica* (= *OL*). Köln: Zetzner, 1597.

Secondary sources

Auroux, S. 1993. *La logique des idées*. Montréal: Bellarmin.
Ayers, M. R. 2005. "Richard Burthogge and the Origins of Modern Conceptualism". In *Analytic Philosophy and History of Philosophy*, T. Sorell & G. A. J. Rogers (eds), 179–200. Oxford: Oxford University Press.
Buickerood, J. 1985. "The Natural History of the Understanding: Locke and the Rise of Facultative Logic in the Eighteenth Century". *History and Philosophy of Logic* **6**: 157–190.
Falkenstein, L. & Easton, P. 1997. "Preface". In *Logic and the Workings of Mind: The Logic of Ideas and Faculty Psychology in Early Modern Philosophy*, Lorne Falkenstein & Patricia Easton (eds), I–III. Atascadero, CA: Ridgeview.
Jardine, N. 1988. "Epistemology of the Sciences". In *The Cambridge History of Renaissance Philosophy*, Q. Skinner & Ch. B. Schmitt (eds), 685–711. Cambridge: Cambridge University Press.
Howell, W. S. 1961. *Logic and Rhetoric in England 1500–1700*. New York: Russell.
Lohr, Ch. 1999. "Metaphysics and Natural Philosophy as Sciences: The Catholic and Protestant Views in the Sixteenth and Seventeenth Centuries". In *Philosophy in the Sixteenth and Seventeenth Centuries*, C. Blackwell & S. Kusukawa (eds), 280–295. Aldershot: Ashgate.
Measell, J. S. 1977. "The Authorship of the Art of Logick (1654)". *Journal of the History of Philosophy* **15**: 321–324.
———. 1978. "Variant Title-Pages in the Art of Logick (1654)". *The Library* **33**: 157–162.
Michael, F. S. 1997. "Why Logic Became Epistemology: Gassendi, Port Royal and the Reformation in Logic". In *Logic and the Workings of Mind: The Logic of Ideas and Faculty Psychology in Early Modern Philosophy*, L. Falkenstein & P. Easton (eds), 1–20. Atascadero: Ridgeview.
Pozzo, R. 1998. "Res considerata and modus considerandi rem: Averroes, Aquinas, Jacopo Zabarella and Cornelius Martini on Reduplication". *Medioevo* **24**: 151–176.
———. 2003. "Ramus and other Renaissance Philosophers on Subjectivity". *Topoi* **22**: 5–13.
———. 2004. "Logic and Metaphysics in German Philosophy From Melanchthon to Hegel". *Approaches to Metaphysics*, W. Sweet (ed.), 61–74. Dordrecht, The Netherlands: Springer.
———. 2012. *Adversus Ramistas. Kontroversen über die Natur der Logik am Ende der Renaissance*. Basel: Schwabe.
Schmitt, Ch. B. 1983. *John Case and Aristotelianism in Renaissance England*. Kingston-Montreal: McGill.

Schuurmann, P. 2004. *Ideas, Mental Faculties and Method: The Logic of Ideas of Descartes and Locke and its reception the Dutch Republic, 1630–1750*. Leiden: Brill.
Serjeantson, R. W. 1999. "Testimony and Proof in Early-Modern England". *Studies in History and Philosophy of Science* **30**: 195–236.
Sgarbi, M. 2010. "Abraham Calov and Immanuel Kant: Aristotelian and Scholastic Traces in Kantian Philosophy". *Historia Philosophica* **8**: 55–62.
———. 2012a. "Towards a Reassessment of British Aristotelianism". *Vivarium* **50**: 85–109.
———. 2012b. "Hume's Source of the 'Impression-Idea' Distinction". *Anales del Seminario de Historia de la Filosofía* **2**: 561–576.
———. 2013. *The Aristotelian Tradition and the Rise of British Empiricism: Logic and Epistemology in the British Isles (1570–1689)*. Dordrecht, The Netherlands: Springer.
Smith, N. 2000. "Plato on Knowledge as a Power". *Journal of the History of Philosophy* **38**: 145–168.
Sparn, W. 2001. "Die Schulphilosophie in den lutherischen Territorien". In *Grundriss der Geschichte der Philosophie: Die Philosophie des 17. Jahrhunderts. Band 4, Das Heilige Römische Reich Deutscher Nation. Nord- und Ost Europa*, H. Holzhey & W. Schmidt-Biggemann (eds), 475–606. Basel: Schwabe.
Trentman, J. A. 1976. "The Study of Logic and Language in England in the Early 17th Century". *Historiographia linguistica* **3**: 179–201.
von Staden, H. 1999. "Dynamis: The Hippocratics and Plato". In *Philosophy and Medicine 29: Studies in Greek Philosophy*, J. Boudouris Konstantinos (ed), 262–279. Athens: International Association for Greek Philosophy.
Wood, A. à. 1817. *Athenae Oxonienses an Exact History of All the Writers and Bishops Who Have Had Their Education in the University of Oxford*. Oxford: Oxford University Press.
Wundt, M. 1939. *Die deutsche Schulmetaphysik des 17. Jahrhunderts*. Tübingen: Mohr Siebeck.
———. 1945. *Die deutsche Schulphilosophie im Zeitalter der Aufklärung*. Tübingen: Mohr Siebeck.

INDEX

abstention, method of 37
abstract thought: Aquinas on 210–211; Telesio on 222
abstractive cognition 105–106, 108–109, 131
Achillini, Alessandro 111, 232
active intellect 230
activity 42
affective magic 200
agent-causation 145, 160n3
agent intellect 168
agent sense: Aristotle on 166; Averroes on 168; Jandun on 166, 169–171; Nifo on 171; Suárez on 174, 178
Airay, Christopher 282
Albert the Great 104
Albertus Magnus 83, 86
Alexander, of Aphrodisias: on *De Anima* 10; doctrine of the soul of 10–11, 90, 111, 218, 230, 240; influence of 112–115, 117, 218, 230; on the intellect 230
Alsted, Johann Heinrich 271, 275–276
Analysis analyticorum posteriorum sive librorum Aristotelis de Demonstratione (Powell) 279
animals: faculties of 50; genetic argument 188; natural soul of 75; nature and 46; unconscious and 47, 52, 58–59
anti-naturalism 104
anti-scholasticism 2, 7–9
Apostolici regiminis 235–236, 239
appetites: concupiscible 48, 250, 255; irascible 48, 250, 255; moderation of 250; rational soul and 146; sensitive 66, 211, 252–255, 261
appetitive faculty 76
Aquinas, Thomas: abstract thought and 210–211; on Averroism 83–85; dualism and 208; on intellect 5, 84–86; on intentionality 102–104; on passions 250–252; on perception 210; Pomponazzi on 237–239; on sensation 211; on the soul 6, 64–66, 73, 209, 230; on species 103–104; on the will xii
archei 52, 56
Arendt, Hannah x, xii
Aristotelianism: British 271, 279–286; Christianity and 104, 116, 146–147, 240; critiques of 152, 234; facultative logic in 270–276, 279–285; hylomorphism and 4–7, 14; intentionality and 102, 104; metaphysical framework of 208; method and 22; mind-body problem and 208–209, 218; moral action and 251, 254; passions and 254–255; philosophy of mind and 3; scholasticism and 1–2, 8–9, 113, 118; soul and 34, 208–209; on soul's powers 64; on universals 105
Aristotle: Averroes on 83; on capacities 4; common sense and 54; on facultative logic 271–274; on the individuation of thought 88; on the intellect 230; on intellectual habits 273–274; on knowledge 272–274, 280; mind and 54; moral virtue and 250; Plato and 218, 233; receptivism and 167, 171; on

291

INDEX

sensation 166–168, 272; on the soul 4–5, 7, 10, 25, 47–49, 63–64, 76, 84, 209, 271; university study of 10, 24; on virtues 251, 254, 256–257, 261; *see also De Anima* (Aristotle)

Aristotle. Works: *Categories* 65, 273; *De Anima* 5, 10, 24, 63, 83, 111, 166–167, 170, 208, 230–231, 240; *Metaphysics* 273; *Nicomachean Ethics* 9–10, 150, 273; *Posterior Analytics* 272–274; *Rhetoric* 273; *Topics* 65

Art of Logick, The (Coke) 282

astral determinism 144, 147

astrology 199

attention 126, 132–137, 138n14, 139n35, 139n36

attentive soul 175

Augustine, Saint 64, 125

Augustinianism: intentionality and 104, 109; mind-body problem and 216; psychology and 104, 108, 114, 116

Aureolus, Petrus 105, 108, 261–262

Averroes: Alexander on 10; on Aristotle 83; Catholic doctrine and 89; Ficino on 13–14, 235; influence of 231–232; on intellectual cognition 111; on material intellect 231; mind-body problem and 218; noetics of 83–85, 88, 90–91; Pietro on 50; plurality of the soul 243n45; Pomponazzi on 237; on sensation 168–169; on the supra-individual intellect 5, 11, 15, 84, 88; on unicity of the intellect 89, 239

Averroism: Aquinas on 83–85; critiques of 83–85, 95; defining 83; form and 95; intellectual representations and 111; Jandun on 90; sensation and 166–167; supra-individual intellect and 110

Avicenna 53–54, 234, 242n34

Bacon, Francis 201, 221, 241

Bañez, Domingo 157

Barozzi, Pietro 232

being 188

Berkeley, George xiv, xv

Biel, Gabriel 157

black bile 196, 258

Blasius of Parma 230–231

body: accidental dispositions of 79n24; form and 93–94; intellect and 86–87; knowledge and 47, 50, 55, 57–59; love and 189–190; sensitive powers and 67–68

Boethius 153, 231

Bonaventure 83

Boudon-Millot, Véronique 43

British Aristotelianism 271, 279–286

Brower, Jeffrey 207

Bruno, Giordano 185–186

Buickerood, James 270

Burckhardt, Jacob 2

Buridan, John: on Alexander's theory of the soul 230; direct signification 25; dualism and 207; on instrumental powers 71–72; on the intellective soul 71–72; as intellectualist 151–152; metaphysics and 28; method and 22; mind-body problem and 213–215; on perception 213–215; on principal powers 71–72; reductionist strategy of 26–27; on sensation 214; on the soul 38n23; on study of the soul 24–27, 36; on voluntary agents 150–151; on the will 151–152

Burthogge, Richard 285

Burton, Robert 55

Cajetan 173, 175, 236

Calov, Abraham 271, 275–279

Calvin, John 156–157

Campanella, Tommaso: on delusions 57; influences on 196; on magic 196, 198–200; on nature 196–197; on passions 186, 199–200; on sensation 197, 201, 223; on the spirit 197–198, 200, 241; vitalistic approach 223

Cardano, Girolamo 43, 51–52

Cartesian dualism: mechanistic philosophy of 208, 224; mind-body problem and xvi, 207, 223

Castellani, Giulio 113

Categories (Aristotle) 65, 273

Catholic doctrine: *De auxiliis* controversy 157; free will and 157; on human intellect 89

INDEX

causality/causation: agent-causation and 145, 160n3; efficient 158; event 160n3; final 158; intentionality and 108; mutual 158
causal relations 29, 31
Champier, Symphorien 44
Chatton, Walter: on abstractive cognition 131; on attention 133–134; "mineness" of acts 132–134; on propositional self-awareness 126, 131–134
Christianity: Aristotelianism and 104, 116, 146–147, 240; Condemnation of 1277 147–148, 152; free will and 156–157; love in 264; pagan philosophy and 240; passion and morality in 250
cognitive faculties 101–103, 275–279
cognitive receptivism 171
"cognitive turn" 270, 281, 286
Coke, Zachary 282–285
Commentaria in De anima Aristotelis (Cajetan) 236
Commentaria in Primam Parte Summae Theologiae (Cajetan) 236
Commentaria una cum quaestionibus in libros Aristotelis De anima (Suárez) 166
Commentarium magnum in Aristotelis De anima (Averroes) 168
common sense 54
compatibilism 153–154, 157, 160n2
concepts 110
Conciliator differentiarum (Pietro d'Abano) 43, 47
concupiscible appetites 48, 250, 255
Condemnation of 1277 147–148, 152
Connection of the Virtues, On the (Ockham) 252
consciousness: acts and objects of 129–130; late medieval theories of 125, 137n2; mind-body problem and 209–210; *see also* self-consciousness
conscious/unconscious mind: medical philosophy of 45–48, 50, 52, 58; plant life and 58–59
Consolation of Philosophy, The (Boethius) 153
Constantine the African 55
constructivism 285
Contarini, Gasparo 231

Contradicentia medica (Cardano) 43
Conway, Anne 201
cosmic spirit 190–191
cosmology: human mind and 185; love and 188; Neoplatonism and 11, 28–29, 179, 217–218; Platonist 11–14
cosmos: Ficino on 13–14, 188–189; hierarchical stages of 188; human mind and 185–186; love and 189; Paracelsus on 52; sensation and 201; Telesio on 201
Crescas, Ḥasdai: as compatibilist 153–154; critique of Aristotelianism 152; on possibility 154–156; on rewards and punishment 154, 156; on will 153–156, 160
Cudworth, Ralph 201

De aegritudinibus capitis (Guaineri) 53
De amore (Ficino) 188
De Anima (Aristotle): Alexander on 10, 231; Averroes on 83, 168, 170; Buridan on 24; Cajetan on 236; on intellect 5, 83, 87, 93, 168, 230; medieval reception of 229; Pomponazzi on 111, 238–239; on sensation 167; Simplicius on 114, 240; on soul's powers 63, 65, 208; study of medicine and 10; Suárez on 116–117, 134, 140n52, 166, 240; in university curriculum 24
De anima et vita (Juan Luis Vives) 45
De auxiliis controversy 157
Decembrio, Pier Candido 232
De cuiuslibet animi peccatorum dignotione et medela (Galen) 43
De immortalitate animae (Gasparo Contarini) 231
De immortalitate animae (Pietro Pomponazzi) 111, 236
De immortalitate humani animi (Pier Candido Decembrio) 232
De indolentia (Galen) 43
Del Medigo, Elijah 232
Del senso delle cose e della magia (Campanella) *196, 198–199*
delusions: imagination and 55–56; medical understanding of 57; mind-body relationship and 53–54, 58–59; perception and 57

293

De mente humana (Simone Porzio) 240
De moribus (Galen) 43
De naturalibus facultatibus (Galen) 41, 46, 50
De perenni philosophia (Agostino Steuco) 240
De placitis Hippocratis et Platonis (Galen) 43
De propriis placitis (Galen) 51
De rerum natura iuxta propria principia (Telesio) 240
Descartes, René: on Aristotelianism 208–209; on free will 266; mind-body problem and 207; passions and 251, 265–266; sense perception and 221
De sensu agente (Nifo) 166
determinism: astral 144, 147; compatibilism and 147, 160n2; condemnation of 147; free choice and 155–156; as a threat to free will 144; types of 144; universal 152
De Trinitate (Augustine) 125
De unitate intellectus contra Averroistas (Aquinas) 83
De vita coelitus comparanda (Ficino) 190
De vita libri tres (Ficino) 187, 190
diabolic magic 198
direct intuition 128–129
direct realism 102, 104, 108–110
direct signification 25
disembodied sensation 212–213, 215, 217
divine magic 198
divine omniscience 153–154
Donato, Girolamo 10, 231
Dretske, F. 126, 129
dualism: Aquinas and 208; Buridan and 207, 215; Ficino on 30; immortality of the soul and 240; medieval philosophers and 208; Ockham on 212; Plato and 208; *see also* Cartesian dualism; mind-body problem
Duns Scotus, John *see* Scotus, John Duns

efficient causality: final causation and 158; sensation and 172–174, 177–179; soul's powers and 73–74
empirical epistemology 279–283, 285–286

empiricist method 36–37
Enchiridion (Erasmus) 257, 264
Enneads (Plotinus) 28, 232
entelecheia 240
Erasistratus 47
Erasmus 257–258, 264, 266
Erophilus 47
Essais (Montaigne) 32
event causation 160n3
Examen de ingenios para la ciencias (Huarte) 44
experience 283–284
explanatory relations 29
external sensation 76, 177–178
extramission 170

FAA *see* formal assimilation account of intentionality (FAA)
fact-awareness 126
facultative logic: Aristotle and 271–274; British Aristotelianism and 279–285; Coke on 282–285; defining 270–271; empirical epistemology of 279–283, 285–286; Flavell on 280–281; gnostology and 276–277; induction and 280–282; knowledge and 272–275, 279–285; method and 284–285; noology and 276–277; Powell on 279–280; in Renaissance Aristotelianism 270–276; sensation and 272; Zabarella and 275
faculty psychology 63–64, 76–77
Fasciculus (Christopher Airay) 282
Fernel, Jean: on faculties of the soul 44, 75–77, 80n61; humanist training of 45; on parts of the soul 75; on the soul's powers 72, 74–75; on vital heat 76
Ficino, Marsilio: on Averroes 235; genetic argument 188; humanism and 3; on immortality of the soul 11, 13–14, 31, 36, 232–235; on love 187–190; on materialism 233–234; on melancholy 56, 187, 190–191; metaphysical levels of 12–14, 28–30, 220; method and 22, 29–30; mind-body problem and 217–219, 221; on passions 186–191; Platonism and 3, 9, 14–15, 28, 188; on reality 12; on the soul 28–30, 44,

218–219; on the spirit 188–191, 219–221; on stages of being 188; tripartition and 188, 191, 200
Fienus, Thomas 55–56
Fifth Lateran Council 235–236, 239
final causation 158
Fish, W. 165
Flavell, John 280–281
flying man 234, 242n34
form: body and 93–94; informing 89; intellect as 90–91; plurality and gradation of 94
formal assimilation account of intentionality (FAA) 102–104, 108–110, 115–116
freedom: compatibilist 157; divine omniscience and 154, 157; libertarian 145, 147, 157–158, 160; will's 146–150, 153–160
Fromme, Valentin 277
Fuchs, O. 261

Gaetano of Thiene 111
Galen, Claudius: on Hippocrates 41; influence of 2; medical philosophy of 43, 47; on nature 41–42, 46–47, 50–51; philosophy of mind and 14, 43; on the soul 43–44, 46; on soul's faculties 77; unconscious and 47
Galenism 2, 15
Gassendi, Pierre 208
Genua, Marcantonio 113
Gersonides 153
Giles of Rome 104
Gilson, E. 95
Gnosticism 250
Gnostologia (Valentin Fromme) 277
gnostology 276–277, 286
God: creation of soul's substance by 74; essence and operative powers in 64, 73; free will and 158–159; intelligible object and 277; logic and understanding of 283–284; omniscience of 153–155; Platonism and 12, 218; as prime mover 172; sensation and 212, 214; soul and 30–31, 74, 234, 238; structure of the world and 28–29
Gorgias (Plato) 250

Gregory of Rimini: on concepts 110; disembodied sensation and 215; on intellect and will 70; on the intellective soul 70; on intentionality 109–110
Guaineri, Antonio 53–55
Gutke, George 276–277

Habitus primorum principiorum seu Intelligentia (Georg Gutke) 277
Harmony of Free Will, The (Luis de Molina) *157*
Hellenistic tradition 22
Helmont, Jan Baptiste van 56–57
Henry of Ghent 104, 175
Hexiologia (Heinrich Alsted) 277
hexiology 276, 285
Higher-Order Perceptual (HOP) theory 138n12
Higher-Order Thought (HOT) theory 138n12
Hippocrates 41–42, 46
Hobbes, Thomas 285
Hobbesian materialism 224
Huarte, Juan 44
human beings: causation and 145; cognitive faculties of 101–103; delusions and 57; faculties of 25–26, 44; intellect and body in 87–88, 92–93; intellective/rational soul and 15, 49, 64, 70–72, 74–75, 145–146; love and 189–190; multiple souls in 27, 63, 66–67, 70, 72; natures of 236–238; proper forms of 94; sentient and natural souls in 75–76; tripartition of 188, 191
humanism: defining 7; education in 10; patronage and 9–10; philosophy of mind and 3; Renaissance 7–11, 14; scholasticism and 2, 8–11
humanistic logic 279, 281
Hume, David 285
hylomorphism: defining 4; Jandun on 93; philosophy of mind and 14; Pomponazzi on 111–112; radical 111–114; rejection of 77; soul and 4–7, 10, 64; Suárez on 116; Zabarella on 114

Iberian scholasticism 110, 116, 240
Ibn Rushd *see* Averroes

INDEX

Idea medicinae philosophicae (Petrus Severinus) 52
illness: imagination and 56; mental 53, 55–57; passions and 200
image: intellective/rational soul and 86–87; separation from 84; soul and 84; thinking and 84, 87
imagination: delusions and 55–56; illnesses and 56; intentionality and 114; location of 54; melancholy and 56; spirit and 199
imaginative species 178
immaterial soul 194, 214, 221, 223
immortality of the soul: affinity and 233; Aristotelianism and 241; Averroes on 235; Blasius on 231; Cajetan on 236; dualism and 240; Ficino on 11, 13–14, 31, 36, 232–235; Galen on 43; Lateran Council on 235–236; medieval philosophers and 229–230; naturalism and 239; Ockham on 230; Platonism and 232; Pomponazzi on 218, 236–239; reason and 230; Renaissance theories of 239–240; Scotus on 230
indirect realism 109, 115, 117
induction 274, 280–282
informing form 89
innatism 280
instrumental powers 71–72
intellect: active 230; agent 168; Alexander on 230; Aquinas on 84–85; Aristotle on 5, 83, 87, 93, 168, 230; Averroes on 83–84; body and 86–87, 90–92; as immaterial faculty of the soul 103; intentionality and 101; as intrinsic agent 91–92; Ockham on 212–213; potential 168; supra-individual 5, 11, 15, 84; unicity of 88–90, 147; universals and 283; will and 146, 148–149, 152
intellective/rational soul: Aquinas on 65, 86–87; Averroes on 231; body and 86; Buridan on 71–72; Gregory on 70; human beings and 14, 49, 64, 70–72, 74–75, 145–146; images and 86–87; Ockham on 66–67; Siger on 86–87; Suárez on 72, 74; Thomas on 68–69
intellectual cognition: abstractive 105–106, 108–109, 131; Averroes on 111; body-dependent 112–113; immateriality of 106; intelligible species in 106; intentionality of 101–104, 111, 115, 118; intuitive 105–109, 131; Jandun on 111; naturalistic approach to 113; Ockham on 106–107; representations in 101, 103, 111; sensible species and 175–176; soul's attention and 116–117; Suárez on 116–117, 136; universals and 107, 115, 117
intellectual determinism 144
intellectual habits: Alsted and 276; Aristotle on 273; cognizing and 278; defining 276; facultative logic and 273–276, 280; knowing and 278; science and 276; understanding and 276, 278–279; Zabarella on 274–275, 280
intellectualism 145, 151–152
intelligible species: Aquinas on 103–106; critiques of 104, 111; intellection and 104, 106, 115, 276; intentionality and 105; Jandun on 110–111; Ockham on 106, 108; phantasms and 112, 114, 117–118; Pomponazzi on 111–113; as representations 103, 105, 113; Suárez on 117, 135; thought in act and 84; Zabarella on 115
intentionality: Aquinas on 102–104; Averroists and 110; causality and 108; direct realism and 102, 104, 108–110; distinctions in 101; formal assimilation and 102–104, 108–110, 115–116; Gregory on 109–110; imagination and 114; Jandun on 110–111; naturalistic approach to 103–104; in nature 42, 58; Ockham on 105–109; representations in 101, 103, 105–106, 110, 118; scholastic Aristotelianism and 102, 113, 118; Scotus on 104–105; sense perception and 101; Zabarella on 114–115
intentional species 175
internal causation 31
internal sensation 76, 176–178
intuitive cognition 105–109, 127–130
irascible appetites 48, 250, 255
irritability 42

INDEX

Ishaq ibn 'Imran 55
Italian naturalists 221–224

Jewish thought 153
John of Jandun: agent sense and 166, 169–171; on Alexander 90; Averroism and 5, 90; on form 90–91, 94; on hylomorphism 93; on intellect and body 90–93, 231; on intentionality 110–111

Keckermann, Bartholomäus 276, 282
Kent, Bonnie 266n5
Kessler, E. 239
Kim, Jaegwon 207
King, Peter 208, 210, 215, 255
knowledge: Aristotle on 272–274; body and 47, 50, 55, 57–59; of causes 279–280; experience and 283–284; nature and 51–53; object of 275, 277–278, 286; observation and 284; perception and 48; plant life and 50; scientific 273–275, 280, 285; sensation and 272, 274–275, 280–281, 284

Lagerlund, Henrik 207
Lamarck, Jean-Baptiste 42
Late Middle Ages: Averroism in 83; defining 1; external/internal senses in 166; Iberian scholasticism in 110; medical view of the mind in 41–59; mind-soul problem in 5; mortality of the soul in 230; psychology and 230–232
Lateran Council 235–236, 239
Lawrence of Lindores 230
Leibniz, Gottfried Wilhelm: cognitive faculties and 279; method and 29; on the mind 201
Leijenhorst, Cees 175
Liber de spiritu et anima (Anonymous) 64
libertarian freedom 145, 147, 157–158, 160
Light of the Lord, The (Ḥasdai Crescas) 153
Locke, John 285
logic: cognition and 283; "cognitive turn" in 270, 281–282, 286; defining 281–282; humanistic 279, 281; intellectual habits and 274; precognition and 275; syllogism and 282; thinking and 284; Valla on 9; *see also* facultative logic
Logicae artis compendium (Sanderson) 281–282
Lohr, Charles 274
Long Commentary on the De Anima *of Aristotle* (Averroes) 83
love: Aquinas on 261; in Christian Neoplatonism 264; as *copula mundi* 189; cosmos and 189; Ficino on 187–189; passions and 187–190, 261–262, 264–265; personal 189
Lucretius 234, 242n30
Luther, Martin 156–157

madness 53, 55
magic: affective 200; Campanella on 196, 198–200; diabolic 198; divine 198; natural 198–199; passions and 199
Maimonides 152
Marsilius of Inghen 230
materialism 233–234
material world 185–186
McGrade, Steve 261
medical philosophy: activity in 42; delusions and 58–59; Galen and 43; irritability in 42; mental illness and 57; mind and nature in 41–42; reactivity in 42; unconscious and 47, 50, 58
Medicinalium iuxta propria principia libri septem (Campanella) 57
medicine: *De Anima* and study of 10; as natural magic 199; passions and 200; philosophy and 41–42, 52; temperaments and 43–44
Meditations (Descartes) 208
melancholy: Ficino on 56, 187, 190–191; Fienus on 56; imagination and 55–56; memory of 54–55; as mental illness 53; as passion 187, 190–191
Melanchthon, Philip 10, 279
memory 54–55
mental illness 53, 55–57
Metaphysical Disputations (Suárez) 158
metaphysical levels of being 12–14, 28–30, 192, 220

metaphysics: method and 23–24; psychology and 23; soul and 24, 28
Metaphysics (Aristotle) 273
method: of abstention 37; empiricist 36–37; facultative logic and 284–285; metaphysical discussions and 23; mind and 22–24; Principle of Perfection (PP) 29; Principle of Sufficient Reason (PSR) 29; Pyrrhonian 31–32; rationalist 36–37; reductionist strategy 26–27
mind: capacity to feel 186; defining 23; delusions and 53–54; digestive self and 57; embodied concept of 186, 200–201; imagination and 54–56; material world and 185–186; medical view of 41–43; medieval philosophers and 208; method and 22–24; nature and 186; operations of 279; Paracelsus on 52–53; as part of a cosmological structure 185; passions and 186; philosophers and 42–43; *see also* soul
mind-body problem: Aristotelian approaches to 208–215, 218, 223; Buridan on 213–215; Cartesian dualism and 207, 223; consciousness and 209–210; Ficino on 217–219, 221; formulation of 209; hylomorphism and 4; Italian naturalists and 221–224; medieval philosophers and 208–209; nature of 207; Ockham on 212–213; Olivi on 216–217; Platonic approaches to 215–219; sense perception and 210; spirit and 219–223; Telesio on 221–223; vitalistic approach 223–224
mind-soul problem: Averroes on 5; medieval philosophers and 5, 23; metaphysical framework of 209; Ockham on 7, 211–212
"mineness" of acts 128–130, 132–134
moderate voluntarism 145, 150
Molière 76
Molina, Luis de 157
Montaigne, Michel de: criticism of faculty psychology 76; on passions 259–260, 262–263, 265; Pyrrhonian method and 23, 32–34; on reason 33–34; on the soul 33–37; on writing 35

moral action/morality: Aquinas on 251; Aristotelianism and 251, 254; early Christian views on 250–251; irascible appetites and 255; Ockham on 252–253; passions and 250–266; rewards and punishments 156; will and 251–253
moral virtue 250, 256–258, 261, 265
More, Henry 201
Musano, Francesco 187

naturalism 221–224, 239
Natural Faculties, On the (Galen) 41
natural magic 198–199
natural soul 75–76
nature: Campanella on 196–197; faculties of 46–47, 50, 57–59; Galen on 41–42, 46–47; Hippocratic notion of 41–42, 46; hot and cold in 192; intentionality in 42, 58; mind and 186; plastic 201; pluralism and 50–51; spirit of 201; Telesio on 191–192; unconscious 47
Neoplatonism: causality/causation and 31; cosmology and 11, 28–29, 179, 217–218; love in 264
Nicholas of Amsterdam 230
Nicomachean Ethics (Aristotle) 9–10, 150, 273
Nifo, Agostino: on Averroes 171–172, 232; intellect and 111; on sensation 166, 171–172; sensible species and 171
noetics 83–85, 88, 90–91
noology 276–277, 279, 286
Norea, C. G. 262

object-awareness 126, 129–130, 132, 134
objectual act-awareness 126–132, 135–136
observation 284
Ockham *see* William of Ockham
Olivi, Peter John 104, 216–217
Ordinatio (Ockham) 127
Ortus medicinae (Jan Baptist van Helmont) 56
Outlines of Scepticism (Sextus Empiricus) 31

pagan philosophy 240
panpsychism/pampsychism 185–186, 202
Paracelsus 52–53, 56
parallelism 114
parsimony principle 67, 69–70
passions: Aquinas on 250–252; Aristotelianism and 254–255; Campanella on 199–200; as chaotic 260–263; corporeal nature of the soul and 194–196; early Christian views on 250–251; Erasmus on 257–258, 264, 266; as feelings 264–265; Ficino on 187–188; love as 187–190, 262, 264–265; magic and 199; melancholy as 187, 190–191; mind and 186; Montaigne on 259–260, 262–263, 265; moral action and 250–266; Ockham on 256, 260–262, 266; in panpsychism 186; physiological view of 256–260; political rule and 255; reason and 196, 250–252; Renaissance theories of 251; scholasticism and 251, 266; spirit and 196, 200; Suárez on 253–256, 265; surrounding world and 200–201; Telesio on 192, 194–196, 201; transformations of 251; vice and 250, 256–257; virtues in 250, 252, 256–258, 261, 264, 266n5; Vives on 258–259, 262, 264–266; will and 251, 253–256
Passions de l'Âme, Les (Descartes) 266
Patrizi, Francesco 185
Pattin, Adriaan 178
Paul of Venice 111, 232
perception: activist 165; agent sense and 169; Aquinas on 210, 213; Buridan on 213–215; as cognitive action 136; consciousness and 210; delusions and 57; knowledge and 48; mind-body problem and 210; Ockham on 213; receptivist 165; self-consciousness and 125; sensible species and 135, 171; sensory 101, 165, 172, 210, 221; soul and 217; spirit and 193
Petrarch, Francesco 9, 11
Phaedo (Plato) 233
Phaedrus (Plato) 250

phantasms: Aquinas on 111; dispositions from 110–111; intellection and 114–115, 117–118; intelligible species and 112; intentionality and 113; Jandun on 111; parallelism and 114
philosopher physician 41, 52–53
philosophers: activity and 42; attitudes towards the mind by 42–43; on natural faculties 50; on the soul 45–46; temperaments and 43
Philosophia digne restituta (Alsted) 276
philosophy: Late Middle Ages 1, 5; medicine and 41–42, 52; Renaissance 1–2, 5; temperaments and 42
philosophy of mind: Aristotelianism and 3; Galen on 14, 43; humanism and 3, 14; hylomorphism and 14; mind-body problem in 5–6; Platonism and 3, 14
physician philosopher 41, 52–53
physicians: attitudes towards the mind by 42–43; delusions and 53–54; on natural faculties 50; reactivity and 42; temperaments and 43–45; unconscious and 50
Physiologia (Jean Fernel) 44
Piccolomini, Francesco 77, 113
Pietro d'Abano: on the faculties of the soul 47–50, 58; medical philosophy of 43
Pironet, F. 151
plant life: knowledge and 50; motion and 50; natural soul of 75; unconscious and 58–59
plastic nature 201
Plato: Aristotle and 218, 233; on dualism 208; Ficino on 28; *Gorgias* 250; on Hippocrates 41; literary qualities of 11; passions and 250, 265; *Phaedo* 233; *Phaedrus* 250; *Republic* 234, 250; *Symposium* 187, 250
Platonic Theology on the Immortality of the Soul (Ficino) 11–13, 28, 217–218, 220, 232
Platonism: ethical purpose and 12; method and 22; mind-body problem and 215–219; philosophy of mind and 3, 14; reality and 12; revival of 9, 11; soul and 11–14, 34; structure of the world in 28

INDEX

Pliny 199
Plotinus 28, 188, 232
pluralism 50–51
Pomponazzi, Pietro: on Alexander's theory of the soul 231; on Aquinas 237–239; on Averroes 237; hylomorphism and 10, 111–113; on immortality of the soul 218, 236–239; on intelligible species 111, 113; on intentionality 113; on soul's faculties 77; on Thomism 238
Porzio, Simone 113, 240
Posterior Analytics (Aristotle) 272–274
potential intellect 168
potentiality 49
Powell, Griffith 279–281
Prassicio, Luca 239
precognition 275
primae notiones 268, 284–285
principal powers 71–72
Principle of Perfection (PP) 29
Principle of Sufficient Reason (PSR) 29
Proclus 28
propositional self-awareness: Chatton on 126, 131–134, 137; Ockham on 126–130, 137; Suárez on 134–137; types of 126; *see also* self-consciousness
Protestant Reformation 156–157
psychology: Aristotelian 104, 112, 116, 118, 129, 208–209, 218; Augustinian 104, 108, 114, 116; Averroistic 111; cognitive 179, 182n39; emergence of 23; facultative logic and 270; faculty 63–64, 76–77; late medieval theories of 230; metaphysical problems and 23–24; naturalistic approach to 115; natural philosophy and 118; Neoplatonic 117–118; philosophical 221–222, 236; radical hylomorphism and 111–114; Renaissance theories of 230
Pyrrhonian method: procedure of 32; scepticism and 23, 31–32; soul and 33–34

Quaestio de immortalitate anime intellective (Lucio Prassicio) 239
Quaestiones de anima (Blasius) 230–231
Quod animi mores corporis temperamenta sequantur (Galen) 43
Quodlibeta (Ockham) 127–128

radical hylomorphism 111–114
radical voluntarism 145, 150
rationalist method 36–37
rational soul: Ficino on 218–219, 234; human beings and 145–146; Telesio on 223; will and 146
reactivity 42
reality: Calov on 277–278; Ficino on 12–14, 187–188, 217, 232; immaterial 14; knowledge and 277; layers of 217–220, 232; material 13–14; mind and 43, 53, 55; natural faculties and 42; representations and 53; senses and 56
reason: body and soul in 44–45; divine perfection and 34; faculties of 34, 49, 94; immortality of the soul and 230; Montaigne on 33–34; passions and 196, 250–252; rational soul and 33–34; spirit and 190; will and 151, 253
receptivism 167, 171, 174
reductionist strategy 26–27
reflexive intuition 128–131
religion 199
Renaissance: defining 1, 17n5; humanism 7–11, 14; mind-soul problem in 5; modernity and 2; psychology and 230; theories of the passions in 251
Renaissance Aristotelianism 270–276, 279, 285
representations: concepts as 110; in intellectual cognition 101, 103, 111; intentionality and 101, 103, 105–106, 108
Republic (Plato) 234, 250
rewards and punishments 154, 156
Rhetoric (Aristotle) 273

Sacred Disease (Anonymous) 53
Sanderson, Robert 281–282
scepticism: Pyrrhonian method and 23, 31–32, 34; science of the soul and 23
Schmitt, Charles B. 281

scholasticism: Aristotelian 1–2, 8–9, 113, 118; humanism and 2, 7–11; Iberian 110, 116, 240; passions and 251, 266; study of 8–9
science 276
scientific knowledge 273–275, 280, 285
Scotism 88, 94, 110
Scotus, John Duns: immortality of the soul and 230; on intentionality 104–105; on psychic powers 66; on sensation 211; on universals 105
secundae notiones 284
self-consciousness: attention and 126, 137; cognizing and 125; intuition and 127–130; Ockham on 127; perceiving and 125; Suárez on 134; *see also* propositional self-awareness
selfhood 57
sensation: agent sense of 166, 168–169; Aquinas on 211; Aristotle on 167–168, 272; Averroes on 168–169; Buridan on 214; Campanella on 197, 201, 223; defining 165; disembodied 212–213, 215, 217; efficient cause of 172–174, 177–179; internal/external 176–178; Jandun on 169–170; knowledge and 272, 274–275, 280–281, 284; memory of experience in 280; Nifo on 171–172; Ockham on 211–215, 224n10; passive sense of 166, 170; pleasure and pain 192–194; spirit and 222; Suárez on 166–167, 172–178; Telesio on 193–194, 221–223; Wodeham on 215; *see also* agent sense
sense/sensory perception: as cognition of singulars 101; efficient causality of 165; mind and 210; Suárez on 172; Telesio on 221
sensible species: accidental and material aspects of 173; cognitive act and 174–176; dead reception and 176; internal/external sense 176; perception and 135, 171; sensation and 103; ontology of 172–173
sensitive appetite 66, 211, 252–256, 261
sensitive soul 64–70

sensory cognition 172–178
Sentences (Ockham) 105, 107, 109
sentient soul 75–76
Severinus, Petrus 52
Sextus, Empiricus 31
Siger of Brabant: on intellective soul and body 86–87, 92, 231; mind-soul problem 5; *operans intrinsecum* concept of 87–88
Simplicius 114, 240
sin: Aquinas on 251; Erasmus on 264; passions and 250–251, 255–256; sensitive appetite and 255
Sophisma de sensu agente (John of Jandun) 169
soul: Aquinas on 6, 64–65, 73, 209, 230; Aristotle on 4–5, 7, 25, 34, 47–49, 63–64, 76, 84, 196, 208–209; Buridan on 24–27, 36, 38n23; conscious/unconscious 45–48, 50, 52; corporeal nature of 194–196; defining 23; dualism and 30; faculties of 47–50, 63–64, 75–77, 257; Ficino on 11, 13–14, 28–31, 36, 44, 218–219; Galen on 43–44, 46; God and 30–31; hylomorphism and 4–7, 10, 64; image and 84; immaterial 194, 214, 221, 223; immortality of 11, 13–14, 31, 36, 43, 218, 229–239; indivisibility of 214–215; materialistic view of 233–234; metaphysical analysis and 23–24, 28; Montaigne on 33–37; physiological view of 258; Platonism and 11–14, 34; Pyrrhonian method and 33–34; rational 145–146, 218–219, 223, 234; reductionist strategy of 26–27; science of 23–27, 36; as spirit 193; temperament and 44–45; *see also* mind
Soul, On the (Aristotle) *see De Anima* (Aristotle)
soul's powers: acts and objects of 65, 67; appetitive faculty 76; Aquinas on 64–66; Aristotelianism and 64–65; Buridan on 71–72; critiques of 76–77; distinction from soul 73–74, 77; diversity of 63; efficient causality and

73–74; emanations 64–65, 74; essence and 65; external sensation 76; Fernel on 74–75; Gregory on 70, 72; homogenous 67–68; instrumental 71–72; intellective/rational 64–72, 74, 231; as intermediary entities 64; internal sensation 76; Ockham on 6–7, 24–25, 27, 66–71; principal 71–72; as proper attributes 65; sensitive 64–70; Suárez on 72–73; Thomas on 68–70, 72; vegetative 64–65; vital heat and 76
species: Aquinas on 103–104; conceptions of 140n57; imaginative 178; intelligible 103–104, 106, 111–112, 115, 135; intentional 175; rejection of 104, 106, 118; *see also* sensible species
spirit: body and 222; Campanella on 197–200; cosmic 190–191; Ficino on 188–191, 219–221; food and 199; imagination and 199; love and 189–190; melancholy and 190; mind-body problem and 219–223; nourishment of 191; passions and 196, 199–200; perception and 193; pleasure and pain 193–194; sensation and 222; as the soul 193; Telesio on 193–195, 221–223, 240–241
Spirit and Soul, On (Anonymous) 216
spiritual ontology 201
Spruit, Leen 175
Steuco, Agostino 240
Stoicism 250, 257, 260–261, 265
Sturm, Johann 10
Suárez, Francisco: on agent sense 174, 178; on attention 126, 134–137; on causation 158; on *De Anima* 240; on distinction of soul and powers 73–74; on efficient causality 177–179; on hylomorphism 116; on immortality of the soul 240; on intentional species 175; on internal/external sense 176–178; on passions 253–256, 264–265; on propositional self-awareness 134–136; on sensible species 172–176; on sensitive appetite 254–255; on sensory cognition 166–167, 172–179; on soul's attention 116–117; on the soul's powers 72–73; on will 156–160, 253–255

supra-individual intellect 5, 11, 15, 84
Symposium (Plato) 187, 250
Systema systematum (Bartholomäus Keckermann) 282

Taddeo da Parma 231
Telesio, Bernardino: on Galen 196; mind-body problem and 221–223; on nature 191–192; on passions 186, 192, 194–196, 201; on sensation 193–194, 221–223; on the spirit 192–196, 221–223, 240–241; vitalistic approach 223
temperaments: functions of life and 51; Galenism and 54; medicine and 43–44; philosophy and 43–44; physicians and 43–44
Tempier, Étienne 5, 147, 231

theological determinism 144
thinking/thought: body and 44, 58; images and 84, 87; individuation of 88, 94–95; intellective/rational soul and 86; logic and 284; soul and 47
Thomas Del Garbo: on the intellective soul 68–69; on the sensitive soul 68–70
Thomas de Vio Caietan *see* Cajetan
Thomism 110, 179, 238, 240, 253, 255–256
Tignosi, Niccolò 232
Timpler, Clemens 276
Toivanen, Juhana 216–217
Tommaso de Vio *see* Cajetan
Topics (Aristotle) 65
Tractatus de anima intellectiva (Siger of Brabant) 86
Tractatus de demonstratione methodicus et polemicus (John Flavell) 280
transcendentals 278
Trinity, On the (Augustine) 64

unconscious *see* conscious/unconscious mind
understanding 276
universal determinism 152
universal essences 105, 107, 115
Universalis philosophia (Campanella) *57*

302

INDEX

Valentino da Camerino 236
Valla, Lorenzo 9
vegetative soul 64–65
Vernia, Nicoletto 111, 232
vice: concupiscible and irascible appetites and 250; Ockham on 256, 260; passions and 250, 256–257; virtue and 258
virtue: Aristotelian 251, 254, 256–257, 261; Montaigne on 265; moral 250–251, 256–258, 261, 265; Ockham on 252–253, 256, 260; passions and 250, 252, 256–258, 261, 264, 266n5; sensitive appetite and 266n5; vice and 258; will and 253
vital heat 76
vitalistic approach 223–224
Vives, Juan Luis 45, 258–259, 262, 264–266
voluntarism: intellectualism and 145, 151–152; moderate 145, 150; passions and 260; radical 145, 150; responsibility and 256; will and 148, 253, 255
voluntary agents 150–151

Watson, W. I. 210
will: acts of 146, 151; agent-causation and 145; Aquinas on xii; Arendt on xii; Augustine on xii; Crescas on 153–156, 160; deferring and 151–152; determinism and 144; divine omniscience and 153–154; freedom of 146–150, 153–160; good as object of 149; intellect and 67, 70, 146, 148–149, 152; moral action and 251–253; nilling and 149, 151; not-willing and 151; passions and 251, 253–256; rational soul and 146; reason and 151, 253; Suárez on 156–160, 253–255
William of Ockham: on abstractive cognition 131; on attention 135; on free will 67, 147–150; on homogenous parts 67–68; immortality of the soul and 230; on intellect 67, 212–213; on intellectual cognition 106–107; on intentionality 105–109; on intuitive cognition 127–131; mind-body problem and 212–213; mind-soul dualism and 27, 211–212; "mineness" of acts 128–130; parsimony principle 67, 69–70; on passions 256, 260–262, 266; on propositional self-awareness 126–130; science of the soul and 24–25; on sensation 211–214, 224n10; on the soul's faculties 148; on the soul's powers 6–7, 66–70; on virtuous action 252–253; on willing to be unhappy 149–150
Wodeham, Adam 215
Wylton, Thomas: on form 89; influences on 88; on unicity of the intellect 89–90

Zabarella, Jacopo: induction and 274, 281–282; influence of 275–280, 285; on intellectual habits 271, 274–275, 280; intentionality and 115; on object of knowledge 275, 277–278; precognition and 275; radical hylomorphism and 114
Zupko, J. 151–152

For Product Safety Concerns and Information please contact our EU
representative GPSR@taylorandfrancis.com
Taylor & Francis Verlag GmbH, Kaufingerstraße 24, 80331 München, Germany

www.ingramcontent.com/pod-product-compliance
Lightning Source LLC
Chambersburg PA
CBHW071802300426
44116CB00009B/1181